ELITE ACCOMMODATION IN CANADIAN POLITICS

Other books by Robert Presthus

The Turkish Conseil d'Etat, Cornell University Press, 1958
The Organizational Society, Alfred Knopf, 1962
Men at the Top: A Study in Community Power, Oxford University Press, 1964
Behavioural Approaches to Public Administration, University of Alabama Press, 1965
Individuum und Organisation, Fischer Verlag, 1967
Public Administration (with John McDonald Pfiffner), Ronald Press, 1968
La Societa Dell'Organizzione, Rizzoli, 1971

ELITE ACCOMMODATION IN CANADIAN POLITICS

ROBERT PRESTHUS

CAMBRIDGE
AT THE UNIVERSITY PRESS 1973

Published by the Syndics of the Cambridge University Press
Bentley House, 200 Euston Road, London NWI 2DB
American Branch: 32 East 57th Street, New York, N.Y. 10022
Canada: The Macmillan Company of Canada Limited,
70 Bond Street, Toronto 2, Ontario

Library of Congress Catalogue Card Number: 72–83598

ISBN: 0 521 08695 7

Typeset in Great Britain
by William Clowes & Sons, Ltd.,
London, Beccles and Colchester

Printed in the United States of America

FOR SARA AND ROBIN

CONTENTS

PREFACE

The work presented here attempts to deal with the Canadian political process at two levels of analysis. One concerns the structure and political behaviour of interest groups seen from a detailed survey perspective. The other attempts to set the interest group phenomenon within the larger framework of Canadian political institutions and culture, and indeed, within the social system itself. Two major theoretical approaches are used for this purpose. At the first level I have relied largely upon George Homans' interaction theory, in which relations between interest groups and governmental elites are conceptualized as a series of mutually beneficial exchanges of valued currencies of several kinds, including information, political support, companionship, advice, and services.

Interaction theory rests essentially upon two propositions, one economic and the other psychological. It holds that individuals sustain interpersonal relations only if each person concerned believes he is 'making a profit', and that, all else being equal, they tend to repeat interactions that are gratifying, while terminating those which prove unsatisfying. In effect, the theory posits that shared activities bring individuals together and the resulting exchanges tend to produce shared sentiments, which in turn, strengthen and encourage further interaction. To this syndrome we have added another, *influence*, which seems to flow logically from the interaction process. The theory is used here to explain interaction and imputations of legitimacy and influence to interest groups among the Canadian political elite, defined here as the 1,150 legislators, senior civil servants, and interest group directors included in the study.

At the second, system-wide level of analysis, I have used the theory of elite accommodation. This theory, worked out mainly by the Dutch scholar, Arend Lijphart, attempts to explain the persistence of stable, democratic government in 'consociational' societies. Such societies are characterized by deep internal cleavages of religion and ethnicity, and thus the theory seemed especially germane in the Canadian political culture which is generally regarded as one of limited national integration, inspired mainly by tensions between its French- and English-Canadian segments, deep-seated regional discontinuities, and a multi-party system which tends to aggravate some of the other cleavages. In such political cultures it becomes the vital task of socio-political elites to play a nation-saving role by a sustained process of negotiation and bargaining among the leaders of major social groups, carried out at the highest political levels and aimed at overcoming the centripetal tendencies of the political system. Although the Cabinet is the centre of elite accommodation, its implementation occurs mainly at the bureaucratic level where, as our data show, the major share of interaction occurs. This theory, as interaction theory at another level, seemed well-suited for an explanation of the larger significance of the interest group data produced in our research. Although no single theory can fit all the exigencies of any complex empirical situation, we found it intellectually attractive and functionally useful.

The proof of this contention, of course, lies in the following analysis.

Toronto
December, 1971   Robert Presthus

ACKNOWLEDGMENTS

I have incurred many debts during this study, which I am glad to acknowledge. Perhaps the greatest of these is to the Canada Council for generous funding of the research during the four years of field work. I am also grateful to York University for providing leave during 1971–2 which greatly facilitated the writing of the present volume. It is a pleasure, too, to thank the legislators, higher civil servants, and interest group leaders in Quebec City, Montreal, Ottawa, Toronto, Vancouver, and Victoria who so kindly gave us their time and thought during the interviews. One is truly gratified at the reservoirs of talent and good-will found among these men and women.

I owe a debt as well to those colleagues and graduate students who helped with the interviewing and the institutional arrangements required to carry out the research. In Toronto, where the survey began, my major assistant during the design and planning stages of the project was Laurence Fast, whose doctoral dissertation is based upon the present research. Other graduate students who assisted in interviewing, coding, translation, and related activities include: Elizabeth Newton, Mary Campbell, Bill Gullett, Allen Mills, Jeff Norquay, André Blais, Rick Kleiman, Scott Bennett, Linda Shinder, Ben Barkow, Ruth and Mark Lerner, Robert Tostevin, and Margo Twohig.

I am especially obligated to Eric Stapleton and Lesta Sanders who pulled together the completed interviews for coding and recording on cards and tape, and maintained order in our research headquarters in Toronto. Programming and computer service was provided by the State University of New York at Buffalo, where I am indebted to Vaughn Blankenship and Lester Milbrath for providing administrative support and counsel. John Sinclair and Debby Dunkel did the programming and processing of the data through the computer system. I owe Sinclair a special debt for his assistance at the analysis stage.

Acknowledgments

In Quebec and Montreal, bilingual interviewing was provided by Francine Depatie, Monique Lord, Almire Lamontagne, Francoise Stanton, Denise Lecler, and Luciano Bozzine. In Ottawa, Corinne Bertrand and Louis Lebreque provided the required secretarial and bilingual skills. In British Columbia, where we received especially kind assistance, my benefactors included Neil Swainson and Ronald Cheffins at the University of Victoria. Larry and Karen Fast were also most helpful in organizing and carrying through the Vancouver part of the research, with the aid of Mary Campbell.

Arend Lijphart read the theoretical parts of the manuscript and I am greatly indebted for his insightful comments, which saved me from many errors. My colleague, Kenneth McRoberts, was especially helpful regarding recent political developments in Quebec which challenge its tradition-oriented culture. George Levenson also read several chapters and made valuable suggestions from a methodological standpoint. I am indebted to Harmon Ziegler and Michael Baer for allowing me to use part of the interview schedule from their study of interaction between legislators and lobbyists in four American states. The *Canadian Journal of Political Science* very kindly gave me permission to use material on federal MP's which first appeared there.

Finally, I want to thank my wife, Sara, for her patience and understanding during the project.

ROBERT PRESTHUS

PART I

POLITICAL THEORY AND POLITICAL CULTURE

As other subsystems, interest groups function within a discrete political and cultural context which shapes their behaviour and, essentially, determines the extent of their legitimacy. This part of the analysis sets down, in broad compass, the political–cultural framework within which Canadian groups exist and outlines the two major theoretical formulations that will be used to order our empirical data: the theories of elite accommodation and interaction. Our intention throughout is to set interest group behaviour within the larger political system of which it is an integral part.

CHAPTER I

THE THEORY OF ELITE ACCOMMODATION

When this study began, its initial theoretical framework was interaction theory; the central focus was upon the process, incentives, and costs of interactions among legislators, bureaucrats, and interest group leaders as they sought to work out mutually satisfactory political decisions. Such a theory is quite specific, concentrating as it does upon individual and small group behaviour. We were not at that stage prepared to commit ourselves to a comprehensive theory which could explain our interest group findings in terms of the larger socio-political system. It seemed preferable to assume that the findings, set in an interaction context, would point the way to such a theory once we had learned more about the role of interest groups in the Canadian political system.

As the research proceeded, we became increasingly impressed with the extent to which the processes of governmental policy determination and implementation seemed to involve (indeed, almost exclusively) continuous exchanges of technical information and normative preferences about issues among the three segments of the 'political elite'.[1] In this sense, the implications of a highly focussed initial theory directed us into the broader field encompassed by the theory of elite accommodation. To put it another way, our search for a general explanatory theory evolved inductively from an initial 'low' level to a comprehensive theory which attempts to set interest group behaviour within the context of the larger political process and, indeed, within the Canadian culture itself.

[1] I shall use the following terms throughout: the 'political elite' includes legislators and bureaucrats in the official government apparatus and private interest group leaders; the 'governmental elite' includes only legislators and bureaucrats; while interest group leaders and their representatives will be characterized as 'private elites'. Since federal and provincial members of parliament will usually be combined for analysis, I shall use the term 'MP's' to characterize both groups. When provincial members are treated separately, they will be designated as 'provincial MP's'.

3

Political theory and political culture

THE ALLOCATIVE FUNCTION OF ELITE ACCOMMODATION

In addition to its nation-saving role, it is important to emphasize that the process of elite accommodation also has the routine, operational function of allocating social resources. Most of our analysis focusses upon this instrumental level of accommodation, which is of course an integral part of the larger process of national integration. In Canada, there is a consensus that a mixed economy, with heavy welfare components, is the appropriate political–economic system. Such a system requires a coordinating mechanism which can ensure some rough equilibrium among the contending group interests. In Western democracies, this mechanism is composed of political elites representing the organized, articulate sectors of society. Its members are found both within government and in the so-called private sphere. In this context, elite accommodation may be regarded as a structural requisite of any democratic society in which policy decisions are the result of negotiation and consultation among the elites concerned. It is more than a 'crisis' mechanism adopted by ethnically and religiously fragmented societies to ease their internal cleavages. Elite accommodation is inherent in the process of democratic government.

Theoretically, then, our analysis proceeds at two analytically discrete, but functionally interrelated levels. The empirical evidence presented here is drawn essentially from the operational level, in which accommodation and the allocation of desired values goes on steadily and virtually invisibly, compared with the occasional, dramatic confrontations occurring in a 'nation-saving' context. Such allocations often occur in the bureaucratic arena, between senior officials and interest group representatives. The imperatives of functional specialization and group representation mean that such consultations usually occur in a context of agency–clientele relations. Consultation with ministers often accompanies such interactions. In a word, elite accommodation and the attending allocation of resources are usually confined to those who have the required substantive interest and political resources.

The explanatory power of the theory of elite accommodation has been demonstrated recently in the analysis of certain political systems of Western Europe.[1] This theory, which is essentially concerned with the conditions of

[1] Arend Lijphart, *The Politics of Accommodation* (Berkeley: University of California Press, 1969); 'Typologies of democratic systems', in Lijphart (ed.), *European Political Systems* (Englewood Cliffs, New Jersey: Prentice-Hall, 1969); 'Consociational democracy', 21 *World Politics* (January, 1969). I am greatly indebted to Lijphart's thoughtful analysis. See also, Roger Girod, 'Geography of the Swiss party system', in Erik Allardt and Ejrjo Littunen (eds.), *Cleavages, Ideologies and Party Systems*, Vol. 10, Wester-

political leadership and stability in fragmented political cultures, has been presented as an alternative or a supplement to traditional explanations which have assumed that the continuity and stability of Western democracies rests upon certain necessary social, ideological, and structural conditions. These include a national consensus upon the so-called political 'rules of the game'; a fairly pervasive sense of nationalism or collective solidarity which eases the strains of class, ethnic, and regional cleavages; and two-party systems of government which effectively displace and compromise the divergent claims of the plethora of interest groups existing in any developed society. Interaction and communication between the social and ethnic subgroups of the political system are another of the necessary conditions of stability often posited in the traditional hypothesis, as well as the existence of extensive cross-cutting group memberships which tend to encourage the will and the capacity for political tolerance and compromise among individuals who belong to several groups whose values and objectives may be inconsistent.

A great deal of theoretical attention has been paid to the presumed effects of such multiple membership in interest groups.[1] The assumption is that individuals belong to several groups with different objectives, points of view, etc. A number of functional consequences for political stability are believed to follow, essentially because the inevitable and competing differences among the different groups temper the claims of citizens and impel them toward the kind of non-ideological, compromising approach to politics which makes stable democratic government possible. Multiple group membership, in effect, is symbolic of a pluralistic societal condition, characterized by considerable but constrained diversity along ethnic, religious, and political lines. Such diversity not only encourages stability, it also increases political interest and competence.

One awkward problem with this rationale is that most people do not belong to more than a single voluntary association, even in highly developed Western societies. As the Almond–Verba data indicate, only one-third of their US sample belong to more than *one* organization; in Britain and Germany, only about 16 per cent; and in Italy and Mexico, less than 6 per cent.[2]

marck Society (Helsinki: Academic Bookstore, 1964); Duncan MacRae, Jr, *Parliament, Parties and Society in France, 1946–58* (New York: St Martins Press, 1967).

[1] Among others, see David Truman, *The Governmental Process* (New York: A. Knopf, 1951), p. 508; Arthur Bentley, *The Process of Government*, p. 208; and William C. Mitchell, 'Interest group theory and "overlapping memberships": a critique', unpublished paper, 1963.
[2] Gabriel Almond and Sidney Verba, *The Civic Culture* (Boston and Toronto: Little, Brown, 1965), p. 264.

5

TABLE I-I *Interest group affiliation, Canada and United States*[a]

Intensity[b]	Canada	United States
	%	%
One	64	57
Two-or-more	36	32
Three-or-more	18	18
	(2,767)	(970)

[a] Adapted from James Curtis, 'Voluntary association joining: a cross-national comparative note', 36 *American Sociological Review* (October, 1971), p. 875.
[b] Union membership is included which tends to inflate rates somewhat. Percentages do not equal 100.

With respect to the US and Canada, one would assume that rates are probably similar, given their similarly high levels of political development and GNP. On the other hand, since membership is highly correlated with educational level, one would expect to find Canadian rates somewhat lower. Fortunately, comparative data are now available which provide reasonably precise answers to the question (see Table 1-1).

Here, we find membership rates fairly similar, but with Canadian adults somewhat more likely to belong to one and two voluntary groups. Some caution is warranted, however, with respect to these findings, for two reasons. The items used to elicit the data were different: for example, the Canadian study used a list of organizations, which probably encourages recall. Equally important, the Canadian study was done (1968) eight years later than the US research. Such a time differential can be important. Wright and Hyman, found in a 1971 replication of their 1958 study that rates had increased from 36 per cent to 43, for single memberships.[1] Despite such possible skewing, we can probably conclude that rates are fairly similar between the two societies, although as indicated later, they differ sharply within Canada, between English- and French-speaking citizens.

As noted, including union memberships exaggerates participation; without them, the rates fall to 50 per cent, i.e. half of Canadian adults belong

[1] 'Trends in voluntary association memberships of American adults', 36 *American Sociological Review* (April, 1972), p. 195. After showing that only *10 per cent* of adults belong to 3 or more groups, they conclude that 'voluntary association membership is not characteristic of the majority of American adults.' p. 191.

to only a single interest group. In the present context, it is important to be aware of such limitations because they form part of an underlying political reality which culminates in accommodation among elites, with relatively limited participation by ordinary citizens. As Arend Lijphart has shown, neither multiple group structures nor homogeneous, highly integrated ethnic and linguistic political cultures are necessary for stable government, as the examples of Austria, Belgium, the Netherlands, and Switzerland show.[1] Our thesis is that Canada fits nicely into this category of politically fragmented, but stable democracies.

In some versions of the traditional hypothesis, a fairly 'high' level of mass political commitment is also included as a functional requisite. More accurately, perhaps, 'more' participation is generally regarded as better than 'less', both normatively and in terms of the stability of the system. Yet, at the same time, 'too intense' a degree of political commitment is usually regarded as dysfunctional, in that it may inhibit the process of bargaining and compromise upon which the stability of the system rests. The effort to restrict the parameters of legitimate access and participation in significant issues is of course a primary characteristic of any political process, and 'too intense' an interest obviously threatens this operational aim and necessity.

Two-party systems have often been regarded as a functional requisite of stable democratic systems. This structural characteristic is held to ensure majority government, the pragmatic compromise of narrow interests, and effective action, contrasted with multi-party systems which often tend to institutionalize conflict by identifying parties with narrow ideological interests. The several parties must then form temporary and shifting coalitions, resulting in diffused responsibility and attending instabilities. Instead of rationalizing and reconciling competing interests, the multi-party structure tends to exacerbate such divergences.

In effect, the absence of some combination of these conditions has often been held to result in political conflict and instability.[2] As noted, however, certain observers have found that some of the most venerable Western democracies exhibit few of the 'functional requisites' posited above. Instead, they have bi- or polylingual, polyethnic, culturally fragmented social

---

[1] 'Typologies of democratic systems', pp. 56–9.
[2] Among others, see Sigmund Neumann (ed.), *Modern Political Parties* (Chicago: University of Chicago Press, 1956); Maurice Duverger, *Political Parties* (New York: Wiley, 1963); Anthony Downs, *An Economic Theory of Democracy* (New York: Harper, 1957); Gabriel Almond and James Coleman, *Politics of the Developing Areas* (Princeton: University Press, 1960).

systems, while their political subsystems are often characterized by several parties representing the dominant ethnic–religious subcultures in the society. Equally significant, their ethnic and religious diversity results in inter-group tensions and intensely felt ideologies that obviate the underlying national consensus assumed as essential by the traditional hypothesis. Such normative and cultural discontinuities are often institutionalized in the political system, as when explicit quotas for proportional allocation of positions in the governmental bureaucracy are established. Or when 'tradition' decrees that certain high elective offices be held by (or rotated between) men from only one or two religio-ethnic groups. Such fragmented cultural systems and their political subsystems have been called 'consociational', i.e. political systems whose 'essential characteristic' is not any particular institutional arrangement, but an 'overarching cooperation at the elite level with the deliberate aim of counteracting disintegrative tendencies in the system'.[1]

The theory of elite accommodation in consociational societies has been offered as an alternative hypothesis which accounts for the theoretical and empirical discontinuities outlined above. While all political systems require elite leadership, accommodation theory posits a critically decisive role for such leaders. It also explicitly and realistically extends the penumbra of 'political elites' to encompass the leaders of private groups. Within the formal governmental apparatus, legislators and top-level bureaucrats remain perhaps the central elements in the decision-making process, while in the private sphere, the leaders of interest groups assume a critical role in formulating the claims of their various constituencies and hammering out an accommodation among such claims with political elites. In addition to direct personal intervention and lobbying, the instruments of their influence include participation in a plethora of joint government–industry committees, administrative boards, and *ad hoc* advisory roles. Meanwhile, the role of the rank-and-file citizen is minimized and, indeed, insofar as mass interaction across religio-ethnic lines tends to be disruptive, limited mass participation becomes functional for the maintenance of stability and continuity in the political system. Limited participation is also functional because it provides elites greater freedom in working out compromises. Finally, the conditions of consociational politics tend to increase the bargaining power of articulate interest groups at the expense of governmental elites, who are constrained

---

[1] Lijphart, 'Typologies of democratic systems', p. 63. Hans Daalder has suggested that elite accommodation may sometimes have become established *before* fragmentation of a political culture occurs, 'On building consociational nations: the cases of the Netherlands and Switzerland', 23 *International Social Science Journal* (1971).

both operationally and symbolically by the need to sustain the precarious equilibrium among their divergent subcultures.

In effect, the major theory to be used here concerns itself with governmental and private leaders who play direct, continuous and active roles in the Canadian political apparatus.[1] The approach is essentially analytical rather than normative. There is no intention to suggest that the process of elite accommodation is covert, undemocratic, or unique. Instead, we assume that some measure of elite hegemony in political affairs is operationally necessary in any complex, functionally differentiated social system. Our essential aim is to present and document a theory of political behaviour which may help explain the Canadian process of government and the vital role of interest groups in that process.

Insofar as the institutional structure of accommodation is concerned, the following analysis differs somewhat from the classical consociational assumption that accommodation occurs *within* the formal political structure. Our research suggests that the process also occurs *between* governmental and private political elites. The latter sometimes become part of the official political structure, but much more often they remain outside it, in terms of formal political roles. Accommodation theory, however, provides for such a structural modification. As Lijphart maintains, 'there are a variety of other responses that serve the same [accommodation] purpose. In fact, the essential characteristic of consociational democracy is not so much any particular institutional arrangement as overarching cooperation at the elite level...'[2]

Elite accommodation in Canada clearly occurs at several levels, most obviously in the Cabinet where regional and subcultural criteria of representation are the central premises of appointment. Accommodation is also institutionalized in federal–provincial relations and in the 'rule of proportionality' in appointments to the civil service,[3] Supreme Court and the Senate. The Prime Minister's extensive patronage power may also be included among its mechanisms. Such aspects of Canadian politics seem too well-known to require more than passing mention. Certainly, recent history indicates the critical role of accommodation politics at the highest level: the felicity with which the Liberals under Pearson played this part of the game,

[1] Other theories to be used in the analysis, including interaction theory will be discussed in Chapter 3.
[2] 'Typologies of democratic systems', p. 63.
[3] Porter, for example, cites a federal Minister to this effect, regarding appointments to the civil service: 'there are two principles to be observed, the efficiency of the service and the promotion of national unity', John Porter, *The Vertical Mosaic* (Toronto: University of Toronto Press, 1965), p. 441.

contrasted with the ineptitude of the Conservatives under Diefenbaker underscores the electoral consequences of neglecting Quebec.

By contrast, the role of interest groups in this process has been comparatively neglected.[1] However dramatic and visible high politics may be, the routine, everyday process of interest group accommodation seems to merit greater attention than it has received. This group process represents not only the whole substantive spectrum of national interests, but subcultural and economic interests as well, and often simultaneously. In this analysis, as a result, we are arguing for an end to any artificial separation between 'political' leaders in the formal apparatus of government and 'private' elites in the institutional sectors of industry, labour, agriculture, and the rest. However compelling our disciplinary urge to compartmentalize the 'political', it seems unrealistic and theoretically inadequate to conceptualize Canadian government in these dimensions. The web between so-called private and public elites is, as we hope to demonstrate, virtually seamless.

The problem of defining elites can be troublesome, but in this study they will be characterized as those who played active roles during 1967–71 in Canadian Parliaments, the higher civil service, and in interest groups. More specifically, elites are defined empirically here as the 1,124 individuals included in our random sample of legislators, civil servants, and directors of interest groups in Ottawa, Quebec, Ontario, and British Columbia. The modified theory of elite accommodation used here assigns the critical role in national policy formulation to the members of these three segments of the political system. In effect, they are the leaders who ensure its survival by continuous interaction and mutual adjustment achieved through a highly institutionalized process of bargaining and compromise.

The theory of accommodation posits a rather limited role for political parties.[2] The assumption again seems to suit Canadian conditions, where

---

[1] Cf. S. J. R. Noel who, in a commentary on Lijphart's theory, cites several areas where accommodation theory applies to Canadian politics, but includes only formal mechanisms, such as the Cabinet, federal–provincial boards, committees, etc. 'Consociational democracy and Canadian federalism', 4 *Canadian Journal of Political Science* (March, 1971), p. 16. On the other hand, he provides the great service of minimizing the role of parties in policy-making.

[2] As S. J. R. Noel concludes, 'it may well be that the importance of parties in the Canadian political system has been (and is) greatly exaggerated...', (unpublished paper, read at the Canadian Political Science Association Meeting, June, 1970), p. 18. Arend Lijphart has noted, however, that parties can be significant if 'they are the organised manifestations of subcultures in a fragmented society', as in Austria, Belgium, and the Netherlands.

interest groups seem more powerful and operationally essential than the parties. Historically, the two major parties have rarely carried out the role of formulating consistent, national policy alternatives and of educating the public by a sustained discussion of such policies. 'They tend to become chiefly agencies for the conquest of power.'[1] Nor have they generally been concerned with, or very successful at, building a national consensus or identity. Indeed, the major parties have tended at times to 'write-off' certain regional areas, since they could win a majority without them. In general, theirs has been essentially a reactive role, confined to brief periods of violent activity (political recruitment in fact is their major function) during elections, after which the system returns to 'normal': i.e. government by an uncoordinated series of pragmatic, *ad hoc* bargains and compromises reached among coalitions of members of the three elites in the substantive and geographical areas concerned.

CONDITIONS OF ELITE ACCOMMODATION IN CONSOCIATIONAL SOCIETIES

The process of accommodation is facilitated by several characteristics of the Canadian political elite.[2] At present, these are offered as hypotheses. First, there is a constant process of personal interaction among its three components. Not only is interaction among them common, but interchanges of roles tend to occur in which a given leader may find himself at one time affiliated with the private component as representative of an interest group, and at another time as a member of either the elected or appointive components of the formal governmental system.[3]

[1] John Porter, *The Vertical Mosaic*, pp. 373–7; André Siegfried, *The Race Question in Canada* (Toronto: McClelland and Stewart, 1966), pp. 112–13.

[2] Although the demands for elite accommodation are less compelling at the provincial level, given its relatively greater ethnic–cultural homogeneity, the process and the generalizations made here would seem to apply generally to provincial politics. In effect, the *process* of elite accommodation seems very similar at both provincial and federal levels, but the *motives* are different. The 'nation-saving' impetus is obviously less compelling among provincial elites. Perhaps we may conclude that whereas federal elites have the dual motivation of nation-saving and the allocation of public largesse, provincial elites tend to be focussed almost exclusively upon the latter. The *relative* influence of each elite section also seems to vary, with (for example) the bureaucratic segment tending to play a more critical (but varying) role in Ottawa than in Victoria, Quebec City and Toronto.

[3] On some unusual occasions, members of the political elite may perform such roles simultaneously, as in the case of one director in our sample who was also a Senator.

Political theory and political culture

A second functional requisite of the accommodation process is a certain degree of shared normative consensus among the three elites. Generally, and with many exceptions, its members share similar preferences about the nation, its dominant collective myths, and their instrumentalization in everyday life. Unlike the fragmented socio-political values of the divided subcultures, members of the governing elite are often committed to the ideal of national unity and the pragmatic compromises required to maintain the political system in a state of shifting equilibrium. There is, in effect, a good deal less ideological polarization among them than among their respective clientele groups. In this context, and at this level, their value system may be seen as essentially pragmatic, contrasted with the mass whose perceptions tend to be rather more ideological.[1]

Finally, the normative consensus and operational effectiveness of the elite is reinforced, if not created, by the pervasive homogeneity in socioeconomic origins of its three component sectors. However diverse their religio-ethnic character, members of both the English- and French-Canadian elite tend to comprise highly advantaged strata of society. Obviously, exceptions occur, but the generalization seems entirely feasible. In effect, the Canadian political elite seems to be bound together by mutual interaction, common social backgrounds, and shared norms. Only our data, of course, can validate this assumption.

The instruments of elite cohesion thus include both structural and normative elements. Its members occupy critical roles in the national economic and political system and in its ethnic and religious substructures. Normatively, they share generally positive beliefs regarding its major value premises, including Christianity, capitalism, and corporatism. They often share a common concern in creating and maintaining *national* identity and integrity.[2] These shared conditions enable them to interact productively across the conflicting interests of class, region, religion, and ethnicity that characterize the highly fragmented Canadian political culture. At the same time, the threat to stability posed by such internal divisions provides a constantly reoccurring motivation which by itself inspires elite response,[3] and sets the broad parameters of what is defined as politically feasible.

[1] For evidence, see Presthus, *Men At The Top: A Study in Community Power*, (Oxford University Press, 1964) pp. 328–36; McClosky *et al.*, 'Issue conflict and consensus among party leaders and followers', 44 *American Political Science Review* (June, 1960), pp. 422–3.

[2] Mackenzie King, asked to name the major achievement of his long political career, replied, 'Keeping Canada united during the war.'

[3] Arend Lijphart, *Politics in Europe* (New York: Prentice-Hall, 1969), p. 70.

12

Specifically, as Lijphart suggests, the political elite must have the following attributes:

1. The capacity to recognize the dangers inherent in a fragmented political system;
2. A positive commitment to maintaining the ongoing system;
3. The ability to transcend at the elite level the cleavages existing at the subcultural level;
4. The capacity to find pragmatic solutions to the demands of the subcultures.[1]

Certain psychological attributes are probably characteristic of the political elite. At this point, they are offered as hypotheses. Their devotion to national unity and identity probably subsumes a generous personal appreciation of their capacity to shape and press through wise policies. Their political confidence and pragmatism are probably shared with significant personal needs for the dividends of power and deference often flowing from higher political roles. Feelings of political efficacy are typically strong. Not astonishingly, their sense of personal achievement and self-esteem tends to manifest itself in a generally positive appreciation of the going system. Conversely, as we shall show, rank-and-file members of society often tend to rank low on several of these values. Personal ambivalence about politicians and government, and about one's capacity to influence them tends to result in relatively reduced levels of participation.[2] Our data will document the relevance of these assumptions in the Canadian political culture, which is characterized by a certain measure of mass distrust of government, especially *vis-à-vis* the federal government whose legitimacy has always been precarious. Somewhat ironically, this condition is accompanied by considerable deference toward those in leadership positions. The explanation probably includes the common popular tendency to exhibit a generalized ambivalence toward 'politicians' collectively, attended by considerable respect for them individually.

Certain conditions are also required among the mass or rank-and-file members of the polity if accommodation among the three political elites is to succeed. These exist at two analytical levels, among the entire culture and within each of its discrete subcultures, and particularly the English-Canadian and French-Canadian components. In the former context, it is essential that

[1] *Ibid.*, pp. 64–5.
[2] See Chapter 2. For cross-national generalizations, see Lester Milbrath, *Political Participation* (Chicago: Rand McNally, 1965).

ordinary citizens are prepared to delegate effective governing authority to leaders. This requisite applies to both their 'private' roles as members of interest groups and to their 'public' roles as citizens. In each case, they must generally be prepared to accept sporadic participation, as seen for example in elections, annual meetings, occasional mobilization on specific issues, etc. One way of characterizing this requisite is in terms of Canadian patterns of authority, in which institutions such as the family, school, and government tend to inculcate what we shall later refer to as *deferential* attitudes toward authority.

We are concerned here with a universal property of social systems: the nature of the bases upon which authority is legitimated by those subject to it. As Max Weber says, 'the basis of every system of authority, and correspondingly of every kind of willingness to obey, is a belief... by virtue of which persons exercising authority are lent prestige.'[1] The beliefs that underlie authority in Canadian life, it seems to me, rest in considerable measure upon hierarchical and class assumptions which reflect its European heritage. These assumptions reflect and reinforce an elitist philosophy of higher education which has, until very recently, delayed the emergence of a countervailing elite based upon technical expertise.[2] Some aspects of this general orientation, which I have characterized as the deferential pattern of authority, will be analysed in the next chapter.

It is also useful to think of this particular requisite of mass behaviour in terms of political participation, i.e. the extent to which individuals take active roles in political affairs, through voting, supporting candidates, contributing time and money to campaigns, serving on committees, etc.

Similarly, at the undifferentiated mass level of analysis, it is essential that a *moderate* level of nationalism persists. While one might assume that intense feelings of nationalism would be more functional since they would blunt the centripetal force of ethnic and religious cleavages, Lijphart shows that only a moderate nationalism exists in the five countries he characterizes as 'consociational', i.e. Austria, Belgium, Lebanon, the Netherlands, and Switzer-

---

[1] *The Theory of Social and Economic Organization* (New York: Oxford University Press, 1947), p. 328.

[2] In 1960, for example, despite its world rank of second in per capita income, Canada ranked somewhat lower in students per 100,000 in higher education. Some comparative figures include: United States, 1,983; The Netherlands, 923; Australia, 856; New Zealand, 839; Canada, 645; Russia, 539; Britain, 460. Considerable expansion of higher education systems has occurred in all these societies since 1960, but one assumes that their relative positions have not changed greatly. Bruce Russett *et al. World Handbook of Political and Social Indicators* (New Haven: Yale University Press, 1964).

land.[1] It will be useful to keep this qualification in mind as the analysis proceeds, since an attenuated degree of nationalism has long been a characteristic of Canadian political culture.

Some appreciation of an *external threat* has also been suggested as a requisite for consociational patterns of governance.[2] Such a perspective tends to moderate the particularistic claims of the several competing groups that threaten the social equilibrium. As is well-known, Canada presents a particularly striking example of this condition. Fear of its powerful neighbour to the south has been, it seems fair to say, a constant factor in Canadian political behaviour. Indeed, the thrust of this appreciation is reinforced by an ironic duality, in which the nation's fears of American cultural and economic imperialism have included a similar apprehension on the part of Quebec *vis-à-vis* English-Canada.

A further requisite at the mass level is a certain degree of social polarization in which members of the various subcultural groups remain relatively isolated from each other. This condition tends to prevent potential conflict among such groups from becoming patent. Here again, the Canadian experience is apposite. The high degree of religious, linguistic, educational and social separatism implicit in the mosaic philosophy tends to ensure the necessary degree of exclusivity. Evidence sustaining this appreciation is seen in a national survey of Canadian youth (N-1,359), the largest single proportions of whom concluded that the most pressing threats to Canadian national unity were 'English–French differences of opinion', and '...regional differences and differences between economic classes'.[3] Considerable empirical evidence indicates, moreover, that members of such segmented groups are likely to be rather more ethnocentric and doctrinaire than their leaders. If accommodation among such groups is to occur, it will probably be through the efforts of leaders who can somehow take a larger national view of the particularistically-defined issues that often characterize Canadian politics.

This condition, parenthetically, illustrates dramatically the discontinuity between conventional explanations of democratic stability and the theory used here. Whereas the existence of overlapping group memberships has been assumed to be a central factor in ensuring stability, the theory of elite

---

[1] *Politics in Europe*, p. 71. Lijphart has recently qualified this condition, maintaining that weak nationalism is merely one attribute of consociational societies, rather than a necessary condition.

[2] *Ibid.*, p. 70.

[3] John C. Johnstone, 'Young people's images of Canadian society', *Royal Commission on Bilingualism and Biculturalism* (Ottawa: Queen's Printer, 1969), p. 48.

accommodation assumes precisely the opposite: *Not only do individuals tend to restrict themselves to groups that have similar values, but such exclusivity encourages political stability.*[1]

A corollary of the subcultural polarization requisite is that *within* each subculture, a fairly high degree of cohesion and organization exists which will ensure that leaders have a relatively free hand in negotiating with elites representing other subcultural elements.[2] Here again, the historic duality of the Two Canadas is germane: Quebec and English-speaking Canada have been accurately characterized as the 'two silences'. The symbiotic relationship between going elitist conceptions of leadership, deferential patterns of authority, and the resulting autonomy of leaders, and effective accommodation among their political elites may now be more apparent.

It should be noted in this context that Canada fails to meet only one of the functional requisites of consociational politics. The major absent condition is a 'relatively low total load' on the governmental system, which obviates great strain upon its resources and permits elites to focus upon the crucial task of maintaining the system. Judged by such indexes as the proportion of Gross National Product spent for all government, now about 38 per cent (1972), the proportion of the total labour force employed by government, about 12 per cent in 1972.[3] and the attending pervasiveness of government in Canadian society,[4] it seems probable that Canada does not meet this

[1] Lijphart, *The Politics of Accommodation*, p. 69.

[2] *Ibid.*

[3] *Ibid.* It seems that Canada differs little from other rich Western societies in depending heavily upon 'big government'; if, for example, the total expenditure for all government is compared, including social security and public enterprises, as a percentage of Gross National Product, Canada ranks tenth in the world, representative nations rank as follows:

1.	Sweden	52.9
6.	The Netherlands	41.2
8.	Italy	39.9
10.	Canada	37.4
11.	Norway	36.5
19.	Denmark	29.9
20.	United States	27.9

Russett, *et al.*, *World Handbook of Political and Social Indicators* p. 63. In effect, although nine countries spend more for government, five of them are 'large' in terms of population, including Britain, Japan, and France. This suggests that Canada does not meet the 'low total load on government' criterion of consociational societies.

[4] Using a sophisticated index of national political development based upon cross-cultural levels of communication, urbanization, education, and employment in agriculture during the period 1940–60, Phillips Cutright finds that Canada is even more highly developed politically than predicted by these measures. 'National political development:

second condition. Indeed, in terms of comparative international levels of over-all development, it ranks seventh, behind the US, UK, Australia, West Germany, Sweden, New Zealand, in that order.[1] Although we are not sure that the two variables are positively associated, it does seem that countries that are highly developed politically would, all else being equal, tend to be characterized by great reliance upon the governmental system. For example, most of the countries mentioned here rank in the highest quartile regarding total expenditure on general government as a percentage of GNP. Their political systems are, in effect carrying a heavy load. Despite this exception, Canada does meet the general conditions of consociational societies in which sustained accommodation among elites representing the various subcultures and their functional interests is the only means of ensuring stability.

In sum, our empirical analysis of interest group interactions with legislators and higher bureaucrats suggests that both the substance and the implementation of public policy in Canada are largely shaped by accommodation among three political elites, comprised of legislators and higher bureaucrats and the leaders of major interest groups. Among them, they possess disproportionate shares of such scarce political resources as legitimacy, expertise, continuity, access, and power. Despite the vaunted institutional autonomy of the Cabinet, it seems clear that in operational terms the national political process is essentially one of continual, *ad hoc* bargaining and compromise, in which the resolution of the claims of a bewildering variety of interests is often the major activating force in the behaviour of governmental elites. At the very least, Government's policy initiative is virtually always shared with members of the private political elite.

At the same time, the Canadian cultural milieu, which provides the framework for the process of elite accommodation, nicely meets the conditions of consociational societies. Political integration is marginal. As John Meisel writes, 'Canada is almost totally lacking in a genuinely shared set of symbols, heroes, historical incidents, enemies, or even ambitions.'[2] Moreover, as

---

measurement and analysis', 28 *American Sociological Review* (April, 1963), p. 262; pp. 253–64.

[1] J. Kyogoku and H. Inoue, 'Multi-dimensional scaling of nations', in Charles L. Taylor (ed.), *Aggregate Data Analysis* (Paris: Mouton and Co., 1968), pp. 188–90. The rankings are based upon 25 'principle components' including population, income, industrial structure, education, mass media, health, and religion, drawn from Russett *et al., World Handbook of Political and Social Indicators*.

[2] Cf. R. H. Leach, ed., *Contemporary Canada* (Durham: Duke University Press, 1968), p. 135.

suggested in the next chapter, the political culture is deeply fragmented, mainly along the English-Canadian–French-Canadian axis, but also in terms of regionalism and the evolving claims of new Canadians for parity in the political system.[1] Four parties, having only marginally discrete policy preferences (with the exception of the New Democratic Party (NDP)), comprise the national Parliament. These parties range ideologically from the left, represented by the socialist NDP, through the middle Liberal and Progressive–Conservative parties, to the Social Credit party, a right-wing splinter group which perhaps alone among the national parties is not a viable, potential contender for decisive political power. At the provincial level, as seen for example in Quebec and British Columbia, some of such minority parties, based upon relatively narrow interests, have been in power. Canada, in sum, meets many of the conditions of consociational democracy.

INTEREST GROUP POLITICS

A major consequence of Canada's fragmented political culture and the attending necessity for the two major parties to avoid principles in favour of an economically-oriented, brokerage system of politics is to insure an especially vital role for interest groups. As André Siegfried concluded three-quarters of a century ago, 'It is the party...that treats with the great forces whose support it requires – railway companies, the Catholic clergy, industrial and commercial companies, etc.'[2] More recently, Frank Underhill reaffirmed this judgment, 'A party which depends for success (i.e. for office) upon the different and often contradictory appeals which it must make to different sectional interests will inevitably in the course of time become mainly dependent upon and responsive to those interest-groups which are themselves best organized and most strategically located for applying effective pressure upon the party leaders. In Canada there are two such groups who have always held a dominating position in our politics because of their superior internal organization – the French Catholic Church in Quebec and the interlocking financial–industrial–commercial interests...The Quebec Church owes its power to the effectiveness with which it can control and

---

[1] The emerging claims of increasingly self-conscious 'new Canadian' groups for a greater share in political decisions will tend to reinforce the consociational character of the Canadian system. In this context, it is interesting that the 'mosaic' policy tends to aggravate ethnic particularism and, hence, the fragmentation of Canadian political culture.

[2] Siegfried, *The Race Question in Canada*, p. 118.

18

direct the mass voting of its parishioners. Big business depends primarily upon campaign contributions, also upon constant official and unofficial lobbying, and upon all the complex economic and social relationships between business and political leaders.[1]

As is well known, the Canadian political experience from Confederation onward has been essentially economic and pragmatic in orientation. Examples are legion: the history of Macdonald and the Canadian Pacific Railway; the 'National Policy' of his Liberal–Conservative party and his genius in pushing it ahead, despite sustained ethnic and religious tensions between Ontario and Quebec; the resurgence of a similar thrust by Laurier, after an unsympathetic interlude under Mackenzie; and the keen appreciation of Mackenzie King that 'the essential task of Canadian statesmanship is to discover the terms on which as many as possible of the significant interest-groups of our country can be induced to work together in a common policy.'[2]

These political and cultural conditions and their consequences for the role of interest groups in the political system seem to lend themselves nicely to analysis using a theory of elite accommodation. Obviously, not every condition of consociational society nor every facet of accommodation theory will fit the Canadian milieu. Theories rarely function in this way. On the whole, however, the theory should be useful in explaining Canadian politics.

This brief and highly generalized outline of accommodation theory will now be set in context by a survey of Canada's fragmented political culture.

[1] *In Search of Canadian Liberalism* (Toronto: Macmillan, 1960), p. 167.
[2] *Ibid.*, p. 126.

CHAPTER 2

THE CANADIAN POLITICAL CULTURE

The Canadian process of elite accommodation is shaped mainly by the nations's dual political culture, French-Canadian and English-Canadian. This culture, which is deeply fragmented along ethnic, religious, institutional, and philosophical lines, not only provides the ideological framework within which political elites exist, it also conditions to a large extent the operational role that such elites play in the national political process. This is essentially because political culture largely determines the legitimacy of both government and the interest groups with which it interacts in designing public policy.

Political culture consists of the attitudes that citizens have about politics; the extent to which they participate in political affairs; the shape and the content of political socialization employed by such agencies as the family and school; and perhaps most important, the extent to which its members regard the political system as *legitimate*, as being reasonably equitable and effective. Political culture, in turn, works hand in hand with the institutional apparatus of government, which reflects and moulds the national legacy of historical experience and assumptions about man and the state. For such reasons we begin with an analysis of four mutually reinforcing elements of the national political culture, each of which seems particularly germane to an understanding of the role of interest groups and the Canadian system of elite accommodation.

These elements include a pragmatic appreciation of government's role in the economy; an underlying corporatist theory of societal life; traditional and deferential patterns of authority; and a quasi-participative political culture insofar as the ordinary citizen is concerned.[1] *These components of Canadian*

---

[1] By 'participative' we mean the opportunity for and the felt capacity of ordinary men and women to play an active personal role, both individually and through interest groups, in shaping the governmental decisions that affect them. In this context, voting is regarded as a necessary but not a sufficient condition.

political culture, culminate, in turn, in a national political process that may be called one of elite accommodation. Essentially, as noted earlier, this is a system in which the major decisions regarding national socioeconomic policy are worked out through interactions between governmental (i.e. legislative and bureaucratic) elites and interest group elites. We shall refer throughout to these three sub-elites as 'the political elite'.

PRAGMATIC APPRECIATION OF GOVERNMENT'S ECONOMIC ROLE

Despite an historical acceptance of capitalist values, government has come to play a critical role in both provincial and national economies. While most English-Canadians have always entertained a pragmatic appreciation of government, perhaps symbolized by the common view that Confederation itself was essentially an economic plan, it is only recently that French-Canadians have come to accept this condition. Today, they share fully the positive view of government's economic role. By 'pragmatic' I mean an essentially utilitarian conception of government which provides a justification for its use to support economic development and to cushion the shocks of the marketplace. This pervasive sanction for direct government intervention in the economy is what is meant here by 'legitimation'. Any radical spirit of *laissez-faire* or fear of government which might have been assumed to characterize Canadian entrepreneurs, and indeed most of those engaged in commerce and industry, rarely seems to have taken hold in English Canada. In Quebec, on the other hand, the painful exigencies of the depression in the 1930s and the reform policies of the Lesage regime were required to overcome the pervasive resistance to state intervention among religious, economic, and political leaders.

In terms of historical political theory, the positive appreciation of the state's role reflects Tory conceptions of society as a collective organic entity in which cooperation is more common than conflict and group claims are prior to those of the individual. In this perspective, government is seen as an integral part of society, rather than as a necessary evil. Such a perception may explain why, in 1970, the federal government's imposition of the stringent War Measures Act was widely supported by a majority of Canadians, including those in Quebec.

At the same time, economic imperatives are often cited as the major reason for *étatism* in Canada.[1] The financial and entrepreneurial resources

[1] Harold Innis, *Essays in Canadian Economic History* (Toronto: University of Toronto Press, 1956).

required for industrial development simply were not available in a new and sparsely populated country. As a result, a sharp distinction has not always been drawn between the use of state resources for private and for public ends.[1] This means that various essential elements of the economy, which might have remained in private hands, have either been state-owned initially or nationalized when this seemed convenient. Air Canada, the Bank of Canada, Canadian National Railways, British Columbia, Ontario and Quebec Hydro, and indeed some 20 Crown proprietary corporations, are among them.

By 1970, this policy had brought subsidy programmes for virtually every sector of the national economy. Moreover, when development is needed or when existing industries encounter difficulty, those concerned turn immediately to Ottawa or the provincial governments for help. They are seldom disappointed. Few attempts are made in English-Canada to rationalize any resulting disparity between the capitalist rhetoric expressed in some quarters and the mixed enterprise reality. Opinion leaders may have made some mild effort to mute government's role in the partnership, and perhaps certain segments of the public remain unaware of its extent, but among articulate elites there seems to be a widely-shared view that government should be used positively for economic development and protection against the strains of the marketplace.

Until the Quiet Revolution of the 1960s French-Canada was quite different. *Etatism* was regarded as anathema by its bourgeoisie, economic, and intellectual elites. Ideological resistance to state intervention was equally characteristic of religious leaders, who may have viewed such as being incompatible with their own welfare programmes. Doctrinally, a comprehensive policy of state intervention was sometimes identified with liberal democratic regimes, whose policies might culminate in urbanization, industrialization, and attending social changes that were long antithetical to time-honoured Church norms. Quebec's religious leaders were quite effective in turning aside any analysis which might conclude that the province's cultural aspirations necessarily required a viable economic base.

French-Canadian intellectuals, whose views until quite recently were at one with those of the clergy, often shared this point of view. As a result,

---

[1] The selective privatization of public assets is nicely illustrated in the city of Toronto where municipal tennis courts are co-opted by certain groups who transform the facility into a quasi-private club, whose members elect officers, pay dues, and prescribe rules, including the hours when ordinary citizens may use the courts and the appropriate uniforms to be worn by them.

traditional values which idealized rural existence, professional and humanistic learning, a French-Canadian cultural mystique, nationalism, limited government, and elitist conceptions of leadership were not effectively challenged until long after the depression of the 1930s which brought elsewhere a dramatic reconceptualization of government's role. Such a change was not to occur in Quebec until the 1960s.

Bourgeoisie industrial and commercial elements endorsed most of these values, and in addition, they had the usual reasons for rejecting welfare statism. Successive governments, moreover, shared their views during and following the depression. Social welfare and educational spending remained minimal until the Lesage Government came to power in 1960. Previous *Union Nationale* and Liberal governments kept taxes low, among other concessions, in order to attract foreign capital into the province. The secularization and expansion of higher education, particularly in neglected technical fields, which might have enabled French-Canadians to compete more effectively for larger shares of opportunity within the province's expanding industrial structure, was probably of limited appeal to all three groups, for mixed reasons, ideological, economic, and competitive. Such factors, and there were many others, delayed the vast expansion of governmental functions that has characterized Western society during this century.

Change, however, was sharply augmented by Quebec's rapid industrialization and rising standards of life during World War II. Since that time, traditional ultramontane intellectual influence in Quebec has been successfully challenged by younger liberal elements. Their 'neo-nationalism', informed largely by secularist values, includes a rejection of Canadianism as a solution for French-Canadian aspirations, the acceptance of industrialization with its implications for the modernization of higher education, and the independence of *Canadien* culture, to be achieved within an autonomous province of Quebec. In the 1960s the Lesage government hammered through a positive new programme, attended by the nationalization of Quebec Hydro, which for many French-Canadians symbolized foreign domination of their economy, and a dramatic expansion of educational opportunity at every level. Since that time, the provincial government has actively promoted economic growth, including a development programme which aggressively encourages investment both from Europe and the United States. At present, then, we may say that both Canadas share the pragmatic appreciation of the role of government in social and economic affairs.

This affirmative ideology is immediately relevant to elite political behaviour in the Canadian milieu. It means that government tends to play an active,

23

brokerage role *vis-à-vis* major social and economic interests. The governmental elite, in a word, invites such groups to organize their claims, rationalize any conflicting demands within their various constituencies, and present them as effectively as possible to a government whose definition of its own role is essentially that of allocating public largesse among them. The pragmatic ethic legitimates precisely this conception of government's role.

Quantitative indexes of the consequences of the positive appreciation of government's role illustrate the recent secular trend. In 1960, for example, all levels of government spent about 27 per cent of gross national product; by 1972, this proportion had risen to 38 per cent, well above the United States and among the highest in Western nations. On the revenue side, the 11 billion dollars that government drew about ten years ago had increased by 1970 to 30 billion. The dramatic increase in federal employees provides another index. In 1960, the number was about 150,000; in 1970, 250,000.

A countervailing dynamism follows among private elites. As government penetrates into new areas, while expanding its role in traditional sectors, interest groups tend to expand in number and scope in order to ensure representation in the struggle for public bounties. As a result, a vast number of groups now confront government with their demands. Obviously, various criteria, explicit and otherwise, are used by the governmental elite to differentiate among their multiple claims, including those of government itself for projects having honorific, symbolic, and economic value. Constant bargaining and negotiation occur, often at some cost to party principles and comprehensive planning, but one may be sure that the relative economic and political resources of the various private contenders are a constant factor in the equation. This point is stressed because our analysis will indicate that Canadian interest groups differ widely in the resources they bring to bear in the political arena, and that their effectiveness is generally roughly proportionate to their resources. Meanwhile, certain other elements in the Canadian political culture ensure that the resulting accommodation between government and interest groups is legitimated by the public.

CORPORATIST THEORY OF SOCIETY

If government itself enjoys a deep-rooted legitimacy because of popular acceptance of its pervasive role, interest groups are equally fortunate in having the support of a venerable corporatist theory of group relations in society.[1] Corporatism is essentially a conception of society in which government delegates many of its functions to private groups, which in turn provide guidance regarding the social and economic legislation required in the modern national state. Although many theoretical and normative doctrines have been joined in corporatist thought and practice, for our purposes, its essential ingredient is an underlying pluralism which gives private groups both normative and functional legitimacy in the political system. As we shall show, this condition is vital for interest group behaviour. Corporatism rests upon an organic view of society in which collective aspirations are seen as prior to those of any discrete individual or group, including the state. For this reason, a typical incentive in corporatist thought has always been the hope of finding some way to overcome pervasive modern schisms between labour and capital, social classes, and indeed, between government and the governed. The usual solution has been to bring private groups directly into the official governing process.

It is important to note initially that corporatism has many faces, including its ugly manifestation in Italian fascism and French Pétainism between 1920 and 1945. An essential difference between these models and the Canadian variant lies in their disparate conceptions of the role of the state. In the classical pluralist version, interest groups are looked upon as prior to the state and fully equal to it normatively and juridically. The state's role is seen as an auxiliary one, in which many of its essential tasks are delegated to groups whose interest and expertise promise a high level of socioeconomic performance. The basis of representation becomes essentially collective, rather than individual. Functional and group imperatives, in effect, take the place of individualistic, class-oriented perspectives of society. The structure and style of the medieval guilds has often provided a model for contemporary advocates of corporatism. In the German, Italian, and Vichy models, on the other hand, private groups were effectively subordinated to the state, although Pétain's view of the state was less monolithic than the Italian and German versions.

The roots of Canadian corporatism go back to the Middle Ages when theorists were searching for some normative rationale which would give private groups a measure of autonomy against the emerging national state.

---

[1] Harry Eckstein, *Pressure Group Politics* (Stanford: Stanford University Press, 1960), pp. 24–33; Mathew Elbow, *French Corporative Theory: 1789–1948* (New York: Octagon, 1966); Louis Baudin, *Corporatisme: Italie, Portugal, Espagne, France* rev. ed. (Paris: *Librairie générale de droit et de juresprudence*, 1942); and Emile Durkheim, *The Division of Labour in Society* (New York: Macmillan, 1933).

French- and English-Canada seem to have shared this view fully, although in different ways. In English-Canada, corporatism has been an unquestioned, latent assumption, while in Quebec it has been widely celebrated by both the Church and many leading intellectuals. One of its earliest affirmations came from Pope Pius XI, who saw it as a desirable form of social organization, and possibly, as a counterpoise to the positive welfare state.

Corporatism also seems to have been seen as an alternative to parliaments elected upon a geographical basis. Instead, it proposes functional or occupational bases of selection. Private groups of every kind would thus provide the organs of government. In Quebec, such an instrument was seen as a means of overcoming any tendency of governments to be dominated by narrow financial interests. Ideally, corporatism would ensure that government represented the common good. On the other hand, some observers, including Pierre Elliott Trudeau, have regarded corporatism as an example of the futile 'monolithic ideology' of Quebec social thought, co-opted as a means of 'taming' trade unionism.[1] However that may be, the theory has a fairly extended history in Quebec, going back at least half a century. As in English-Canada, its major effects include a philosophical basis for interest group legitimacy *vis-à-vis* government. Indeed, an essential element of corporatism is that private groups are regarded as being fully as legitimate a part of society as government. Their ends should have equal weight with those of government. Both pluralist thought and natural law doctrines are set against any claims of state hegemony.

This essentially normative argument is reinforced by a decisive functional one: given the variety of groups in society, the diversity and complexity of their substantive interests, and the magnitude of their claims upon the state, it seems virtually impossible for government alone to adjudicate among them, much less make intelligent decisions about the policies required to fit their endlessly varied circumstances. The awareness and information which government needs to carry on its comprehensive role must in part be supplied by the groups themselves. Virtue and necessity are again combined to present a powerful justification for a system of group politics based upon elite accommodation.

Corporatist theory holds, then, that society is properly conceived as a congeries of interest groups, each of which enjoys legitimacy and the free-

[1] *La Grève de l'amiante* (Montreal: Editions Cité Libre, 1956) pp. 10–37. Regarding corporatism in Quebec, Trudeau claims that 'during this period [1930s] nearly all French-Canadian thinkers, politicians, journalists, and editors advocated corporatism as a kind of extraordinary panacea...' *Federalism and the French Canadians*, p. xxiii.

dom to put its demands to government. Such an ideology has immediate implications for individual participation in the political system. Corporatism, indeed, has an anti-individualistic bias.[1] It tends, on balance, to weaken the thrust of purely individual claims, both on normative and operational grounds. In effect, unless an individual's demands are part of the claims put by a larger collectivity, they tend to be regarded by political elites as both questionable and quixotic. Operationally, moreover, government usually finds it difficult to handle individual claims; both its size and its mentality find them inapposite. This condition suggests again a decisive functional property of interest groups: they have the critical task of refining and synthesizing the claims of vast numbers of individuals for presentation to government. This collectivization of demands is a crucial labour-saving device, given the number and complexity of popular claims, the scope of government in Canadian society, and the attending overload of governmental institutions. Indeed, the functional role of interest groups is so vital that Max Weber could say, 'The management of politics through parties simply means management through interest groups.'[2]

The institutionalization of the corporatist ethic in the Canadian political milieu is seen in the federal Senate, a body of 102 (1970) individuals appointed on political bases, with a substantial property qualification, presumably to exercise a moderating effect upon the popularly elected House of Commons. Essentially, in the context of this analysis, the Senate provides a basis for functional representation of a select group of interests, among which the main ones are corporate and financial. Analysis of the backgrounds of Senators, for example, suggests the going pattern of representation (see Table 2-1).

Business, finance, and industry is the largest category of occupational representation, and when combined with law, which is symbiotically and representationally related to it, we find that fully two-thirds of the Senators represent this general area. A fairly substantial minority has been active in politics and government service at both federal and provincial levels. Almost 10 per cent of the Senate is made up of professionals, other than law, and almost half of these are medical doctors. Farm operators are relatively few and only one representative of labour is included. Virtually all of the Senators are from the two charter groups, and the only so-called ethnic representatives are one Indian and one Ukranian.

[1] Eckstein, *Pressure Group Politics*, p. 24.
[2] 'Politics as a vocation' *From Max Weber: Essays in Sociology*, trans. and ed. by H. H. Gerth and C. W. Mills (New York: Oxford University Press, 1946), p. 94.

TABLE 2-1 *Functional representation in the Canadian Senate*

Area	Proportion of Senate
	%
Business, industry, and finance	37
Law	30
Government and politics[a]	16
Professions (other than law)	9
Agriculture	6
Labour	1
	(102)

[a] This category includes those Senators for whom either political or bureaucratic roles have been their *primary* occupational role.

It should be emphasized that I am not maintaining that the Senate exercises great influence over federal policy. The vital point here is symbolic: the extent to which Canadian political culture legitimates corporatist theory by bringing directly into the formal political apparatus a large and socially powerful group of individuals who patently represent the dominant private business, financial, industrial, and professional interests of the society.

The federal Senate, in effect, dramatizes the pervasive synthesis between government and interest group elites, while providing yet another example of the survival of traditional bases of authority in Canadian society. Corporatist theory also seems closely linked with the positive view of government outlined earlier. Together, they provide a normative justification for a group system of politics that would have been functionally necessary in any event. Compared with other liberal, 'atomistic' societies such as the United States and France, where the ordinary citizen often regards interest groups as anathema, this 'organic', legitimative aspect of Canadian political culture is probably a decisive factor in interest group behaviour. Although the shape and extent of government's interactions with interest groups are perhaps not widely known, corporatist assumptions tend to give the system both legitimacy and viability.

DEFERENTIAL PATTERNS OF AUTHORITY

Both Canadas retain significant residues of two venerable forms of authority, which Max Weber, the German scholar, has defined as 'traditional' and 'charismatic'. Both forms tend to encourage deferential patterns of authority in interpersonal relations. The bases of socio-political legitimacy also include an alternative form called 'legal–rational', which in Weber's words rests upon 'a belief in the legality patterns of normative rules and the right of those elevated to authority under such rules to issue commands'[1] Although at any given time society reveals traces of all three authority systems, there has been a secular tendency throughout Western history for societies to evolve from traditional and charismatic bases toward legal–rational ones. As the term suggests, traditional authority is based upon the 'eternal yesterday', upon the weight of custom and convention. One does things because they have always been done this way. In thus looking to the past, traditional authority is perhaps inevitably conservative.

Charismatic authority, on the other hand, is based upon a subjective incentive whereby leaders who possess charismatic (literally, 'gift of grace') qualities are able to inspire followers with the desire to obey on grounds of trust and confidence in their extraordinary powers. Charismatic authority may be either conservative or revolutionary in its social consequences, but is clearly antithetical to legal–rational authority. Over time, as the thrust of science, technology and secularism becomes stronger, the two 'earlier' bases of authority are challenged, and in some societies, overcome by an essentially bureaucratic impulse in which the breakdown of ancient values, the substitution of contract for status relationships among men, and the rationalization of production dominate. Man enters, in Weber's evocative phrase, 'the iron cage' of history. In effect, technological, legal–rational bases of authority tend to supersede traditional-and-charismatic claims for deference and submission.

In any society certain structural conditions tend to perpetuate traditional–charismatic values. These may include monarchical rule, elitist educational norms, pervasive class differentiations, highly bureaucratized institutional structures, and marginal levels of economic development. Little need be said about the tradition-serving function of monarchy. Elitist educational norms with their emphasis upon classical and professional education, as opposed to scientific and technical training, reinforced by limited educational opportunity at the university level, resistance to the introduction of 'universalistic' (i.e. objective) bases of recruitment, and the idealization of leadership based upon subjective factors of presence, accent, generalist–amateur qualities – all similarly tend to perpetuate traditional–charismatic bases of authority. A common result is the survival of ascriptive (i.e. inherited,

[1] *The Theory of Social and Economic Organization*, ed. and intro. by T. Parsons (New York: Free Press, 1947), p. 328, pp. 324–92.

class-based) criteria of personal evaluation, along with those based upon achievement.

Class differentiations have a similar effect, since they tend to separate individuals into enclaves of education and social interaction which through a process of mutual reinforcement give traditional values a great deal of continuity. If, for example, the premises of recruitment to strategic decision-making roles in the society are controlled by members of a certain class stratum, such values will of course tend to persist, even though they are patently minoritarian and only precariously related to its functional needs. Some such bases of selectivity have often existed in Canadian politics and industry,[1] perhaps most obviously in the appointive federal Senate.[2]

The impact of economic development upon traditional and charismatic values is well established. Essentially, it accelerates the breakdown of the traditional, *Gemeinschaft* values which tend to characterize so-called developing nations. One of the first institutions to be transformed is the extended family system, whose behaviour tends to rest upon 'particularistic' (subjective) premises of time, kinship, and religion that often blunt the needs of an industrializing society for achievement, discipline, expertise, transitory loyalties, and interpersonal relations strongly influenced by individual self-interest. Despite some obvious personal dysfunctions, the nuclear family structure often proves better adapted to these imperatives. As Everett Hughes has shown, some such process has occurred in Quebec during this century as its rural, farm peasant class was gradually transformed under industrialization into an urban proletariat.[3]

Industrializing societies require great numbers of technically skilled engineers, scientists, chemists, and managers. Thus the typically professional, humanistic, and elitist oriented higher educational systems of developing societies must also be transformed. In effect, both their elitist assumptions and substantive content must be modified. Whatever weight may be given to resulting claims that 'more means worse', industrial predominance at this historical moment seems to require a higher educational system radically different from that provided by tradition-oriented societies.

[1] John Porter, *The Vertical Mosaic*, pp. 215–24; Chapters IX, XIII, and XVII.
[2] As Norman Ward says, after referring to the Senate as almost a 'vestigial' institution, 'Some measure of reform, however, should not be impossible. The prime difficulty is that the Senate can be improved in so many ways that the multitude of alternatives smothers any particular measure of reform which may be advanced', R. M. Dawson, *The Government of Canada*, fourth ed., revised by Norman Ward (Toronto: 1970) p. 329.
[3] *French Canada in Transition* (Chicago: University of Chicago Press, 1943).

Certain residues of such traditional–charismatic assumptions and their institutional manifestations seem to characterize some sectors of Canadian society.[1] Moreover, while the origins and the intensity of the deferential model obviously differ in French- and English-Canada, their respective feudal and anti-republican legacies have had many similar consequences for their political cultures. Summarily, the going normative prescriptions some-times include certain tendencies toward elitism, a hierarchical view of society, ascriptive bases of personal evaluation, ambivalence about the alleged materialistic individualism of the neighbour to the south, and some tension between traditional social values and pressing demands for conditions more apposite to an industrial society. In English-Canada, such tendencies may be viewed as a residue of that constellation of values brought to Canada by the Empire Loyalists following the American Revolution. As Arthur Lower says, 'Needless to say, a change of residence did not work a change of philosophy. In its new wilderness home, and its new aspect of British North Americanism, colonial Toryism made its second attempt to erect on American soil a copy of the English social edifice. From one point of view this is the most significant thing about the Loyalist movement: it withdrew a class concept of life from the south, moved it up north and gave it a second chance.'[2] While there is some argument as to how completely the socio-political values of the Empire Loyalists were transmuted to Canada, considerable evidence exists for the view that, in the main, their anti-republican, hierarchi-cal, counter-revolutionary preferences were resurrected in their newly established political institutions and indeed prevailed until at least the mid-eighteenth century. Lord Durham noted that 'Upper Canada...has long been entirely governed by a party, commonly designated as the Family Compact...For a long time, this body of men...possessed almost all the highest public offices, by means of which, and of its influence in the Executive Council, it wielded all the powers of government.'[3] Moreover, as S. F. Wise concludes, such colonial aristocracies 'left behind them a legacy of social

[1] The term 'residues' is used here to indicate that, relatively speaking, legal–rational norms are dominant in perhaps most sectors of Canadian society, which in terms of most socioeconomic indexes is one of the highly developed nations of the world. For relevant quantitative indexes, see Russett *et al., World Handbook of Political and Social Indicators.*

[2] *Colony to Nation* (Toronto: Longmans, 1964), p. 118. Again, speaking of the effects of the Mackenzie Rebellion, which included 'a purge of forward-looking elements from Upper Canada', Lower concludes, 'the rebellion thus reinforced the American Revolu-tion in creating a conservative and even reactionary province.' p. 245.

[3] Cited in David W. T. Earl, *The Family Compact: Aristocracy or Oligarchy* (Toronto: Clark, 1967), p. 6.

Political theory and political culture

and political conservatism which has had much to do with shaping the Canadian character'.[1]

As S. D. Clark has shown, this legacy has been reinforced by the pervasive bureaucratization of Canadian institutions. 'Typically, the Canadian middle-class person has been an office-holder, whether in the service of the government, a business corporation, church or other such type of bureaucratic organization.' Such individuals, he believes, have maintained their positions less by engaging in a competitive struggle than by building about themselves 'a very largely closed bureaucratic system of control. Such a middle-class has inevitably remained small but it has been one which, in control of the strategic institutions of the Canadian society, could wield enormous influence and power.'[2] As a result, socialization has included considerable emphasis upon classical bureaucratic virtues of order, deference, hierarchy, security, and collective limitations upon individual autonomy. To some extent, the social structure has retained somewhat greater residues of the traditional and charismatic bases of bureaucratic authority than expected, given its diversity.

Certain differences, of course, characterize the English- and French-

TABLE 2-2 'Achievement' v. 'Ascription' Among French- and English-Canadians

	Per cent saying each factor was 'very important' in getting ahead in Canadian life	
Factor	English (793)	French (529)
Getting good grades	95	69
Working hard	94	47
Having a nice personality	85	69
Getting a university education	80	49
Knowing the right people	50	51
Being able to speak both French and English	39	57
Coming from the right family	23	27
Having the right religion	11	32
Being born in Canada	10	22
Having parents with money	6	11

[1] Ibid., p. 145.
[2] The Developing Canadian Community, second ed. (Toronto: University of Toronto Press, 1968), p. 234.

32

Canadian subcultures. English-Canadians for example, are apparently considerably more likely to accept the individualistic, 'Protestant Ethic' norms often required for economic growth.[1] Among a national sample of young people of English and French origin (aged 13–20), for example, differences are found which are shown in Table 2-2.[2]

In effect, with the exception of 'having a nice personality' all 'achievement' (universalistic) indexes, e.g. working hard, getting good grades, earning a degree, are rated higher by those of English origin, while 'ascribed' (particularistic) indices, e.g. religion, family, place of birth, are ranked higher by the French-Canadians.

In the context of divergent bases of authority, the English-Canadian respondents tend to elect legal–rational bases, whereas the French-Canadians prefer traditional ones. Interestingly enough, Johnstone also found that those of French origin in Quebec ranked legal–rational norms lower than French-Canadians in other parts of Canada.

Norman Taylor has shown how similar values influence industrial structure in Quebec.[3] Familial cohesion and attending particularistic norms tend to inhibit the demands of industry for discipline, recruitment on objective bases, risk-taking, and growth. Ironically, this condition symbolizes the pervasive individualism of French-Canadian culture. Yet it is not a 'rugged' individualism, but rather, as Everett Hughes has shown, 'an individualism of the family'.[4]

In the context of interest group behaviour, French-Canadian individualism provides the basis for an interesting hypothesis. One might predict that it would tend to inhibit associational development, which is sometimes held to rest upon the capacity for collective action and loyalty to social units larger than either the nuclear or extended family. Although other factors undoubtedly intervene, if we find that the gross proportion of groups in Quebec is significantly less than in English-Canada, we shall have some supporting evidence for this hypothesis.

Although English-Canadians are probably more achievement and success-oriented than French-Canadians, they also appear to oscillate between the

[1] The classic study here, of course, is Max Weber, *The Protestant Ethic and the Spirit of Capitalism*, (New York: Scribners, 1930); see also, 'The Protestant sects and the spirit of capitalism', in Weber, from *Max Weber: Essays in Sociology*, pp. 302–22.

[2] Adapted from John C. Johnstone, 'Young people's images of Canadian society', *Royal Commission on Bilingualism and Biculturalism*, p. 8.

[3] 'French Canadians as industrial entrepreneurs', 68 *Journal of Economic History* (February, 1960), pp. 37–52.

[4] *French Canada in Transition*, p. 172.

conflicting poles of traditional–charismatic and legal–rational authority, of ascription and achievement. One sees, for example, both in industry and government, strong traces of the 'generalist', amateur approach to administration. The Canadian higher civil service is patterned rather closely after the British administrative class, which even today tends to symbolize traditional and charismatic bases of authority. Technical aspects of government programmes tend to be de-emphasized, while policy-making and the amateur-classicist syndrome are magnified.[1] As is well known, despite increasing entry from the executive class, the bulk of British higher civil servants have been recruited from Oxford and Cambridge, with degrees in literature and humanities predominating. The going assumption, stemming from a system of recruitment introduced in 1854, holds that classically educated officials are competent to handle most technical aspects of government. Several observers have challenged this assumption and its results, but we need not consider the functional consequences of the system here.[2] It is sufficient to note that its assumptions reflect traditional patterns of thought and recruitment, which have been followed to some extent in the highest levels of the Canadian civil service.

One consequence is to insulate government somewhat from the citizen, who is inhibited not only by the residues of traditional authority structure and the complexity of public affairs but also by the superior forensic, intellectual, and class status of the higher civil servant. Another consequence is to blunt the claims of the electorate for change, as the civil service assumes the role of ensuring continuity and gradualism in national policy.

As our data will show, similar assumptions and consequences tend to underlie recruitment in the national political arena. Politics is rarely a vocation. Fully half of our legislative sample (*N*–269) has served four years or less and John Porter has shown, at the federal level, that the political role in Canada is usually less a career commitment than a transitory experience in a legal or business career.[3] Such a pattern tends to reinforce the

[1] Among others, see Rupert Wilkinson, *Gentlemanly Power: British Leadership and the Public School Tradition* (New York and London: Oxford University Press, 1964).

[2] Among others, see Brian Chapman, *British Government Observed* (London: 1963); Thomas Balogh, *Unequal Partners* (London: Blackwell, 1963); for a relevant stricture regarding the Canadian foreign service, see R. Barry Farrell, *The Making of Canadian Foreign Policy* (Scarborough: 1969), p. 91.

[3] *The Vertical Mosaic*, pp. 400–2; for some of the negative effects of high turnover on professionalism and the development of the expertise that might enable back-benchers to play a viable role in policy making, see Allan Kornberg, 'Parliament in Canadian society', in A. Kornberg and L. Musolf, *Legislatures in Developmental Perspective* (Durham: Duke University Press, 1970), pp. 7–2; 121–8.

symbiotic relationship existing between governmental and interest group elites. Equally important, as the higher civil service, the Canadian House of Commons is in no sense a mirror of the national social structure.[1] With rare exception among the minor parties, its members are from highly advantaged social groups. My research in the 28th Parliament (1968–70) shows, for example, that fully 73 per cent of them are in the upper-middle-class stratum, based upon occupation and education.[2] Porter has shown similarly the favoured class status of Canadian national political leaders and the virtual absence in the federal cabinet during the entire period from 1920–60, of any men of working-class origin.[3]

One index of deferential interpersonal relations is whether or not individuals subjectively perceive themselves, and others, as occupying a certain social class stratum. If they do, data on class rankings should range along the entire scale, from upper-class to lower-class. If they do not, the distribution should cluster around the 'middle-class' point in the scale, since those who are not sensitive to the existence of class stratifications tend to classify everyone as being 'middle-class'.[4]

A 1965 national survey of political values (N–2,741) included a subjective measure of class, i.e. respondents were asked to indicate their own felt class status. The distribution was as follows:[5]

	%
upper-class	10
middle-class	40
working-class	49
lower-class	1

The broad range of responses and the symbolic relevance of the 'working class' category provide some evidence that class sensitivity and, hence, stratification, exists.

---

[1] A similar generalization, of course, holds for all Western nations.

[2] Education and occupation have been used here to determine social class status. Hollingshead, upon whom this index is based, also included place of residence as an index. However, since education and occupation determine almost all the variation, we have used them. For a full description of the index, see A. B. Hollingshead and F. Redlich, *Social Class and Mental Illness* (New York: Wiley, 1958), Appendix 2.

[3] *The Vertical Mosaic*, pp. 395, 398.

[4] Cf. Joseph Kahl, *The American Class Structure* (New York: Holt, Rinehart and Winston, 1957), p. 160.

[5] Rick van Loon 'Political participation in Canada: the 1965 election', 3 *Canadian Journal of Political Science* (September, 1970), p. 384.

Once again, the signal point is the effect of such structural conditions upon perceptions of authority in Canadian society. They seem to include another incentive to deferential patterns of behaviour on the part of the ordinary citizen. For example, a national sample (1965) of Canadians, asked to rank over 200 occupations in terms of their relative prestige, placed MP's very near the top, slightly above lawyers and university professors, and slightly below physicians. The results probably include some incentive to accept the legitimacy and authority of legislators, despite any generalized ambivalence about politics. Another consequence is to augment both the autonomy and responsibility of political elites for the course of political events. Yet another is considerable delegation of authority to leaders. The shape and consequences of this characteristic obviously vary, yet the generalization holds. In English-Canada, a considerable amount of discretion has always been delegated to leaders, yet citizens seem to have retained some feeling of participation. In French-Canada, fulsome deference and delegation have been similarly apparent, but perhaps the relationship between leaders and followers has been less consensual, while the sense of participation and of being effectively represented has been somewhat less viable. Social stratification, too, has been somewhat more marked in Quebec, with an attending sharpening of the deferential perspective.

Thus, although the incentives to deference may be similar, the mechanisms appear to be somewhat different. In English-Canada, the internalization of authoritative political norms seems to have been more pervasive, so that obedience has probably more often been experienced as noncoercive. In French-Canada, on the other hand, deference to legal prescriptions and hierarchical personal relations has perhaps been more formal and coercive, with somewhat less evidence of feelings of individual responsibility for compliance. One of the results might be a tendency for rank-and-file *Québécois* to feel less trustful of and less identified with government. Although, as we saw earlier, young people in Quebec are strongly supportive of their provincial government,[1] this attitude probably reflects the current claims of Quebec nationalism rather more than the legitimation of its political leaders. Moreover, an often invidious distinction between the state and the political elites who direct it is common in Canada and must be regarded as a qualification of the deferential mould. In sum, although it is tempting to characterize deference in English-Canada as 'positive', and that in French-Canada as 'negative', our data on political values and participation indicate that defer-

[1] Johnstone, 'Young people's images of Canadian society', pp. 78, 79, 85, 88.

ence in both contexts is not always accompanied by high trust of political elites by ordinary citizens. To some extent, deference is based upon class dependency, as well as upon more positive incentives.

Within English-Canada at least, the consensus (with many exceptions, as our data will indicate in a moment) seems to be that government leaders will probably act in the best interests of the nation. As Michel Brunet says (with, as we shall see, some exaggeration), in contrasting the political cultures of the two societies, 'Throughout English-Canada no one seriously questions the legitimacy of the aims pursued by the central government.'[1] In French-Canada, a pervasive hierarchical tradition and the classical French residue of *incivisme* mean that, while the aims of government may be questioned, the power of leaders to control public affairs and to dispense government's largesse on a selective political basis has rarely been challenged. In both milieux, the superior educational and class status of governmental elites tends to legitimate their authority, an authority which is some cases clearly reflects charismatic residues. Certain elitist leadership assumptions tend to persist, exemplified in the 'dictatorship of the Cabinet' and, within it, the dominant role of the prime minister.

In both cultures, deferential social assumptions are institutionalized in the parliamentary system. Essentially, this system provides for a dramatic centralization of power and authority in some two-dozen members of the Cabinet. But even within this presidium, there is a further narrowing of power since the prime minister is clearly more than first among equals. Here again, the results include deferential patterns of behaviour within the formal political apparatus. Power breeds deference and the promise of a Cabinet post or a parliamentary secretaryship no doubt provides a powerful reinforcement. The venerable tradition of party loyalty has a similar impact.[2] Once more, the consequences include limitations on participation, as seen in the ranks of back-benchers whose disenchantment with their ineffectual role is well known. Moreover, if such limits on effective participation are characteristic of the formal political apparatus, it hardly seems surprising that they would be even more patent among ordinary citizens. Such conditions lead us to characterize the Canadian political culture as 'quasi-participative'.

[1] *Canadians and Canadiens* (Montreal; Paris: 1954), p. 18.
[2] As Siegfried noted about 1902, 'In Canada, the party is almost a sacred institution, to be forsaken only at the cost of one's reputation and career', *The Race Question in Canada*, p. 114.

Political theory and political culture

We are concerned here with the extent to which the ordinary citizen[1] feels able to (and does) participate actively in the shaping of the political decisions that affect him. We shall use the term 'quasi-participative' to describe Canadian political culture. Several problems are raised by this characterization. One concerns the basis of comparison and evaluation one uses. In effect, how intensive *should* political participation be in Canada, given its demographic character? As the second richest country in the world, with accordingly high rates of literacy, newspaper readership, educational achievement, etc. it seems equitable to set a fairly demanding standard of participation.

A related problem is the determination of precisely what various levels of quantitative evidence *mean* in rough terms such as 'high', 'medium', and 'low'. In effect, how significant is the fact that, say, one-third of Canadians in a national sample rank 'low', on political efficacy? Is 'one-third' a significant proportion of any universe? I feel it is, but I grant that the conclusion is subjective.

Despite this problem, we shall see in a moment that significantly 'large' proportions, (e.g. 30–40 per cent) of Canadian citizens exhibit 'low' rates of trust, political interest, knowledge, and participation. Only in *voting* do we find more than a small proportion 'highly' engaged in politics. Voting, moreover, is probably the least demanding and effectual of several means of participation. Such conditions have led one observer to use the term 'spectator–participant' to define Canadian political culture.[2] This characterization rests upon both quantitative evidence and psychological dispositions, such as one's sense of efficacy, and precisely why he participates in the political process. Does he vote because of a sense of civic duty or because he really feels he can influence events? Such considerations suggest that certain qualifications of the conventional conclusions regarding 'high' participation may be in order.

Fortunately, some systematic evidence is available on participation and efficacy, from which significant conclusions can be drawn. Other conclusions include logical deductions from theoretical and historical aspects of Canadian political culture. In effect, if, as we have argued, Canadian society tends to

---

[1] The term 'ordinary citizen' may be taken to include all those who are not categorized as members of the political elite. The latter can be defined empirically as those political activists who, for example, make up our sample of legislators, higher civil servants, and interest group leaders.

[2] Van Loon, 'Political participation in Canada', p. 396; pp. 396–9.

retain residues of hierarchy and elitist conceptions of leadership, its political culture will tend to limit rank-and-file participation. More specifically, citizen action groups will tend to be regarded as intrusive and even illegitimate. Significant proportions of individual citizens will tend to regard themselves as relatively ineffectual *vis-à-vis* government. Voting may be low among certain strata of society. Correlates of participation such as political interest, knowledge, efficacy, and trust in government will tend to cluster around the 'low-to-medium' end of the scale.

It is clear, of course, that electoral participation in national elections is reasonably high in Canada,[1] and comparable with other Western democracies at the provincial and local levels. For example, the 1965 national survey, which compared turnout over an extended period indicated that an average of 56 per cent of all respondents had voted in federal elections, and 47 per cent in provincial.[2] Voting, however, is only one of several means of participation, including office-holding, service on relevant committees, actively campaigning for a candidate, attending political meetings, discussing political affairs, etc. Moreover, in the context of elite accommodation in a parliamentary system, voting provides only an infrequent, *post hoc* means of holding parties responsible and granting a new mandate to an alternative set of political elites.

Some systematic evidence indicates, moreover, that voting is widely regarded as the *only* form of political influence possessed by the ordinary Canadian. A national *Government Information* survey, for example, found in 1968 that 70 per cent of a random sample of all Canadians over 15 years of age believed that 'Voting is the only way that people like me can have any say about how the federal government runs things.'[3] This datum does not tell us, of course, precisely how effective these respondents thought voting was, but it does indicate that it is widely regarded as the only effective means among those available.

Equally significant is the general level of *political efficacy* felt by the so-called average man. Here, the same national survey provides some evidence, using an item which asks respondents how much influence they feel individuals have regarding government (see Table 2-3).[4]

'Political efficacy' here is defined positively as the belief that one is able

---

[1] See also John Meisel, *Papers on the 1962 Election* (Toronto: 1964); and Robert Alford, *Party and Society* (Chicago: Rand McNally, 1963.)

[2] Van Loon, 'Political participation in Canada', p. 376, p. 388.

[3] Institute of Behavioural Research (unpublished data) ,York University, 1968.

[4] R. N. Morris, R. Morris, D. Hoffman, F. Schindeler and C. M. Lanphier, 'Attitudes toward federal government information', Institute for Behavioural Research, (Toronto: York University, 1969), p. 161.

TABLE 2-3
French–English differences in feelings of political efficacy

Efficacy	English (9,352)	French (3,600)
	%	%
Low	9	7
Fairly low	23	18
Medium	21	33
Fairly high	32	32
High	15	10
	(100)	(100)

to influence Parliament, the civil service, and 'government'. While just under half of the respondents fall in the 'high' and 'fairly high' categories, these data also indicate that a substantial proportion (almost 30 per cent of Canadians feel that the average man has little or no influence upon government. It should be noted, however, that this sample includes not only citizens, but landed immigrants, some of whom would not be eligible to vote, nor would they always have the language facility required for participation. On the whole, few differences exist among specific groups; surprisingly, level of education is not related to efficacy. French-speaking Canadians, however, are somewhat less likely to feel highly efficacious, and those in Quebec are somewhat more likely to express this view.

Feelings of efficacy are sharply lower regarding the bureaucracy where fully 63 per cent (N–12,952) believe that 'when you walk into a government office, you become just a number.' Fifty-three per cent, moreover, maintain that 'public officials do not care what people like me think.'

More useful for our purposes are data on efficacy from two national surveys of federal elections carried out under the direction of John Meisel. The distribution shown in Table 2-4 occurred among Canadian respondents.[1]

Whereas the preceding survey found almost 45 per cent of ordinary citizens ranking 'high' or 'fairly high' on efficacy, here we find a significantly lower proportion (29 per cent) at this level. Some comparative data are available. Using the same scale in a national sample in the United States, Campbell *et al.* found that 36 per cent of respondents indicated a 'high' level of efficacy.[2] More recently, again using the same items in a United States city

---

[1] Adapted from van Loon, 'Political participation in Canada', p. 393.
[2] *The Voter Decides* (Evanston: Row, Peterson, 1954), p. 192.

TABLE 2-4

Political efficacy among
Canadian citizens, 1965

Efficacy[a]	Distribution	
	%	
High	29	(778)
Medium	46	(1243)
Low	26	(700)

[a] This scale comprises four items:
(1) I don't think the government cares what people like me think.
(2) Sometimes politics and government seem so complicated that a person like me can't really understand what's going on.
(3) People like me don't have any say about what the government does.
(4) Generally, those elected to Parliament soon lose touch with the people.

(N-186), Form and Huber found that 32 per cent ranked high.[1] Other international comparisons are available, but unfortunately they do not use the same items. In research in New York State, using three items ('Anyone in (Edgewood or Riverview) who wants to, gets a chance to have his say about important issues'; 'Most decisions in...are made by a small group that pretty well runs the city'; and, 'The old saying, "You can't fight City Hall" is still generally true'), Presthus found that only 48 per cent of a sample of two (N-1,198) communities ranked 'high' compared with 71 per cent of community leaders (N-81).[2] Almond and Verba used a 'political and adminstrative competence' index to characterize respondents who believed they could influence local and national governments, and that their point of view would be seriously considered in a government office, with the

[1] 'Income, race, and the ideology of political efficacy', 33 *Journal of Politics* (August, 1971), p. 669.
[2] *Men at the Top: A Study in Community Power*, p. 334.

following results: United States, 44 per cent; Britain, 53; Germany, 55; Italy, 29, and Mexico, 8 per cent.[1] Although the different cut-off points used in each analysis make comparison difficult, perhaps we may conclude that around 30 per cent of the electorate experiences considerable doubt as to its political influence.

As might be expected, efficacy and participation are positively associated: just over one-third of those ranking 'high' on efficacy in 1965 were 'highly' or 'medium' active, compared with one-fifth of those who ranked 'low' on efficacy.[2] At the same time, it is significant that of the entire sample an impressive majority ranked 'low' on 'participation' (voting, reading about politics; persuading someone how to vote; and belonging to and working for a party during the campaign), as seen in Table 2-5.[3]

TABLE 2-5 *Participation in the 1965 campaign*

Level of participation	Proportion ranking	
	%	
High	5	(105)
Medium	22	(462)
Low	73	(1533)

These data indicate that political participation in Canada occurs predominately at the 'low' level, subject to any special circumstances of the 1965 election. Almost three-fourths of those interviewed are found in this category. Here again, comparative data from the United States may be useful: Campbell, *et al.* found that 27 per cent of a national sample ranked 'high' on participation, whereas Form and Huber found 31 per cent.[4]

Comparison with Table 2-4, moreover, indicates that high feelings of efficacy do not always culminate in the high level of political participation one might expect. A major correlate of participation is social class, usually measured by education and occupation. The 1965 data reinforce this generalization: 49 per cent of upper-middle-class respondents ranked high on efficacy, compared with 38 per cent of middle-class, 18 per cent of working-class and 8 per cent of lower-class respondents.[5] As van Loon concludes, 'In addition to not expressing their discontent through the electoral system,

[1] *The Civic Culture*, p. 181.
[2] Van Loon, 'Political participation in Canada'.   [3] Adapted from *ibid.*
[4] 'Income, race, and the ideology of political efficacy', p. 669; *The Voter Decides*, p. 31.
[5] *Ibid.*, p. 394.

TABLE 2-6   *Comparative data on efficacy, 1965 and 1968*

| | Distribution[a] | | | | | |
| | 1965 | | | 1968 | | |
Item	Agree	Disagree	NA/DK	Agree	Disagree	NA/DK
'I don't think that the government cares what people like me think.'	% 46	% 49	% 6	% 42	% 51	% 7
'Sometimes politics and government seem so complicated that a person like me can't really understand what's going on.'	69	28	3	69	26	4
'People like me don't have any say about what the government does.'	49	47	4	47	49	5
'Generally, those elected to Parliament soon lose touch with the people.'	56	37	8	56	36	8
'Voting is the only way that people like me can have any say about how the government runs things.'[b]	76	22	2	76	20	3

[a] Totals do not always equal 100, due to rounding.
[b] This item was not included in the 1965 efficacy scale, but is cited here in view of our concern with participation.

then, a high proportion of the Canadians who have the most to be discontent about do not feel that they are capable of having any influence over political allocations. To some extent, they may be right.'[1] In comparative terms, subject to any limitations of the samples and any variation due to differences in the times at which the surveys were completed, it seems that political participation in Canada, with the exception of voting, tends to be somewhat lower than in the United States.

Regarding feelings of political efficacy, the national survey of 1968 reveals virtually the same results found in the 1965 research, as shown in Table 2-6.[2] Suggestive conclusions emerge regarding national attitudes toward efficacy and participation. On four of the five items a majority of respondents agree

[1] *Ibid.*
[2] I am greatly indebted to Professor Meisel for releasing these data before publication of the results of his 1968 survey.

in both surveys with these rather jaundiced statements concerning their personal efficacy. Only one change in direction occurs between the two periods, in the item concerning the influence 'people like me have about what government does', where the small majority recorded in 1965 is reversed in 1968. The effects of the problem of 'response set', which occurs when statements are presented affirmatively, as these are, is unknown, but this effect should be counteracted by their negative tone.

Among the most significant implications for participation is the compelling proportion (76 per cent) who conclude that voting is 'the only way' they can influence the government. Voting, of course, is in many ways a marginal aspect of participation, since it occurs relatively infrequently, requires minimal social resources, and is sometimes essentially ritualistic, in the sense that it is motivated less by feelings of efficacy than by a sense of civic duty. Some reinforcement of this negative valence is probably implicit in responses to the item stressing the complexity of modern politics and attending difficulties in understanding the issues, where over two-thirds of the respondents 'agree'. Certainly while judgments about the significance of these data may differ, it is clear that substantial proportions of average Canadians have serious reservations about their ability to influence governmental elites, and particularly bureaucrats.

A similar valence is apparent regarding the degree of confidence ordinary individuals have in the federal government. An index based upon responses to two items[1] was used to construct Table 2-7; drawn from the *Government Information Study*, 1968.[2]

TABLE 2-7
Faith in the federal government

Level of faith	Proportion (12,952)
	%
Low	19
Fairly low	26
Moderate	23
Fairly high	24
High	8
	(100)

[1] The two items concerned the belief that the federal government supplies honest information and that it usually lives up to its promises.
[2] *Ibid.*, p. 163.

44

Table 2-7 indicates that close to half of Canadian citizens rank in the 'low' or 'fairly low' category. Another way of interpreting the findings is that, whereas 45 per cent of the respondents ranked 'low' or 'fairly low' on faith, 32 per cent ranked 'high'. Rather surprisingly, when English- and French-Canadians are compared, the latter rank somewhat higher in confidence in the *federal* government.[1]

Some items in the 1965 and 1968 Meisel surveys provide similar evidence. One such asks, 'Do you think that *all people* who are high in government give *everyone* a fair break – big shots and ordinary people alike – or do you think some of them pay more attention to what the big interests want?' Almost 80 per cent of those interviewed in the two periods believed that government tended to pay more attention to the 'big interests'. This judgment, moreover is confirmed by an earlier finding of the Canadian Institute of Public Opinion[2] that 52 per cent of Canadians believed that 'big business had the greatest influence on Government.' Meanwhile, one-quarter believed that labour unions had the greatest influence.

On the other hand, when asked how much of the time do you think you can trust the government to do what is right, 58 per cent of those in the 1965 and 1968 surveys said 'always' or 'most of the time'. Moreover, only 24 per cent believed that 'quite a few' of the people running the government were 'crooked'.

Any popular ambivalence about confidence in government revealed here may be reinforced by a relatively low degree of political interest and commitment. It is well-known, for example, that party identification is weak among Canadian voters, whose allegiance may shift dramatically from one election to another, and who indeed may split their vote, provincially and federally, in the same election.[3] Regarding interest in politics, the 1968 national *Government Information* survey is again helpful.[4] If our hypothesis about the 'quasi-participative' character of Canadian political culture is valid, we should find a significant proportion of respondents ranking low on this variable. Table 2-8, which shows that almost one-third of the sample rank 'low' in interest, lends some support to the hypothesis.

Here, the largest proportion of respondents fall in the 'high' category, yet once again almost one-third rank 'low' in interest. Data from the 1965

[1] *Ibid.*, p. 165.
[2] May 30, 1964.
[3] John Wilson and David Hoffman, 'The Liberal Party in contemporary Ontario politics', 3 *Canadian Journal of Political Science* (June, 1970), pp. 177–204.
[4] This table is adapted from *ibid.*, p. 174.

TABLE 2-8
*Interest in governmental affairs
in general*

Level of interest	Proportion (12,952)
	%
High	38
Moderate	31
Low	31
	(100)

Meisel survey provide additional evidence: twenty-six per cent ranked 'high' on interest; 44 per cent ranked 'medium' and 30 per cent ranked 'low'. Comparing these findings with those in Table 2-8, we find a significantly smaller proportion (26 *v.* 38) ranking 'high'.[1] Perhaps it is valid to conclude that about one-third of Canadians rank 'high' in political interest. This conclusion is underscored by the conclusion that *political interest* was the major variable explaining participation in the 1965 survey.[2]

A major thrust of our analysis is that this ambivalence about personal efficacy and marginal degree of political interest is in part a residue of both Empire Loyalist and early French-Canadian preferences for hierarchy and restricted participation in political affairs.

There is considerable historical evidence that responsible democratic government was won in English-Canada only over the deep-seated opposition of the Loyalist gentry. As Frank Underhill concludes, 'another point worth noting is the effect of British influences in slowing down all movements throughout the nineteenth century in the direction of the democratization of politics and society.'[3] The franchise was extended slowly, and not until 1900 did the first one 'with some semblance of manhood suffrage' appear.[4] As Norman Ward shows, in the election of 1911 only one-fourth of the population was enfranchised; by 1921, the proportion had risen to one-half.[5] Manhood suffrage, in fact, did not come to Canada until late in the nineteenth century, almost 100 years after it appeared in the United States. Meanwhile, women suffrage did not occur in Quebec until 1940. This comparatively recent experience of popular sovereignty plus low general

[1] Van Loon, 'Political participation in Canada', p. 395.   [2] *Ibid.*
[3] *In Search of Canadian Liberalism*, p. 15.   [4] Porter, *The Vertical Mosaic*, p. 371.
[5] *The Canadian House of Commons: Representation* (Toronto: University of Toronto Press, 1950), p. 230.

educational levels, especially in Quebec, has probably inhibited the development of collective feelings of participation.[1] The positive association between
education and both efficacy and participation is well-known. Hoffman and
Schindeler found in their survey of some 800 Ontario citizens in 1968 that
higher education was the principal explanatory variable in both instances.[2]
It would seem, in addition, that the significant proportion of recent immigrants in Canadian society, who possess neither the franchise nor,
presumably, the requisite feelings of political efficacy, must also have a
dampening effect upon mass participation.

The Ontario survey cited earlier found that *political knowledge* had a highly
positive association with political participation.[3] Fortunately, knowledge-
about-government was also included in the 1968 *Government Information*
survey regarding attitudes toward information programmes of the federal
government. The level of political knowledge among the national sample
should therefore provide a useful index of political participation among rank
and-file members of Canadian society. Table 2-9 presents the data.[4]

The data suggest that knowledge about government, and by inference,
political participation, among Canadians is somewhat limited. For example,
in only three of the 15 areas of government responsibility, foreign policy,
education, and homeless children, do more than half of those interviewed
correctly identify the proper locus of jurisdiction. Interesting variations are
found among the provinces. Quebec is first in awareness with 31 per cent
of its respondents ranking 'high'. British Columbia follows closely at 30 per
cent, while Ontario ranks much lower, with only 17 per cent. It is surprising
that immigrants and native Canadians, as well as urban and rural residents,
are equally well informed,[5] which makes Ontario's position hard to explain.
If the authors of the national study are correct in their conclusion that
'Those who are poorly informed seldom discuss politics and rarely participate in the political process', we have some confidence that the characterization of Canadian political culture as 'quasi-participative' has some empirical
basis.

[1] Porter, *The Vertical Mosaic*, p. 371.
[2] 'Social and political attitudes in Ontario', unpublished data, Institute of Behavioural
Research, York University, Toronto (1968).
[3] 'Participation' was defined as engaging in political discussion; voting; attending protest
meetings; keeping informed about politics; teaching children loyalty to Canada; trying
to convince people to vote your way; working for a party; and giving money to a party
or a candidate.
[4] Adapted from Morris *et al.* 'Attitudes toward federal government information', p. 18.
[5] *Ibid.*, p. 22.

TABLE 2-9   *Level of citizen knowledge about politics and government, 1968*

Government responsibilities	Correct answer	Most freq. wrong answer	Least freq. wrong answer	Don't know
	%	%	%	%
	Federal	Both	Provincial	
Foreign policy	62	14	2	22
Public and high schools	Provincial 60	Both 20	Federal 7	13
Homeless children	Provincial 54	Both 20	Federal 10	16
Unemployment insurance	Federal 48	Provincial 23	Both 18	11
Income tax	Both 41	Federal 46	Provincial 6	7
Colleges and universities	Provincial 36	Both 31	Federal 17	16
Trans-Canada highway	Both 33	Federal 42	Provincial 11	13
Medicare	Both 26	Federal 43	Provincial 16	15
Scientific research	Both 26	Federal 49	Provincial 5	29
Public housing	Both 25	Provincial 33	Federal 21	20
Protection of language and culture	Both 24	Federal 36	Provincial 15	25
Retraining unemployed	Both 24	Provincial 32	Federal 26	18
Maintaining farm prices	Both 20	Federal 41	Provincial 16	23
ARDA	Both 20	Federal 29	Provincial 17	24
Sending experts to underdeveloped countries	Both 13	Federal 62	Provincial 3	22

Historical factors again tend to reinforce this judgment. The British legacy, for example, is clearly apparent in English-Canadian conceptions of leadership and, on the other side of the coin, limited rank-and-file participation, extending to elected representatives. Both are likely to be affected by British societal models, including what has been called 'The Old Tory Theory of Authority: the tendency both in British government and British voluntary associations to delegate inordinately wide powers to leaders and spokesmen, to ratify decisions taken by leaders almost as a matter of form, which affords such leaders a wide range of manoeuvre when they come face to face in negotiation.' [1] The implications of this condition for the process of elite accommodation are patent.

Attitudes toward participation are probably influenced in similar directions by French-Canadian conceptions of leadership. Here, it seems, elitist forms also have deep historical and institutional roots. As Esdras Minville writes, a 'special characteristic' of French-Canadian cultural attitudes is 'a practically spontaneous acceptance of authority and hierarchy in the family, in society, and in the State. French Canadians like to be ruled.' [2] In terms of socialization, it seems that the inculcation of deferential attitudes in Quebec has been considerably strengthened by the continuity and cohesion among the major agents of socialization. Church, state, and family norms regarding authority have, in effect, been virtually unchallenged until the recent past. This cultural exclusiveness is also apparent in group life. As with most fragmented political cultures, group memberships tend to be concentrated within the French subculture, thereby exacerbating the cleavage between French- and English-Canada by obviating any moderating effect that overlapping membership might bring.

The Quebec political culture requires further comment. As Herbert Quinn says; 'Three main factors have always been dominant in the French-Canadian's approach to politics: his preoccupation with the maintenance of his cultural values and the safeguarding of his interests against the English-speaking majority in Canada; his strong adherence to the doctrines and philosophy of Roman Catholicism as interpreted by his clergy; [3] and his lack of democratic convictions and of an adequate understanding of parliamentary government.' [4]

A subjected people, professing a religion deeply distrusted by their Protestant conquerers, determined to preserve their cultural uniqueness, French-Canadians have had a difficult political history. A recurring theme is their lack of democratic experience and understanding. This condition has deep historical roots. Gustave Lanctot writes of the early *habitant* culture, 'Without any type of organization which could have assembled and

---

[1] Eckstein, *Pressure Group Politics*, pp. 24–5.
[2] *L'Avenir de notre bourgeoisie* (Montreal: 1939), p. 34; also, Lionel Groulx, *L'Action Nationale* (Montreal: 1934), p. 61.
[3] It is noteworthy that French-Canadians are deeply religious, in 1955, for example, 93 per cent of *Québécois* attended church at least once per week, compared with only 44 per cent of English-Canadians in Ontario (Gallup Poll).
[4] *The Union Nationale* (Toronto: 1963), p. 3.

governed them, they acquired the habit of passively deferring to the or-
dinances of the intendants, to the orders of the governor, and to the edicts of
Versailles.'[1] Nor did things change much during the entire nineteenth
century. Writing in 1903, André Siegfrid documents the extent to which lay
political opinion was dominated by the *curés*. He refers also to the *entente*
between the Church and the British civil authorities whereby, in exchange
for virtually complete autonomy in ecclesiastical affairs, the Church kept the
'French Canadians submissive, loyal, and calm.'[2]

Despite their cohesion in the face of external challenges, French-Canadians
have been divided along several axes. While nationalism has provided a
strong integrative force, class differences have had a centripetal effect.
Motivated by well-meant aspirations for economic development, their
political leaders sometimes colluded with foreign economic interests at the
expense of the working-class. More recently, and possibly encouraged by
somewhat flamboyant federal spending policies, competitive cultural and
economic aspirations have encouraged certain government expenditures that,
in Montreal particularly, seem at times to ignore basic social needs. The
Church, which enjoyed full legitimacy in virtually every sphere, inculcated
values that often seemed inapposite to the social and economic aspirations
of its members. Thus agrarian life and prolificacy continued to be idealized
at a time when the land required to sustain them was disappearing. Educational values, which remained within the tradition of the classical college,
sometimes proved inapposite to emerging needs.[3] The mystique which
honoured poverty as spiritual and regarded industrialization and urbanization as twin evils proved to be socially dysfunctional. Meanwhile, the
educated elite sometimes regarded the majority as incapable of political
participation, resulting in an anachronistic paternalism which probably
inhibited the development of political interest and skill on the part of the
average citizen.

Elitism, paternalism, and the dysfunctional socioeconomic policies of the
Church have thus been critical factors in shaping the political culture of
Quebec. A wealth of human, mineral, and water resources were at hand, yet
until World War II, her economic and political development was painfully

---

[1] 'La participation du peuple dans le gouvernement de la Nouvelle-France', XV *Revue
trimestrielle canadienne* (Septembre, 1929), in M. Rioux and Y. Martin, *French Canadian
Society* (Toronto, Montreal: McClelland and Stewart, 1964), p. 21.

[2] *The Race Question in Canada*, p. 48.

[3] As John Porter says, 'A fourth source of inequality arises from the great influence that
religion has had on educational policies', *The Vertical Mosaic*, p. 169.

slow.[1] Perhaps the explanation is essentially one of the ambivalence of a society torn between traditional–charismatic forms of authority and the emerging demands for legal–rational bases of social and economic organization. Certainly, some of its leaders were too often occupied with maintaining inapposite values in social, economic, and educational spheres. Meanwhile a certain preoccupation with the symbols of grandeur tended to deflect resources and attention away from pressing needs of education and economic security.[2] No doubt, the deep-seated popular concern with preserving French-Canadian culture made it easier for leaders to secure support for such adventures.

Politically, these several norms encouraged a conception of government in which the forms were democratic but the process was often one of machine control, made possible by the use of public funds for patronage purposes. This conception of politics was undoubtedly encouraged by the prevailing lack of popular interest and participation in decision-making and the acceptance of an hierarchical system of authority in practically every social sphere.

The historic religiosity of French-Canadians similarly affects Quebec political values. As S. D. Clark has shown, religious influences have been particularly strong in moulding national character and institutions, in both Canadas. The perpetuation of aristocratic values; the uncertain development of industrial capitalism; and the strength of traditional educational orientations are among the legacies. 'The heavy drain upon the material resources of the country in maintaining institutions of religious worship has weakened the economic energies of the population... The strength of the aristocratic tradition in Canada owes much to the influence of religion. In Roman Catholic Quebec the notion of a socially superior class based upon family connections, education, and usually, the ownership of land has been deeply rooted in the teachings of the church; there has been an aristocracy of old families that has proved itself on the whole inadept in promoting new forms of

---

[1] Here, perhaps, Max Weber's formulations regarding the antithesis between Catholicism and economic development are germane, *The Protestant Ethic and the Spirit of Capitalism* (New York: Scribner's, 1958). Insofar as Weber found the Protestant belief in one's capacity to achieve active mastery over the world a central element in the development of capitalism, the Quebec Church's 'other-worldly' orientation and its strictures against 'materialism' may have been decisive.

[2] Some of the human costs of this dualism are suggested by a provincial health report (1970) which revealed that death rates from infant mortality, tuberculosis, cancer and coronary seizures in Quebec were the highest in Canada, and that whereas average life expectancy in 1966 for males and females was 74 in Canada, the rate in Quebec was 71.

economic enterprise.'[1] Nor is religiosity and its historical influence limited to Quebec. 'In English-speaking Canada, if the relation between religion and the class structure has been less obvious, it has been little less important. Church establishment in colonial times placed a considerable dependence upon a close alliance with a privileged upper class that lacked the imagination or inclination to take any sort of lead in the economic development of the country.'[2]

Before the Conquest, as Herbert Quinn shows, two official sources of political authority existed in Quebec, the Bishop of Quebec and the French governor. However, once French civil authority was displaced by British colonial administration, both the legitimacy and the loyalty of *Canadiens* were confined to leaders of the Church. The latter's prescriptions, moreover, covered virtually every vital question, including not only moral issues, but relations between citizen and state, marriage and property, education, welfare, unionism, and agricultural organization.

These conditions relate directly to the quasi-participative character of Quebec political culture.[3] Long before any true governmental organization appeared in the parish, an hierarchical system existed among Church members, prescribed by French law and ecclesiastical regulations. A colony within a colony, French-Canadians throughout much of their history have not had the opportunity to learn the art of self-government. Until this century, the values of the Church, which honoured authority, hierarchy and obedience, must have contributed little to prepare the majority of French-Canadians for an active, understanding role in politics. Until well into the present century, the Church saw a positive, welfare-oriented government as in some sense a competitor to its own ideology and programmes which covered similar areas. Doctrinally, moreover, the Church could not accept the democratic ideal that power and ultimate sovereignty rests in the majority of the ordinary people, since this would countermand its historic reliance upon natural law for the norms governing human conduct.[4]

Much of what has just been said about religious influence, is of course historically oriented, and the question must be raised as to how much such

---

[1] *The Developing Canadian Community*, pp. 172–3; see also Clark, *Church and Sect in Canada* (Toronto: University of Toronto Press, 1948).
[2] *Ibid.*, p. 173.
[3] Among others, see Pierre Elliot Trudeau, 'Some obstacles to democracy in Quebec', *Federalism and the French Canadians*, pp. 103–23.
[4] Mason Wade, *The French Canadians, 1760–1967*, Vol. 1 (Toronto and London: Macmillan, 1968), Chapter 7.

factors affect contemporary political behaviour in Quebec. Certainly, important institutional changes have occurred during the past decade, perhaps most significantly in the area of education. In the universities, the system is entirely non-confessional; the lower schools are controlled by the provincial government and the teachers are laymen. Welfare organizations and hospitals, similarly, have come under governmental control. The high rate of church attendance mentioned earlier has fallen off sharply: in one working-class area, Hochelaga-Maisonneuve in Montreal, whereas over half the French-Canadian residents attended Mass in 1960, by 1971 just under one-quarter did. Moreover, among younger French-Canadians, between 20 and 35 years of age, the rate fell to only about 12 per cent.[1]

A final crucial element in French-Canadian political culture is the family, in which the historical condition has been essentially one of traditional *Gemeinschaft* norms, reinforced by an hierarchical structure which reflects the differentiations of authority found in the Church, the *rang* and the parish Here again, no doubt, significant changes are occurring as greater educational opportunity and youth's challenge of authority modify traditional patterns of authority in the French-Canadian family. It is hard to determine, however, to what extent the older structure has been replaced. There is a well-known association between family socialization, interest group membership and political participation.[2] The family milieu has a decisive influence on the desire and the capacity for political activism. Permissive, democratic patterns of decision-making within the family tend to prepare children for active participation in adult politics. An authoritarian family structure tends to have the opposite effect, inhibiting the development of the attitudes and skills required for participation in group life. In turn, individuals who belong to such groups are more likely to be informed, interested and active in politics, and to believe that they are politically effective. A reasonably high degree of interest group ubiquity and membership, in effect, are functional requisites in democratic political systems.

Here again, it seems, the historical legacy of Quebec includes a structural element which tends to inhibit participation by inculcating hierarchical, inward-looking familial perspectives that do not always encourage group membership. Political modernization, *inter alia*, seems to require that

[1] I am indebted here to my colleague, Kenneth McRoberts, for providing these examples of recent changes in Quebec's institutional structure.
[2] G. Almond and S. Verba, *The Civic Culture* (Princeton: Princeton University Press, 1963), Chapter 11; Alex Inkeles, 'Participant citizenship in six developing countries', 53 *American Political Science Review* (December, 1969), pp. 1120–41, esp. 1125.

TABLE 2-10   *Group membership among English- and French-speaking Canadians, by education and sex*

Education	Proportion belonging to one group:			
	English-speaking		French-speaking	
	Male	Female	Male	Female
	%	%	%	%
Some college	80	86	71	62
Secondary school	60	56	47	35
	(961)	(943)	(354)	(93)

individuals develop 'social trust', including loyalties of a broader compass than either family or immediate community. Some larger conception of a national interest and identity has been found essential for participative democracy which, in turn, is often characterized by prolific interest group activity.[1]

Comparative data on group membership indicate that rates are substantially lower among French-speaking than English-speaking Canadians. Not including union membership, differences exist as shown in Table 2-10.[2] The greatest variation here appears among female members of the two universes. French-speaking women, even with education controlled, are considerably less likely to be members of voluntary groups than English speaking women. It is also noteworthy that, among the latter, membership rates are higher than those for English-speaking men. Here, it seems, is another indication of the somewhat greater traditionalism of French-Canadian society. It is also an indication that the larger 'community consciousness' of which extensive group membership is often a symbol, is less developed in Quebec than in English-Canada. Finally, although it is premature to generalize at the moment, insofar as group membership is a necessary condition for participation in the process of elite accommodation, these data indicate that participation is less frequent among Quebec citizens, compared with those in Ontario and British Columbia.

Whether the precarious community values of French-Canadians have changed enough to provide this kind of solidarity in Quebec is difficult to say. On the one hand, cultural nationalism undoubtedly provides an impulse toward political integration and identity. At the same time, it seems clear

[1] Almond and Verba, *The Civic Culture*.
[2] I am indebted to James Curtis for providing these data, based upon secondary analysis of Professor John Meisel's national survey of the 1968 federal election.

that pervasive class and ideological cleavages exist.[1] Nor does the contemporary economic uncertainty provide the basis often regarded as necessary for democratic stability. The striking fluctuations that unemployment and uncertainty can bring are perhaps suggested by the fact that the proportion of young people attending Quebec colleges and universities decreased by about one-fourth between 1967–8 and 1968–9.

While the support of some one-third of the electorate in the 1971 elections for the *Parti Québécois* is impressive, the tradition of weak party loyalty and highly fragmented and ideological party structures in Quebec suggests that this may be only a protest vote, rather than the beginning of a trend in the direction of dramatic political change. Perhaps even more than the rest of Canada, Quebec is faced by certain brute economic imperatives, including solving her unemployment problem and finding capital, which make radical solutions by government unlikely. Undoubtedly, many university students and their teachers support such solutions, but her political and economic elites hardly seem prepared at the moment to choose either separatism or socialism, much less the violence of the *Front de Liberation de Quebec* (FLQ).

Meanwhile, societies change slowly. The technological patina of North America gives the appearance and the promise of radical cultural change, but the underlying inherited social norms often show an amazing survival value. Just as the traces of Empire Loyalist values, early bureaucratic structures, and the reliance upon government for economic development remain viable in English-Canada, so the residues of English domination, ecclesiastical influence and the idealization of rural life persist in Quebec. Traditional societies such as Quebec perhaps find evolutionary change especially difficult. Certainly, it seems unlikely that she will, in effect, skip a stage in economic development and move directly into a post-industrial era, which would seem necessary to meet the philosophical aspirations of the intellectuals who largely interpret the course of events in Quebec today. Speaking in terms of a hierarchy of human needs, it seems that too many elementary material needs remain to be filled before the majority of *Québécois* can become engaged in a struggle to achieve the ideal society prescribed by its intellectuals of the Left.

[1] The religious and ethnic homogeneity of Quebec has tended to deflect attention from its internal social cleavages. For analyses of this aspect of Quebec society, see Maurice Pinard, 'Working class politics: an interpretation of the Quebec case', 7 *Canadian Review of Sociology and Anthropology* (May, 1970), pp. 87–109; Pinard, 'One party dominance and third parties', 33 *Canadian Journal of Economics and Political Science* (August, 1957), pp. 358–73; Jacques Dofny and M. Garon-Audy, 'Mobilités professionnelles au Quebec', 1 *Sociologie et Société* (November, 1969), pp. 277–301.

Political theory and political culture

Historical conditions thus shape the political culture of contemporary French-Canada. They must diminish the sense of political effectiveness held by many French-Canadians and the extent to which they conclude that government can be influenced by individuals and organized groups pressing for non-revolutionary change. Perhaps, as Herbert Quinn maintains, parliamentary government and representative democracy have always been regarded negatively in Quebec, as a counterpoise against English-Canadian dominance rather than as a means of participatory government.

Dramatic changes, resulting mainly from rapid industrialization beginning about 1939, have of course modified many aspects of Quebec's traditional social structure. Between 1939 and 1950, for example, the volume of manufacturing output rose by over 90 per cent, an increase equalling that achieved during the entire preceding century. However, this *Gesellschaft* impulse was to a large extent the product of exogenous influences, such as heavy American capital investment. It seems to have depended somewhat less upon cultural factors within Quebec, some of which continue to resist change. As John Porter has shown, French Canadians have shared only to a limited extent in the occupational up-grading accompanying this industrial take-off.[1] Among the economic elite in Canada in 1951, only 6.7 per cent could be classified as French-Canadian.[2] Of 760 company directors only 10 per cent were Catholic.[3] Two decades later, the situation had not changed much. Among 12,741 directors of major Canadian corporations, only 9.48 per cent were French-Canadians, although the members of this charter group constituted about 40 per cent of the population.[4]

This condition has usually been attributed to cultural factors, including the classical educational system and lack of facility in the English language. The use of English in many industries has, of course, inspired much resentment among the French in Quebec; this resentment has been institutionalized in several interest groups devoted to the encouragement of the use of the French language in the professions and industry. But unequal chances for educational achievement also have a great deal to do with such unequal social mobility. In 1951 and 1961, French-Canadians, along with Italians and Indians were highly under-represented among Canadian males at school between the ages of 5 and 24.[5] In general, as a result, occupational mobility tends to be lower among French-Canadians, compared with those

---

[1] *The Vertical Mosaic*, pp. 86–8.   [2] *Ibid.*, p. 286.   [3] *Ibid.*, p. 289.
[4] Computed according to the *Directory of Directors* (Toronto: *Financial Post*, vol. 25, 1971). Ambiguities were resolved by recourse to *Who's Who*.
[5] Porter, *ibid.*, pp. 88–9.

of British origin. As de Jocas and Rocher found, for both fathers and sons, the latter were concentrated in white-collar jobs, while the *Canadiens* were found mainly in blue-collar occupations.[1]

In the present context of quasi-participative politics, it is important to determine the extent to which recent social changes in Quebec have modified political behaviour there. Have industrialization, urbanization and secularization resulted in increased levels of participation, as assumed by the theory of political development? Has turnout increased in Quebec in provincial and federal elections? One test of this latter question is available in comparative electoral statistics. It should be noted initially that voting has usually been quite high in the province. In provincial elections during the past 40 years, for example, turnout has averaged around 74 per cent. Moreover, the rate has been steadily increasing since World War II. On the surface, such evidence might seem to support the claim that politics has changed during the recent past, as a result of socioeconomic change.

However, as a careful student of the problem concludes, 'if we scratch below the aggregate surface, we find this explanation is invalid.'[2] High turnout proves to be a consequence of consistently high participation in *rural* areas, whereas in the urban, industrialized areas of Montreal, rates are only 50–65 per cent. One explanation for this condition is the patronage system in rural areas, augmented by relatively low participation by English-Canadian elements in Montreal ridings.[3] Turning to federal elections, there is again no evidence of increased voting as a result of modernization. '*There are no clear increases in turnout over the three decades and there is no positive relationship between participation and urbanization/industrialization*' (italics added).[4]

Some observers have suggested that the emergence of new parties, such as the *Parti Québécois*, which has a mass basis, such pressure groups as the *Estates Generale*, and even the appearance of such terrorist groups as the *Front de Liberation de Quebec* are symbols of increased participation. It seems, however, that such parties and pressure groups have tended to appear rather frequently in the province throughout its political history. In sum, as

---

[1] 'Intergenerational occupational mobility in the Province of Quebec', 23 *Canadian Journal of Economics and Political Science* (February, 1957), pp. 58–66; Porter, *The Vertical Mosaic*, pp. 96–103.

[2] Dale Posgate, *Social Mobilization and Social Change in Quebec*, Doctoral dissertation, State University of New York: Buffalo (1972), p. 227.

[3] *Ibid.*, p. 232; see also Vincent Lemieux, *Parenté et Politique: l'organisation sociale dans l'Ile d'Orleans* (Quebec: University of Lavel Press, 1971).

[4] Posgate, *Ibid.*, p. 232.

Posgate concludes, 'The aggregate analysis of census characteristics and political participation (i.e. voter turnout) reveals a clearly negative relationship between social mobilization and political participation [in Quebec].'[1]

To find evidence of unprecedented political change in Quebec, one must probably resort to qualitative evidence. Such factors as a more positive view of the role of government; the strengthening of French-Canadian nationalism; the modernization and liberalization of party structure; and a general reshaping of traditional goals into a more positive pattern – such seem to be among the political developments that have occurred recently in Quebec.[2] Meanwhile, quantitative measures such as turnout and voluntary group membership indicate that participation remains relatively unchanged.[3]

Despite industrialization and changing political fortunes, one constant value has persisted, the determination of Quebec's people to preserve their unique culture and language.[4] This commitment has fostered a certain displacement of interest from social and economic issues to nationalistic concerns, which may explain in part the uncertain path of economic development and political stability in Quebec. It may also explain the apparent inconsistency between limited mass participation and respect for politics and the generally positive view that the *Québécois* have of their provincial government, compared with Ottawa. Nationalism and cultural integration, in effect, bring about the internal cohesion often found among groups which feel threatened from without. By 1972, although social and economic concerns had become more vocal, they remained at best co-equal with the time-honoured theme of cultural nationalism. To some extent, perhaps, the two goals were incompatible, in the sense that lower- and middle-class opposition to separatism was in part based upon fear of its disruptive economic consequences.[5]

Despite the 'Quiet Revolution' and rapid industrialization following World War II, Quebec seems to retain at least some of the characteristics of a

[1] *Ibid.*, p. 315.
[2] *Ibid.*, pp. 324–40.
[3] For comparative data on group membership among French-speaking and English-speaking Canadians, see Chapter 10.
[4] Quinn, *The Union Nationale*, p. 3.
[5] Some observers maintain that the major support for separatism exists in the new, bureaucratic middle-class, but no precise data are offered to support this claim. Cf. Hubert Guindon, 'Social unrest, social class, and Quebec's bureaucratic revolution', 7 *Queen's Quarterly* (Summer, 1964) pp. 150–62. Meanwhile, one is perhaps well advised to reserve his judgment, especially since neither bureaucratic nor middle-class elements have historically shown much liking for either the iconoclasm or the uncertainty that separatism would entail.

traditional society. Undoubtedly, the social and economic changes that have occurred seem striking to those who have lived in the province for an extended period.[1] For others, however, the residues of the past remain patent. Writing in 1965, John Porter could still speak of 'the low occupational level of French-Canadians, the rigidity of French-Canadian class structure, and the authoritarian character of French-Canadian institutions...'[2] And in 1967, Pierre Elliott Trudeau could conclude, 'Well, times [in Quebec] have not changed much.'[3] In Weberian terms, the transition from traditional and charismatic bases of authority to legal–rational ones has been slow and painful.

Thus in both French- and English-Canada, certain attitudinal and structural factors tend to inhibit rank-and-file participation. There is recent evidence, of course, that this condition is changing. Within the federal Parliament, for example, the Committee system has been strengthened. Disenchanted back-benchers have been outspoken and the Government has made assurances that greater popular participation will be forthcoming. Meanwhile, in Quebec, the discontents and violence symbolized by FLQ terrorism have made politicians more sensitive to popular expectations. Yet, for the great majority of Canadians, Arthur Lower's generalization probably remains tenable. Cabinet government is a system in which the ordinary citizen 'gives full power of attorney to a small committee each four years or so, well knowing that virtually nothing he can do in the interval will have much effect on the group to whom he has given his blank check'.[4]

CONCLUSION: THE THEORY OF ELITE ACCOMMODATION RESTATED

Our aim in this chapter has been to provide a theoretical framework for an empirical analysis of Canadian interest groups and their interactions with members of the legislative and bureaucratic elites. Four components of the national political culture and their implications for such behaviour have been outlined. At this point, a major consequence of these elements for decision-making in the political system can be restated. Viewed in the round, they seem to result in a political process that may be called *elite accommodation*.

---

[1] For analyses of the evolution of Quebec from an essentially rural–agrarian to an urban–industrial society, see Everett Hughes, *French Canada in Transition*; and Hubert Guindon, 'The social evolution of Quebec reconsidered', 26 *Canadian Journal of Economics and Political Science* (November, 1960).
[2] *The Vertical Mosaic*, p. 383.
[3] *Federalism and the French Canadians*, p. xxiii.
[4] *Canadians in the Making* (Toronto: 1958), p. 281.

Political theory and political culture

As used here, the theory relates only peripherally to party government and its ideological dimensions. The essential focus is upon the often routine attempts of 'private' and 'public' elites (i.e. interest group and official political elites) to work out pragmatic solutions to the problem of allocating national resources and reconciling the tensions of a political culture deeply fragmented along ethnic, religious, and regional lines. The need for political elites to accommodate the tensions among religious and ethnic subcultures is only part of the process as conceptualized here, although a vital part given the instability of Canada's political history and the obvious difficulty of maintaining national integration.

In this context, parties themselves may be defined as interest groups or congeries of interest groups. Weber's admonition that party government is government by interest groups may be useful in clarifying the theoretical orientation employed here. In effect, the following process seems to occur. In oversimplified terms, the pragmatic appreciation of government's role in the national economy tends to justify its expansion. This general thrust tends, in turn, to inspire a countervailing mobilization on the part of interest groups, whose penetration into the formal political system is normatively sanctioned by the corporatist ethic, as well as by the demands of functional rationality. This process of mutual accommodation between government and articulate private groups is encouraged by deferential authority relations and a quasi-participative style of rank-and-file political behaviour, which, as we have seen, ensures a great deal of delegation to elites in many contexts. The centralization of authority and power in the Cabinet system reflects and hardens this mould.

The larger consequence of such institutional and normative conditions is a *modus vivendi* in which political decisions are worked out, case by uncoordinated case, through consultation, negotiation, and compromise among substantively concerned group elites, on the one hand, and political and bureaucratic elites on the other. 'Elites' may be defined as that minority in any society who possess and manipulate disproportionate shares of such scarce and highly valued resources as prestige, security, education, income, authority, power, and influence. Empirically, the political elite is defined here as the some 1,100 interest group directors, members of parliament, and officials included in this study. 'Accommodation' is the outcome of the process of consultation, negotiation, compromise, and conflict whereby such elites allocate public resources. Between elections, which provide the essential means of mass participation, such elite accommodation becomes the norm. With many exceptions, interaction among the political elite is consensual and cooperative. Their relationship is often symbolic, and we assume that they share many ideological and cognitive values. Such continuities enable them to define situations similarly, to engage in concerted action, and to make the necessary reciprocal adjustments. This process occurs largely in two contexts: among private groups and between them and government.

A common stratagem is for interest group elites to form coalitions, usually temporary, for combining their resources on behalf of one or another interest. In this way, they honour the going rule-of-the-game that interest groups will hammer out their own consensus and build their own avenues of support before approaching government. Indeed, such behaviour is a functional necessity since governmental elites cannot handle a plethora of uncoordinated claims.

The role of the ordinary citizen in this process is largely confined to elect-ing leaders and, for some, expressing his will through membership in private groups. In English-Canada, the deferential tradition, reinforced by some trust in leaders, mediates the system; in French-Canada, the primary ele-ment is probably deference, augmented by negative nationalism. Elites are thereby able to reconcile or at least to adequately compromise the conflicting claims of region, religion, ethnicity, and class that characterize Canada's fragmented political culture.

This conception of the political system has sometimes been called 'elitist democracy'.[1] Its essential assumptions, some of which are based upon the work of classical elite theorists such as Pareto, Mosca, and Michels, include the conclusion that political resources are unequally distributed among the members of any society or other collectivity. As a result, those who possess larger amounts of intelligence, skill, energy, political acumen, and income necessarily become leaders, in order to meet the functional needs of society for individuals capable of playing certain strategic roles. A sociological variant of this thesis is the functional theory of stratification which holds, briefly, that only a minority of individuals in any society possess the talent and the will to qualify for and to play critical social roles. Society must provide them disproportionate rewards in status, prestige, and income.[2]

---

[1] Perhaps the foremost exponent of democratic elitism is J. A. Schumpeter, *Capitalism, Socialism, and Democracy* (New York: Harper, 1956); for a critical view, see P. Bachrach, *The Theory of Democratic Elitism* (Boston: Little, Brown, 1967); for a clear review of various views of elitist and 'radical' democracy, see Geraint Parry, *Political Elites* (New York: Praeger, 1969).

[2] K. Davis and W. Moore, 'Some principles of stratification', 10 *American Sociological Review* (April, 1945), pp. 242–9; for a rebuttal of functional theory in this context,

Average men, through the ballot, ultimately control such elites and thus ensure that their decisions reflect the larger community interest. A related assumption is that leaders require a certain shielding from mass intervention in order that they may reach more rational decisions than would be possible under so-called direct democracy. Thus, both on normative and operational grounds, but perhaps mainly on the latter, the essential conclusion is that elites must rule in any type of political system.

In the Canadian system, a vital consequence of this preference is the critical role in the political process assumed by interest groups, or, more precisely, their leaders.[1] Beyond the legitimation derived from the corporatist ethic, such elites enjoy various practical advantages that ensure their decisive participation. Possessing the cohesiveness of those who share a focussed interest, responsible essentially to their limited constituency, not required to compete in the electoral arena, enjoying fulsome resources, relatively unrestricted access into the formal system (based in many cases upon legal and institutional guarantees), tending to monopolize experience and expertise in their own sphere, which governmental elites must draw upon, they often become powerful indeed.

Equally important, such elites seem able to function in a relatively non-ideological context. The need for pragmatic solutions to national problems tends to dominate their definition of the decisional situation. At the same time, the 'closed', deferential style of Canadian politics; the counter-revolutionary, ascriptive strain in its historical experience; weak party identification and the lack of concern with national political symbols, in effect, the precarious Canadian political culture – all contribute to the persistence of elite accommodation as the norm in national politics.

The functional reasons for the system of elite accommodation are often supra-political and extra-ideological. They probably rest mainly upon the need for legal–rational bases of authority and procedure in complex, highly differentiated modern society. Such technical and decisional imperatives are often opposed to the assumptions of participative democracy. They often require the narrowing of the range of access and participation which are characteristic of elite accommodation. Essentially, such a conclusion reflects the informational and structural conditions of industrial society: problems are complex and they demand action. Given such premises, governmental

---

see M. Tumin, 'Some principles of stratification: a critical analysis', 18 *American Sociological Review* (August, 1953), pp. 387–94.
[1] Some normative implications and costs of the process of elite accommodation will be discussed in our concluding chapter.

elites, and the private citizen too, turn to the sources of technical knowledge and political influence. These are often found among interest groups.

Obviously, the incentives for the role of political elites in such a system are more than technological and personal. They include the efforts of elites of the two major subcultures to avoid the disintegration of the national political system, which is threatened by French-Canadian nationalism within as well as American economic and cultural imperialism. As noted earlier, this 'nation-saving' incentive is a necessary condition of elite accommodation as used here, but the process also includes a more pragmatic 'non-ideological' incentive in which a broad range of other desired values are at issue.

In sum, the Canadian process of elite accommodation is sustained by several analytically discrete incentives, including the sustained, 'non-ideological' allocation of public resources; a technical imperative which demands considerable amounts of information, much of which emanates from interest groups; and a 'political' one which necessarily claims the attention of governmental elites constitutionally charged with accommodating the claims of divergent national subcultures. Such incentives enhance interest group legitimacy and power, while dampening the role and appeal of participatory democracy.

Considerable empirical data is available to test the major propositions of the theory of elite accommodation. For example, elite effectiveness probably requires a certain degree of ideological consensus among governmental and interest group leaders. They must, in effect, support the going social system and its major normative assumptions. Our indexes of political values will show to what extent the three elites in fact share such common norms. An equally significant requisite of collective action is a condition of social homogeneity among the three elite groups. Analysis of the extent to which they share common backgrounds of education and occupation will provide a vital test of this condition. Finally, elites probably share a rough cognitive consensus about the operational nature of the political–economic system and the role of interest groups within it. The evidence will be considered later. In the next chapter, certain theoretical aspects of interest group analysis are presented.

CHAPTER 3

THEORETICAL ASPECTS OF INTEREST GROUP ANALYSIS

Canadian society has a rich and varied group life in which, it seems, very few interests remain unorganized. What are the correlates of this condition? Basically, there is a strong association between national wealth and the ubiquity of groups. In terms of per capita income, Canada ranks second in the world and, despite her relatively small population, she ranks seventh in gross national product. Such conditions ensure the economic resources and the diversified industrial and commercial system required to support a pervasive group infrastructure.

Developed group systems are also a result of the growth of modern economic and technical specialization, which is again characteristic of relatively wealthy societies. Specialization, as Emile Durkheim shows, is a function of social and economic development.[1] As occupational roles become increasingly differentiated, new socioeconomic interests evolve, and men tend to organize themselves into self-conscious groups which attempt to stake out a unique role and function in society.[2] It is characteristic of members

[1] *The Division of Labour in Society*, trans. and intro. by George Simpson (New York: Macmillan, 1933), pp. 60–4.

[2] We hope to avoid the problem of reifying interest groups, thereby attributing to them some existence apart and different from that of their members. Use of the phrase 'the members of' or 'the director of' before the term 'interest group' would help obviate this problem, but would soon become redundant. Thus, all allusions here to interest groups and their behaviour refer to the individuals in them. This nomalist view of groups is opposed by several schools, including social realism which maintains that a group is an independent reality that must be conceptualized in terms of the meaning it has for its members. As Znaniecki concluded, 'Every fully developed social group is imagined, remembered and conceived as a super-individual objective whole with definite content and meaning', 'Social organizations and institutions' in G. Gurvitch and W. E. Moore, *Twentieth Century Sociology* (Philadelphia: Philosophical Library, 1945), p. 206. Such a position recognizes that groups are essentially a fiction created by their members, but maintains that the fiction is analytically relevant because

of such groups to turn to the state to gain a legal monopoly in their given sector, especially when, in Weber's words, 'the number of competitors increase in relation to the profit span,'[1] that is, when competition becomes keen.

Such goals are often articulated in terms of some larger 'public interest'. The enhancement of group interests may indeed be consonant with the welfare of the larger community, but as Arthur Bentley insisted, there is no way of demonstrating 'a group interest of society as a whole'. The going assumption, borrowed from *laissez-faire* economic theory (and reinforced, perhaps, by the common tendency to rationalize existing realities), is, nevertheless, that the uncoordinated efforts of a multiplicity of groups to achieve their specific interests culminate in the general welfare, or, at least, in its closest possible approximation in an imperfect world.

The efforts of most groups to monopolize a sector of social activity and to present themselves as its only legitimate representative encourages us to conceptualize groups basically in terms of *interest*. As Bentley maintained, without an interest there is no group, and both can only be analysed by their actions. 'There exists only the one thing, that is, so many men bound together in or along the path of a certain activity.'[2] This interest and activity, moreover, are always directed against other groups. In his view, the concepts 'group', 'interests', and 'activity', are precisely synonymous. 'Society is nothing other than the complex of the groups that compose it.'[3]

Thus the better realization of its 'interest' is usually the primary motive for a group's existence. Bentley was not much concerned with the problem that the members of groups have several interests because he defined

---

it conditions individual and collective behaviour. Behaviourists, however, are probably more comfortable with a nominalist conception of groups that focusses essentially upon the measurement of the activities and values of the individuals who constitute the group. Certainly, when we speak of a group as being 'powerful', 'prestigeful', 'conservative', 'active', or 'moribund', the reference is usually to properties exhibited by their members. Some of these attributes are no doubt collective, including cohesion, morale, etc., but perhaps a decisive point is that they are discernable only through systematic analysis of individuals. For analysis of such aspects of interest group theory, see Leon Dion, *Societé et Politique: La Vie des Groupes* (Quebec: Les Presses de l'Université Laval, 1971), pp. 55–108.

[1] Max Weber, *Economy and Society*, Vol. 1, ed. by Guenther Roth and Claus Wittich (New York: Bedminister Press, 1968), pp. 341–2.

[2] *The Process of Government*, ed. by Peter Odegard (Cambridge: Harvard University Press, 1967), p. 211; pp. 211–15.

[3] *Ibid.*, p. 222.

groups in terms of their *collective*, rather than their 'individual' interests. Our data will enable us to treat this theoretical discontinuity since our information includes the director's definition of his group's 'essential purpose', and also any service or benefit which it provides its members. In addition, we have his judgment as to the major reasons why his members belong to the group. We shall argue in a moment that a group's major 'interest' can be specified, in rebuttal of the criticism that to say a group is motivated by 'self-interest' or some over-riding 'interest' doesn't tell us very much.

But interest groups have other motives and by-products. Their primal interest often becomes a vehicle for the exchange of valued activities and sentiments. Such activities and sentiments pay dividends in terms of individual self-realization, which may become more gratifying as one's sense of personal efficacy is enhanced by the collective influence of his group. Such personal incentives include the desire to serve others; to engage in social interaction; to feel personally useful; to overcome feelings of alienation or ineffectuality; to gain personal power and prestige; and to achieve social exclusiveness. Analytically distinct and prior, however, is the single major collective interest or goal which typically inspired the organization's creation, and from which these other activities and incentives are in this sense derived. It is important to add that many interest groups were initially established negatively, as it were, in response to some exogenous threat, but this fact does not invalidate the previous assumption regarding the priority of their primal interest, as revealed through their interactions with government and the way their resources are allocated.

THE PROBLEM OF DEFINITION

In a somewhat different context, groups are often characterized in terms of the character of the interest that activates them, i.e. as business, professional, political, fraternal, religious, and/or service groups. As our data will show, these types are often quite similar in terms of internal structure, the *process* by which they interact with governmental elites (i.e. legislators and bureaucrats), and the fringe benefits or 'selective inducements' offered their members.

A useful taxonomy of interest groups can also be provided by dichotomizing them into the following types, using 'paired opposite' categories:

66

Compulsory	*v.*	Voluntary
Temporary	*v.*	Permanent
Economic	*v.*	Instrumental
Mass	*v.*	Selective
Producer	*v.*	Consumer
Local–provincial	*v.*	Federal
Federated	*v.*	Unitary
Oligarchic	*v.*	Participative
Private	*v.*	Public

Many of the groups in our sample fit nicely under one or more of these categories. The distinction between economic and instrumental groups is helpful, with 'economic' referring to large, producer-oriented groups whose objectives often include direct financial and market benefits to individual members, contrasted with 'instrumental' groups whose members tend to seek humanitarian, political, or other eleemosynary gratifications. The distinction between compulsory and voluntary groups is sometimes useful. However, it has some obvious limitations. Professional associations for example, are often categorized as voluntary associations, yet membership is sometimes explicitly required before one can work, while at other times it is 'expected' of all those in the guild. The 'producer–consumer' dichotomy is also useful, and topical, given the rapid emergence of 'consumer' associations. As a rule, however, it seems that such organizations are less effectual than most other types, often precisely because they do not have a primal, focussed interest around which action can be galvanized and commitment sustained. By contrast, most industrial, professional, agricultural, business and labour groups present themselves and represent their members essentially as *producers*. It is only recently that collective solidarities based upon the definition of one's role as a consumer have widely inspired this type of interest group.

Many important aspects of interest groups, however, are not revealed by such categorizations. These relate to such questions as their political role and influence; how precisely they reflect the distribution of social power in Canada; how their functions and objectives influence their structure; and what, if any, seem to be the functional requisites of all types of interest groups.[1] As suggested earlier, two related analytical foci are the ways in

---

[1] A useful survey of research orientations in the field of interest groups is Sam Eldersveld, 'American interest groups', in H. W. Ehrmann, *Interest Groups on Four Continents* (Pittsburgh: University of Pittsburgh Press, 1958), pp. 173–96.

which the parliamentary system affects interest groups and how their behaviour is constrained by the political culture of Canadian society. These are central questions in the present analysis.

Research in interest group behaviour runs into some difficult conceptual questions, beginning with how best to define such groups. Sometimes, the term 'interest groups', which we shall use for all types of groups regardless of their primal interest, is restricted to 'economic' types such as agricultural, business, or labour groups. Again, a dichotomy has been suggested between 'economic' and 'expressive' or 'instrumental' types of associations. 'Political' groups have been distinguished from 'non-political' types, but as noted this classification does not hold up empirically, since the most unlikely type of association is likely at one time or another to act politically. In general, dichotomies seem less useful than continua for definitional purposes.

Max Weber was among the first to emphasize the utility of group analysis as a means of understanding social structure. He begins by distinguishing 'communal' and 'associative' social relationships. The first is based upon the subjective feeling of the parties concerned that 'they belong together'. Associative groups, on the other hand, are those in which 'the orientation of social actions...rests upon a rationally motivated adjustment of interests... whether the basis of rational judgments be absolute values or reasons of expediency.'[1] These might be called 'economic' and 'instrumental' in our terms. A major distinction between them seems to be the *rationality* of the motivations and the need for the conscious adjustment of mutual interests, which are presumably less compelling in the case of communally based groupings. Here, also, there is the suggestion that whereas communal types are characteristic of the pre-industrial *Gemeinschaft* stage of social and economic development, associative types reflect the emergence of *Gesellschaft*, contract-based industrial society.[2] Such collectivities, moreover, may be open or closed with respect to membership. Open types are those which have no restrictions on membership of an affective, ethnic, social or other nature, whereas closed types are typically those which have special rights, usually monopolistically held, which they are able to guarantee to members. Weber cites various combinations and gradations of such types which need not be repeated here. Associative groups, in turn, are divided into two types, compulsory and voluntary. The latter (*Verein*) claim authority

---

[1] *Economy and Society*, Vol. 1, ed. by G. Roth and C. Wittich (New York: Bedminister Press, 1968), pp. 40–53.
[2] *Ibid.*, pp. 40–1.

only over voluntary members, while the former (*Anstalt*) refers to organizations which impose, within their delimited context, successful control over all behaviour conforming to certain patent criteria. Both types of associations are distinguished by rationally established rules and a bureaucratic staff. Such distinctions, of course, refer to ideal types and considerable overlapping is always found in empirical situations. Nevertheless, the concepts of voluntary and compulsory association seem useful in differentiating interest groups that tend to have a specific ulterior motive, such as economic security, from those are bound together by normative ties that seek to advance a 'cause'.

Such a rough dichotomy appears when we differentiate interest groups in terms of their primary goals: business, professional, and labour groups tend to stress 'specific ulterior interests', while welfare, educational, religious, ethnic, social–recreational, and fraternal types emphasize 'cause' or eleemosynary kinds of incentives. Here again, of course, pure types rarely exist, as seen in the fact that even the most economically oriented groups express certain ideological norms, while the elites who direct many 'cause' types of groups may exhibit a keen appreciation for financial and bureaucratic survival. The distinction between voluntary and compulsory associations is especially difficult to sustain, since both labour unions and professional groups, which are typically included in the voluntary category, are hardly pure types.

Research in interest group behaviour thus runs into some difficult conceptual problems, beginning with the question of how best to define such groups. Some observers have conceptualized interest groups as being essentially 'private', but here again, although the great majority of groups in our study are 'private' (i.e. non-governmental), this label is not always adequate because the patterns of interaction, shared premises, and overlapping institutional alliances between private and governmental elites are so intertwined that the distinction is often useful only in a formal, expository sense.

Our research indicates, moreover, that organized *public* groups now engage in a good deal of interaction among various levels of government, as well as within each level and *vis-à-vis* the general public. Not only do some provinces, for example, maintain representatives in Ottawa, but each discrete element of government often has a representative who seeks to influence other parts of the political system, as for example, when a department has an official who maintains liaison with Parliament. Thus, while our perspective of interest group behaviour formally conceptualizes such activity as typically

69

occurring between private groups and government, a great deal of such behaviour now occurs within and between governments.

The term 'pressure group' has also enjoyed rather wide currency, suggesting of course that groups bring 'pressure' to bear upon those in political roles to achieve their ends. Here again, however evocative the metaphor, the characterization is inapposite, for at least two reasons. Not only has the term become somewhat invidious, but some of the groups which fall into our net are, in a formal sense, either 'non-political' (i.e. they do not interact with government) or if they are political, their efforts to influence government are too jejune to be characterized as 'pressure'. One of our aims, moreover, is to demonstrate the *relative degree* of 'politicization' of Canadian interest groups; to characterize all of them as 'pressure groups' defeats this purpose.

The categories 'political' or 'non-political' are not very useful for another reason: the conception of 'political' used here includes not only the interactions that groups have with the formal governmental apparatus, but it also comprehends their *internal governance* and their attempts to influence other private groups and the public. In this context, there is little utility in attempting to build a taxonomy of interest groups which differentiates sharply between 'political' and presumably 'non-political' groups. This attempt confuses means and ends.[1] All groups have *interests* (ends) of many kinds, economic, welfare, professional, etc., which they seek to enhance. Directors of such groups have little difficulty in specifying what these 'interests' are. Such ends, however, are often far removed from 'politics', in the usual denotation of the term. Instead, it is the *process* by which groups seek to protect and advance their varied ends that is essentially political. This seems true, moreover, whether the resultant behaviour involves governmental or private centres of power. If 'politics' is essentially concerned with the use of power and authority and influence to allocate certain scarce values, all groups are 'political'. Some are clearly more 'political' than others, but all are 'political' in the above sense.

In effect, all groups may be defined as *political* in the following terms: (1) Their internal process of governance includes a range of behaviour commonly defined as 'political', i.e. they often follow democratic forms of election and participation; their members often combine into subgroups for purposes of conflict and cooperation about certain policy choices. Not only are the

---

[1] This confusion appears again and again among some professional and business groups who make demands upon government but maintain all the while that 'they have nothing to do with politics', by which they mean partisan, electoral politics.

common political values of power, influence, and authority constantly sought *within* the group, but (2) their interactions with other private groups, again both competitive and cooperative, reveal many of the same incentives and activities, and finally (3) many of them, including some which seem only marginally 'political', and so define their activities, expend considerable energy making demands upon governmental elites.

Having conceptualized interest groups as essentially political, it seems useful to add an important qualification. All interest groups are political but not all political groups will be defined here as interest groups. Some observers have argued that political parties, ministers, backbenchers, the bureaucracy and government itself are all interest groups. While such elements often behave in ways similar to those of interest groups, and while they share certain incentives such as survival and security, this conceptualization has some analytical disadvantages. If only because they have assumed a formal obligation to run the official apparatus and hence, have a degree of legitimacy and power unmatched by most private interest groups, it seems questionable to place them in the same category. Certainly, as an 'interest group' government lacks the autonomy, cohesiveness, and exclusivity that enable most private interest groups to press their claims singlemindedly.

I prefer to view the government apparatus (parties, executive, legislature, and courts) as the official system *through* and *with* which interest groups work in translating various kinds of social power into legitimate political power. This is not to say that government is a cipher, without any independent influence upon this process. It obviously has highly valued dividends to allocate, including prestige, legal sanctions, material largesse, and legitimated violence, and it may have some independent calculus of the proper distribution of such values. These are usually allocated, however, after considerable bargaining and conflict among its own internal centres of power, as well as with relevant interest groups. At times, of course, government agencies act very much like interest groups, lobbying both within the official apparatus and among private arenas of power. However, the essential distinction remains: *interest groups never assume formal authority and responsibility for running the government.*

It seems helpful to think of the formal political apparatus as an instrument (not without self-interest and initiative) through which the prior claims of articulate social groups are realized. As Bentley says, 'the interest groups create the government and work through it.'[1] Their claims provide much of the energy that activates the formal political structure and often determine

[1] *The Process of Government*, p. 270.

71

the ends to which it is put. Certainly, one would be hard pressed to find any significant policy or programme conceived independently by governmental elites. As we shall show, the interlocking between political and private elites is too pervasive, sustained, and symbiotic for such to be the general case.

Although our sample includes a cross-section of virtually all types of interest groups, one common characteristic is that none of them are 'profit making'. Many, of course, are creatures of activities which are themselves profit-making; chambers of commerce and trade associations of one kind or another fall into this category. But none of them is directly engaged in profit-making. In addition to 'business' groups, which constitute the largest single proportion (one-fifth) of interest groups in Canada, our sample includes the following types of groups: professional associations, labour unions, agricultural groups, service clubs such as Lions or Kiwanis, ethnic groups such as the Jewish Association of Hungarian Descent, fraternal associations such as Loyal Orange and *St Jean Baptiste*, recreational groups such as the *Association Cycliste Canadienne*, welfare groups such as the Canadian Welfare Council, and religious groups such as the Association for the Advancement of Christian Scholarship.

A fairly abstract definition is needed to comprehend so broad a spectrum of groups. For our purposes, the following seems useful: *interest groups are collectivities organized around an explicit aggregate value on behalf of which essentially political claims are made* vis-à-vis *government, other groups, and the general public*. This definition includes most of the essential qualities of such groups: membership, organization, which implies structure and roles, a basic, official *raison d'être* or collective 'mission', attended by latent goals such as security, prestige, and income for its permanent staff, and certain claims sought through an essentially political process involving negotiation and consultation with public and private targets.

This definition incorporates the peripheral goals and benefits touched upon earlier. However, in the terms of their most basic characterization, it is interesting to speculate whether the latter are not really only secondary aspects of group life. Without their primal collective interest, would such groups persist? We may have exaggerated the significance of this manifest goal somewhat, partly because interest group directors usually feel constrained to underscore it. The generalization may apply only to large professional and economic groups, which represent their members in one of their most crucial life contexts, occupational role. Our research will probably show that both the director of an interest group and its members participate for several reasons,[1] but it will also enable us to rank such incentives. This should reveal the extent to which members are concerned with certain direct material benefits that are distinct from the larger 'political' goal of the association. Such questions raise an interesting theoretical issue.

THE THEORY OF 'SELECTIVE INCENTIVES'

The economist Mancur Olson has suggested that the 'common characteristic' of large economic interest groups who lobby extensively for some collective goal is that they are also organized for some *other* purpose.[2] This other purpose is usually some personal, instrumental incentive, such as preferential rates on insurance, cooperative purchasing, and technical information. Such selective incentives, Olson maintains, are the main reason members remain in large economic groups. This fact, in turn, enables their leaders to seek the large, collective goals which formally activate the group. 'The lobby is then a by-product of whatever function [the] organization performs that enables it to have a captive membership.'[3] Examples are cited from labour unions, professional associations, and farm organizations. Of unions, he concludes that 'their political power is a by-product of their non-political activities.' Members are interested in the bread-and-butter issues of wages and hours of work, not in the larger political concerns of their union, which encompass a broad range of welfare issues. Professional lobbies and farm organizations exhibit a similar pattern of selective inducements.

In contrast to Bentley, who insisted that interest groups should be defined by their major collective interest, Olson argues that such groups really have two types of 'interest', a collective one and a selective individual one. The latter, moreover, is more vital than the primal interest, since it provides the inducements required to insure the groups' survival, as well as its capacity to lobby for its collective goal. In effect, Bentley's theory is extended and sharply modified, in ways that will be noted in a moment.

One analytical problem is to differentiate between what we have called the group's primal interest and the by-products which, in Olson's theory,

---

[1] Each director was asked to indicate the perceived incentives of members for belonging to his group. It would, perhaps, have been better to ask this question directly of members but our resources did not permit a survey of their attitudes.

[2] *The Logic of Collective Action* (Cambridge: Harvard University Press, 1965), p. 132, pp. 132–40 *passim*.

[3] *Ibid.*, p. 136.

provide the selective incentives which really keep members in the organization. An obvious question is precisely *what* is their primal interest, and who defines it? Such an interest could be the larger 'public interest' which some interest groups insist they seek. It could be the collective economic interest of its members. Certainly, the primal interest is often rationalized as a public interest, encompassing the entire community. It could also be the material fringe benefits provided by most groups.

Our data enable us to partially test Olson's theory by differentiating groups in terms of the perceived incentives of members, and also by an analysis of the types of benefits provided by Canadian groups. Olson insists that the real test is whether groups that fail to provide selective incentives *survive*, but this requires an historical kind of analysis rarely possible in survey research. Obviously, if all types of groups are considered, some long-lived 'cause' groups appear which often fail to offer their members any tangible, personal incentives. But Olson, of course, restricts his theory to 'economic' groups. In this context, he shows that some agricultural groups, for example, which fail to offer such incentives have either disappeared or had great difficulty in surviving.

Olson also rejects Bentley's and Truman's assumption that the outcome of group conflict is the best possible manifestation of the 'public interest', and that two countervailing mechanisms, 'overlapping membership' and 'potential groups', prevent any single interest group from abusing its power. In effect, because any given individual belongs to several groups with discrete goals, which weakens the thrust of any particular value, and because latent interests are always prepared to arise whenever existing groups became too powerful, the politics of the interest group process is generally viewed as benign and self-equilibrating.[1]

If these two assumptions are valid, it should be possible to demonstrate that competition exists among groups in specific functional areas. Our data may enable us to test the extent to which, in certain given 'interest' sectors, competitive behaviour in fact exists among groups as a result of overlapping memberships. As noted earlier, the idea that overlapping group memberships are a necessary condition of political stability has been severely challenged by analyses of certain multi-party systems, which exist in fragmented ethnic and linguistic political cultures, yet are among the most stable democracies in the world.[2]

[1] David Truman, *The Governmental Process* (New York: Alfred Knopf, 1951).
[2] Arend Lijphart, *The Politics of Accommodation*; 'Typologies of democratic systems', 1 *Comparative Political Studies* (April, 1968), pp. 3–44.

The question of 'potential groups' is more difficult to handle since it is very hard to test empirically. It does seem that latent, unorganized 'interests' exist, but the process and conditions under which they become active and organized remain obscure. *Post hoc* examples of such phenomena abound, but it seems that the test of prediction has not been met. Certainly, until such latent groups acquire a 'collective conscience' and other political and organizational requisites, they are likely to remain passive.

One suggestive theoretical approach which proved fruitless was our attempt to divide groups into '*status quo*' and 'innovative' types, as a means of determining their relative effectiveness. During the field research, it often seemed that certain marginal types of groups, in terms of budget and social prestige, were mainly concerned with attempting to change the existing distribution of social resources. Meanwhile, other groups, which usually enjoyed larger shares of legitimacy and possessed more hard resources, were mainly occupied with maintaining the *status quo*. Since we were informed again and again by directors that the *status quo* role was much easier to perform, this construct seemed especially useful in analysing effectiveness. It appeared that a nice typology of groups might be developed from these conditions, based upon the differing resources, methods, and effectiveness of each type. As a result, all case study issues were coded as being either 'innovative' or '*status quo*'. Here, as often happens, although a theory was intriguing enough to merit testing, the data failed to support it.[1]

First, as noted earlier, over 80 per cent of the case study issues turned out to be innovative in character. When directors were asked in what two substantive areas they had been most successful in dealing with governmental elites, the largest single proportion (20 per cent) replied 'having favourable legislation passed'. 'Having favourable administrative practices adopted' was ranked, although narrowly, as second by 17 per cent. More important, when the empirical test was made, the assumed relationships did not appear. For example, insofar as the association between effectiveness and type of issue was concerned, virtually no differences appeared. Little or no variation was explained by either 'hard' or psychopolitical resources, including number of members, legitimacy imputed to the group, or identification of members with group goals. Virtually equal proportions of all types of groups, possessing various types and amounts of resources were equally involved in both kinds of issues.

---

[1] For similar experience, see Lester Milbrath, *The Washington Lobbyists* (Chicago: Rand McNally, 1963).

COLLECTIVITIES DEFINED AS 'INTEREST GROUPS'

Despite some problems, perhaps the most useful way to define the organizations analysed in this study is as 'interest groups'. Such a term seems to denote their principal character: their focus upon a single, dominant aggregate *interest*, consciously shared, and around which members organize in order to better seek collectively what they desire individually. This 'interest' may, of course, range from the most direct and narrow economic motive to an abstract humanitarian aspiration. It may be a 'tangible' economic goal such as the maintenance of 'fair trade' pricing or jurisdiction over an industrial process by a union. On the other hand, it may be a 'selfless' aspiration such as the efforts of French language groups in Quebec to preserve the cultural heritage of the province. It is important to add that while members of a given group tend to agree on this collective goal, they are not likely to share common attitudes on other aspects of social or political life. Although it is fashionable to maintain that they belong to groups with conflicting values, it is probably more accurate to say that they may have membership in one or two groups whose primal interests are quite unrelated to each other.

This primary, collective interest usually provides the impulse upon which is built a superstructure of organized resources, strategic policies, ideological rationalizations, and derivative individual benefits. But in the end, it seems, the association's major concern is to enhance the probability that the major goal will be achieved. Perhaps, as Olson maintains, one of the best ways to do this is to provide its members with an abundance of personal inducements. There are undoubtedly some groups in which peripheral incentives strongly challenge putatively major goals, yet our research suggests that, at any given time, most group leaders and their members are seriously identified with the latter. More precisely, the major incentives of most members tend to be defined in terms that require for their fulfilment the achievement of the group's primal, collective interest.

INTEREST GROUPS AND POLITICAL PARTIES

To some extent, our emphasis upon the salience of the group's collective goal is the result of the fact that interest groups, unlike political parties, are not *expected* to articulate and represent a plethora of discrete interests. Interest groups are not 'pluralistic' in this sense, although the fact that a vast number of them exist and (in some contexts) compete lends some credence to the view that a given political culture is 'pluralistic'. Other differences between interest groups and political parties may be helpful in conceptualizing such groups. Basically, of course, most parties seek to gain the power to govern, to control funds and offices, interest groups are usually content to influence those who displace such power. A small proportion of them, of course, try to nominate and elect candidates, but this is not among their prescribed or legitimated functions, as it is with parties. The need to function within a political structure whose members change periodically means that interest groups typically avoid partisan politics and work towards a specific goal within the prevailing political structure.[1] Because their objectives are much more sustained and focussed than those of parties, they enjoy a great deal more ideological cohesion and programmatic continuity. These conditions may explain their occasional protestation that they are 'non-political', even though they admittedly seek to influence governmental elites.

Structurally, interest groups are sometimes viewed as subsystems within the party system, as seen in the case of labour unions and the NDP. As we shall show, relationships between interest groups and government are often extremely close, as when legislators or bureaucrats are members of the very interest groups who appear before them. Indeed, MP's are sometimes named by interest group executives and by other MP's as being lobbyists for certain substantive interests. In addition, of course, private groups are often 'built into' the formal political process through membership on joint committees charged with policy-making and appointments.

Nevertheless, the two systems are distinct in that the role of private elites in the political decision-making process is probably not fully legitimated by rank-and-file citizens, as suggested by the ambivalence with which the practice of lobbying is regarded. Certainly, a crucial factor about interest groups is their informal, extra-constitutional position in the political system. Since this condition has little effect upon their functional role and importance, one can think of such groups spatially and operationally as existing at some intermediate level between the parties and government and the unorganized mass of citizens, with the vital function of synthesizing individual and group claims into a coherent policy for presentation to party leaders and to members of the formal political apparatus.[2]

---

[1] A few groups, including mainly consumer associations and labour unions, are directly concerned with electoral politics and with the larger shape of government policy across several areas.

[2] Some observers maintain that interest groups 'articulate' presumably discrete interests which in turn are 'aggregated' by political parties. Our research suggests that such

This function is very similar to that often ascribed to political parties, which suggests that the difference between them and interest groups may be rather tenuous in some contexts. Certainly, the comprehensive role of synthesizing and formulating policy which parties may contribute at the provincial and national levels is carried out largely *within* any given substantive sector by interest groups. Such a delegation is functionally necessary. One of its limitations, of course, is that parties in power do not usually, in any system, find themselves willing or able to carry out all the commitments implied by this process. This fact provides interest group elites with a great deal of work and frustration between elections.

This aspect of party government suggests another explanation for the pervasive role of interest groups. Since Canadian parties rarely coordinate and synthesize group claims, other than in the most highly generalized form, interest groups must enter the policy-making arena to supply the detailed claims and expertise which the parties either cannot or will not commit themselves to. Moreover, even when parties do make a specific commitment, the process of hammering any policy into legislative and programmatic form is so complex and detailed that relevant interest groups must be brought in to supply technical guidance.[1]

The strength of interest groups is further ramified by the accommodation role of the federal government, which is contingent upon the fragmented Canadian political culture and aggravated by the doctrine of federalism, and which weakens its potential as a legitimate centre for the control and direction of national social and economic policy.

FUNCTIONAL BASES OF ELITE ACCOMMODATION

Government departments and agencies are organized upon a basis of functional representation, which means that interactions between them and their major client groups tend to be sustained and focussed. The institutionalization of such relationships is extensive: joint membership of political elites upon advisory committees; clearance of major agency appointments with relevant interest groups; *ad hoc* joint committees for the drafting of

groups also spend considerable time 'aggregating' the interests of coalitions of 'mutually-interested' groups.

[1] Another rationale for interest group participation is provided by the normative belief that such groups 'should' be brought into the policy-making process. Here, an interesting difference between political elites and ordinary citizens exists, in which interest group participation (with the possible exception of *ad hoc* citizen groups) is usually legitimated by elites but highly suspected by ordinary citizens.

legislation and administrative rules; government delegation of the administration of a programme to an interest group; membership of agency officials in the interest group – these are among the common synthetic elements. Equally germane is the little-known practice whereby an agency creates an interest group to make claims upon its resources. Our research indicates that close to half of all departments have at some time inspired such groups. As government's net has spread more widely into new and highly technical areas, its reliance upon such liaisons has inevitably increased.

Since judgments about the proper allocation of public resources will always differ, and some groups will receive less than others, accommodation is not always smooth. On the whole, however, the more common condition is one of consensus and cooperation, if only because most exchanges occur within the boundaries of given agency–client contexts. Interest group elites, as we shall show, see legislators and bureaucrats as helpful expeditors. In Canada, where private group participation in government has usually been viewed positively in line with the dominant corporatist theory, this relationship enjoys much greater legitimation than in countries such as France and the United States where a tradition of Lockeian individualism has often stigmatized it.

In all Western states, however, it seems that evaluations of this nexus differ more than its institutionalization, which has been similarly pervasive everywhere. As a result, many private and putatively non-political groups, such as physical scientists, have become very intimately involved in governmental policy-making. To this extent, the traditional distinction between the 'private' and 'public' status and roles of interest groups and government is no longer very helpful. Our research shows that many Canadian interest groups and their lobbyists consciously attempt to influence government. (Obviously, the intensity and effectiveness of such attempts vary considerably, a condition we shall attempt to document.) The main reasons include the secular increase in the scale and intensity of government activity and the apparently infinite growth of functional specialization in modern, industrial society. An unanticipated consequence is that both parties and government are increasingly less able to integrate the conflicting demands and needs of the many groups in society. Interest group elites thus assume a larger role in the determination of public policy. This formulation seems to fit the Canadian political system nicely, in terms of the positive appreciation of government's partnership in the private economy, corporatist theory, and the brokerage role forced upon parties by ethnic, religious, and regional cleavages, as well as by their desire to win elections.

Political theory and political culture

LOBBYING

Another important conceptual problem involves the appropriate characterization of the role played by interest group elites in attempting to influence
legislators, bureaucrats, other interest groups, and the unorganized public.
Such activities are often referred to as 'lobbying'. As noted earlier, we
found some reluctance among Canadian governmental elites to discuss
these activities, which were sometimes defined in a pejorative way. Some
Canadian legislators maintained that a 'lobbyist', unlike the head of an
interest group, was a person who hired himself out to represent *any* interest,
had no organization behind him, and was somewhat suspect ethically because
he often attempted to use contacts developed earlier in government service
to advance the interests of his clients.[1] Some interest group leaders share
this ambivalence, while at the same time carrying out political activities
that can only be defined as lobbying, in its general connotation as any effort
to influence MP's, bureaucrats or the public in order to shape governmental
policy.[2]

A survey of the literature and journalistic commentaries on Canadian
politics, however, indicates that these characterizations present only part
of the ongoing reality. Not only is the term 'lobbyist' apparently more
current than our informants believed, but the role itself is more common
than indicated. The *Monetary Times*, for example, speaks of the 'Federal
government's lobby system and its several hundred members'.[3] In 1970, a
federal NDP member prepared a private bill which would have required
the registration of lobbyists.[4] The *Times* cited the Pharmaceutical Manufacturers' Association as the lobby which had inspired the member's concern

[1] In effect, a distinction is made between the head of an organized interest group and the
agent of a specific company or interest, even though each individual plays the same
political role. In the first case, lobbying is apparently legitimate, but not in the other.
[2] For an interesting example, see Helen Jones Dawson, 'The consumers association of
Canada', 6 *Canadian Public Administration* (March, 1963), pp. 92–118. As she concludes,
'The Association has also been hamstrung by its own rather ostrich-like attitude put
forward in the constantly reiterated maxim that CAC must not be allowed to become
a pressure group.' p. 320.
[3] 'Inside the Ottawa lobby', July, 1968, p. 11. *The Globe and Mail* carried a story, 'Lobbying flourishes behind euphemisms', which maintained 'there are hundreds of lobbyists
in the capital', March 10, 1969. The *Globe Magazine*, February 27, 1971 also carried a
piece by Hugh Winsor called, somewhat expansively, 'Lobbying: a comprehensive
report on the art and its practitioners', pp. 2–7. See also, *Parliamentarian*, January,
1970, for a résumé of lobbying in Canada.
[4] As is customary with private bills, this one (C-38) was 'talked out', under the direction
of the Government whip. See *House of Commons Debates*, April 14, 1970, pp. 5850–7.

by its intense opposition to the Government's unsuccessful attempt in 1969 to pass legislation which would weaken patent protection for drugs. That at least one lobbyist has been the head of an interest group is indicated by the fact that Dr William Wigle, lobbyist for the PMAC, was president of the group and had earlier been president of the Canadian Medical Association.[1] The *Times* also reported that over 200 national associations had their headquarters in Ottawa and that 'many companies maintain their own man in the capital'.[2]

Such representations, reinforced by our functionalist assumption that any modern political system necessarily requires information and support from a broad range of private groups, suggest that the term 'lobbying' does indeed have empirical referents in the Canadian political milieu. We decided to entertain the hypothesis and to incorporate it in our research instrument. However, in an effort to ease any pejorative connotation of the term, we defined 'lobbying' broadly to respondents as 'any effort on the part of any individual or group to influence political elites and the public by direct or indirect persuasion.'

For our purposes, then, 'lobbying' is conceptualized in the following broad terms: It includes both direct (e.g. letter-writing and personal interactions) and indirect (e.g. organizing influence at the constituency level) attempts by directors to influence the decisions of governmental and other political elites and the general public. Such attempts are aimed at the following targets: parliament, administration, judiciary, their own members, other interest groups, and the ordinary citizen. Our parameters here are broader than those usually set by political scientists, who tend to limit their scope to legislators and bureaucrats, and sometimes only to the former. Our research indicates, however, that interest group directors spend a great deal of time attempting to influence other private groups to behave in some desired way to influence governmental policy. Regarding the general public as target, here again many interest groups attempt to influence individual citizens to make representations to governmental elites on their behalf. Such groups seek to influence political opinion indirectly, i.e. their hope and expectation is that those contacted will influence other individuals and, ultimately, governmental elites.

The characteristic *means* of such influence is the communication of information regarding the group's reaction to proposed governmental action or its wish to have some new policy introduced. Information is perhaps the most valued currency mediating the exchanges between lobbyists and

[1] *Ibid.*, p. 15.　　[2] *Ibid.*

governmental elites. It is useful to differentiate two analytically discrete elements of such information, which we shall call *substantive* and *ideological*. Substantive elements refer to the objective, technical, 'feasibility' components of a policy issue, while ideological elements concern its 'party' and 'political survival' aspects. Both elements act as constraints upon governmental elites and are constant situational factors for lobbyists attempting to influence a given member. Both the substantive and ideological information supplied to a legislator often provide, if he wishes, a necessary rationale for whatever decision he decides to take on a given issue in caucus or before the Government has taken a firm position.

The content, frequency, and form of such communication are central variables in the analysis of interest group behaviour.[1] In part, their content provides the incentive for the establishment of mutually productive liaisons between governmental and private elites. More important, it reveals the policy position of the group concerned and, as we shall suggest, the weight its representations carry with the individual or agency concerned. Frequency, in turn, tells us something about both the continuity of interaction and the influence enjoyed by a group. Form reveals the sociometric intensity of such interaction, whether, for example, contacts are merely 'official' or whether more personal kinds of interaction are characteristic of certain group executives, compared with others. Informal negotiations among political elites are often said to be characteristic of Canadian policy determination. Our data should permit a test of this judgment.

SEMANTIC AND LINGUISTIC PROBLEMS OF CROSS-CULTURAL ANALYSIS

The ambivalent conception of lobbying held by some respondents suggests the importance of semantic differentials in survey research. In effect, cultural orientations may distort cross-national findings because formally equivalent terms are not always functionally equivalent. Data which appear to be comparative are not really so because the verbal stimulus of a term, 'lobbying' for example, may evoke a different conceptual response-set than that assumed by the interviewer. We encountered such problems in translating our interview schedules into French. For example, the term 'interest

---

[1] We shall test later, for example, the hypothesis that the influence imputed to interest group leaders and their agents by governmental elites is positively associated with the frequency of personal interaction between them.

group' could be translated as *groupes de pression* or *corps intermédiaire*. We finally chose the latter, since it seemed to provide a better index of Durkheim's useful conception of such groups as essential links between the individual and government, and was also more neutral.

This and related experiences suggested that similar, deep-seated semantical differences might also affect communication with our English-Canadian respondents, especially since our research was based upon American experience. Only a few analyses of semantic differentials between English-Canadians and Americans exist, but some of them proved useful. Insofar as semantical distortion is the result of subtle cultural differences, some evidence indicates that some segments of English-Canadian and American societies hold very similar values in certain contexts. In a study of values based upon 'thirteen possible ways to live' among a sample of students from the United States, (N–2,015) Canada (N–170), India, Japan, China, and Norway, Charles Morris found it unnecessary to present his Canadian data separately, because there was so little difference between the United States and the Canadian groups.[1] Canadian students ranked somewhat higher on self-restraint and self-control, i.e. 'the stress is upon responsible, conscientious, intelligent participation in human affairs' and somewhat lower on enjoyment and 'progress in action' (the latter is defined as 'the stress upon delight in vigorous action for the overcoming of obstacles', an emphasis upon 'the initiation of change', and 'confidence in man's powers rather than one of caution and restraint'.)[2] In general, however, very little difference was found between the two samples. Indeed, the mean ratings on the thirteen 'value-orientations' on male respondents from the two countries were identical.[3]

Morris' findings, however, are not entirely consistent with other, mainly sociological, interpretations of Canadian and American character differences. John Porter, for example, after citing many cultural influences that tend to erode traditional differences between the two societies, finds it 'difficult to disagree' with S. M. Lipset's conclusion that 'Canadians...are conservative, authoritarian, oriented to tradition, hierarchy, and elitism in the sense of showing deference to those in high status. Canadian values have been shaped by a distinct antirevolutionary past which contrasts with the strong egalitarianism of the United States with its emphasis on opportunity and personal achievement as the basis of social rewards.[4]

[1] *Varieties of Human Value* (Chicago: University of Chicago Press, 1956), p. 42, pp. 47–8.
[2] *Ibid.*, p. 42, Table 8. [3] *Ibid.*, p. 47; pp. 32–4.
[4] 'Canadian national character', *Cultural Affairs* (Spring, 1969), pp. 49–50.

Porter insists, moreover, that English- and French-Canadians are more alike in these values 'than spokesmen of either group are prepared to admit'. Selecting certain values such as religiosity, humanistic and elitist educational orientations, ruralism, and the tendency toward an authoritarian political culture, Porter suggests that the differences are not as great as the similarities. Perhaps, he concludes, there is a 'single culture in Canada in which the core values are conservative, and on the matter of lesser values the French and the English are subcultural variants'.[1]

Both semantical and conceptual barriers to cross-cultural political research are probably raised by such fundamental value cleavages between Canada and the United States. Certain political symbols, for example, evoke different responses among political elites in the two societies.[2] We are not concerned here with symbols which have patently different meanings such as the term 'civic', which is used in Canada to denote the local or municipal level of government, whereas in the United States it commonly characterizes politics and government generally. Our concern is with more subtle cultural frames of reference in which the denotative meaning of symbols is less at issue than the normative and objective connotation attached to them.

Among Canadians, it seems, certain assumptions about the parliamentary system quite naturally colour such reactions, and similar phenomena are equally present among Americans regarding the presidential system. The phenomenon of party discipline seems particularly germane. Generally acceptable in the Canadian milieu since it is consistent with the hierarchical and systemic assumptions mentioned above, the practice is often antithetical to Americans whose egalitarianism tends to honour independence among politicians. The term lobbying evokes similarly discrete reactions, again reflecting in part the differing assumptions of respondents. In parliamentary convention, if not practice, interest groups and their agents are seen as having a minor role because an all-powerful Government can presumably carry out its electoral mandate without much need for concessions to private groups. The American view, among most political elites, is more likely to assume that lobbying and interest group influence are necessary and proper elements of an individualistic political system in which power is widely shared.

[1] *Ibid.*, p. 50.
[2] Some observers have found, however, that the difficulties of semantic and linguistic differences in cross-national research have been exaggerated. As Robert Marsh concludes 'certain aspects of human cognition – evaluative and dynamic factors – are relatively independent of the structure of language,' *Comparative Sociology* (New York: Harcourt Brace and World, 1967), p. 277.

The historic self-consciousness and traditionalism of French-Canadians[1] also plays a part in semantic discontinuity and precarious rapport. For example, the nationalistic, humanistic thrust of higher education in Quebec tends to foster, among some members of the political elite, a bias against behavioural research.[2] This cultural orientation is perhaps associated with the consistently higher refusal rates we encountered among all three political elites in Quebec. Allied with this bias was some defensiveness about participation in a study directed by an 'outsider', from an English-Canadian university. Cultural particularism also had its functional side, however, as when our Quebec respondents found the French translations of our interview schedule to be quite well done. The strong deference toward authority noted by many observers of French-Canadian society was also apparent in the responses of some deputies to items regarding the political influence of interest groups. In several cases, the reply indicated that their *party leader* was the paramount source of decision, both within the parties and *vis-à-vis* private interests.

Certain other political symbols and values have been found to be highly culture-bound. We noted in an earlier chapter that English-Canadians tended to exhibit a somewhat more positive internalization of legal–political norms of conduct than French-Canadians who were perhaps more likely to regard them as idealistic impositions. Here, one may suggest that any resulting *incivisme* in Quebec is a cultural fragment imported from France, and characterized by that paradoxical blending of authoritarianism and individualism that tends to make French politics comparatively less stable than that of other Western countries. Political alienation, as a result, tends to be higher among French-Canadians, with attending consequences for the evaluation of political symbols and political institutions.[3] Such orientations probably affect political research in unknown and perhaps unknowable ways,

---

[1] Cf., for example, responses to an item in a national sample (1968) in which respondents were asked, 'How do you think of yourself?' 58 per cent of English-Canadians and 61 per cent of other ethnic groups replied, 'Simply as a Canadian', compared with only one-third of French-Canadians. Similarly, almost one-third of French-Canadians believed Quebec should have a 'special status' among Canadian provinces, compared with only 10 and 7 per cent of English and 'other' Canadians respectively. Unpublished data provided by John Meisel from his survey of the 1968 election.

[2] A similar but less pervasive attitude exists in English-Canada as well. Naturally, there are many exceptions to these generalizations.

[3] John Meisel, for example, found in two national surveys (1965 and 1968) that French-Canadians were consistently more likely than English-Canadians to agree with standard 'alienation' items.

85

but it may be that the attending variations among individual responses are randomized to the extent that their effect is neutralized.

CONSULTATION OR NEGOTIATION

More significant than the content, form, and frequency of communication between interest groups and the governmental elite is its *impact* upon policy. A useful distinction has been made between *consultation* and *negotiation*, which provides a rough index of the effectiveness of a given interest group.[1] Consultation refers to a situation in which the opinions of a group are solicited by the officials concerned but are not decisive insofar as the ultimate decision is concerned. Negotiation, on the other hand, occurs when the approval of the group concerned is the vital factor in the final decision. In effect, negotiation gives the group a veto power. Our data include a recorded 'case study' of a vital decision experienced by each interest group director as a demand upon a governmental agency, and vice versa. Despite some difficulties in interpretation, these data should help determine the decisional significance attributed by the agency to the representations of the group concerned. Hopefully, groups can be differentiated along that dimension, while the characteristic modes of interaction between different agencies and their clientele groups can also be specified.

THE IMPORTANCE OF LEGITIMATION

Our earlier remarks suggest that some Canadian governmental elites may sometimes feel quite ambivalent about the role of interest groups and those who represent them in what we have defined non-pejoratively as a 'lobbying' role. As some observers have emphasized,[2] national attitudes provide a normative framework which strongly affects the legitimacy of interest groups in politics. If the political culture generally supports the principle of group participation in governmental policy determination, such groups will probably enjoy a generally sympathetic reception. In British political theory, as noted earlier, an essentially corporatist view of the state has usually insured pervasive consultation and negotiation between government and relevant private groups. Since the political structure and assumptions of Canadian government are essentially a British legacy, we have assumed that interest

[1] Eckstein, *Pressure Group Politics*, pp. 22–5.
[2] Cf. Eckstein, *ibid.*, pp. 27–9.

86

groups and their agents tend to enjoy a similar fulsome acceptance here from political elites.

Some attempts, nevertheless, were made to deny the existence of the kinds of activities which are called lobbying in other Western political systems. Several considerations seem relevant in explaining this ambivalance. One is the fact that Canadian political scientists have almost completely neglected the role of interest groups.[1] This might suggest that such groups have not been significant enough to merit analysis. On the other hand, and this seems to have been the case in Britain, such groups may have played so vital and unquestioned a role in the governmental process that it was apparently assumed, until quite recently, that neither analysis nor ventilation were required.[2] It may be, too, that any patent recognition of the central role of interest groups presented too sharp a revision of the traditional assumption that Cabinet government in Canada functions autonomously, without the accommodation of exogenous interests often apparent in separation-of-power systems.

THREE THEORETICAL PERSPECTIVES

If empirical data are to be meaningful, they must be anchored in an explicit theoretical framework. Facts by themselves are useless until they are ordered by theories which explain how they are related in some larger set of propositions. Explicitness is stressed because some kind of theory is always present in social analysis, and since this is so, it is best to make it known. A theory is essentially an *explanation* of relationships between a deductively related set of variables. It is usually not considered sufficient to merely demonstrate that such a relationship exists. Although a theory must do this, its ultimate task and obligation is to explain 'why'. To order our interest group data, we shall employ three theoretical perspectives; structural-functionalism, interaction theory, and the theory of elite accommodation.

It is important to note that these theories include system, subsystem, and individual levels of analysis. While elite accommodation and functionalism deal with the contribution that interest groups make to the larger political and social systems, interaction theory seems useful in explaining the dynamics

[1] The most authoritative text on Canadian government, for example, as late as 1970, includes no section on interest groups and neither the terms 'pressure groups' nor 'lobbyist' appear in the index. Dawson, *The Government of Canada*.

[2] The first analysis of British pressure groups seems to have appeared in 1955, W. J. M. Mackenzie, 'Pressure groups: the conceptual framework', 3 *Political Studies* (October, 1955).

of personal, face-to-face relationships between interest group and governmental elites. In focussing initially on the reasons why individuals remain members of groups, the latter also provides an explanation of the origin and survival of the interest group and political subsystems.

The theory of elite accommodation draws upon elements of both functional and interaction theory. Functionally, the process of accommodation between governmental and interest group elites may be explained as a means whereby institutional structures mediate societal needs of resource allocation and conflict resolution. Elite accommodation is a functional requisite of co-ordination between government and 'private' structures which are inevitably affected by such allocations of desired values. As noted earlier, this process is functionally critical in the fragmented Canadian political culture with its high potential for disruptive conflict among diverse ethnic and linguistic subcultures. Interaction theory relates to elite accommodation at its most basic psychological and economic levels, by explaining the incentives for sustained participation by political actors in both 'public' and 'private' roles. Security, patriotism, nation-building, prestige, ideology, and income are among the incentives which impel political elites to perform such system-maintaining roles. We can now turn to a brief outline of functional and interaction theory.[1]

STRUCTURAL–FUNCTIONAL ANALYSIS

Structural–functional analysis holds that social institutions and norms serve a 'functional' (i.e. operationally necessary) role in maintaining the stability of society by providing some process or institution that is essential to its survival.[2] Thus the function of the monogamous family, which appears in almost all societies, is to perpetuate social life by procreating and socializing the young. Judicial systems are 'functional' in meeting an essential need of all societies, the peaceful reconciliation of conflict. The ceremonial rain-dances of certain North American Indian tribes serve a function of socio-religious cohesion. The functional role of violent sports such as hockey and football is often held to be essentially cathartical, i.e. to provide a socially acceptable and minimally harmful means of releasing aggression. More directly, the function of elite accommodation is ultimately

---

[1] The theory of elite accommodation was outlined earlier.

[2] Robert K. Merton, *Social Theory and Social Structure* (New York: Free Press, 1957); for a critique of functionalism, see George C. Homans, 'Bringing men back in', 29 *American Sociological Review* (1964), pp. 809–18.

the preservation of the stability of the national social system. We are more concerned, however with its routine, operational role of allocating governmental largesse among major, organized interests.

Two concepts of functional analysis have been used to differentiate the objective consequences of such institutions that are intended and recognized from those which are neither intended nor recognized.[1] The former are called manifest functions, and the latter latent. In time, latent functions may be transferred into manifest ones, as certain informal patterns of behaviour become institutionalized. This conception helps clarify the 'potential groups' formulation mentioned earlier. Such language is useful in characterizing interest group functions, as we hope to show.

From an analytical point of view, it is always important to ask the question, 'functional for whom?' In most cases, the 'disinterested' observer tends to analyse a given role or institution from a society-wide perspective. Obviously, the point is critical since one's conclusions will be heavily influenced by the perspective from which he views a given activity. It is clear that certain kinds of interest group behaviour, lobbying for example, might be deemed functional from the limited perspective of a given group's welfare, while at the same time their consequences might be neutral or even dysfunctional for the larger society.

Structure, moreover, may provide clues as to the functional role of various institutions. Just as the bills of water-birds, shaped over vast periods of time, sustain their food-gathering habits, so the structure of an organization is often shaped to fulfil its essential functions. Although they were extant in ancient Rome and Greece, interest groups are still young, historically speaking, so that the bewildering variety of structural modifications seen among birds and animals has not yet evolved. Indeed, one is impressed by the homogeneity of interest group structures in Canada, despite the broad range of functional areas they serve and the great diversity of interests they represent. Just over one-quarter of the groups in our sample, for example, are organized on a 'local-only' basis, while the second most common form, local–provincial–national, accounts for another one-fifth, followed by the 'provincial-only' form (13 per cent) and 'national-only' (11 per cent), with the other one-third covering five remaining structural departures. In effect, our 640 groups include only nine different structures, and half of them have only three.

Most interest groups, moreover, are essentially concerned with sustaining some primal goal and the processes and structures best adapted to this end

[1] Merton, op. cit., p. 51.

have become fairly stereotyped, given both their limited ends and the rather constricted *modus operandi* into which they are channelled by the imperatives of the formal political structure and the constraints imposed by the political culture. If the manifest goal or process of interest groups is essentially one of enhancing the security, prestige, income, and self-realization of its members in a given functional context, as symbolized by its primal interest, perhaps we may conclude that interest group goals have become quite standardized. The infinitely variable element is the peculiar substantive milieu in which the interest group exists. Here, it seems, we are coming close to Bentley's dictum that *interest* and *activities* and *group* are synonymous concepts.

THE FUNCTIONAL ROLE OF INTEREST GROUPS

Perhaps the clearest rationale explaining the functional systemic role of private groups was set down by Emile Durkheim, the French sociologist, who saw such groups as a necessary element for binding modern society together. Some mechanism was required to bring the remote individual into the mainstream of collective social life. For Durkheim, professional and occupational groups mediated this functional requisite of any advanced society. As he put it: 'Collective activity is always too complex to be able to be expressed through the single and unique organ of the state. Moreover, the state is too remote from individuals, its relations with them too external and intermittent to penetrate deeply within individual consciences and socialize them within. When the state is the only environment in which men can live communal lives, they inevitably lose contact, become detached and society disintegrates. A nation can be maintained only if, between the state and the individual, there is intercalated a whole series of secondary groups near enough to the individuals to attract them strongly in their sphere of action and drag them, in this way, into the general torrent of social life.' [1]

In a more specific context, interest groups can be viewed as structural mechanisms linking the atomic individual through a congeries of interest collectivities with a subsystem of the larger society, i.e. the formal political apparatus. This interlacing of 'private' and 'public' spheres is again a functional requisite for both elements, giving shape and direction to individual claims and providing policy guidelines and information without which political elites would find it difficult to act wisely. This condition underscores the theoretical inadequacy of conceptualizing 'government' and the 'private' sphere as separate entities.

[1] *The Division of Labour* (Glencoe: Free Press, 1947), p. 28.

The functional role of interest groups is apparent in the way their leaders are often brought *directly* into the governmental system in order that their expertise and experience can be used in administering a government programme. The role that Medical and Dental Societies have played in Canadian health programmes provides one example. Such groups have assumed a leading role in drafting legislation affecting many aspects of public health and their own occupational role; they have sat on government committees concerned with expanding health care; they have helped draft legislation in such spheres; they have promulgated licensing statutes and disciplinary codes which receive the stamp of governmental authority; and they have been charged with the administration and the actual enforcement of the provisions of such statutes. In such areas the boundaries between private and public government are virtually imperceptible. Government, in effect, delegates part of its authority and legitimacy to a private group to better carry through a vital public programme. In many such cases, the expertise and public confidence enjoyed by the group concerned are functional requisites of the first order.

Here, of course, we have been interpreting 'functional' in essentially analytical terms. Viewed from a mixed normative and functional perspective, interest groups also serve the functional requisite of *democratic participation*. In this context, such groups are functional because they provide a badly needed means of citizen participation in the interest group and political subsystems. Certainly, in many cases, such participation may be only symbolic, in that the individual member may be far removed from the decision-centres in his own association and party. But even this minimal degree of influence may be acceptable to him, given the propensity of men to accept such imperatives of organizational life as the so-called 'iron law of oligarchy' which tends to limit rank-and-file participation in large organizations.[1]

The resulting symbiotic relationship between interest group elites and governmental elites is one example of functionalism, which attempts to analyse institutions objectively, from the standpoint of their observable consequences for the system of which they are a part. In this context, to regard interest groups and their lobbying as undemocratic or unresponsible is perhaps beside the point. Some of their consequences are no doubt debatable, but the burden of our research is that they are functionally

---

[1] For the classical analysis of such conditions of participation in modern political organizations, see Robert Michels, *Political Parties: A Sociological Study of the Oligarchical Tendencies of Modern Democracy* (New York: Hearst International Library, 1915).

necessary, in both substantive and ideological contexts. Perhaps some other way of providing the requisites they contribute is possible, but as corporatist theory suggests, they seem to be essential components of complex, highly differentiated societies such as Canada.

INTERACTION THEORY

A major theoretical approach to be used in ordering our data on Canadian groups is interaction theory. Interaction theory rests upon two basic assumptions: the psychological proposition that all behaviour is determined by differential reinforcement and the version of economic theory that explains behaviour in terms of costs and benefits. Typical postulates include the following:[1]

1. If in the past the occurrence of a particular stimulus-situation has been the occasion on which a man's activity has been rewarded, then the more similar the present stimulus-situation is to the past one, the more likely he is to emit the activity, or some similar activity now.

2. The more often within a given period of time a man's activity rewards the activity of any other, the more often the other will emit the activity.

3. The more valuable to a man a unit of the activity another gives him, the more often he will emit activity rewarded by the activity of the other.

4. The more often a man has in the recent past received a rewarding activity from another, the less valuable any further units of that activity becomes to him.

5. The more to a man's disadvantage the rule of distributive justice fails of realization, the more likely he is to display the emotional behaviour we call anger.

Essentially, interaction theory holds that social behaviour is a process of reciprocity or exchange in which individuals initiate and sustain activities and personal interactions that prove rewarding.[2] The process may be

[1] George C. Homans, *Social Behavior: Its Elementary Forms*, pp. 53–5, p. 75.
[2] For a clear early statement of interaction theory, see Homans, *The Human Group* (New York: Harcourt Brace and World, 1950), especially Chapter 4; refinements appear in Homans, *Social Behavior: Its Elementary Forms* (New York: Harcourt Brace and World, 1961), particularly Chapter 4; and Peter Blau, *Exchange and Power in Social Life* (New York: John Wiley, 1964). For a test of Homans' major propositions, see Ronald Maris, 'The logical adequacy of Homans' social theory', 35 *American Sociological Review* (December, 1970), pp. 1069–81. In Europe, interaction theory was central in the work of Georg Simmel, *Sociology* (Leipzig: Duncker and Humblot,

expressed by the following equation: $I - L - I$, in which I is the interaction inspired by the accommodation process, L is the legitimacy that follows the exchange of reciprocal values, and I is the influence which is a behavioural consequence of interaction and legitimacy. The currency which mediates this process, including that between governmental and interest group elites, covers a broad range of values, including affection, empathy, companionship, information, influence, and money. Such values, it should be noted, include both emotional and instrumental gratifications. Individuals, in effect, bring a variety of contributions to such interpersonal situations as committees, work groups, friendship, and marriage. Such contributions are characteristic of formal and informal relations, brief encounters, and permanent associations, of small groups and large, of dyadic and larger collective relationships. In all cases, however, a certain measure of continuity is required to meet the assumptions of interaction theory.

As noted, the incentive for such sustained interactions is the rewards experienced by those concerned. As a result, an opportunity is provided for a reinforcement of the sentiments which the activities enable the actors to share. This gratification, in turn, provides the incentive for further interactions, giving an active, closed-loop character to the process. Both the situations and the incentives which inspire their continuity are highly varied.

Interaction theory, as a result, has the advantage of generality; it covers a broad range of social activity and encompasses an extensive variety of values and behaviour. Equally significant, it rests firmly upon observable behaviour rather than upon abstract 'needs of the system' and similar extra-empirical explanations of political behaviour.

The explanatory power of interaction theory is suggested by its capacity to explain why some social relationships persist while others languish. Its motivational assumptions are essentially egocentric. Interactions persist because they are personally gratifying to the actors. Obviously this is a psychological explanation: men sustain relationships because they provide a net balance of satisfactions. One need not assume a balance-sheet model of calculation to conclude that, in some trial and error fashion, individuals attempt in varying measure with varying degrees of success, to achieve a rough cost–benefit equilibrium. Each party may hope to achieve the most positive balance between his own contributions and rewards, but we can

1908); and *The Sociology of Georg Simmel* (Glencoe: Free Press, 1950) For an application of interaction theory to interest group activity, see Harmon Zeigler and Michael Baer, *Lobbying: Interaction and Influence in American Legislatures* (Belmont: Wadsworth, 1969).

93

also assume that his appreciation of the expectations of other participants for a similar satisfying accommodation will curtail unreasonable demands. Empirically, it seems, one may observe that individuals in a dyadic relation often sustain a relationship because each contributes certain mutually complementary qualities to it. In the commercial milieu, a judicious welding of capital and brains may occur; nicely symbiotic needs for dominance and submission characterize some marriages; while in friendships, compatibility may be achieved through a happy accommodation of ego's need for self-expression attended by a singular capacity for listening on the part of alter.

The interaction process has an active, reinforcing quality in which frequent and sustained contact tends to reinforce normative solidarity among the actors, with the result that interaction persists, which in turn further strengthens the shared sentiments and activities that sustain the relationship. This theoretical formulation should enable us to handle the vital question of legitimacy and the resultant degree of influence ascribed to directors in their interactions with legislators and bureaucrats. The frequency and continuity of such interactions can be empirically determined, and these data in turn can provide a basis for conclusions about the legitimacy imputed to interest groups and the extent to which their agents are regarded as effective.

THE EMPIRICAL BASE

Before turning to our findings, it may be useful to describe briefly the research upon which the following analysis is based. Essentially, this study concerns the structure, resources, values, and roles of Canadian political elites as revealed by an analysis of interest group directors (N–640), legislators (N–269) and higher civil servants (N–214) in Ottawa and three Canadian provinces, Quebec, Ontario, and British Columbia. These regions were selected arbitrarily for study, mainly because they seemed to be among the most significant in Canada in terms of population, industrialization, divergent political cultures and parties. At the beginning of the field study, (1967), Quebec was in the hands of the *Union Nationale* party and by the end (1971) the Liberals were in office; the Conservatives reigned throughout in Ontario; W. A. C. Bennett's Social Credit party was in power in British Columbia; and a Liberal government held the reins in Ottawa.

Strictly speaking, our sample permits us to generalize only to these three provinces and Ottawa. At the same time, in considering the extent to which our findings may be applied nationally, it is well to remember that these provinces contain 77 per cent of Canada's population and its three largest cities, and produce almost 80 per cent of its Gross National Product. Moreover, the 140 members of the national Parliament included in the sample represent every province, while the interest group sample in Ottawa includes organizations representing most provinces. Even though federal legislators, as we shall show, are hardly a representative cross-section of Canadian society, they probably embody the dominant opinion of the nation.

Random samples were drawn of the three categories of respondents who were given interviews of from one to one-and-one-half hours, during the period 1967–71. Further details regarding the sample, research methods, and interview schedules can be found in the Appendix. Since the samples are random, one can feel reasonably secure in generalizing to the universes from which they were drawn. In the case of civil servants, given the vast size of the universe and our plan to include only those who seemed to be most likely to interact with private group elites, we drew the sample from the highest stratum of the various services, which includes only about two per cent of the entire civil service. The interest group and legislative samples, on the other hand, are based upon the entire universe in each research site, and include approximately half of all legislators and about 20 per cent of all interest groups. In each province the capital and the largest city, if it were other than the capital, were surveyed. In Quebec, for example, Quebec City and Montreal were included, as were Victoria and Vancouver in British Columbia.

One final remark about terminology. For brevity, I shall often reduce 'interest group' to 'group'; similarly, 'interest group director' will often be referred to as 'director'; while 'higher civil servants' will be denoted as 'bureaucrats'. No invidious connotation is intended by the latter term; bureaucrats are simply public officials working in a highly rationalized and routinized kind of organizational milieu, historically characterized by administration through bureaus, hence 'bureaucrats'.

PART II

CANADIAN INTEREST GROUPS: STRUCTURE, ROLE, RESOURCES, EFFECTIVENESS

Our aim in this section is twofold: to present a taxonomy of interest group structure and behaviour from which generalizations may be made about this vital sector of Canadian society; and to provide an empirical base for a theoretical explanation of the symbiotic role that interest groups play in the allocation of national resources. The analysis begins with a review of the shape and intensity of interest group structure.

CHAPTER 4

THE STRUCTURE OF INTEREST
GROUPS

Canadian society includes a multiplicity of highly differentiated interest groups, reflecting its relatively great affluence, literacy, and degree of functional specialization in most socioeconomic areas. Although some sectors, including labour and consumer groups, were slow to affiliate, by the 1970s very few interests remained unorganized. This is not to say, of course, that all of them were equally articulate, resourceful, or politically conscious. Here, the variations remain substantial. One of our main tasks is to present such differences systemically, using various indexes to differentiate groups along these and related dimensions. Before this is done, however, a brief introductory survey of the structure, functions, and goals of such groups is required.

INTRODUCTORY NOTES *208388*

Interest groups in this analysis have been defined, rather abstractly, as *collectivities organized around an explicit value on behalf of which essentially political demands are made* vis-à-vis *government, other groups, and the general public.* For present purposes, however, the groups included in this study may perhaps be more usefully defined in terms of the substantive areas they represent. Such a characterization punctuates their major interest and enables one to compare them in terms of their relative size, numbers, and political resources. Thus business, labour, agricultural, and professional groups, among which are found some of the oldest Canadian interest groups, including for example, the Agricultural Association of Quebec, founded in 1792 and the Quebec Chamber of Commerce, 1890.[1] The Montreal Board

[1] F. Ouellet, *Histoire de la Chamber de Commerce de Quebéc, 1809–1959* (Quebec: Université Laval, 1959); see also, M. Belanger, 'L'Association Volontaire: le Cas des Chambres de Commerce', unpublished doctoral dissertation, Sociology, Université

of Trade appeared shortly after, in 1822. Augmenting these are fraternal, ethnic, religious, consumer, welfare, and educational groups. Among the oldest of these are the Literary and Historial Society of Quebec, 1824, the Society for Relief of Strangers in Distress, in York, 1827, the Royal Institution for the Advancement of Learning within the Province of Quebec, 1829, the Orange Order founded in Ontario in 1830 and the *Société Saint-Jean-Baptiste* established in Quebec in 1834.

Within each of these categories a great deal of variation exists, reflecting again the scope and diversity of collective life made possible by the wealth, functional specialization, and ethno-cultural heterogeneity of Canada. The exquisite specialization of group life is perhaps suggested by the existence of a *Canadian Institute of Association Executives*. One is hard pressed indeed to think of *any* social interest that is not represented by one or another organized group. Although the range and diversity of such groups is virtually unbounded, our data enable us to give some order to the complex reality of associational life, at the inevitable cost of some over-simplification.

Despite such diversity, interest groups are rather similar along certain dimensions. Legally, for example, those which are national in scope are typically established under the Companies Act (Revised Statutes of Canada, 1952) which provides that the Secretary of State may 'by letters patent under his seal of office grant a charter to any number of persons under three (3)...for the purpose of carrying on in more than one (1) province of Canada, without pecuniary gain to its members, objects of a natural, patriotic, religious, philanthropic, charitable, scientific, artistic, social, professional, or sporting character...' In certain cases such as the Royal Canadian Air Force Association (1948), some have been established by orders-in-council. For associations operating exclusively within a given province, similar charter provisions obtain, usually under the aegis of the Provincial Secretary's office.

Another area in which interest groups tend to be similar is in their statement of objectives, typically incorporated in their constitutions immediately following the group's name. Such prescriptions, which usually focus on the primal interest of the members, sometimes include a specific linking of the group's interest with that of the general public. The Canadian Gas Association, for example, lists as the first of several objectives: 'to promote the development of the Canadian Gas Industry in all its activities to the end

Laval (1969); for a useful source of French-Canadian groups, see Robert Boily, *Quebec 1940–69 Bibliographie* (Montreal: Les Presses de L'Université de Montreal, 1971).

that it may serve to the fullest extent the best interests of the public'.[1] The Canadian Textiles Institute has a rather more focussed objective, existing '*entirely* for the purpose of supporting the efforts of members to develop, maintain and extend a favorable business climate in which to operate', (italics added). The Montreal Board of Trade similarly 'voices the outlook of business in matters of public concern, encourages active exchange of ideas and opinions among businessmen, provides information on government legislation and regulations, and seeks equitable conditions should the latter be unduly restrictive or burdensome'. The National Home Builders Association's first object is 'to associate the home builders of Canada for purposes of mutual advantage and cooperation', followed by a commitment, 'to improve the quality and character of homes for the Canadian people'.

Professional, labour, and consumer associations give their public interest objectives a similarly varying priority in their constitutions. The Ontario Dental Association, for example, lists as its first objective 'to encourage the improvement of the health of the public'. This aspiration is followed by a more specific aim: 'to promote the mutual improvement of its members and the advancement of the art and science of dentistry'. The Canadian Medical Association's first aim is 'to promote the medical and related arts and sciences and to maintain the honour and the interests of the medical profession', followed by 'measures designed to improve the public health...' The Canadian Dietetic Association, however, focusses entirely upon its collective interest: 'the purpose and objective of the Corporation shall be to promote, encourage, and improve the status of dieticians in Canada.' A similar priority is apparent in the objectives of the Toronto Musicians' Association which seeks to 'unite into one organization all persons who become members, to secure for the members improved wages, hours, working conditions, and other economic advantages through collective negotiations and bargaining'. The Consumers' Association of Canada aims 'to unite the strength of consumers to improve the standards of living in Canadian homes...'

High among the priorities listed among most groups is their function of political representation, usually aimed at both the general public and government. Often this function is included under some such charter proposition as, 'to represent its members in matters of national, provincial, and local policy and legislation affecting...' In the round, however, the representational function tends to be emphasized mainly in various publications

[1] We are assuming here that such formal objectives are ranked in terms of their felt priority. It may be, however, that this is not so.

provided for members and/or the public. In these, any political activities of the director, president, board of directors, and prominent members are presented, sometimes as a status report, indicating the stage of the representation or the leaders' estimate of probable outcomes. A Canadian Mining Association brochure, for example, states that its 'main role is to project the views of the industry on a national scale and co-ordinate its efforts with those of government departments in regard to policies affecting exploration, mining and processing, and the development of exports'.[1]

The Retail Council of Canada similarly 'presents the trade's point of view to Governments and Royal Commissions and Committees established by Governments on all matters affecting the interests of its members'. This function, moreover, is listed first among the six principal objectives of the association. An example of the Council's lobbying efforts is a brief presented to the federal government protesting against the proposed Competition Act, which seeks among other things to protect the consumer. Among the terms used to characterize the draft legislation are 'preposterous', 'regrettable', 'narrow', 'restrictive', and 'a travesty on justice'. As with many such briefs, which are among the most common of group political activities, this one received due publicity and thus, potentially at least, an opportunity to marshall public opinion against the measure.[2]

Service to members is another common theme incorporated in the constitutional aims of most groups, often taking the form of the exchange of information deemed useful to members and the provision of specific technical aid. Here again, a Canadian Manufacturers' Association's statement is illustrative, 'The guiding principles of the CMA are simple and straightforward. Its prime functions are to promote the interests of Canadian manufacturing industries and their employees and to supply services and assistance to Canadian manufacturers and exporters.[3]

Another area of similarity among interest groups is their internal organization, which typically includes a full-time director, appointed by and (formally at least) subject to the direction of a board of directors, usually elected by the members[4] for variable periods and functioning through an executive committee. Depending upon membership size and resources, the director will have a staff. In almost all associations, he has at least a full-time

[1] *Mining Association of Canada*, 'Mining: what it means to Canada' (1968), p. A–1.
[2] Toronto *Globe and Mail* (November 27, 1971), p. B2.
[3] *Canadian Manufacturers' Association*, 'At your service' undated, p. 3.
[4] 'Members' can, of course, be individuals, companies, federations of companies, associations, etc. Some associations include several of these types of members, with membership dues varying accordingly.

secretary. In many business *cum* trade types of associations, several departments are found, including research, public relations, finance, etc. Such associations often provide their members a broad range of management services, which requires extensive and highly skilled staff. The national headquarters of the Canadian Manufacturers' Association, for example, has a staff (1971) of over 100 members, providing information to members on 'labour relations, customs and excise, export and import procedures, transportation, taxation, public relations, to mention but some'.[1]

The financing of associations is equally standardized. In most cases (60 per cent of Canadian interest groups), their basic income is from membership dues, which are set in various ways, depending upon the substantive area involved. Often, in trade associations a graduated fee according to the size or volume of business of the member is set; in other types of organizations, which may combine individual and company members, a differentiated scale of dues exists. Several other sources of income exist as well. Some associations offer seminars which bring in substantial amounts; others receive local, federal, and/or provincial grants of various kinds; some produce and sell directories, research studies, and journals from which advertising income may be obtained. Annual conventions at which space may be sold to relevant commercial enterprises provide another common source of income. Yet others, although this is less frequent, receive annual subsidies from affiliated associations or from other interest groups who are related in some symbolic way. For example, the National Home Builders' Association received (1971) over $100,000 from the NHBA Manufacturers' Council.

The third common structural element among associations is a president, usually elected annually by the members. This role is often filled by an outstanding, senior member of the interest represented by the group. Annual elections, among other purposes, provide an opportunity for groups to publicize their activities and underscore their general policy orientation, as well as their collective reaction to current issues affecting their primal interest.[2] Annual conventions provide a simliar opportunity to ventilate their views and, as will be shown, to nourish their relations with govern-

---

[1] *Canadian Manufacturers' Association*, 'At your service' 1971. For the definitive work on the CMA, and the only comprehensive analysis of a Canadian interest group, see S. D. Clark, *The Canadian Manufacturers' Association* (Toronto: University of Toronto Press, 1936).

[2] The Toronto *Globe and Mail* for example, faithfully reports the election of presidents of major economic groups in its business section, which is a valuable source of information on such groups, their policies, and activities.

mental elites. We shall see that such public relations activities rank high among the typical director's functions.

In many ways, the most important element in the interest group structure is the director. Several names are used to designate his position. In unions, the term 'business agent' or 'treasurer' is common; in fraternal groups, certain rather esoteric terms, such as 'exalted leader' or 'grand master' appear; among business and professional groups, the term 'executive director' is most common. In several types of groups, 'president', 'executive secretary' or 'general manager' may appear. In the round, 'executive director' is most common and we shall therefore use it (often abbreviated to 'director') throughout to refer to the permanent head of an interest group.

Interest groups themselves have a similar variety of names, ranging from 'association' through 'club', 'commission', 'conference', 'council', 'federation', 'institute', 'lodge', 'order', and 'society' to 'union'. Nor do the names always provide precise denotations of their object: some musicians' unions, for example, call themselves 'associations'. Here again, fortunately, the term 'association' is by far the most common, and it will accordingly be used as the generic name for interest groups when the term itself is not used.

Another fairly standard departure is for an association to be organized into several divisions or sections according to the specific functional components found in the activity it represents. Thus divisions of finance, research, public affairs, etc. Perhaps more frequent is the federated type of structure, organized upon a geographical basis, having several provincial 'divisions' affiliated with a national headquarters, often situated in Montreal, Toronto, or less frequently, in Ottawa. In some cases, regional rather than provincial bases are used for such federations. In others, a three-tier structure is found in which national and provincial units are augmented by a local branch. In yet others, a two-tier structure exists, including only national and local affiliates. Structures of authority and responsibility vary widely among such levels and we are unable to generalize about them. Less frequently, except among unions, a Canadian federation is affiliated with an international section. The National Retail Merchants' Association, for example, is a segment of the American parent association, which has branches in '40 other nations of the free world'. A subsequent table will show the proportions of Canadian associations using each of the various structural categories. Such functional and geographic specialization may result in certain kinds of activity, political representation, for example, being delegated to only one level of the association. Among some labour unions, for example, political activities (e.g. direct lobbying) are centralized at the national level.

Generalization about relationships between the permanent executive director and the temporary president and board is hazardous. Many directors insist that they virtually monopolize policy-determination in their association, that their board typically and readily gives its consent to policies initiated by them, while others view themselves essentially as agents of the board. Regardless of the objective state of affairs, we may suspect that most directors present themselves to their boards as managers, whose role is essentially ministerial. Where the association represents highly-paid, prestigeful occupations or industry, we may also assume that the president plays a significant role *vis-à-vis* the director. Indeed, it is common practice for executive directors to remain relatively obscure, with the groups' publicity focussed upon the annually-elected president or chairman, as he is sometimes called. On the other hand, the director enjoys all the advantages accruing to permanent officials in a bureaucratic structure, including expertise and continuity, often augmented by considerable political acumen.

It is significant that many groups stress the participative character of their association, indicating again their sensitivity to ongoing democratic norms of responsibility. Presidents and boards of directors are elected at annual meetings for one- or two-year terms. Committees of members present recommendations and resolutions for consideration by the total membership. Meetings follow parliamentary procedures. Permanent staff are appointed and subject to the will of the board of directors, etc.[1]

The Canadian Manufacturers Association, for example, declares that it is an 'industrial democracy', with a structure and procedures which form an 'interesting comparison' with 'existing forms of federal, provincial and municipal governments'.[2] Some 1,500 of Canada's industrial managers are among the membership of the Association. Each has one vote in electing its executive council. The council corresponds to the federal parliament; since it is elected on a representative basis from every province, and 'represents every type of manufacturing in the land'. The executive committee of the council, moreover, corresponds to the federal cabinet, made up of 26 members, including the chairmen of the Association's standing committees. Each chairman is analogous to ministers in Ottawa, since he is in charge of ten head-office service departments. The Association's six geographical divisions are similarly compared to provincial governments, and their 30 branches to municipal governments.

---

[1] Despite such forms, however, the generalization is that most private associations tend to be oligarchic.

[2] *Canadian Manufacturers' Association*, 'At your service', undated, p. 5.

Since our major interest is in the external political activities of interest groups, we did not gather systematic evidence on the quality of their internal governance. However, organizational theory and research provide some general conclusions. As Robert Michels, the Swiss political scientist found, the internal politics of organizations often tend to be oligarchic, for a variety of reasons, including the apathy of members, the complexity of decision-making in many sectors, the superior forensic and managerial skills of leaders, the frequent need for dispatch which makes consultation difficult, and the long tenure often characteristic of officials.[1]

For such reasons, the tendency is for executive directors to enjoy considerable latitude in shaping and carrying through decisions affecting their members. As will be shown, most directors possess generous shares of such political resources as education, income, and socioeconomic status. That some tension may nevertheless exist between them and members is clear since one-third of directors believe that most people in their role experience some conflict with members. The reasons for such conflict, in their view, include mainly, as Michels suggested (among other reasons), 'differences in prestige, pay, and education between directors and members' (one-third). Labour, welfare, and business directors account, in equal proportions, for almost two-thirds of those who present such differences as the major source of tension. Other directors insist that 'it is impossible to satisfy everyone' (15 per cent), and that 'members often do not see the "broad picture"', (14 per cent). We find that directors in business (one-fifth), labour (just under one-fifth), welfare (16 per cent), and professional (15 per cent) tend to perceive more conflict than those in the remaining categories. On the other hand, one suspects that the personality attributes of the director may be quite significant in shaping such perceptions.

FUNCTIONS AND METHODS

At this orienting point in the analysis, we shall merely indicate very generally the functions and methods of interest groups. Here again they exhibit considerable similarity. Formally, as their charters usually stipulate, their major function is to augment the security, self-realization, influence, and income of their members in their role as legatees of the primal interest which inspired the creation of the group. Certainly, our interviews with directors suggest that their own motivations are essentially pragmatic; constraints

[1] *Political Parties.* See also, Robert Presthus, *The Organizational Society* (New York: Vintage Books, 1965.)

of time, energy, and competition rarely permit them to adopt a broader, 'public interest' conception of their role. (The expectations of their members are equally practical, with the exception of a minority of 'instrumental' groups.) While only a few of them regard legislators as 'competitors' and while temporary alliances are made with other relevant groups, their definition of their role is essentially one of representing their own focussed interest, in indirect and muted competition with other groups for public support, legislative aid, and assistance from bureaucrats. Since governmental elites are beset with similar claims from a variety of other equally legitimate groups, among whom they must allocate their time, attention, and funds, all interest groups do not and cannot, receive equal shares of these values. As a result, the most articulate and persuasive groups tend to receive the major shares of government largesse. This condition provides a major basis for the director's highly pragmatic definition of his situation.

In addition to enhancing their primal interest, groups have several other related functions, which again are fairly standardized. These include social and recreational activities and providing an opportunity for self-realization among their members. All of these, of course, may be defined broadly as contributing to the group's primal interest, but some of them, such as social and recreational affairs, seem relatively peripheral compared with such other functions as communication, research, and technical services which are directed toward the association's major goal. While it is true that members may have varying appreciations of this 'major goal' we shall show later that most directors and members have a very pragmatic 'bread and butter' conception of the association's role, which is generally to advance the security, welfare, and income of its members, individually and collectively.

It may be useful to conceptualize directors as existing at the centre of a communications net, with their members at one extremity and several relevant publics including government and the mass public at the other. Essentially, the director's role involves transmitting the demands of his members to government and other relevant publics; their reactions, in turn, are brought back to members. Obviously, a considerable amount of tailoring occurs during this process, and perhaps especially at the director's level. As the man in the middle, he must synthesize, programme, and modulate the demands of his clients who will sometimes tend to be politically naive or unrealistic in their expectations. Communication in the other direction, between political elites and members, will be similarly tailored by the director, who is often viewed in very pragmatic terms by his members. As a result, group gains will tend to be emphasized while losses will be muted.

The communication role of the director also includes increasing the awareness of his members regarding changes in the environment of the group's major interest or activity. Members tend to be preoccupied with routine affairs, they tend to become settled in their ways, finding change difficult. The director attempts to ease the strains of change by anticipating its direction and impact. Needless to say, he is also preoccupied more positively with favourably *changing* the conditions of participation for his interest group, through influencing public opinion and legislative and bureaucratic decisions, often in an attempt to enlist the legitimacy and coercive power of government to structure and stabilize his interest's marketplace, or among groups with eleemosynary interests, to achieve some broader, 'consumer-oriented' goal. In the main, however, he and his group are probably as often the victim of change as its master. Theirs is often a reactive role.

It is also a truism that interest groups are forced to work within the existing framework of government and, as emphasized earlier, within the existing political structure. These conditions are 'givens' in their operational calculus. But whatever the pattern of governmental structure, interest groups seek access where power lies, an imperative which accounts for the similarities in their own structure and behaviour.

Other typical functions of interest group directors (and selected members) include serving on government committees; consulting and negotiating with government; preparing and presenting briefs to legislative and departmental committees outlining the group's policy or its reaction to relevant government policy; carrying out and sponsoring research; providing technical information to members; providing various other kinds of services, including group plans for insurance, purchasing, and travel.

Recommending individuals for government posts in their respective areas; publishing association journals and newsletters; rebutting attacks against their association or interest; interceding for members in specific cases involving government subsidies and welfare payments; administering continuing education and apprentice training programmes; sponsoring awards and fellowships in areas of the association's primal interest; arranging annual meetings and inviting high-level bureaucrats to address them;[1]

---

[1] Examples are legion, but the following random cases indicate that some interest groups interact at the top levels of political power. The Canadian Construction Association, for example, had Prime Minister Pearson as the keynote speaker at its 50th annual meeting in 1968. Mr Pearson was made an honorary life member of the Association. Premier Jean-Jacques Bertrand of Quebec played a similar role at the 16th annual convention (1969) of the Quebec Lumber Manufacturers' Association, attended by

conferring honours and awards, including presidencies and directors' positions in their association upon politicians or civil servants who have served them well; and forming coalitions with other interest groups who share similar objectives and problems – all are among the common activities of such groups. They provide nice examples of the exchange process. Meanwhile, most associations carry on substained efforts to improve their internal administration with a view to providing more and better service to their members.

Hopefully, these generalizations have provided an overview of the kinds of groups included in this study. We now turn to a more systematic analysis, based upon a random Canadian sample of 640 groups. Table 4-1 presents the distribution of such groups in the four research sites.

It is immediately clear that six categories of associations tend to dominate

TABLE 4-1   *Interest group sample, by category and frequency*

	Proportion of total distribution					
Category	Ottawa (107)	Quebec (195)	Ontario (223)	British Col. (114)	Sample (639)	
	%	%	%	%	%	
Business	13	23	26	15	20	(126)
Welfare	14	14	17	18	16	(100)
Labour	14	15	10	18	14	(89)
Professional	11	12	9	14	12	(77)
Educational	18	11	9	5	10	(64)
Social–recreational	15	7	9	12	10	(62)
Religious	1	6	9	5	6	(37)
Fraternal–service	5	5	3	6	4	(25)
Ethnic	1	2	3	1	4	(24)
Agricultural	1	1	2	—	1	(8)
Other	6	5	3	2	4	(27)
					(100)	(639)

Honourable Claude Gosselin, Quebec Minister of Lands and Forests, who during the preceding month had received the title of *Grand Officier de l'Ordre du mérite forestier* at the 30th Congress of the *Association de Quebec Forestiere* in recognition of 'his exceptional service to the cause of forestry'. About the same time, Honourable Jack Davis, Federal Minister of Fisheries and Forestry gave the initial speech at the 61st annual convention of the Canadian Lumbermens' Association in Montreal. This practice of honouring high-level politicians and bureaucrats at such meetings is very common among the more significant groups.

Canadian interest groups

Canadian interest-group structure: business, welfare, labour, professional, educational, and social–recreational interests account for four-fifths of all organized groups. As the N's in each category indicate, business and industrial interests of various kinds rank at the top, followed closely by welfare associations, labour and professional groups. Business–industrial and welfare groups are most numerous, accounting for over one-third of the total. The extent to which the former surpasses the others suggests the extent to which economic incentives underlie interest group organization. Labour's total proportion is slightly reduced by the fact that refusal rates were somewhat higher among such directors. Again, had the field research been done in 1972, instead of 1968, the proportion of welfare groups would have been even higher, since these have been proliferating at a great rate. By 1972, for example, there were some 150 'poor people's', welfare-type groups in Ontario alone.

Interest group specialization varies substantially among the four geopolitical areas. While Ontario includes the largest proportion of business groups, British Columbia enjoys an advantage in welfare groups. Ottawa is obviously the centre for educational representation. Parenthetically, this latter condition is especially interesting in view of the fact that constitutionally, we are told, education is a provincial responsibility. Here, as elsewhere, interest groups are perhaps less interested in legalisms than in the realities of power and public largesse. The distribution of religious associations shows an even greater disparity, with Ontario exhibiting fully nine times the intensity of organization found in Ottawa. Since Quebec, which by such standards as church attendance ranks high among the provinces in religiosity, it is somewhat unexpected to find this variation. On the other hand, the ubiquity and strength of religious influence in Ontario is well-known.[1]

The regional pattern of labour organization also reflects the larger socioeconomic context. Historically, British Columbia, of course, has been highly unionized, reflecting in turn its economic reliance upon extractive industries, such as mining, fishing and lumbering, which (as well as shipping) tend to include relatively large proportions of class-conscious, militant workers. Quebec ranks high in the same area for somewhat similar reasons. One might expect that Southwestern Ontario with its high degree of industrialization would account for a larger proportion of labour groups, but it seems that many of the headquarters of the larger industrial unions are situated in Ottawa due to their international structure, while many of the smaller industries of Ontario are not unionized. A similar explanation, it should be

[1] See, for example, S. D. Clark, *Church and Sect in Canada*.

noted, accounts for Ontario's (i.e. Toronto's) dominance of business groups, several of which are the national unit of their federal association.

The over-all distribution seems anomalous in the extent to which agricultural groups contribute so small a proportion of all groups, given the central role of agriculture in the Canadian economy. However, a check of the universes from which the present sample was drawn indicates that the agricultural sector tends to be organizationally atypical.[1] Essentially, its group structure tends to be much less proliferated than other major economic sectors such as labour and industry.[2] Four major associations, the Canadian Federation of Agriculture, the Grange, the National Farmers' Union, and the *Union Catholique des Cultivateurs* incorporate the overwhelming majority of farmers.[3] This structural pattern also reflects considerably less specialization than is characteristic of the other economic giants. Yet, other factors must be present, because agriculture still reveals a great deal of differentiation in terms of crops, methods, income, and farm size. The economic uncertainty which characterizes agriculture probably tends to work against the continuity and stability of interest group structure found in other vital elements of the national economy. The secular decline in the proportion of farmers in the labour force, which reflects increasing farm size and concentration, may also have decreased the impetus and the need for specialized agricultural associations.

Perhaps, too, politically speaking, the historic overrepresentation of rural–agricultural interests in federal and provincial parliaments has provided an effective surrogate for alternative representative mechanisms among farmers. This fortunate but diminishing circumstance (as electoral boundaries are redrawn to reflect population changes) probably means that many services and functions, which in other economic sectors have had to be provided by private associations, have been built into government programmes, thereby reducing the need for interest groups in agriculture. Whatever the reasons, agriculture remains an 'underorganized' sector.

Another rather underorganized category is ethnic groups, which constitute

---

[1] For example, the 1971 Toronto telephone directory includes only one agricultural association, the *Ontario Federation of Agriculture*, among over 1,150 entries which met our criteria of 'interest groups'.

[2] Almond and Verba found similarly low proportions of agricultural groups averaging only 2 per cent of all types of groups, in their 5-nation study. *The Civic Culture*, p. 247.

[3] For an analysis of various aspects of agricultural organization in Canada, see Helen Jones Dawson, 'An interest group: the Canadian Federation of Agriculture', 3 *Canadian Public Administration* (June, 1960), pp. 134–49; also, D. Beaudin, *l'U.C.C. d'aujourd'hui*, (Montreal: Editions de l'U.C.C., 1952).

only about four per cent of our sample. Given the historical federal policy of encouraging immigration and the resulting ethnic–cultural diversity of the Canadian social structure, one would have expected a larger proportion of such groups. Perhaps, since interest group representation is positively associated with advantaged socioeconomic position[1] this condition may persist until 'new Canadians' have become more closely integrated into the national socioeconomic culture. Here, one necessarily speaks in generational periods of time. It is also true that such groups tend, along with labour unions, to have somewhat higher refusal rates than other types of associations. Moreover, 'ethnic' groups are difficult to categorize, since they often encompass educational, welfare, recreational, and religious aims and activities. For this reason, some of them may have been covered in such other categories.

MEMBERSHIP STRUCTURE

The interest groups in our sample have essentially four types of membership: individual; firm; individual and firm; and no members as such. Most common is the association made up of individual members which comprises fully 60 per cent of the sample; those comprising firms only contribute 20 per cent; individuals and firms, 6 per cent; while groups with no members[2] account for the remaining 14 per cent. The vast majority of the first class of memberships is found in professional, labour, recreational–social–fraternal, agricultural, and ethnic categories. The Canadian Labour Congress, for example, has 1,600,000 individual members, through its various affiliated unions. Similarly, the Canadian Medical Association has 20,000 individual members throughout Canada. The second and third categories are typically found in business–industrial and welfare types of associations. The Canadian Welfare Council, for example, has some 1,500 individual members, 500 social agencies and another 500 corporations. The Canadian Manufacturers Association, similarly, includes some 6,450 members, almost 5,000 of whom

---

[1] For example, 43 per cent of the members of the groups in the sample are of middle-class origin, according to the judgment of their executive directors, compared with a national proportion of less than 12 per cent, as based upon occupational classes I and II breakdown in B. R. Blishen, 'The construction and use of an occupational class scale', 24 *Canadian Journal of Economics and Political Science* (March, 1958), pp. 519–31.

[2] Although our initial definition of interest groups referred to them as 'collectivities' which quite explicitly connotes members, our sample includes a certain proportion of nonmembership groups which despite this structural anomaly have most of the other properties and objectives of 'normal' interest groups.

are companies who appoint representatives as individual members of the association. Non-membership groups occur almost exclusively in the social welfare area.

ORGANIZATIONAL STRUCTURE

As indicated earlier, interest groups are either unitary or federated. The latter are usually organized in line with traditional divisions within the political system. Considerable variation exists within this scheme, however, with group structure ranging from a one-tier to a four-tier design. In the main, structure follows function, i.e. groups whose essential interests are confined to intra-provincial affairs quite naturally have a one or two-tier structure, whereas those whose interests encompass regional and national boundaries exhibit a three- or four-tier scheme. Table 4-2 presents the proportions of groups in each category.

Some diversity of structure is apparent. While over half of the sample has a unitary or one-tier design, a significant proportion have a multi-tiered or federated structure which enables them to function cross-provincially, nationally and even internationally, and to delegate specific responsibilities according to the functional needs and jurisdictional design of their particular interest. The two-tier system, either local–provincial, local–national, or provincial–national, plus the regional type of organization, account for precisely one-quarter of the total sample. Differences across the four sampling areas are not great and hence are not presented in the table. However, regarding the three-tier structure, it is interesting that eight of our ten categories of interest groups use this form; only agricultural and

TABLE 4-2 *Organizational structure, by frequency*

Structure	Proportion of total	
Local only	25 %	(158)
Local–provincial–national	18	(114)
Provincial only	13	(81)
National only	11	(72)
Local–national	9	(58)
Provincial–national	8	(52)
International	8	(49)
Local–provincial	7	(46)
Regional	1	(5)
	(100)	(635)

ethnic groups do not. As might be expected, Ottawa and Ontario have significantly larger proportions (19 and 16 per cent respectively) of such local–provincial–national structures. British Columbia, on the other hand, has less than one per cent of such among her groups.

'Local-only' structures are dominated by social–recreational and welfare types of organizations. Ottawa, meanwhile, has a significantly smaller proportion of 'local-only' structures, compared with the other three areas, which of course reflects its status as the national capital and its attending attraction for national and federal-type of interest group structures.

SOURCES OF REVENUE

As will be specified later, interest groups tend to enjoy considerable financial support. Obviously, this happy condition varies considerably among types of groups, with those having large and relatively prosperous members typically enjoying the greatest affluence. Beyond this truism, however, one finds that one-third of Canadian associations have rather large memberships of 1,600 or more, with the result that even though individual dues and contributions may be small, the sum total is often impressive. Other means of income also exist. At the moment, only the source of such funds will be presented, leaving for the next chapter the relative financial status of various types of groups.

Essentially, interest groups receive their funds from five sources: dues, investments and rent, voluntary contributions, government grants, and a residual category defined here as 'other'. Table 4-3 presents the distribution.

With the exception of labour, all groups rely upon several sources of income. Dues, however, are the primary source for almost 60 per cent of

TABLE 4-3 *Sources of income, by group and proportion* (*percentage of total income*)

Source	Business	Wel.	Lab.	Prof.	Educ.	Rel.	F–S.	S–R.	Ethnic	Agr.	Sample
	%	%	%	%	%	%	%	%	%	%	%
Dues	81	12	100	79	44	7	61	47	55	33	57
Vol. centrs.	—	36	—	2	11	71	4	—	14	—	12
Gov't. grants	5	14	—	6	20	—	21	4	—	25	8
Invest.–rent	4	3	—	2	4	—	3	15	26	25	5
Other	10	36	—	11	20	20	10	33	5	17	18
	(126)	(100)	(89)	(77)	(64)	(37)	(25)	(62)	(24)	(8)	(630)

114

them, yet in such cases as social–recreational, religious, and welfare associations, other forms of income play a critical role. Only labour, religious and ethnic groups fail to receive some funding from local, provincial, or federal governments. Here again is some evidence of the operationalization of the corporatist norms noted earlier. Such grants take a variety of forms, including unrestricted subsidies, research support, payments for contractual services, and seed-money for new programmes. The most-favoured status of agricultural groups in this context probably stems, as suggested earlier, from the political strength they have possessed through traditional patterns of rural overrepresentation in provincial and national parliaments. Fraternal–service groups, under which we have coded military and patriotic associations such as the Royal Canadian Air Force, sometimes receive small annual grants from the federal government. Consumer groups such as the Canadian Association of Consumers receive an annual subsidy from Ottawa, upon which they have relied quite heavily since their membership has not reached the levels one might have expected, given the huge potential. The special structural circumstances and difficulties of consumer and 'cause' types of associations will be analysed in detail elsewhere.

In the investment–rent category, it is noteworthy that agricultural and ethnic groups receive the largest share of such income. Such groups often own property or other investments that provide rental and other income.

The substantial 'other' category of income covers a wide range of services and products which most kinds of associations provide for their members and others. Welfare associations rely greatly upon several kinds of special fund-raising programmes to augment their incomes. Social–recreational associations are also heavily dependent upon such sources, which often include income from liquor sales and an occasional game of chance. Industrial, commercial, and professional (among other) associations typically publish journals which often earn considerable advertising revenue. The journals of medical and dental associations, for example, carry heavy loadings of advertising for medical equipment, pharmaceutical, and hospital supply firms, and may contribute a major share of their annual income.[1]

The annual conventions of many associations provide yet another source of income through the sale of display space and booths for commercial firms

---

[1] In 1965, the *Canadian Medical Association Journal*, for example, enjoyed a profit of $100,000. However, revenues from advertising, mainly from pharmaceuticals, apparently vary considerably, since the *Journal's* profit fluctuated from $59,006 in 1962, to $35,909 in 1963, to $71,531 in 1964. Report of the Managing Editor, *CMAJ*, Vol. 94 (January 15, 1966), pp. 148–52.

in relevant fields. Some trade associations receive annual grants from manufacturers in such fields.

Technical–professional associations sometimes carry out research programmes which provide additional income. The Canadian Gas Association, for example, tests and certifies gas-burning equipment for manufacturers, and in 1971 earned $500,000 in this way. It provides inspection services for new installations, which again produce income. Other professional and business associations carry on training seminars which can be quite profitable.

In those substantive areas and jurisdictions in which associations have taken on the function of supervising, training and licensing practitioners in their fields, a part of the prescribed fee is sometimes shared with the association. Here, of course, is a common example of the conditions under which private associations share directly in the process of government, bringing their organizations, expertise and public esteem to the aid of government which is not always able to administer such programmes independently, nor is it always ideologically prepared to assume full control over such activities, as in the well-known case of health insurance. This practice, once confined mainly to the learned professions, has now become common in virtually every functional area and tends, along with its advantages, to result in certain restrictive behaviours in which the incentives of public service are challenged by group efforts to control the terms of occupational participation. It is important to recognize that such interlacings go beyond the process of consultation and negotiation mentioned earlier to the point where the very administration of a government programme is delegated to the interest group concerned. As most legislators agree, however, the delegation of government's authority to such groups is essential, given the technical complexity of modern services in many areas.

Since dues are the primary source of income for almost 60 percent of Canadian interest groups, it may be useful to offer some generalizations about them. Almost every type of association has a flexible dues structure, usually providing for graduated fees for different categories of members, such as student, member, and fellow in professional associations and apprentice, journeyman, and master in some labour unions. Business and industrial associations often determine their dues by a pro-rated schedule based upon such indexes as total volume of business, percentage of sales, number of employees, etc.

The range of dues varies widely, but once again striking continuities appear. Among purely individual memberships, fully 87 per cent of all types of groups have dues in the 0–99 dollar range, while the next level,

100–199 dollars, includes another 9 per cent. Within the 0–199 category, moreover, over half fall in the 0–24 dollar range. In effect, annual dues of over $100 are rare indeed, with professional, labour, and business associations being most likely to reach or surpass this level. Among corporate-type memberships, which number only about 100 in the entire sample, 80 per cent are in the 0–1,999 dollar category; 12 per cent fall in the 2,000–9,999 category; and the remaining 8 per cent range from 10,000–16,000, and upward.

THE STRUCTURE OF INTEREST GROUP GOALS

We mentioned earlier the 'primal interest' of groups, and suggested that this interest was usually symbolized by the substantive nature of the group and its conception of its 'mission'. In effect, the definitive interest of any group is typically its *manifest* collective function. Members sometimes define this interest in terms different from those of the association's staff, and interest groups obviously have several 'interests', which may be defined as *latent* since they are not public, recognized functions but are by-products or fringe benefits. In an effort to specify more precisely the nature of interest-group goals, we asked each director to indicate in his own words the primary objective of his association. The combined responses from all types of groups enable us to rank the 'primal interest' of the associations, as these are perceived by the director (see Table 4-4).

From the perspective of directors, who are closely identified with their groups, it is clear that pragmatic, highly personalized incentives motivate one-third of Canadian interest groups. Nicely in line with the theory of selective inducements mentioned earlier, their politics has a predominately 'mercantile complexion'. Interesting regional variations in goal structure

TABLE 4-4 *Primary interest group goal, as per-ceived by directors*

	Proportion of total distribution	
Economic interests	35 %	(218)
Public interest	15	(94)
Social–recreational	14	(84)
Prestige of members	6	(36)
Spiritual–religious	6	(35)
Other	25	(160)
	(101)	(627)

appear, however, since British Columbia and Quebec rank above the mean (35 per cent) on economic incentives, while Ottawa and Ontario rank below. While Ontario is almost at the mean, Ottawa is somewhat below at 29 per cent. Ottawa ranks highest on the 'public interest' goal, while British Columbia is lowest, followed closely by Quebec. The prestige valence also provides suggestive contrasts: whereas Quebec is highest above the mean (6 per cent), and Ottawa and Ontario rank very close to it, British Columbia exhibits the absolute minimum of prestige-seeking members, one per cent. Since she also ranks highest on economic interest and lowest on public interest, we may perhaps assume that interest groups in British Columbia have the most sharply focussed goal among the four areas. Such differences, of course, may be to some extent artifacts of the sample, which included, it may be recalled, the following areal concentrations among group categories: educational groups dominated in Ottawa; business groups in Ontario and Quebec; and labour in British Columbia. However, random selection of groups ensures that such variations in group density and goal structure also reflect what might be called the modal 'community consciousness' of each geographical area.

The vast majority of economically-oriented groups, four-fifths, equally shared, are found among business and labour categories, and indeed, there remain only about two dozen other groups who share this priority. In terms of Weber's taxonomy of groups, they are a 'pure voluntary association based on self-interest (*Zweckverein*), a case of agreement as to a long-run course of action oriented purely to the promotion of specific ulterior interests, economic or other, of its members'.[1] Further analysis reveals that almost half of those groups with a 'public interest' orientation are found among welfare groups, with educational and professional groups accounting for another one-third. The tendency, mentioned earlier, for groups to equate their own interests with those of the public may be apparent in the high ranking of the 'public interest'. The large 'other' category reflects the difficulty of coding the directors' open-ended responses to this item.

The analysis of the primary goals of interest groups bears upon the theory of selective incentives outlined earlier. One of its major propositions is that men view large organizations rationally and become members only if there is some selective, individual by-product accruing as a result of membership.[2] The collective goals of groups, which we have called 'primal', are often too

---

[1] *Economy and Society*, Vol. 1, ed. by G. Roth and F. Wittich (New York: Bedminster Press, 1968), p. 41.
[2] Olson, *The Logic of Collective Action*, pp. 131–3.

remote and ill-defined to provide the incentive required for continued membership. In the language of economics, collective benefits are likely to be sub-optimal.

Table 4-4 indicates that the largest single proportion of members do indeed belong for self-oriented reasons, in order to secure certain individual benefits that are contingent upon membership. On the other hand, many directors maintain that their group is motivated mainly by affective rewards such as prestige, serving the public interest, and even spiritual ones. Moreover, regarding such special incentives, we found that virtually every group director indicated that his group provided some material by-product or service, such as group insurance, travel plans, publications, technical information, etc. The extent to which all types of organizations tend to offer such incentives is suggested by the fact that almost no directors regarded these services as atypical, i.e. as something that his members could obtain only by joining the group. Olson tends to restrict his theory to large producer and professional types of groups, including trade unions and farm groups, as well as medical societies. When we analyse our sample in terms of the type of groups in which economic interests are the principal incentive, we find that almost all of them are found in labour and business–industrial categories. Thus his theory seems to hold for such groups.

When we analyse professional groups separately, we find that 34 per cent of the directors indicate that their members belong for personal, essentially economic reasons. The usual example is medical doctors who receive group insurance programmes against malpractice suits and journals which are occupationally essential. Similar incentives probably motivate many other professionals, such as those in university work, who find the collective goals of their associations too vague to provide a viable incentive, with the result that their expectations are transferred to more tangible inducements, including journals, job-aid, and personal prestige through office-holding within the association.

The fact that almost every type of interest group now tends to offer what Olson calls 'selective inducements', however, remains a problem, since if this is true, and if members still retain, as our research suggests, collective and affective interests, some modification of the theory seems required. To some extent, it seems most suggestive when applied to the incentives of the permanent officials of an interest group, for whom collective benefits, which are usually uncertain and abstract, could hardly hope to compete with the tangible incentives of security, prestige, and income attending office. At the same time, similar tensions between collective and personal benefits are likely to occur in many institutional environments, and certainly one of the most rewarding personal skills in any bureaucratic arena is the capacity to identify oneself intensely with the collective goals of the organization.

CHAPTER 5

POLITICAL RESOURCES OF
INTEREST GROUPS

Political activism and effectiveness are essentially a function of resources. Generally, individuals and associations who possess larger shares of such resources as income, interest, legitimacy, and socioeconomic status tend to participate more frequently in politics than those who have fewer of these resources.[1] This seems to be the case regarding several forms of participation, including voting, group membership, actively supporting candidates, joining committees, discussing political affairs, and interacting with governmental elites. In this chapter the cumulative political resources displaced by Canadian interest groups will be compared. Our assumption is that differential amounts of such resources will probably be manifested in varying levels of political access and interaction among the several categories of interest groups. At the same time, there is almost surely no one-to-one relationship between such resources and political effectiveness, a difficult question which will be dealt with later.

POLITICAL RESOURCES OF DIRECTORS

Interest group directors may be viewed as the cutting edge of group efforts to influence public opinion and governmental policy. Almost three-fourths of directors (N–640) occupy full-time positions with their respective groups,

---

[1] Canadian data based upon two national surveys in 1965 and 1968 indicate that political participation is positively associated with such variables. Rick van Loon, 'Political participation in Canada'; Russett et al. conclude similarly, that 'in the United States and Western Europe it has generally been found that voting participation is highest among citizens of high education, income and social status, and higher in cities than in rural areas', *World Handbook of Political and Social Indicators*, p. 83; and N. H. Nie, G. B. Powell, and K. O. Prewitt, 'Social structure and political participation: developmental relationships, I, II,' 63 *American Political Science Review* (June and September, 1969), pp. 361–78, 808–32.

and many have had long experience in the functional areas with which their group is concerned. Indeed, over half of them have spent from 10 to 40 years in their own association. Less than one-fifth play a part-time, voluntary role as director. Ethnic groups are most likely to have such directors (72 per cent), followed by social–recreational, fraternal–service and rather unexpectedly, professional groups, about one-third of which have part-time directors. Within limits prescribed by their boards of directors, public legitimation of their mission, and the political resources of their group, directors are free to work positively toward its primal interest. Their capacity for such movement is also a function of the personal resources they command in the form of commitment, access, and socioeconomic status.

Political resources, in effect, can be divided into those of the director and of the organization. As the following paradigm suggests (Table 5-1), the former may be further divided into socioeconomic and psychopolitical categories.

TABLE 5-1   *Taxonomy of interest group resources*

	Socioeconomic	Psychopolitical
Director:	Access	Political efficacy
	SES	Legitimacy, elite
	Memberships	Commitment, members
	Income	Persuasiveness
	Experience	Cooperative ethic
Organisation:	Membership: size and SES	
	Budget	
	Staff	
	Age	

While it is tempting to ascribe certain psychopolitical resources, such as public legitimacy, to interest groups, such would probably be an example of the dubious tendency to reify organizations, as mentioned earlier.

The psychopolitical resources of directors include five types: commitment, political efficacy, persuasiveness, legitimacy, and what may be called 'the cooperative ethic'. Commitment refers to the extent to which directors believe their members are personally identified with the major collective goals of their associations, compared with other incentives such as information and prestige. The operational consequences of commitment, in turn, are highly dependent upon the director's sense of his own political efficacy, defined as the belief that he can influence events by personal effort. Persuasiveness concerns the extent to which directors believe their efforts to influence governmental elites have been successful. To what extent does the director believe that his role and his group are regarded as legitimate by the governmental elites with whom he interacts? The 'cooperative ethic' relates to the quality of the perception that directors have of the political environment: in effect, do they generally perceive governmental elites as being friendly, cooperative and manipulable or are they seen as hostile competitors?

Following logically after such psychopolitical variables is a most vital socioeconomic resource, access. This variable refers to the frequency with which directors penetrate the formal political apparatus. While lobbying includes important indirect attempts to influence governmental elites, e.g. letter-writing campaigns, one suspects that direct intervention in the formal political process is both more frequent and more effective.[1] Here, interest group representatives can cash in political obligations built up in countless informal ways; and indeed exchange any or all of the broad range of benefits that mediate interaction between them and governmental elites. Access, of course, is a necessary, rather than a sufficient condition of effectiveness, but it is clearly a prime element in the director's battery of political resources.

We look next at other socioeconomic kinds of personal resources, including education, income, and experience. Socioeconomic status (based upon occupation and education) is a critical political resource because it typically subsumes such resources as higher education, which tends to increase the parameters of one's political interest and knowledge while providing the conceptual and forensic tools often required for an active role in politics. Other well-established correlates of advantaged SES include political knowledge and sense of civic duty, and another vital socioeconomic resource, membership in voluntary groups.[2]

Although income is hardly a perfect index of personal competence, we may assume some rational association between them. Using salaries as a rough index of the calibre of directors, we find that fully two-thirds of them

---

[1] It may be useful here to repeat our earlier non-pejorative definition of lobbying as 'any effort on the part of any individual or group to influence political elites (i.e. either or both private and governmental elites) by direct or indirect persuasion.' The definition includes both direct (e.g. letter-writing and personal interactions) and indirect attempts (e.g. organizing influence at the constituency level) to influence the decisions of governmental and/or other individual or interest group elites.

[2] Among others, see Lester Milbrath, *Political Participation* (Chicago: Rand McNally. 1965); and Nie *et al.* 'Social structure and political participation'.

enjoy incomes of $10,000 to $15,000, almost one-quarter are in the $15,000 to $22,500 category, while the remaining 10 per cent have incomes above $22,500. In effect, two-thirds of these men and women are in the top 12 per cent of salaried individuals in Canada (1970). Interest groups not only provide attractive salaries, but various fringe-benefits such as expense accounts which directors require since they often engage in extensive travel and social interaction with other members of the political elite.

Table 5-2 presents a comparative distribution of socioeconomic political resources among directors in several group categories.

TABLE 5-2   *Socioeconomic resources of directors*

Resource	Proportion ranking 'high'[a]					
	Business	Labour	Prof–Ed.	Welfare	Instrumental[b]	
	%	%	%	%	%	
SES	76	30	86	81	58	(404)
Income	58	18	38	30	12	(148)
Experience	21	24	15	16	18	(111)
Membership	57	30	60	50	33	(222)
Access	31	13	21	18	16	(98)

[a] 'High' refers to the following conditions: SES, based upon education and occupation, in the two highest levels (I and II) in the Hollingshead index, *Social Class and Mental Illness*. Income: $15,000 or above; Experience: 10 years or more as director; Membership: 3-or-more social groups; Access: direct, personal contact with governmental elites, 'frequently'.
[b] 'Instrumental' groups refers to a residual category, comprising 'non-economic' groups, including religious, social–recreational, ethnic, fraternal–social, etc.

A most striking aspect of these data is the highly advantaged SES enjoyed by this segment of the Canadian political elite. Whereas about 10 per cent of the population is found in upper-middle-class strata, two-thirds of all directors are in these strata. Only about 8 per cent of Canadians are university graduates, but our sample includes almost 50 per cent. While only 5 per cent of salaried Canadians earned over $15,000 in 1970, almost one-third of our respondents did. Again, although only 18 per cent of all Canadians belong to 3-or-more voluntary groups,[1] almost half of those responding to this item (N–461) did. Defining access as contact with both MP's and bureaucrats, it seems that 16 per cent of group leaders are in the most active level, i.e. twice a week or more.

[1] James Curtis, 'Voluntary association joining: a cross-national comparative note', 36 *American Sociological Review* (October, 1971), pp. 872–80.

Despite such generally favourable circumstances, political resources are not distributed equally among the directors. Those in business and professional–educational, tend to be most favoured along most dimensions, compared with those in labour, welfare and instrumental groups. Although all the data are not shown here, social–recreational, fraternal–service, labour and ethnic groups tend to rank lower on several resource dimensions, but not on all of them. The data for some of the following generalizations are not shown in the table, since they deal with groups covered into the 'instrumental' category, as well as with more detailed aspects of the summary evidence presented.

The directors of certain types of groups, for example, tend to monopolize certain values. Those in religious, professional, welfare, and educational groups possess disproportionate shares of higher education. Religious directors also rank highest on SES, with almost three-fourths of them in the upper-middle-class category. They apparently pay dearly for their distinction, however, since none of them appear in the $15,000-plus income category. Directors of professional groups rank a poor second on socio-economic status. Regarding access, directors of business groups rank substantially higher than the others, with professional–educational directors second and labour directors last. Labour's low rank, however, is partly due to the union policy of restricting political contacts to certain levels of the hierarchy, often the regional level. Not astonishingly, business associations have the largest proportion of highly paid executives, with well over half receiving $15,000 or more per year. Indeed, further analysis reveals that one-fifth of them are in the $22,500-and-over category. There is a considerable range, however, with three times as many directors receiving this amount in Ottawa, compared with British Columbia. Regional variations in top salaries are shown by the relative proportions of all directors receiving $22,500 and above: Ottawa, 22 per cent; Ontario, 10; Quebec, 6; and British Columbia, 2 per cent. Directors in education, over one-third of whom enjoy incomes in the higher reaches, rank second, followed closely by those of professional associations.

As noted earlier, we assume that the capacity of an interest group to pay at such levels often enables them, all else being equal, to bring into their service men of considerable ability, well-educated and well-spoken, capable of interacting felicitously with other political elites. These variables are highly correlated with occupational status and it is noteworthy that fully four-fifths of these men are found in the two highest occupational strata, which include proprietors, managers, and professionals, who account for only about 28 per cent of the total Canadian labour force.[1] Religious, professional, educational, welfare, and business groups rank highest in proportion of directors at the top of the occupational scale, with professional and religious groups enjoying a substantial margin over the others at this level. Indeed, these five groups account for four-fifths of all those in this category. At the other end of the scale, labour ranks highest with 36 per cent of directors in a skilled or semi-skilled occupational status.[2] However, only about one-tenth of the entire sample is found in these categories. It is also apparent that most directors are mature individuals, almost half over 50, which gives them the opportunity to have developed a wide range of acquaintances.

Near the bottom of the resource scale are the directors of labour, social–recreational, fraternal–service and ethnic groups. The former are particularly disadvantaged in socioeconomic status, memberships, and income. This distribution of resources follows rather closely the overall pattern among Canadian interest groups, in which business, welfare, professional, and educational groups account for about 60 per cent of all groups. In effect, the capacity to dominate the national interest-group spectrum quantitatively is apparently accompanied by a similar ability to attract qualitatively-advantaged directors.

An unexpected finding is the relatively brief period that most directors have held their current positions. Throughout the four regions, for example, we find that almost 60 per cent have served only 1–4 years, with approximately another quarter having been in harness 5–9 years. At first glance, this distribution seems disadvantageous in such terms as experience, knowledge of the area concerned, and useful connections. The situation, however, is eased considerably by a common tendency among directors to have had a fairly extensive experience in a given association before assuming its directorship. A comparison of tenure-as-director with time-in-association reveals that most of them have come up through the ranks and become directors only after an extended apprenticeship.

For example, among all groups in all sites, over one-half have been

[1] See H. D. Woods and S. Ostry, *Labour Policy and Labour Economics in Canada* (Toronto: Macmillan Co., 1962), Table 26.
[2] Although labour's somewhat anomalous position will be commented upon later, it can be said here that its marginal political influence seems to reflect social and organizational factors, including marginal legitimacy in the conservative Canadian political culture and its structural relationship with international unions. On the latter point, see David Kwavnick, 'Pressure group demands and the struggle for organizational status', 3 *Canadian Journal of Political Science* (March, 1970), pp. 56–72.

members of the association of which they are now director for a decade or longer, and one-fifth have been members for 20-or-more years. This pattern of cumulative tenure suggests that considerable experience in their functional sector is among the important political resources shared by these men and women. Our research did not cover the reasons for their brief tenures as directors, but they reflect in part the fact that our sample includes some, presidents of ethnic, social–recreational, and fraternal–service associations, who usually hold office for one- and two-year terms. On the other hand, about half of the directors of groups which had full-time appointed executives had been in office only 1–4 years. The only exceptions were labour and agricultural groups where the proportion dropped to 40 per cent. Only about 12 per cent of all directors had had their jobs for 15-or-more years.

Regarding access, defined as the intensity of directors' interaction with governmental elites, business groups rank substantially higher than other types. Labour and instrumental groups fall at the low end of the scale, with professional–educational types in the middle. A similar distribution, significant at .01, appears when interaction with MP's is considered separately: business groups again lead, with 11 per cent, followed by professional–educational (8 per cent), labour (6 per cent), and instrumental groups (2 per cent). Such variations disappear when interaction with bureaucrats is analysed, where about one-quarter of all types of directors interact 'frequently', i.e. twice a week or more. These data confirm that the bureaucracy is the major target of interest groups and that any differentiation in patterns of access occurs regarding MP's.

In addition to such socioeconomic resources, directors also share certain other kinds of attributes which we have called psychopolitical resources. Perhaps the most signal of these is legitimacy, which may be defined as the extent of felt normative approbation enjoyed by a director. The roots of legitimation go deep into the social and political culture of a society. We saw earlier that the corporatist theory of society, initially brought to Canada by the Empire Loyalists, provides a persuasive normative justification for interest group participation in the formulation of public policy and the use of public resources to develop the national economy. Allied with this time-honoured rationale is the 'Old Tory theory of leadership' which encourages fulsome delegation to elites by rank-and-file members of governmental and private groups. Our empirical index of group legitimacy is the responses of directors to an item indicating the extent to which they believe legislators regarded as legitimate any efforts by their groups to influence them.

Canadian interest groups

By some extended process of socialization, interest groups become differentiated along a rough scale of evaluation according to which they are ranked by those publics for whom they are salient.[1] The resulting consensus decrees that some groups will enjoy a full measure of legitimation while others will be quite marginal in this respect. The bench-marks for such evaluations stem from certain community norms and preferences about the structure of major social institutions such as religion, politics, and property. In contemporary North America, it seems that the doctrine of natural rights has been transmuted into individual property rights to give a large measure of legitimacy to institutions that preserve and enhance this value, while denying such to those that seem to threaten it. An obvious benefactor is 'free enterprise' and its battery of honourific preferences.

As a result, in general, and with many exceptions, industrial and business activities, those institutional sectors who share their values, and the interest groups they sustain tend to enjoy generous shares of legitimation. Politics, by the same standard, is likely to receive only a marginal legitimation since it can be presented as the antithesis of free enterprise and private ownership values. The ambivalence with which politics is regarded in Canada, despite the positive influence of the corporatist ethic amd the historical appreciation of government as a generally benign presence, is well-known.

Organized labour endures an even more precarious status on the scale of popular legitimacy, as indicated by some of the national survey data reported earlier. While it enjoys considerable potential power, which will probably grow as industrialization spreads, the leaders of organized labour do not interact fulsomely with other institutional elites, nor do they receive the prizes that symbolize power and legitimacy, such as appointments to the Cabinet or Senate, to the governing boards of universities, and to prestigeful private clubs. This is essentially because labour's philosophy and aspirations challenge fundamentally the assumptions of the largely unquestioned system of Canadian private property and 'free enterprise'.[2]

Other psychopolitical resources include the director's generalized feelings of political efficacy, derived from an index composed of standardized items measuring this quality; his perceived effectiveness as a persuader of govern-

---

[1] It is perhaps impossible to categorize legitimation as either purely a personal resource of the director or an institutional resource of the group concerned. In both sociological and historical terms, however, it seems that legitimacy is mainly attached to institutions, and from which members may benefit or suffer, as the case may be. Legitimation resides in the institution as a resource upon which its members may draw, and to which of course they can contribute by appropriate behaviour.

[2] Porter, *The Vertical Mosaic*, pp. 310–14.

mental elites on issues affecting his group; the extent to which he believes members of his group support its objectives and policies; and the extent, to which he views legislators as being generally friendly and cooperative rather than as opponents. One would expect to find considerable variation among the various types of groups, indicating that directors define their operational situation differently. As emphasized earlier, such perceptions have operational consequences.

Such valuational perspectives not only define part of the director's perceptual framework, but governmental elites are fully aware of the public legitimation enjoyed by the various groups who present their claims. In this respect, some groups are more equal than others. The resulting legitimation gradient provides governmental elites with a useful selective index, as well as an instrument for enhancing their own autonomy. MP's and bureaucrats who wish to avoid any dependence upon private groups may conclude that the claims of those groups which displace only marginal legitimacy can be rejected with impunity. The distribution of legitimacy and other psychopolitical resources is presented in Table 5-3.

Here again, business–industrial types of directors possess the largest shares of those political resources defined here as psychopolitical, in contrast to the 'hard' socioeconomic resources presented earlier. On the whole, the resources analysed here are perceptual, in that they reflect each director's judgment or perception of the conditions included. Such evaluations certainly seem less firm than evidence about a group's socioeconomic resources. Nevertheless, when we turn to the measurement of interest group effectiveness in a subsequent chapter, the director's role becomes much more significant than the organization's resources in determining a group's political efficacy.

It is immediately clear that directors impute a high measure of legitimacy to their associations. Since the data are based upon their own perceptions of legislators' evaluations, some caution is in order. On the other hand, one should note that such subjective perceptions often have behavioural consequences similar to those of more objective images of reality. As W. I. Thomas insisted, 'Situations that are defined as real, are real in their consequences.' If a director believes that governmental elites think well of his group, his own estimation of its legitimacy and effectiveness will probably be reinforced, with attending behavioural consequences.

Regarding commitment, strongly significant variations (.001) exist among the various kinds of groups. With the notable exception of welfare, over half of all directors are convinced that their members are only 'moderately'

TABLE 5-3 *Psychopolitical resources of directors*

Resource	Proportion ranking 'high'[a]					
	Business	Labour	Prof–Ed.	Welfare	Instrumental	
	%	%	%	%	%	
Legitimacy	44	24	44	43	47	(187)[b]
Political efficacy	34	17	27	38	29	(232)
Cooperative ethic	72	58	67	70	61	(612)
Commitment	43	22	38	52	47	(239)
Persuasiveness	36	16	28	18	3	(102)

[a] 'High' refers here to the following conditions: Legitimacy, the proportion ranking 'always' regarding perceptions of legislators' approval of their group; Political efficacy, ranking of 'high' on achievement of group's goal in case study; Cooperative ethic, rejection of the proposition that legislators are 'competitors in a struggle to shape public policy'; Commitment, proportion of members 'intensely' identified with the group's goals; Persuasiveness, proportion ranking at the 'high' level on a weighted index of influence the director felt he had exerted over governmental elites through lobbying.

[b] The *N*'s in this table are quite small because the analysis from which they are derived was controlled for both frequency of contact and type of organization, and multiple-item indexes were used. When this is done, many cases are dropped because respondents fail to answer one or more of the items required to make up such indexes. Also, the table includes only the 'highs' in each resource category. The explanation for the large *N* in the 'cooperative ethic' row is that this was a simple 'yes' or 'no' type of response, unlike the others. Despite such problems, the relative position of the groups on each resource is probably accurate.

identified with their group's goals. Welfare groups, it will be recalled, also ranked strongly on 'public interest' incentives, and their directors do enjoy unusually strong support from this source. On the other hand, it is interesting to note that two economic groups, business and labour, both of whom share the same major pecuniary incentive, should rank differently on commitment. Labour also ranks low on the experienced persuasiveness of its directors *vis-à-vis* governmental elites, while business–industrial directors appear at the top of the scale in this regard.

In generalizing about resources, it is important to note that even though directors personally command disproportionate shares, their role is circumscribed to some unknown extent by their status as salaried employees, as well as by the collective political resources of their association. No matter how effectively they represent an interest, they do not typically own or manage the tangible resources which produce the revenue and the primal interest that sustain their associations. On the other hand, it is clear in modern society that control of organizational resources is often an effective route to power. In acting as the legitimate spokesmen for an organized interest, directors are able to share in the dividends of its power. They can, for example, draw upon prestigeful members of their group for political assistance and, indeed, this is the single most effective tactic cited by them. They also enjoy the right of access to governmental elites, and once inside, they can speak authoritatively for their association.

Our essential point here is that their personal resources, augmented by the collective solidarity and legitimacy of their groups, often enable them to be effective spokesmen for that interest. Indeed, the largest proportion of them define their role in precisely these terms. We are not suggesting, however, that as a class they are at the summit of the Canadian social or economic power structure, which as elsewhere tends to require either the possession of wealth or the direct control of it through management of large-scale business and industrial enterprise.

ORGANIZATIONAL RESOURCES

We have been concerned with the personal resources of directors, including socioeconomic status, efficacy, and experience. Equally important, it seems, are certain organizational resources such as staff, income, members, and continuity. Among the most crucial of an association's socioeconomic resources is probably the size and quality of its membership. Although vast membership does not guarantee stability and effectiveness, it can provide many benefits. Since dues are the major source of their funds, groups rely heavily upon members, more of which tend to mean more income. Volume of membership, moreover, can sometimes serve as a surrogate for other basic resources which an association may lack. It is well-known for example that the political strength of labour groups is in good part a function of the support and sanctions they can bring to bear through their votes at the riding level and elsewhere. Moreover, in terms of power and impact, it is clear that the number of members represented by an interest group director has a great deal to do with the weight given his testimony before committees, the attention accorded his pronouncements by the mass media, and the intensity with which politicians seek his support during campaigns.

A caveat is required here regarding the importance of membership size. As noted, some 100 of the groups in our sample have *corporate* members, which makes them small in gross numerical terms, although members may contribute large amounts of dues and other kinds of political support. Such

TABLE 5-4 *Socioeconomic resources of interest groups*

Resource	Business	Labour	Prof.–Ed.	Welfare	Instrumental	
	%	%	%	%	%	
Size: membership						
0–199	59	7	27	54	32	(192)
200–1,399	25	26	36	29	39	(173)
1,400–plus	16	67	38	17	29	(180)
Budget:						
0–39,000	35	28	41	22	39	(191)
40,000–139,999	33	28	28	32	34	(172)
140,000–plus	33	45	31	46	27	(192)
SES, members:						
upper-middle	76	16	67	27	40	(270)
middle	23	21	29	54	47	(201)
working	2	63	4	19	14	(101)
Employees:						
0–9	76	66	76	47	59	(384)
10–19	15	14	12	15	19	(71)
20–plus	9	21	12	38	22	(111)
Age:						
0–20	40	19	35	34	26	(188)
21–50	40	34	40	30	32	(212)
51–plus	21	47	25	36	41	(199)

memberships are typically found in business and industrial groups, as suggested by the fact that they rank lowest in 400-plus memberships among the sample. While the absolute size of membership probably remains a positive resource, it must be qualified in this and other qualitative ways.

Although size is a relative value, an obvious yet basic generalization about interest group membership in Canada is that it tends to cluster around either the low or the high end of the scale. Fully one-third of all groups are in the smallest (0–199) category, whereas another one-third are in the 200–1,399 category. The remainder are distributed throughout the 1,400-plus range. The relation between size of membership and type of group is shown in Table 5-4, which also presents the distribution of various other socioeconomic group resources.

Labour groups dominate in terms of membership size, with two-thirds of them at the 1,400 level and above. Some of the medical and other independent professions and the huge teacher's associations account for the large proportion of professional–educational groups in this category. As suggested earlier, it is well to qualify any assumption that size of membership is necessarily associated with political effectiveness. Indeed, the association is inverse in some cases.

Perhaps the most precise index of the potential political resources of groups is the size of their budgets, which of course incorporate their major allocations of funds and provide another quantitative index of the amounts spent for political activity. The range, averaged among the four sites, is from $500 to $8,199,749 annually. The median is $75,094, with considerable variation existing among the provinces, ranging from a low of $50,875 in British Columbia through $75,500 in Ontario, $85,000 in Quebec, to a high of $89,000 in Ottawa. Fully 85 per cent of all interest groups spend less than $421,000 annually; put another way, only one quarter of them spend over $260,000 per year. Of this select group, 36 per cent are found in Ontario, the most wealthy Canadian province.

Labour's high ranking in size of membership is repeated regarding budgetary resources, where it is matched only by welfare. As always, this summary presentation hides much of the financial picture. Welfare, for example, has the largest proportion of groups in the uppermost part of the scale. While the mean is $120,000, 12 per cent of groups of all types are in the $500,000-plus range. Several have annual budgets in the 2–5 million range. One-half of all groups, however, have budgets of $80,000 per year and less; and two-thirds have $140,000 per year and less. Although we have combined professional and educational groups to simplify the presentation, their comparative financial resources are quite different: whereas almost a fifth of the former have budgets of $300,000 per year and over, only 4 per cent of the latter do. Similarly in the 'instrumental' category: about a fifth of religious, ethnic and social–recreational groups enjoy budgets of $300,000-plus, compared with none among fraternal–service groups.

A related concern is any pattern among interest groups in terms of their major areas of spending. Directors were asked to rank their first three categories of expenditures in terms of the proportion of their total budget spent for each. We assume these estimates are accurate because directors are likely to be quite aware of where the largest proportions of their budgets are spent. The distribution among all types of groups is as follows: the largest single proportion, 46 per cent, of all directors ranked staff salaries, rent and operating expenses first; information produced for members of the association was ranked second, by one-third; while information for the public was ranked third by one-fifth of the sample. One of the major reasons for any group's existence, of course, is the services it can provide its members, which accounts for the high priority ascribed to 'information for members'.

TABLE 5-5 *Corporate and individual dues structure*

Corporate		Individual	
Range in dollars	Proportion	Range in dollars	Proportion
0–1,999	81	0–24	54
2,000–3,999	4	25–49	13
4,000–5,999	4	50–74	13
8,000–9,999	4	75–99	6
10,000–11,999	1	100–124	4
14,000–15,000	1	125–149	2
16,000–plus	5	150–plus	7
	(96)		(397)

As expected, the overwhelming majority of groups spend most of their funds for internal operating expenses. More interesting is the amounts spent for 'political purposes', defined as providing information and services to MP's, bureaucrats and the general public. As noted, information for the public ranks first at the third level. Only at this level does information for MP's and bureaucrats become at all significant, amounting to 11 per cent of the total.

In this financial context, a review of the dues structures of interest groups is useful. Dues are of two kinds, individual and corporate. Some 12 per cent of all groups use both sources, including labour, business, social–recreational, fraternal–service, and educational associations. As noted earlier, corporate dues are typically calculated as a proportion of the member's annual sales, number of employees, or in the case of federated non-business associations, on the number of members or the global amount of dues collected.

The range of such dues is wide, from a few hundred to 16,000 dollars annually. Table 5-5 presents the combined distribution.

Once again, looking at corporate dues, although the dispersion is wide indeed, four-fifths of all groups are in the $0–1,999 range, and within this category (not shown here) fully 60 per cent are in the $0–249 range. Of the 96 groups using the corporate system, the highest dues are found among a small number of business and educational groups in Quebec and Ontario, with the exception of one international labour union in British Columbia with annual dues of $12,000.

Vastly more significant in terms of total income and frequency is the individual dues structure. Here the overall distribution reveals the familiar cluster effect, at the lower end of the scale. Not only are over four-fifths of the groups found in the $0–99 category, but within this category the distribution is skewed toward the low end, with over half at the $0–24 level. Indeed, only 7 per cent of all Canadian interest groups have individual dues of over $150 per year. About a quarter of these, moreover, are found among social–recreational associations in Quebec and Ontario, with the remainder scattered among business and professional groups. On the whole, a good deal of uniformity exists among given types of interest groups across all categories. Business and professional associations naturally command higher dues than fraternal, ethnic, welfare and religious groups whose primal interests are probably less salient to most members than their occupational interests. Nevertheless, the clustering of both corporate and individual dues around the lower end of the scale is characteristic.

QUALITATIVE ASPECTS OF MEMBERSHIP RESOURCES

Reinforcing such essentially quantitative aspects of membership are certain qualitative resources. The degree of organizational commitment is probably quite important (see Table 5-3). Highly committed members provide leaders with an important resource upon which they can draw in working toward group goals. Closely related to commitment as a positive attribute is a productive relationship between director and members. Such a condition, which may be defined as 'rapport', is measured here by the responses of directors to an item regarding the existence of any tension between them and their members. The theoretical underpinning for this conception rests upon the work of Robert Michels, the Swiss political scientist, who found that estrangement between leaders and followers tended to occur in democratic socialist parties.[1] Earlier research indicates that members of some groups may regard directors as 'hired-hands' who do not always understand the operating problems of those in the sector represented by the group. Much depends here upon the prestige and income of members of the group concerned. It is difficult to believe, for example, that the high-level managers who form part of the Canadian Manufacturers Association feel deferential toward its staff. Yet, in a labour union, the business agent may be regarded with considerable respect by ordinary members.

Among our Canadian sample, it seems that the tension potential is quite salient, since fully 36 per cent of directors agree that such estrangement exists. Differences in income, prestige, and education between themselves and members is the major reason.

[1] *Political Parties.*

The personal political resources of members provide another vital interest group resource. As noted earlier, such personal attributes are incorporated in the concept of socioeconomic status, which rests upon occupation and education. This probably explains why certain groups, such as legal and medical associations, despite their limited size, seem to enjoy considerable political influence.[1] They tend, in effect, to possess disproportionate amounts of esteem, income, and technical skill, as seen in Table 5–4. Their control of a vital technology, the improper use of which constitutes a public danger, often enables such groups to employ considerable political leverage in controlling the conditions of participation in their respective spheres. Indeed, and despite variations among them, a firm political generalization is that virtually all types of groups tend to include a substantial proportion of socially-advantaged individuals. Interest groups do not characteristically represent a cross-section of those involved in the interest or activity concerned. Instead, it is usually the most advantaged segments that are organized. Membership rates increase linearly with occupational and education level. Among our sample of over 600 groups, fully four-fifths of members are in middle- and upper-middle-class strata, according to the judgment of their directors.[2] Certain regional variations are found, with Quebec having the highest proportion of members in these strata, followed by Ottawa and Ontario who share equal proportions at the mean, while British Columbia ranks significantly below the mean. In sum, size and quality of members are probably among the major political resources of interest groups, but at this point this judgment remains a hypothesis, to be tested later when effectiveness is analysed. As we shall show, Canadian interest groups vary considerably in their possession of such resources, not all of which are equally significant for political effectiveness.

The presumably critical role of income in group life was mentioned earlier, in the context of annual budgets and directors' salaries. In some sense, income is probably the most signal organizational resource, and we assume that size of annual budget will prove to be positively related to political effectiveness. Among the advantages money can ensure is adequate staff, which in turn expands the battery of technical services an interest group

[1] For an account of the structure, tactics, and influence of the Canadian Medical Association, see Malcolm Taylor, 'Role of the medical profession in the formulation and execution of public policy', 3 *Canadian Public Administration* (September, 1960), pp. 233–55.

[2] Since they are based upon the subjective perceptions of directors, we cannot be as confident about these data as about the SES of the political elite, which is determined by objective indexes of occupation and education.

can provide its members, thereby increasing its membership potential with attending financial inputs, culminating (one assumes) in an enhanced capacity to provide additional staff. The over-all distribution indicates that fully three-fourths of all Canadian groups have from 1–19 employees, with one-quarter of these being only one- and two-man operations. At the other end of the spectrum, only one-tenth have 50 or more employees. The distribution of staff, in effect, is heavily skewed toward the small end of the scale. But staff size varies considerably according to type of association, with welfare groups having the highest proportion of 'large' (20-plus) staffs.

Yet another potential organizational resource is age or continuity, and any cumulative advantages that may accompany them. While its hazards are well known, age can bring valuable dividends, including a loyal and expanding clientele, the emergence of an institutional tradition, the popular esteem attending the recognition that it has met the 'test of time', time-honoured alliances with governmental elites, and opportunities to reap the benefits of inflation. The range in longevity among our group sample varies considerably, with the mean at 35 years. The distribution is very flat, with the largest single proportion of groups, only 6 per cent, appearing at the 99-year level. Not unexpectedly, as the original Canadian charter group, Quebec has the largest proportion of century-old associations; these are found among professional, labour, welfare, and religious groups, in that order.

One other aspect of group resources should be considered: the use of part-time technical specialists in accounting, law, public relations, lobbying, etc. Such resources probably increase the director's capacity to deal with both internal problems of management and his interaction with governmental elites. In the area of legislation, for example, and particularly in group attempts to amend a proposed statute, to draft amendments for consideration by a committee, or to prepare a brief on some Government proposal, legal and financial counsel is often required. Interest groups which character-istically employ such aides are probably more politically effective than those whose lack of resources or interest prevents them from doing so. Since lobbying will be analysed later in a more specifically political context, we will consider it only briefly here.

Regarding the total distribution, the major conclusion is that the use of specialists of any kind is fairly limited among interest groups, even though all of them use such services at one time or another. The total N, it will be shown (Table 6-5) includes about one-third of all groups. The remaining two-thirds, we may assume, do not have the resources or the incentive to use such aides. If our *a priori* assumption is correct that the use of such services is a valid index of high *potential* political efficacy, we must conclude that only about one-third of Canadian groups possess it.

Following American practice and the increasing functional specialization of occupational life, there is a tendency for lobbying to become institutionalized, so to speak. Such services are often provided by 'legislative representatives' who have sometimes had considerable experience at fairly senior levels inside the governmental system. This enables them to offer their clients, who are usually individual corporations, but may also include interest groups, a vital ingredient of lobbying effectiveness: access to decisive points of official power and authority on a personal, first-name basis. Here again, parenthetically, we see the 'circulation of elites' which accounts in part for the cohesiveness of the political elite. Systematic analysis of the structure and behaviour of this new occupational group is impossible at present, since no data are available.

Turning to an inter-group perspective, the use of lobbyists on a selective basis is narrowly the most common technical service (one-third) used by interest groups, with business, labour, and professional (when analysed separately from education) groups ranking above the mean on this activity, although only business reveals any significant difference. Meanwhile, 31 per cent of all types of groups indicate that they use legal aid; labour's high ranking in this context probably reflects periodic contractual negotiations. Ethnic groups, covered under 'instrumental' groups, also rank high, and probably require such help for immigration cases, upon which they spend considerable time. Other technical aids, including annual auditing, consulting services, and fund-raising assistance, the latter often managed by specialized firms on a percentage basis, account for the largest remaining category.

Insofar as the implications of staff assistance for potential political effectiveness are concerned, business and professional groups rank highest on lobbying, although it should be noted that legal assistance too is often used as a form of lobbying, so groups that rank high here may be regarded as having considerable potential political influence, assuming for the moment that lobbying is effective.

A final index regarding comparative staff resources is whether the director's position is a full-time salaried one or merely a part-time assignment. An obvious advantage of full-time representation is continuity. A permanent executive is far more likely to exercise the sustained influence upon governmental elites which is a crucial element in political effectiveness. As one

Ontario MP put it. 'They [interest groups] are only interested in us when a bill is before the House. Their approach is not continuous. They could be a lot more effective if they kept up a steady influence.' All else being equal, one may assume that groups directed by permanent, full-time executives will be more effective than those without such resources. This variable is also a fairly useful index of the relative financial capacity of groups. Here again, the distribution suggests that the large membership and/or economically-oriented types are the most advantaged. Over 90 per cent of labour and agriculture groups have full-time, salaried directors, followed closely by business and welfare with over four-fifths, and religious, educational, and professional groups with about two-thirds. At the other end of the scale, we find ethnic groups, almost three-quarters of which depend upon part-time, voluntary directors, followed not very closely by one-third of social–recreational and fraternal–service groups. The relatively greater *potential* political influence of labour, agricultural, business, and welfare groups is indicated by the fact that less than one-tenth of such groups rely upon voluntary directors, *either full-time or part-time.*

In sum, welfare groups, which include such organizations as United Fund, Crippled Civilians, and the Canadian Association for Retarded Children, enjoy a fairly substantial advantage in two resource areas: size of budget and size of staff. As suggested earlier, these properties often tend to be closely related. Labour has a similar advantage in size of membership, while religious groups have any benefits accruing to long-established associations. These are all impressive quantitative values, but it would be premature to conclude that they are decisive politically. Business groups, for example, which possess various useful political resources, rank lowest on membership and age, nor are they at the top in size of annual budgets. Some other variables probably account for the high level of influence often attributed to them. We shall look into this matter more closely when political effectiveness is considered.

CHAPTER 6

THE POLITICAL ROLE OF INTEREST GROUPS

Broadly speaking, all social systems require a political subsystem to provide a central mechanism of integration and conflict resolution, as well as a widely legitimated institution for allocating the major values of the larger society. Ideally, at least, government enjoys this monopoly of authority and power. It represents in some rather exclusive sense the ultimate centre of control, direction, and disinterest in the modern state. Such a conception is most germane in organic societies such as Canada where government has usually been looked upon as a benign presence, contrasted with the anti-government drift of individualistic societies such as France and the United States. In this chapter, we shall consider the political role of interest groups, which consists essentially of providing governments with the claims and the information required for it to perform this crucial social role.

FUNCTIONAL ROLE OF INTEREST GROUPS

Canadian interest groups have several functions, in addition to their political role. Here again, considerable similarity is found among them. Most groups provide a variety of services and activities for their members, many of which may be regarded as by-products of their primal interest. As our data indicate, individuals tend to have a very pragmatic view of membership, symbolized by the fact that 'personal, economic benefits' are their most common single incentive. Social and recreational affairs, aimed at enhancing group solidarity and rapport, are common, and these are sometimes more salient than the group's collective goal. In some cases, of course, groups are formed for precisely such objects. Most associations also spend considerable effort attempting to influence public opinion, often not in any specifically political sense, but rather to fashion a generalized popular awareness of and sympathy for their mission.

Such activities may be regarded as part of the interest groups' essential *social* role which is to bring together like-minded individuals who share some common interest. This collective impulse can of course range from an unrestrained pecuniary interest to the most quixotic cause. In any context, as Durkheim insisted, the prime function of such groups is to create and nourish a sense of collective consciousness among mass individuals, 'to drag them into the general torrent of social life.' This function is nicely illustrated by the socialization role of ethnic groups in informing 'new Canadians' of the ground rules of the political culture, including the sobering truth that governmental elites tend to listen most closely to organized, articulate groups.

Another of Durkheim's insights regarding the functional role of interest groups is their effect in displacing a purely 'mechanical' social solidarity with an affirmative 'organic' solidarity. The former condition refers to a 'primitive' societal situation in which men are constrained essentially by legal and coercive prescriptions. However, with the advent of a pervasive group structure, based upon the specialization of labour and the need for a freer basis of exchange, this negative social framework can be replaced, or at least considerably eased, by a voluntaristic ethic in which solidarity is based upon functionally inter-related and dependent individuals and groups.[1] Despite the fact that interest groups today are likely to be viewed by the ordinary citizen as contributing to social conflict, as instruments of mechanical solidarity, political elites are inclined to define them as agents of cooperation and cohesion. The continuity between the conception of organic solidarity and Canadian corporatist philosophy is immediately apparent.

Interest groups, in sum, are a functional requisite of all modern societies. In addition to their larger social function, they have a vital political role. Indeed, it is questionable that interest groups and lobbyists are any less functionally germane for one type of political system than for another. Certainly, our research indicates that they are prolific and politically active in both parliamentary and presidential systems.[2]

[1] *The Division of Labour in Society*, trans. and intro. by George Simpson, (New York: Macmillan, 1933).

[2] For a systematic comparison of the political behaviour of Canadian and American interest groups, see Robert Presthus, *The Third House: Interest Groups in Politics* (forthcoming). See also, S. Beer for the generalization that interest groups are better organized and more decisive in the British parliamentary system than in the United States, 'Pressure groups and parties in Britain'.

INTEREST GROUPS IN POLITICS

Our focus is on the narrower *political* role of interest groups, not because this role is functionally separable from their social role, nor because this is their major role *qua* interest groups, but because this aspect of Canadian political behaviour has been somewhat neglected. This is all the more surprising because many Canadian interest groups seem to be quite active politically. Although the data are hardly comparative, Almond and Verba found that one-quarter of group members in the United States believed their groups were actively involved in politics.[1] Definitions of 'actively involved' vary, of course, but our research suggests that a similar proportion of Canadian groups are politically active, even when politics is stringently defined as direct interaction with governmental elites to make a demand.

One index of such politicization is found in our case study data, which asked directors to present issues that involved an interaction with government. Of over 600 groups, well over two-thirds reported such a case. This figure, of course, says nothing about the frequency of such behaviour, but only that in the recent past, this proportion of groups had been politically engaged at least once. It is also possible that if members, instead of directors, had been asked this question, the proportion might have been lower, possibly because of the ordinary member's tangential interest in politics and the low visibility of group political activity, which after all is only one facet of their activities. On the other hand, as we shall see in a moment, the primary political tactic of groups is to appeal to their members for support and action regarding government, which indicates that political activity should be quite salient for them. This finding may possibly reflect the pervasiveness of government in Canada which reaches into virtually every sector of social activity, as suggested by data indicating that the proportion of GNP spent in Canada for government is among the highest in Western countries and that, by several quantitative indexes, the nation is very highly organized politically.

We are concerned essentially with the *linkage function* of interest group elites, which consists of integrating and articulating collective social demands for presentation to governmental elites through a process of negotiation and consultation. The following data will indicate that their contribution to government's task of allocating social resources is probably as important as that of the elites who direct the formal political apparatus. Government policy, in effect, is worked out through a process of symbiotic interaction

[1] *The Civic Culture*, p. 251.

between the three segments of its political elite: members, bureaucrats, and interest group leaders. The larger social implications of this system will be explained by the theory of elite accommodation.

This critical role occurs essentially because government cannot act in a vacuum, either politically or substantively. To perform its formidable synthesizing role, it must carry on sustained interaction with every major sector of the national institutional structure, including business, industry, labour, agriculture, religion, education, the mass media, to name only the most obvious. Interest groups may be regarded as the legitimate and rationalized social instruments for carrying on such interactions.[1] They provide the impetus, the organization, and the expertise required to order a multitude of socioeconomic demands and to present them to appropriate governmental elites in a coherent form. The functional specialization found in government is thus paralleled by a similar structural design within the social system. As suggested earlier, political elites tend to identify strongly with the resulting system, which allocates legitimacy, power, and jurisdictional autonomy among them in this fashion.

As André Siegfried and John Porter concluded, some half-century apart, the essential role of Canadian parties has been to act as a broker among the claims of such various articulate interests. Ideally, of course, governmental elites should include all social interests in their distributive scheme, but constraints of time, ideology, and political support decree that political representation will be selective and imperfect. In theory, too, the several parties should function as instruments of selective differentiation among the universe of contending social interests.

In an imperfect world, however, in which political resources are unequally shared and in which government, too, must include potential reciprocal benefits in its own decisional calculus, it is perhaps inevitable that it sometimes fails to represent the whole spectrum of social interests. One remedy, widely apparent in contemporary politics, is for historically dispossessed 'potential' groups to turn to new and dramatic ways of breaking existing patterns of value allocation.

Essentially, then, the political role of interest groups is to reconcile and synthesize demands within their own sector for presentation to governmental

---

[1] This highly positive perception of interest groups requires some qualification. As all human institutions, they have another, less attractive face: often oligarchic, they tend to represent advantaged minorities, while their purposes and perspectives are sometimes unduly narrow. Nevertheless, their very ubiquity and continuity provide an impressive *prima facie* case for their functional role in society and government.

elites with the hope of obtaining legislative sanction and financial support. The context within which such bargaining occurs is prescribed by the norms broadly encapsulated in the national political culture. Often, of course, as is true of any collectivity, a given interest group will exhibit considerable internal diversity of opinion, which must be rationalized by the leaders before any demand can be brought before governmental elites. Given the constraints mentioned earlier, the latter cannot entertain any but such mandated claims. It is the essential function and the great sociopolitical contribution of private elites to present such rationalized claims to government.

The collective effect is to provide the parties, parliament, and the bureaucracy with the technical information and the impetus needed to carry out their own brokerage function. In this sense, government is a mechanism for accommodating group demands. Such demands, as noted earlier, may be conceptualized in two ways: on the one hand they consist of *substantive information* about a policy or programme; on the other, they transmit the *ideological position* of the group concerned regarding the proposed action. Because politicians and bureaucrats themselves are confronted by these two decisional imperatives, and because policy issues characteristically present themselves in this dual perspective, interest groups tend to shape their own claims similarly.

One other condition of interest group participation in politics remains to be considered. This is the extent to which different groups perceive themselves as being involved in such a role. Our interviews suggest that the directors of many types of groups are politically deaf, to paraphrase Freud. In some cases, this reflects a lack of political consciousness on the director's part. More often, it seems to involve the group's function, which may be only peripherally related to government. Such depoliticized groups include social–recreational, fraternal–service, ethnic and religious associations. On the other hand, there is considerable variation along these lines even among potentially powerful economic types, such as business and labour. The difference between these two interests is clearly apparent in the weight each attaches to the various services or benefits provided their members: whereas just over one-fifth of business directors cite 'the opportunity to influence government' as the *major* benefit they provide, only 4 per cent of labour directors do.

PATTERNS OF SELECTIVE ACCESS AMONG INTEREST GROUPS

In generalizing about the political behaviour of Canadian interest groups, it is useful to determine any patterns of selective access existing among them in their interactions with government. It is often concluded, for example, that the Cabinet is their primary target because it is the centre of power in the political system. The conditions of access, however, are several. The substantive character of groups tends, in some cases, to propel them toward certain 'natural' targets. Interaction between functionally-structured agencies and their private clientele groups provides an example. Again, certain group interests are subject to regulation under organic statutes which are interpreted in specific cases by bureaucrats; as a result, such groups have a primarily bureaucratic orientation. The nature of an issue and its stage in its normal procedural evolution provide yet other bases for selective access. Our data enable us to differentiate interest groups along some of these dimensions.

It may be useful here to conceptualize interactions among the political elite as a process of trade-offs. Indeed, as Bentley insisted, and interaction theory explicitly maintains, trading is the essence of politics. The currencies are infinitely varied and each bargaining situation presents them in different combinations and permutations. The relative significance of each in a given situation, moreover, is clouded by the rhetoric and parliamentary and bureaucratic manoeuvres that often surround issues. It is not necessary, however, to know the details of each issue in order to provide the generalizations in which analysis deals.[1] In this chapter, we shall present comparative data covering all interest groups and dealing with a great range of issues. *Ad hoc* illustrative material will be used only to dramatize or clarify, and not as a basis for generalization.

In this context, it is theoretically essential that one not prejudge the relative political activism of interest groups. This is precisely an empirical question. Our research suggests that the most unlikely type of group may prove to have been intensely, if only sporadically active. Political influence, in effect, is not, as commonsense might lead one to assume, entirely a function of affluence and large membership, nor is it confined to the great 'economic' associations of business, industry, labour, and the professions. While an example can only be illustrative, it may be useful as an indication of the improbable sources from which effective political action can spring. This particular group is a Burial Society, with a part-time director who possesses relatively limited amounts of psychopolitical resources. The Society has only one full-time employee and two part-time aides. Its membership is entirely individual and amounts to about 15,000, most of whom according to the director are only 'moderately' identified with its

[1] In this context, see Bentley, *The Process of Government*, pp. 377–8.

goals. The Society's major purpose is 'to provide people with a low-cost funeral, yet with dignity and simplicity'. One might conclude from this that the group's vital concerns were other-worldly.

Such unpromising resources, however, were galvanized into successful political action by what seemed to be a threat to the group's survival in the form of proposed legislation sponsored by the Funeral Service Association, a rival private group which sought (its third attempt in three years) to secure from the government certain legislation 'similar to that governing dental mechanics, insurance salesmen, and so forth.' Under the proposed standards, the Society believed it might be forced out of existence, that certain forms of burial would become compulsory and that a board, administered by undertakers, would be given authority to grant and deny licenses: 'We were afraid they might try to knock our undertaker out. . . because he does work for us and its [sic] just one type of coffin.' Of special concern to the Society's director was the possibility that the Funeral Service Association might pass the proposed legislation through an Order-in-Council, which would permit the Cabinet to bypass back-benchers, upon whom the Society had relied in the past in preventing similar legislation.

The Society responded in several ways. A lawyer was hired to determine the effects of the proposed legislation. Lists of MP's were sent to all members 'so they could write in opposing the legislation'. The director appeared on TV and before several local groups (mainly labour and religious) presenting the Society's position. The primary focus was at the political level, although 'we didn't want to make it a party issue because our members are from all different parties'. The Society's ideological theme was that the proposed legislation, which involved compulsory embalming, was an abrogation of individual rights. The director 'wanted the right to dictate what she wanted done with her body; she didn't want anybody telling her she had to be embalmed'. Although unable to estimate what proportion of members had been involved, the director felt sure that the most effective tactic had been letters of protest to MP's from Society members. Moreover, she had done a survey of MP's during the Funeral Service Association's previous campaign which revealed that each legislator had received between 50 and 100 letters against the proposal. In the end, as in each of the previous attempts, no legislator could be found who would sponsor the bill.

In addition to suggesting the multiple facets of group political activity, this example provides some evidence of the extent to which group efforts are channelized by political culture and structure. Although the choice of tactics surely varies in terms of group resources, several common activities occurred: ventilation of the group's position through the mass media; individual approaches to MP's; letters by members to MP's; discussion of the issue at group meetings, usually followed by the passage of a resolution; and when the status of the group permits, which it apparently did not in this case, personal representations to relevant Cabinet members. Letters were sent to ministers, but personal contacts did not occur.

Political culture, broadly speaking, provided the group with the morale and legitimacy which inspired its positive response; community norms of personal liberty enabled its leaders to put their case in honourific terms. Meanwhile, the possibility that the Government might authorize the legislation through Orders-in-Council provided another fillip to the moral position of the Society which suggested that responsible government was in danger of being short-circuited: 'The government does a lot of legislation by order-in-council.' Although the Society was clearly effective in this issue, two qualifications should probably be mentioned: not only were they attempting to *prevent* an undesired change, which is typically easier than effecting change, but the proposed legislation had been unsuccessfully raised twice previously. As a result, the Society was armed to a degree rarely possible in the usual case.

In sum, as this example suggests and the systematic evidence to be presented confirms, regardless of their substantive character, Canadian interest groups tend to employ a similar and relatively limited repertoire of tactics. At one time or another, most of them use the entire battery of tactics, but all tend to rely mainly upon a select few. There is, moreover, a virtual consensus among them that certain tactics are preferable in certain situations. Why is this so? One suspects that it is a case of functional determinism: *The structure of group tactics conforms to the specialization of function institutionalized in the political system.* Interest groups seek that point in the political structure where the authority and expertise required to reconcile an issue reside.

In addition, however, groups focus upon such centres of power and function in terms of the current stage of a given issue. When legislation is being formulated, the Cabinet, caucus, other groups, and the public are the logical foci of attention; once it has been accepted in principle, the committees and the back-benchers become sensible targets. Following its passage, attention shifts to those charged with its implementation, typically the bureaucracy and its regulatory agencies.

Functional specificity is further enhanced by the fact that certain groups will usually have an interest which is affected mainly by only one of the centres of formal authority and power. Some groups, for example, deal almost exclusively with one or two departments because their particular substantive interest falls within the jurisdiction of such departments, often exercised through regulations occurring within the framework of statutes. Given the vast areas of administrative discretion existing in provincial and federal governments under the 'delegated legislation' authority, it is not surprising that the largest single proportion of groups indicate that they interact mainly with bureaucrats.

Other groups, for similar reasons, focus upon one or another of the remaining centres of authority. Some groups deal mainly with federal and provincial regulatory agencies. Here again, structure follows function: many areas including agricultural marketing, stock issues, and insurance are regulated mainly at the provincial level. As a result, interest groups representing these sectors tend to focus upon agencies at this level. Our data, for example, indicate that 12 per cent of our sample rank approaching regulatory agencies as their 'most effective' tactic. Agriculture and business account for 45 per cent of the total use of this avenue, followed by welfare, social–recreational, and educational groups.

On the other hand, it is also apparent that the scope of some groups is broader than their specific primal interest. A survey of the briefs presented to the Carter Commission on tax reform and to the Minister of Finance indicates that a very broad spectrum of organized interests was involved in such representations. Such a phenomenon is, of course, not only a function of the fact that taxation is of the broadest public concern, but also that the proposed legislation, following upon the Carter Report, was in an embryonic state, and indeed was apparently thrown out to evoke widespread public reaction. Parenthetically, the extensive modification of the Government's original legislation in this area punctuates the inadequacy of the easy generalization that the role of interest groups in parliamentary government is sharply reduced by the virtually dictatorial power of the Cabinet which can, presumably, in Jenning's oft-quoted hyperbole, 'do anything but turn a man into a woman'. . .

The fate of the Carter proposals becomes clearer when one considers the political experience and resources possessed by some of the groups who presented briefs and actively opposed the proposed measures. One illustrative case may be presented, concerning the director of a provincial Chamber of Mines. The Carter Report, of course, advocated the phasing out of tax concessions to extractive industries. The director presented his group's response to the Report in the following words:

Well, the one [issue] we've been most strongly involved in during the past two years is the Carter Report. We filed a report with the Commission in the beginning. We didn't meet them here, but we filed a report later and mailed it to Ottawa, before they brought their report down, you see. We explained why it was essential that Canada retain these tax incentives. When the Report was brought down, I knew it was coming. And of course, I was ready for it; having been involved for a year or so, you might say I was all primed. After reading through it, with my years of experience, I saw the weakness of it and I figured I had to give a quick reaction. I knew the newspapers would ask (respondent), manager of the Chamber of Mines, what do you think about it? So, I sat down on the Saturday morning and started writing. And I wrote my ideas out, rather hurriedly I might say, but they were fundamental expressions of what's involved. And I took a copy of it down to the daily newspapers, that's on Sunday night, and they all gave it good coverage on Monday morning.

We got a blast out against Carter's thinking quick. Some people maintained – I haven't been accused of it myself, but some people have, and say, 'Well, you should read the report before you express yourself,' I didn't need to read other than his press releases. It was obvious what he was driving at, and I didn't need to read all the fine print to know that he was hitting at the fundamental requirements for a flourishing mining industry in Canada. So, I expressed myself in this vein and got widespread publicity; I also delivered it to the Canadian press and was given publicity right across Canada. It hit every newspaper in the country, or a lot of them, and also a lot of backwoods papers, which is where we wanted to get. I realize the importance of getting your methods through to, shall I say, the backwoods newspaper. Oh yes, I think its very effective politically. This was to a large degree a political issue. I mean, how could we as a group attack it any other way? We're a public organization and its the prospectors in the hills, the guy we help get a job, the geologist working out there, it's the big mining corporations, and the little stock company. It's everybody that I know who's involved in the mining business; the fellow who sells mining equipment, he also has a deep interest in this thing. So, we wanted to get right into the backwoods areas and we did...

So, we expressed ourselves on that occasion and the message was carried right through across Canada, well, to a degree anyway...and it stirred these fellows up and gave them something tangible to base their opposition to Carter on. After all, somebody has to take the lead in these things and a man like myself, its been thirty-eight years of my life involved in it. They count on me to, shall I say, act as leader to express an opinion. And when I do, these boys living in the hinterlands, they undoubtedly proceed to take action themselves. So, we built up a strong public feeling against the Carter recommendations across Canada. I think Carter asked for it. I mean we had to hit him hard and we did hit him hard. He asked for it because he wanted not to modify our existing legislation, but to turn things completely over. In other words, he was saying that what had gone before was no good...Well, we thought he was wrong and we could see a great injury to Canada and to the mining industry, and it was very interesting to note that, after a few weeks, top-flight mining people all across Canada, including heads of some of the biggest corporations and various organizations, Canadian Metal Mining Association and others, expressed themselves pretty well along the same line that I did on that occasion.

Q. Did you work with any other groups like the mining associations?

A. Well we did to a degree, yes. But after this blast of mine, if I might use such a word because it was a blast really, then we got down to cases and we decided we should do something more tangible to make a more proper presentation to government. So this is when we hired...and...to do this study for us. We spent a couple of thousand dollars and we got a thousand copies out, and we distributed these to all the political people in Ottawa and most of the political people in...Then we mailed copies to pretty well most of the Cabinet ministers of every province across Canada so they would know what mining people thought about Carter.

Well, we wanted to get to him so we mailed copies to other organizations around the country, etc. Our brief or reply to the Carter commission was a very effective thing because we got a lot of comments on it. Then there were a lot of groups that got a lot of other groups to write letters. Now we believe when you have a membership, a large membership, we want to use them and it's one thing for a membership like ours to file a brief with Ottawa, but you know as well as I do that political people are affected by letters and protests by the public which they should be.

So there were many prospectors who wrote letters and there were many engineers and geologists who wrote letters to the Carter report because it was their livelihood. So we instigated them, and I don't think there is anything wrong in that. I don't think I'm being wrong in telling you this, but we did everything we could to instigate action to protest against Carter. We felt strongly about it, so strongly that we had to fight, and so we instigated the action of prospectors all over the country, small mining companies, large mining companies and so on. I told I don't know how many hundreds of them, write a letter to Ottawa. Tell them what you think about it, tell them how it will affect you as a prospector, as a geologist or as a little stock company. And also express yourself to your local MP and they did. A lot of letters were sent to these MP's around here. Well, naturally, they sit in Parliament and they are making representations to the government. I feel and I hope I'm not doing too much wishful thinking or being too egotistical, but I feel and its been commented, that we were very effective. I've had some good people, solid people, tell me that the campaign conducted by the Chamber of Mines was the most effective campaign against Carter in Canada. We hit him hard, we hit him right where it hurts and we based it on solid honest facts. We thought we were right or we wouldn't have done it.

Public officials? We did our best, yes. I don't know that we specifically asked anybody to do it. I might have mentioned to..., Deputy Minister of Mines that it would be a good thing if our Minister of Mines was to oppose it, or something like that, you know. We probably did this kind of thing. I can't remember all the things done, but we didn't specifically go out of our way to get the Minister of Mines to oppose it or Premier... to oppose it. But we used every possible way to build up opposition. I'll be honest about it. We did everything a man can reasonably do to oppose something that you feel can destroy your industry.

Q. How effective were you in this case? Were you able to achieve most of your goals?

A. Oh yes, I think so, I really do. I may be kidding myself, because its hard to judge. But I think as an effort by the Chamber of Mines, we were probably one of the most effective efforts in Canada against Carter. I think we achieved everything we were after. We brought it right out into the open, we made it into a hot political issue. We got all the facts, we got every little guy in the country as well as the big ones. The big ones are always involved, they always get in, but we got all the little fellows involved, and we got the equipment supply people involved too. Because a lot of them are members of the Chambers of Mines and they do a lot of business for the mining industry service groups. And we got them involved. I talked to dozens and dozens of them. We got a series of articles in the daily press and we gave a series of talks around the country and expressed our opinion on it. And I think we were very effective. Yes, I really do. I think the government felt that they had got a number one hot potato. They never asked for it. It wasn't the Liberal government that introduced it. It wasn't their fault but we had to make them realize they had a hot potato here and they'd better be awfully careful before they started tampering with the mining tax laws of Canada or they'd have a real continuing battle. And I think this was effective because it was the opinion of everybody. If you got in any mining camp and talked, this was the reaction. They realized that if Carter had his way they would be hurt. They had been told so, and they realized that what we were saying was true.

Q. Did you try and get your ideas across more to MP's in Ottawa, or to the Cabinet?

A. To everybody. We went to the Cabinet, we didn't go there actually, we mailed our brief in, but we worked with the Cabinet and we tried to get all the MP's too. And also to all the MLA's across Canada. Because, after all, if the provinces would oppose it ... Incidentally, in that regard, nobody in the mining industry would argue, certainly I couldn't honestly argue, against some modifications and changes – I mean you've got to go with some changes in anything, but nobody would argue against that. But it was just the complete changing over and the destruction of everything that we opposed.[1]

The many facets of interest group behaviour presented here may provide a useful orienting framework for the summary data to be presented below. Perhaps most notable is the political resources commanded by this director, which in turn were reinforced by his strong personal commitment to the interest he represents.

We suggested earlier that functional specialization probably results in considerable channeling of interest group access. The hypothesis is that certain types of groups have 'natural' points of access within government, and that these provide a useful basis of differentiation. Table 6-1 presents the frequencies for groups according to the target ranked first, and according to their general, *over-all* experience. We shall see in a moment that the distribution changes dramatically in another context.

The distribution indicates clearly that there is considerable specialization of access among Canadian interest groups, but that the civil service is substantially more likely to be the primary target among all groups, except professional, labour, and fraternal–service. Legislature and Cabinet receive

[1] *Verbatim* interview, August 22, 1968. I am grateful indeed to this executive director for permission to quote him here.

TABLE 6-1   *Primary general targets of interest groups*

Target[b]	Prof.	Lab.	S–R.	Bus.	Rel.	Wel.	F–S.	Ed.	Sample
	Proportion ranking each target first[a]								
	%	%	%	%	%	%	%	%	%
Civil service	23	32	50	51	31	50	21	46	40	(178)
Legislature	27	37	11	11	13	17	43	16	21	(90)
Cabinet	22	4	7	25	31	17	21	27	19	(83)
Leg. committees	7	14	0	8	6	4	14	0	7	(30)
Ex. assts. cab.	10	5	4	2	—	6	—	4	5	(20)
Other[c]	8	7	26	2	19	5	—	7	7	(29)
	(73)	(74)	(32)	(91)	(16)	(74)	(14)	(56)		(430)

[a] In this and all succeeding tables, all figures have been rounded and will not always total 100. Agriculture and ethnic groups are not included in this and the three tables following due to very small *N*'s.

[b] The item used here was: 'Which *three* of the following elements receive the greatest amount of attention from you and your organization?' Only the first response is presented in the table.

[c] In addition to this category, we included the judiciary which was ranked first by only 2 per cent of all groups (*N*–11) including labour, welfare, and social–recreational, in that order. Thus the breakdowns were too small to report.

virtually the same degree of access, and the remaining elements in the system also receive quite similar, although lesser, amounts of attention. It is not unexpected, of course, to find the judiciary (see footnote *c* of Table 6-1) ranking at the bottom, given its tradition of autonomy and isolation. Significantly, among the few groups that do turn to the courts, the main ones tend to have somewhat marginal status in the larger society. Perhaps their relative lack of conventional political resources forces them to rely upon rear-guard stands before the courts.

More interesting, perhaps, is the differentiation among group types in terms of their primary targets. Business, welfare, and social–recreational groups spend one-half their time interacting with civil servants, followed very closely by educational and agricultural groups. Fraternal–service types rank lowest in this regard. Concerning access to MP's, the latter group ranks highest, which suggests that these two points of access, i.e. bureaucracy and legislature, are to some extent polar in their attraction and perceived utility for such kinds of groups. The position of business groups illustrates a similar phenomenon; such groups rank *lowest* on legislative access, finding it more efficacious to allocate fully three-quarters of their time to civil servants and Cabinet. Since business groups are often regarded as being quite powerful politically,[1] perhaps their focus upon these two avenues provides a rough index of power *within* the formal political apparatus.

The comparative position of the Cabinet as a target differs considerably among the several types of groups. It is perhaps an index of the survival of religious influence in Canada, to which Porter alludes,[2] that religious groups rank highest in the use of this vital point of access.[3] Ranking next are educational groups, followed very closely by business types. Professional and fraternal–service groups rank next, while social–recreational and labour appear at the bottom. It is an interesting reflection of the marginal social and political position of organized labour that it should be found in this position, despite its vast membership and economic significance in Canadian society. Here again is evidence to support our 'polarization thesis', whereby access in the Canadian political system is conditioned to some extent by the relative legitimacy enjoyed by the social interest represented by the various groups. Labour and welfare activities, summarily, have at best a precarious legitimation in capitalist societies. Thus, whereas business, religious, and educational groups tend to focus upon the apex of political power, the Cabinet, labour, and welfare groups turn mainly to the legislature and the civil service.

Turning to the targets ranked second (not shown here) the over-all pattern of intensity varies considerably and selectivity among targets is much less evident. The Cabinet ranks first, with 22 per cent of the total, followed closely by the civil service and legislature, with one-fifth each, while legislative committees, which had been a poor fourth, virtually close the gap with 19 per cent. Business now allocates its access almost equally among each of the above targets, while labour ranks the Cabinet highest. Welfare still focusses mainly upon the civil service, although recourse to executive assistants rises sharply. Social–recreational and welfare–service groups now turn strongly to legislative committees, having ranked the civil service and legislature highest as their first target. Labour and welfare continue to rank highest in point of access to the judiciary.

---

[1] The Meisel national sample, for example, reveals that four-fifths (combined average 1965 and 1968) of Canadian adults believe that some high officials in government 'pay more attention to what the big interests want', among which one would probably include business.

[2] *The Vertical Mosaic*, pp. 511–29.

[3] It should be noted that our underlying theoretical assumption here is that interaction is initiated by interest group elites. One should, however, at least entertain the hypothesis that the process occurs in the other direction. In this case, it could be that governmental elites initiate interaction with religious elites to secure such benefits as divine guidance.

In sum, the impressive majority enjoyed by the civil service as the primary target of all groups now disappears; the Cabinet becomes the top second choice, but by a very small margin, and the linear trend is for the four major targets to receive virtually the same amounts of attention. Regarding access to the Cabinet, it is important to note that it is a common practice for groups to use a prestigeful member to handle such a contact. At other times, a group may employ a former legislator, a lawyer, or some well-connected person to act on its behalf.

It will be recalled that we included a case study of a vital issue in the research design. One of the items used in this context asked directors to indicate the targets they focussed upon in that issue. An analysis of these responses will provide a check upon the data just present. However, some caveats are required. We should not necessarily expect the two distributions to be highly similar, since one involves generalized patterns of access, while the other deals with a specific issue. Moreover, interest group directors agree that it is much easier to *prevent* the passage of new legislation or administrative regulations than it is to effect such measures. Since fully four-fifths of the case study issues involve innovative situations, we are dealing here with the more difficult task faced by directors, in which their strategy might be atypical. It is also possible that the cases selected by the directors are more important than the general run of issues encountered by their associations. Finally, the element of ego involvement may have conditioned these responses, in the sense that each director might quite understandably prefer to present himself as a person having access to members of the Cabinet. These conditions should be kept in mind when interpreting the data in Table 6-2.

A different pattern of access emerges here, with the Cabinet displacing the civil service and the legislature as reported in the previous table. Moreover, whereas the Cabinet and legislature had been virtually equal, we now find the civil service significantly more likely to be ranked second. In addition to the explanation for this change suggested above, it may be that the substantive nature of the cases lies behind the new pattern. We shall return to this point later when the case study issues are analysed more closely. Regarding the distribution among groups, fraternal–service has displaced the religious elite as the group most likely to turn to the Cabinet, and only welfare groups remain committed to the civil service as their primary target. A summary observation is that, as with the previous table, four-fifths of all interactions are accounted for by the Cabinet, legislature, and civil service.

TABLE 6-2 *Primary governmental target in case study*[a]

Target	Prof.	Lab.	S-R.	Bus.	Rel.	Wel.	F-S.	Ed.	Sample	
	%	%	%	%	%	%	%	%	%	
Cabinet	41	41	10	40	43	33	46	44	38	(155)
Civil service	25	12	21	36	14	39	27	24	27	(107)
Legislature	16	24	24	7	14	10	27	9	14	(57)
Exec. assts.	6	5	—	4	—	—	—	13	4	(18)
Other[b]	11	18	45	14	29	18	—	9	17	(68)
	(65)	(68)	(31)	(83)	(14)	(72)	(18)	(54)		(405)

[a] The item used was: 'In this issue, on which of the following governmental bodies did you focus your *main* attention?' (italics in original).

[b] The 'other' category is large because some of the politically moribund groups presented an issue that did not involve government.

Regarding the association between social prestige and preferred target, it is again interesting to note that most of the groups which rely mainly upon the legislature are somewhat marginal in this respect, including fraternal–service, labour, and social–recreational groups. It does seem, moreover, that the index of their marginality is both social and economic; certainly labour unions, for example, possess large amounts of the latter type of resource, yet continue to rely mainly upon the legislature for political access.

This generalization is reinforced by data (not shown here) regarding the *second* choice of access in the case study issue. Here again, labour and fraternal–service groups rank back-benchers highest, with an average of almost 50 per cent, compared with only 23 per cent for business, professional and educational groups. Comparative figures for the same two sets of groups regarding reliance on the Cabinet are 13 *v.* 20 per cent.

On the other hand, some groups range widely among all three major centres of access. Social–recreational groups, for example, rank the civil service as their primary *general* target by a wide margin, with legislative committees second; in the case study context, they turn first to the legislature and then to the Cabinet as their major second choice.

INTEREST GROUP TACTICS

We now turn from interest group targets to the *tactics* used in their interaction with governmental elites. Here one would expect to find a limited repertoire

TABLE 6-3 *Primary tactic used by interest groups in case study*[a]

Tactic	Proportion ranking each tactic first								
	Prof.	Lab.	S–R.	Bus.	Rel.	Wel.	F–S.	Ed.	Sample
	%	%	%	%	%	%	%	%	%
Enlisting members	46	27	26	33	17	23	44	34	32	(148)
Pub. camp.	18	22	6	12	17	23	33	11	17	(81)
Seeing pols. +bur.	10	10	23	12	13	21	11	21	15	(70)
Seeing cab.	10	9	11	19	8	5	6	20	12	(60)
Other groups	4	12	11	7	4	13	0	5	8	(37)
Exec. assts.	3	3	—	2	—	1	—	2	2	(8)
Other	10	17	23	15	33	14	6	7	15	(71)
	(72)	(77)	(35)	(91)	(24)	(77)	(18)	(56)		(469)

[a] The item used here is: 'Please indicate all the methods you used in working toward this objective' (ask him to rank).

of established tactics, accompanied by some variation by type of group. The data in Table 6-3 are taken from the case study, and are subject to the strictures noted earlier. The frequency of direct appeals to Cabinet can be assessed again, which is useful given the conventional belief that most interest group representations occur there. Here again, it should be repeated, we are presenting data from issues that seem to be critically salient to the directors concerned.

Looking first at the over-all distribution, it is clear that a substantially large proportion of all groups, one-third, with professional associations leading, rely mainly upon galvanizing the support of their members in handling government policies that directly affect them. The heavy reliance of professional associations upon such appeals probably reflects the fulsome amounts of personal political resources enjoyed by members of such groups who, as noted earlier, rank near the top in terms of cohesion, education, and income.

The usual pattern is for directors to secure a mandate from their members in the form of a resolution which is then, as the data suggest, ventilated in the mass media. Indeed, the initiative for this action may stem from government: as one Quebec director reported, 'The government insists we have the support of our members as evidenced by a resolution.' Members are also urged to contact their MP's at the time directors or prestigeful members approach government to present their case. If access can be gained, the latter will see relevant members of the Cabinet.[1] Note, parenthetically, how closely the tactics cited earlier in the Burial Society case resemble those used here. As suggested earlier, the recourse to executive assistants is likely to be used only when ministers prove to be unavailable. Some respondents stressed the strategic role of the executive assistant, indicating that his ready access to his master and influence over his agenda and sources of information give him considerable influence. However, as the data indicate, this avenue is not highly travelled by lobbyists.

Several groups fail to follow the pattern of tactical priorities revealed here: social–recreational, labour, welfare, and religious groups are well below the mean regarding appeals to membership. Here again, it seems that these groups are distinctive, compared with 'old line' economic groups such as professional, business, and agriculture, which tend to set the over-all pattern. Meanwhile, fraternal–service groups rank dramatically above the mean in the use of publicity. Labour's tendency to rely less upon the Cabinet is again apparent, while professional, business, agriculture, and education rank significantly above the sample mean on this variable.

On the whole, however, the impressive finding here is not the diversity shown among tactics, but the tendency for the distribution to be spread rather evenly among all of the various activities, except enlisting the aid of members. This finding reinforces our earlier observation that similarities in the political behaviour of Canadian interest groups are probably greater than differences. Variations in emphasis upon one or another target or tactic obviously exist, as we have seen, but the main drift is toward standardization.

When we turn to the method ranked *second* in frequency, (not shown here) we find that 'seeing politicians and bureaucrats' is ranked at the top by almost 30 per cent of all directors. The appeal to members now becomes second, with 23 per cent, and all other methods decline sharply in use, ranging through forming coalitions with other groups, approaching Cabinet members, publicity campaigns and executive assistants, in that order. However, since these data are based upon only one issue, it would be well to look at the over-all record before attempting to generalize.

[1] Although the difficulty of gaining access to Cabinet Ministers no doubt varies according to many conditions, it is not always possible, even for the director of an important industrial group residing in Ottawa. As this director told the story, he had tried for 32 weeks to see a certain Minister and indeed, had become so frustrated that he kept a diary of his attempts, which he showed to me. Finally, I asked, 'But why didn't he want to see you?' The director replied, 'Because he *knew* what I wanted and he didn't want to do it.'

We turn next to interest group tactics in the context of their reactive or 'rear-guard' stratagems. It seems that groups are often involved in attempts to prevent government or other groups from making disadvantageous changes in the conditions of participation in their sphere. Such consequences usually occur through inadvertence on the part of the government which, understandably, cannot always foresee all the implications of its policies. Although negotiation and consultation with the major interests obviously affected by such policy usually eases this problem. the 'ripple' effect of policy upon peripherally involved groups often inspires the kind of tactics presented here. In some cases, of course, such tactics are launched during the developmental stage of policy formation, but they often seem to be *post hoc* reactions, which serve a valuable, if occasionally embarrassing, feed-back function for governmental elites.

Reviewing the over-all distribution in Table 6-4, a great deal of continuity exists: almost half of all directors testify that their most common tactic is to discuss the issue with their members at their annual meeting or through special meetings. Here again, a resolution is typically drafted deploring or supporting the policy concerned, and providing the director with a symbol

TABLE 6-4 *Primary 'reactive' tactics of interest groups*[a]

Tactic	Proportion ranking each tactic first									
	Prof.	Lab.	S–R.	Bus.	Rel.	Wel.	F–S.	Ed.	Sample	
	%	%	%	%	%	%	%	%	%	
Enlist members	59	50	64	36	60	39	45	30	45	(21)
Write MP's	19	15	18	19	10	14	30	16	16	(84)
See bureaucrats	4	5	3	19	5	21	5	12	11	(7)
Testify in committee	11	9	6	12	10	6	—	10	9	(46)
Mass media	3	9	3	3	10	9	10	16	7	(36)
Newsletter	1	3	—	10	5	6	10	12	6	(29)
Protest rally	1	8	—	—	—	—	—	2	2	(9)
Other	3	1	6	2	—	5	—	3	3	(14)
	(84)	(82)	(33)	(104)	(20)	(87)	(24)	(63)		(497)

[a] Responses are based upon the following item: 'From time to time government probably takes action which directly affects the interests of your group. In such situations, has your group done any of the following?' (please rank in terms of importance).

of collective legitimacy to reinforce his subsequent interactions with government and other targets. A request to members to write their MP's typically follows, often focussed at the riding level in order to punctuate the 'grass roots' quality of the association's position.

Meanwhile, civil servants are approached to make perfectly clear the effects of the change upon the group's primal interest, and to present its evaluation of the proposed measure. Directors often turn to the mass media, conveying their views to a wider audience with the hope of enlisting public support and educating the public as to the implications of the policy, viewed generally, one fears, from a somewhat one-eyed perspective. On the other hand, rebuttals from opposing groups and disinterested citizens, if such exist, may round out the picture. The marginal ranking of 'testifying before committees' is interestingly at odds with our earlier finding that federal legislators regard this activity as the most effective single tactic employed by interest groups.[1] It may be, however, that its relatively low frequency is the result of the 'reactive' context in which these responses occurred. Also the recent strengthening of committee structure in Ottawa may not have occurred to the same extent among provincial governments.[2]

Substantial differences exist among the groups. Business, welfare, and educational groups are significantly below the mean on 'enlisting membership, as their major tactic. Perhaps we may assume that the internal governance of these types of groups is less participatory than in professional, social–recreational, religious, and labour types which rank above the mean. Another possible explanation is that their individual avenues of access are so open and productive that they need not be as concerned about generating mass support. Business and welfare, on the other hand, are similar in being significantly above the mean regarding the use of 'approaching bureaucrats' as a tactic. Education is noteworthy for its intense use of the mass media, compared with other types of groups.

Protest rallies, however currently fashionable, are obviously exceptional, and confined mainly to labour and ethnic (not shown) groups. Their use

[1] Robert Presthus, 'Interest Groups and the Federal Parliament', 4 *Canadian Journal of Political Science* (December, 1971) pp. 444–60.
[2] Thomas Hockin, 'The Advance of Standing Committees in Canada's House of Commons', 13 *Public Administration* (Summer, 1970), pp. 185–202. Some observers are less convinced that the change has been significant, especially since resulting modifications of Government legislation tend to be mainly procedural rather than substantive, cf. C. E. S. Franks, 'Dilemma of the standing committees of the Canadian House of Commons', 4 *Canadian Journal of Political Science* (December, 1971), pp. 461–76.

of such tactics lends support to conclusions about the marginal socio-political status of such groups, which forces them, in effect, to go outside the system to work toward ends which their resources do not always enable them to achieve within it. On the other hand, such tactics are becoming more salient and undoubtedly have considerable impact upon governmental elites who resent the resulting pressure and patent implication that they have been unrepresentative, but at the same time become fully aware of the disenchantment of the group concerned. It is clear that political elites generally regard such tactics as illegitimate;[1] indeed, a common rule among experienced lobbyists is never to apply pressure in such patent ways. The bases of elite rejection are two. Groups that use dramatic protest tactics such as rallies violate established political ground-rules. Such tactics, moreover, are anathema to members of the political elite who, as we have seen, represent social strata among whom manipulation rather than coercion is the modal interpersonal style.

A related tactic sometimes employed by interest groups is the forming of coalitions with other sympathetic groups. Such strategies are not illogical, especially if one discards the questionable premise that groups are locked in pluralistic competition. While conflict obviously occurs, our research suggests that cooperation is often more typical. In some sense, for example, most groups in an area such as business and industry share certain core values, including perhaps an aversion to increased taxation and government intervention in marketing practices, a preference for government protection and support without 'undue interference', and generally, the maintenance of a sympathetic climate for their operations.[2] Obviously, there are many tensions within this sector, including those between small entrepreneurs and national or internationally organized companies, importers and ex-porters, 'solid money' advocates such as banking and insurance *v.* easy money advocates such as the housing industry. In the round, however, continuities in their interests probably outweigh such bases of conflict. It

---

[1] In 1971, for example, Health and Welfare Minister John Munro cancelled a grant to an Ontario poverty group because it had become too militant, saying 'Confrontation tactics by people on welfare do not work...Groups reverting to such tactics have and will be denied support. Anything constructive that such groups have accomplished has been more than outweighed by the resort to destructive techniques'. *Globe and Mail*, (December 9, 1971), p. 12. The group had used sit-in and picketing tactics.

[2] As Thorburn remarks regarding efforts of various groups to amend the anti-combines legislation during 1959–60, 'There was a common attitude among the big business groups that Canadian anti-combines legislation was too stringent and consequently hobbled legitimate business in its activities', 'Pressure groups in Canadian Politics', 30 *Canadian Journal of Economics and Political Science* (May, 1964), p. 162.

is such commonalities of interest that partially explain the coalition phenomenon often seen among interest groups.

One *ad hoc* example, which is only illustrative, occurred during the Pearson Government's attempts to push through legislation (1962–8) which might reduce drug prices by limitations upon existing patent protection enjoyed by pharmaceutical manufacturers. The campaign against the Government's programme was led by the Pharmaceutical Manufacturers Association, which carried out a hard-hitting, yet only marginally successful fight against the legislation which was finally passed in 1969. For our purposes, the salient point is the coalition strategy employed by the Association which was able to bring together several concerned groups in opposition to the Government. These included the Canadian Medical Association, Quebec College of Physicians and Surgeons, Association of Deans of Pharmacy of Canada, Canadian Manufacturers Association, Chamber of Commerce, Canadian Chemical Producers Association, Chemical Institute of Canada, Canadian Pharmaceutical Association (both national and provincial), Canadian Electrical Manufacturers Association, and the Connaught Medical Research Laboratories of the University of Toronto.

The PMAC's coalition included not only groups directly concerned in the substantive issues, but also some like the Canadian Manufacturers Association and the Chamber of Commerce which symbolized the larger general commercial interest mentioned earlier. Since MP's are highly sensitive to articulate opinion, it may perhaps be assumed that the combined efforts of these well-organized and technically competent groups would, in the ordinary run of events, have considerable influence. Although the efforts of the PMAC and its allies in this case were not notably successful, insofar as effectiveness is measured by blocking legislation perceived as generally detrimental to their interests,[1] the conclusion seems to be that drug prices have not been visibly affected by the legislation.[2] In the context, however, the instructive point is the example of a fairly common stratagem which enables groups to combine their resources and to create obligations for use in the future.

One interesting group tactic not included in our interviews, but volunteered occasionally by respondants is the planting of questions to be raised in the House by sympathetic back-benchers. Such tactics enable directors

[1] For a definitive analysis of the case, see Ronald Lang, 'The politics of drugs: The Pharmaceutical Manufacturers Association of Canada and the Association of the British Pharmaceutical Industry (1930–70)', doctoral dissertation, University of London (1972).

[2] *Toronto Daily Star* (May 16, 1970).

to punctuate their position on an issue, to bring it to public attention, and perhaps, to embarrass ministers who have failed to respond to more traditional stratagems. A more dramatic, but less frequent, variant of this tactic is the practice of securing information for a back-bencher during the course of debate, which enables him to return armed with specific rebuttals or rationalizations of awkward points raised by opposing members.

LOBBYING AS AN INTEREST GROUP TACTIC

We referred earlier to the reactions of the political elite regarding lobbying, which ranged from occasional rejections of the very possibility that such activity could occur, to frank acceptance that lobbying did flourish, and indeed, was a functional requisite of effective policy-making. In order to accommodate this ambivalence, we put the question in a neutral form, as follows: 'Some observers believe it is fairly common for interest groups to engage men with special knowledge and contacts to represent their organization on matters of crucial importance. Has your organization done this?' If probing seemed warranted, we also indicated that such assistance sometimes included lobbying, which was defined non-pejoratively as any attempt, direct or indirect, to influence governmental decisions. Some directors replied immediately, 'Well, I handle that sort of activity myself.' Such responses would not be included in the data presented here, so that Table 6-5 probably understates the frequency of lobbying.

Business groups tend to use lobbyists most frequently and lobbying and legal aid are the most used of the various services. As the total N indicates, only about one-third of the entire sample employs specialists. With some

TABLE 6-5 *Interest group use of lobbyists and other specialists*

Service	Proportion ranking each service							
	Business	Prof.	Ed.	Labour	Welfare	Others[a]	Sample	
	%	%	%	%	%	%	%	
Lobbying	41	36	28	32	30	18	32	(64)
Legal aid	28	24	27	49	15	30	31	(62)
Tech. aid	13	15	27	11	18	26	15	(30)
Publicity	9	3	13	—	18	9	10	(16)
Other	7	20	12	8	18	14	13	(28)
	(46)	(33)	(15)	(37)	(33)	(36)		(200)

[a] Religious, ethnic, social–recreational, agricultural, and fraternal–service groups have been combined because their N's were too small for meaningful percentaging.

163

exceptions, most types of groups tend to use most services, although publicity varies more than the others.

By a narrow margin, lobbying proves to be the most common type of *ad hoc* technical assistance used by interest groups, with business ranking highest. The ubiquity of lobbying is suggested by the fact (not shown here) that of the ten group categories, only ethnic and fraternal–service have not employed aides in this role. Lobbying and legal services combined account for almost two-thirds of all assistance. Legal services present an interesting analytical problem, since it is quite possible that such services often include lobbying. For example, the drafting of a technical brief for presentation to government is often the work of legal advisors. Since such briefs, by definition, are *ex parte* statements of an interest group's position, they often constitute a form of lobbying activity; it thus seems valid to categorize those who prepare them as lobbyists. It has been shown, for example, that corporation lawyers played a notable role in drafting and presenting amendments to the federal anti-combines legislation in 1959–60.[1]

Fortunately, our evidence provides some indication of the extent to which legal aid is actually a form of lobbying. We have two categories of data related to lobbying: one specifies the *function* performed by the individual employed by the group, while the other indicates the *type of individual* hired. As Table 6-5 shows, under the legal services function, 62 lawyers were employed. However, under the type-of-individual category, (not shown here) we find a total of 92 lawyers. Since all these men were not providing 'legal services', we may assume that they were employed in direct lobbying. In effect, the difference between these totals, i.e. 30, suggests that at least one-third of all lawyers employed by interest groups functioned as lobbyists. Such a conclusion raises the total proportion of lobbyists among all types of technical aides to over 40 per cent.

Another corroborative index of the extent of lobbying activity is available from a set of items which asked directors to estimate the degree of influence they had been able to exert on governmental elites through personal lobbying. Here, we find another addition to the net volume of such activity. Whereas the previous table indicated that one-third of the interest groups had employed lobbyists, we now find that over two-thirds of directors also play direct, independent lobbying roles at one time or another. Although the precise total probably rests somewhere between the three estimates, it seems that the combined figure is probably the most accurate index of total lobbying activity.

[1] Hugh Thorburn, 'Pressure groups in Canadian politics', pp. 157–74.

Other types of technical services account for about 15 per cent of the total, and include such assistance as accounting, fund raising, and consulting services. Public relations firms are also engaged by interest groups to assist in fund-raising drives and campaigns for or against government measures.

Business, social–recreational, and professional groups, in that order, tend to rank highest on lobbying activities, and when lobbying and the related activity of legal services are combined, we find that labour, religious and social–recreational groups tend to dominate these kinds of activities. However, labour's high reliance upon legal services is probably related to its periodic contract negotiations, while the equally high-ranking of religious groups is difficult to explain. Fraternal–service groups rank significantly above the mean in 'other' technical services, which probably reflects their concern with community-service kinds of programmes.

Although we are anticipating the next chapter somewhat, it seems useful here to provide some evidence of the role of lobbying in shaping the perceptions of governmental elites regarding interest groups. One signal element in such perceptions is the extent to which interaction is related to the general significance attributed to such groups by bureaucrats. Table 6-6 indicates that such an effect does occur.

A highly positive and significant relationship exists between the degree of exposure to lobbyists experienced by bureaucrats and their perceptions of the significance of interest groups in influencing policy in their own departments. Two other facets of these data are suggestive: not only do over three-fourths of bureaucrats impute a high or moderate degree of significance to groups, but the largest single proportion (36 per cent) interact 'frequently' (twice a week or more) with representatives of such interests. From evidence to be presented in a moment, it appears that such representations are usually made by prominent members of the interest

TABLE 6-6   *Interaction with lobbyists and imputed significance of groups*

Significance	Intensity of interaction				
	Frequently	Occasionally	Seldom	Rarely	
	%	%	%	%	
High	47	31	18	4	(51)
Medium	37	34	22	7	(100)
Low	17	26	29	29	(43)
	(70)	(62)	(43)	(19)	(194)

X = significant at .01 K's tau C = .22   Gamma = .35

165

groups, rather than by the director himself or by specialists hired for this purpose. If this is true, it may partially explain any reluctance to recognize the existence of lobbying among the political elite, in the sense that they, as well as the prestigeful members concerned, may tend to sublimate the occasional performance of this role by men who share their own assumptions. Perhaps also, if such a role became stigmatized, it would tend to deprive directors and their groups of one of their most effective tactics.

The data on tactics presented above have been confined to two somewhat special contexts, the case study and the reactive stratagems of interest groups. We now turn to a broader context in which directors are asked to differentiate among eight characteristic tactics *generally* used by interest groups, and to rank the five *most effective*. On the whole, these data should be useful as a basis for a final generalization about the relative frequency and effectiveness of interest group tactics. It should be noted that several of the tactics included in earlier tables were included here, yet as Table 6-7 shows, *directors* in this particular context turn overwhelmingly to a new form of activity. Once again, the distribution is presented by type of group.

There is obviously an overriding consensus among directors that 'personal representations to government by prominent members of your organization' is the most effective tactic in their political arsenal. Not only do well over one-third of all directors rank it highest, but the tactic ranked second at

TABLE 6-7 *Effectiveness of interest group tactics*

Effectiveness ranking[a]	Proportion ranking each tactic first, second, third, fourth, and fifth											
	Prof.	Lab.	S–R.	Agri.	Bus.	Rel.	Wel.	Eth.	F–S.	Ed.	Sample[b]	
	%	%	%	%	%	%	%	%	%	%	%	
1. Personal reps. to government	41	31	60	44	32	25	35	29	43	33	37	(171)
2. Personal reps. to government	11	17	14	44	36	27	19	17	36	30	25	(101)
3. Personal reps. to government	17	28	13	—	9	25	22	—	8	24	18	(63)
4. Testimony at hearings	21	12	11	—	32	—	8	—	13	8	16	(40)
5. Briefs to committees	5	15	—	25	19	11	26	—	13	17	16	(39)
	(55)	(60)	(24)	(9)	(111)	(13)	(72)	(5)	(14)	(51)		(414)

[a] The following item was used here: 'Insofar as your own organization is concerned, how would you *rank* the following methods in terms of their *effectiveness* in attaining your goals?' (italics in original).

[b] Columns will not total 100 because scores are not cumulative.

this level, briefs to the Cabinet (not shown here), accounted for only 15 per cent of the total, while appeals to the general public through the mass media ranked third, at 12 per cent. The pre-eminence of this tactic, moreover, is punctuated by the fact that it scores first in effectiveness on each of the three highest levels of the scale. Only at the fourth and fifth levels do two other tactics emerge.

Among the groups ranking 'personal representations' first, social–recreational, professional, agricultural, and fraternal–service groups are well above the mean. The great economic interests of business and labour rank below the mean, which seems unusual, although when the first three categories are combined, all groups assign over two-thirds of their total attributions to this variable.

TARGETS AND TACTICS: SUMMARY AND IMPLICATIONS

Several generalizations may be offered concerning political interaction among the Canadian political elite. Regarding the preferred *targets* to which interest groups are oriented and considering first the *general* experience of directors, the civil service is the major point of access, preferred by 40 per cent of all groups, followed by the legislature and Cabinet which rank virtually the same, about one-fifth each. These three targets account for four-fifths of the total attributions. Business ranks highest regarding access to the bureaucracy, by a very small margin, followed by welfare and social–recreational groups. An interesting finding here is that religious groups rank highest above the mean in reliance upon the Cabinet, which is their major point of access.

When the *case study* is used as the basis for such differentiations, the pattern changes and the Cabinet becomes the major point of access, favoured again by almost 40 per cent of all groups, followed by the civil service, with back-benchers a poor third. Agricultural groups rank highest on access to the Cabinet by a significant margin, but the sample is small (N–9) which makes the generalization tenuous. Among the five categories of groups which account for about two-thirds of all groups, education ranks highest.

Turning to the *tactics* used by groups in the case study context, once again there is a clear first preference, amounting to one-third of the total, for enlisting the support of group members. The use of publicity campaigns and approaching the governmental elite ranks next, with only a minor difference between them. Confirmation of this valence is provided by the fact that using members of the group ranks first by an overwhelming minority,

45 per cent, as the tactic preferred when the groups are *reacting* to some governmental initiative. Writing members ranks a very poor second, at 16 per cent.

Regarding tactics in a more general context, according to their perceived effectiveness, we again find a decisive consensus (37 per cent) among the directors that a personal appeal to governmental elites by prominent members of their association is the most effective tactic available to them. In a sense, this stratagem may be regarded as a corollary of the consensus regarding enlisting the help of members as the foremost tactic of interest groups. The only challenger is testimony before special hearings, in which business groups rank dramatically higher than the other types of groups.

Finally, our data on lobbying and related activities indicate that about 40 per cent of all groups, led by business, social–recreational, and professional groups, have at one time or another employed a lobbyist or a lawyer to represent them before governmental elites. Over two-thirds of all directors indicated that they also performed this role at one time or another. Our conclusion, moreover, is that these analytical tools tend to underestimate the total amount of lobbying since they do not include the category of 'legal services' which can include a substantial amount of lobbying, along with its technical contributions.

These findings seem to provide empirical reinforcement for certain conclusions by John Porter regarding the persistence of religious influence in Canadian political culture and the extent to which 'there has been throughout the present century a close coalition between political leadership and the corporate world.'[1] Similarly germane are his observations that 'labour leaders rarely share in the informal aspects of the confraternity of power,' and 'that they do not, as we have seen, have the range of honorific roles that the corporate elite does. Nor does the power of labour leaders extend beyond their institutional roles.'[2] In effect, they play only a marginal role in the process of elite accommodation which often occurs through the integration of social, economic, and political roles in Canadian society.

In this context, we find that business ranks highest in the use of lobbying tactics, which require political sophistication, shared norms among the political elite and attending easy access. Business groups also rank above the mean, although not at the top, in access to the Cabinet, which also seems to reflect 'a close coalition' between such groups and the higher governmental elite. Directors of religious groups, meanwhile, rank direct

[1] *The Vertical Mosaic*, p. 539, pp. 511–19; pp. 532–40.
[2] *Ibid.*

access to the Cabinet (in both the case study and general contexts) as their most common stratagem, which suggests the continuity of religious influence in Canadian society. The tendency of labour groups to seek access mainly at the secondary level of power, i.e. the legislature, tends similarly to support the generalization that organized labour in Canada fails to enjoy the legitimacy imputed to other economic groups such as business, agriculture, and professional groups including law, medicine, and accountancy.[1]

Popular ambivalence about labour's socio-political role is apparent in Canadian Institute of Public Opinion national surveys, which show (1967) that only one-fifth of Canadians believe that unions *should* engage in political activities. Moreover, this proportion has ranged between 13 and 26 per cent for the past 20 years, and indeed, is slightly lower today than it was in 1950 and 1955. The pervasive conservatism of Canadian political opinion is perhaps evident (1967) in the fact that union members themselves share this view in almost the same proportion as other sectors of society, 60 *v.* 58 per cent.[2] Regarding popular appreciations of labour's political influence, the same surveys indicate that whereas an average of 60 per cent (during 1945–60) of Canadians believed that 'big business' had 'the most influence on the laws passed in this country', an average of only 22 per cent believed that labour has this level of influence; meanwhile, 36 per cent of a national sample (1972) believed that 'big labour' posed the greatest threat to Canada in years to come, compared with big business (27 per cent) and big government (only 22 per cent).[3]

Certain other factors in the Canadian political culture also account in part for labour's apparently limited political efficacy. In the larger sense of generalized attitudes toward work and the prestige attached to occupational roles, it is clear that those who work with their brains enjoy advantages over those who work with their hands.[4] Such an appreciation is likely to be reinforced by class differentiations in English and French-Canadian society, especially since limited educational opportunity, as well as the elitist classical college tradition in Quebec, have made such gradations highly visible. Undoubtedly, the expansion of university facilities during the 1960s will smooth out such differentiations, but this is an inter-generational process

[1] *Ibid.*, pp. 307–53.　　[2] See release dated July 26, 1967.
[3] *Ibid.*, dated November 30, 1955; March 12, 1960; July 26, 1967; July 22, 1972.
[4] Here, perhaps, is one of the few generalizations of social science which hold good across time and space. The prestige ranking of occupations has been found to be very similar throughout the world and the distinction between manual and non-manual work remains highly salient, see A. Inkeles and P. J. Rossi, 'National comparisons of occupational prestige' 61 *American Journal of Sociology* (January, 1956), pp. 329–39.

which has little affect upon existing political elites and their citizen contemporaries.

It is also possible that labour suffers from what Everett Hughes has called 'an internationalist taint'. Any latent anti-Americanism of Canadians may find labour's affiliation with huge American international unions another seductive reason for challenging its legitimacy and full participation in political affairs, as indicated in the national survey evidence cited earlier. Among the more interesting theoretical conclusions is that interest group effectiveness depends strongly upon a sympathetic political culture and rather subtle kinds of political resources such as popular legitimacy and social acceptance. As will be seen in the following chapter, Canadian labour's experience indicates that even generous shares of such hard resources as membership, income, and functional economic role are not sufficient to overcome the lack of such 'subjective' resources.

More broadly, our data underscore the generalizations advanced by several respondents that access among 'economic' groups in the Canadian political system tends to be somewhat polarized, with business, industrial, and financial interests tending to approach the Cabinet and higher bureaucratic sectors of the governmental elite, whereas labour relies to a much greater extent upon parliament, standing committees and party caucuses. Regarding labour's *general* pattern of access, it may be recalled, the Cabinet was a very poor third, only 4 per cent, compared with legislature and bureaucracy which ranked 37 *v.* 32 per cent, respectively. On the other hand, it should be noted that in the *case study* issue, directors of labour groups ranked the Cabinet first, with parliament a strong second. There is some indication, however, that the case study examples represent issues of critical significance to the groups concerned, in which recourse to the Cabinet becomes an effective but atypical tactic.

Having analysed the functional role of interest groups in the political system, the kinds of issues that mediate interaction between them and governmental elites, and their major tactics and targets, we turn next to the more difficult question of their relative effectiveness.

CHAPTER 7

THE POLITICAL EFFECTIVENESS
OF INTEREST GROUPS

We turn next to the difficult but vital question of the comparative effectiveness of Canadian interest groups in making good the claims they make upon government. The preceding analysis of their resources may be looked upon as providing a rough scale of their potential effectiveness, as a plausible hypothesis that those groups which possess most resources should generally prove to be most successful. Although a logical leap is often made from this premise to the proximate conclusion, we shall attempt to determine empirically under what conditions the assumption is valid. Several indexes will be used, including subjective perceptions of group effectiveness by political elites, the comparative utility of selected targets and tactics, and the amount of success groups experience in achieving their demands. Before turning to the data, however, some of the conditions of interest group competition and the difficulties of measuring effectiveness should be reviewed.

THE STRUCTURE OF INTEREST GROUP COMPETITION

Political effectiveness can be defined as the capacity of group elites to achieve their goals *vis-à-vis* government. Interest groups obviously have several goals, but we are concerned here with those that are 'political' in the sense that they require direct interaction with governmental elites to attain them. Our conception of effectiveness is similar to Max Weber's view of power as 'the chances of a man or a group of men to realize their own will in a communal action even against the resistance of others who are participating in the action.'[1] However, as the data will show, Weber's

[1] *From Max Weber: Essays in Sociology*, trans. and edited by H. H. Gerth and C. Wright Mills (New York: Oxford University Press, 1946), p. 180.

condition regarding *opposition* as a test of effectiveness needs to be qualified somewhat. We find, for example, that fully three-quarters of directors *disagree* with the view that 'MP's are [their] competitors in a struggle to shape government policy.' Moreover, regarding their perspective of their own environment, including that provided by other groups, 71 per cent of them maintain that they encounter no consistent opposition from any source.

The essential reason is the specialization existing among interest groups. As Durkheim saw, the growth of functional specialization enables men and groups to live cooperatively in a state of organic solidarity, as long as each confines his activities to his peculiar sector. Men, in effect, prosper more when they differ more. 'In the same city, different occupations can co-exist without being obliged mutually to destroy each other, for they pursue different objects. The soldier seeks military glory, the priest moral authority, the statesman power, the businessman riches, the scholar scientific renown. Each of them can attain his end without preventing the others from attaining theirs.' [1]

The milieu of interest groups is similarly constituted. In other than the abstract sense that governmental expenditures have some finite limit, they do not compete for the same resources. With many exceptions, lobbyists and bureaucrats are bound together by corporatist social norms and common functional orientations. Theirs seems less a Hobbesian world than a co-operative commonwealth, in which specific claims and common overarching norms make elite accommodation a seductive *modus vivendi*.

PROBLEMS OF MEASURING EFFECTIVENESS

'Effectiveness' is conceptualized here as the quality of being able to bring power to bear upon objects, to effect one's will in the political arena. Less abstractly, it relates to the relative capacity of interest group directors to achieve their collective goals. The interest group process, in effect, is essentially one of making demands upon government (and the public) and effectiveness refers to the ability of groups to make such demands good. Presumably, this capacity is associated with the political resources

[1] *The Division of Labour in Society* (New York: Free Press, 1964 ed.), p. 267, Durkheim apparently drew some of his analysis from the animal world. Citing Darwin, he writes of a piece of turf which nourished 'twenty species of plants belonging to eighteen genera and eight classes'. Again, 'on an oak tree, there were found two hundred species of insects...some feed upon the fruit of the tree, others on the leaves, others on the bark and roots.' pp. 266-7.

possessed by any given group. Since resources are unequally distributed, we assume that effectiveness will also vary along a continuum, ranging from relatively high to relatively low.

Effectiveness is operationalized in several ways. Broadly and over-simply, we may distinguish between 'objective', behavioural and 'subjective', attitudinal indexes. The former derive from the direct personal experience of the political actors, whereas the latter reflect symbolic, 'reputational' judgments, usually acquired over a long time through an amalgam of *ad hoc*, impressionistic, ideologically-shaped perceptions of the behaviour and legitimacy of such groups. Although this distinction is clearly overdrawn, it rests upon such differences as that between directly observed and hearsay evidence in jurisprudence. Our major objective instrument is the outcomes realized in the case study issues. Another crucial behavioural index is the extent to which directors believe they have been able to influence governmental elites through lobbying. Yet another behavioural index is the effectiveness attributed to interest groups by bureaucrats, not in a case study context, but regarding the relative efficacy of those groups with whom they interact most frequently. Finally, various subjective indexes are available, including the perceptions that political elites have of the relative capacity of various types of groups to effect their will *vis-à-vis* government.

As always, however, conceptual elegance is clouded by empirical untidiness. Measuring effectiveness in any context is probably one of the most difficult social science enterprises.

A review of the case study procedure indicates some of these difficulties. Our interviews with directors and bureaucrats include a case study regarding a specific demand, either pressed by an interest group or received by a department from such a group. Almost 500 cases were compiled, most of which were recorded for detailed analysis.[1] The information included the substance of the issue, the level of government involved, major targets and methods used by the group, the access and legitimacy accorded the groups by bureaucrats, the point in the political system at which access was made, and whether the issue involved retaining the *status quo* or effecting change. Regarding spatial distribution of the cases, one-third of them involved the provincial level only, another one-fifth involved the federal level, 12 per cent occurred at the local level, while the remainder were

---

[1] Despite some initial concern that respondents might resist recording the case study, we received excellent cooperation. Although respondents were encouraged to describe the case in their own words, we structured the discussion to some extent by including several specific items which provided a basis for systematic comparison.

scattered about fairly evenly among local–provincial, provincial–federal, local–provincial–federal, international, and intra-association levels.

Substance of the issues ranged similarly, with the largest proportion (70 per cent) involving legislation, administrative regulation, and intra-organizational policy and procedures. Each case includes judgments made by a director or a bureaucrat as to the degree of success achieved in the issue. Such information is very useful, permitting correlations of many kinds and providing our major operational definition and test of political effectiveness. But it also has a basic, perhaps inevitable, weakness: the comparability of the data is compromised by the fact that the difficulty of achieving group goals varies to some unknown extent. As a result, one interest group may be ranked 'completely successful' on an easy-to-achieve objective, while another will be ranked 'partially successful' on a difficult issue, with attending distortion of the effectiveness index.

A related problem is that although our case studies were randomly selected by respondents, there may have been a tendency for some directors, motivated by ego-involvement or the human desire to repress failure, to select only cases in which their goal was achieved.[1] Here, as elsewhere, we must rely to some extent on the random distribution and large size of our sample to overcome any such bias.

Similar observations must be made about our use of subjective perceptions of political elites as a basis for making judgments about relative effectiveness. Such a departure can be justified in two ways. The first is to acknowledge at the outset that such judgments are subjective, but to argue that human behaviour is often determined by such premises. In effect, whether such perceptions are 'objectively' accurate is less significant than the fact that one often assumes they are, and acts accordingly. If a certain category of interest group is thought to be powerful by governmental elites, they will often act accordingly, in a classic example of the self-fulfilling prophecy. The second defense is to argue that the considered judgment of political elites, who interact frequently with a range of interest groups is really more than an impressionistic observation. If, as one expects, we find an overwhelming consensus among the political elite regarding the effectiveness of selected interest groups, we may have one useful basis for measuring this admittedly elusive quality.

Other measurement difficulties relate to our use of combinations of different indicators to produce a scale of effectiveness for types of groups.

---

[1] Fortunately, as will be shown, this does not seem to have occurred, since the case outcomes are distributed along the entire effectiveness scale.

Should, for example, a subjective judgment regarding the effectiveness or 'power' of a group by a legislator or bureaucrat be weighted equally with an experiential index based upon its success in attaining a specific demand? Even if such indexes are presented separately, the problem of weighting them remains. There is, moreover, an understandable tendency for MP's and bureaucrats to attribute the greatest effectiveness to those groups with which they have the most frequent interaction, and which are most significant to them in substantive terms. As noted elsewhere, bureaucratic elites tend to develop clientele groups based in part upon such substantive cohesion. Such groups may as a result seem to be very effective when, in fact, they are merely better known or more germane to the political interests of the elites concerned.

Another aspect of effectiveness which requires attention is the common view that the 'really effective' lobbying in Canadian politics is done, as an Ottawa director put it, 'by individuals of stature who are representative of capital and who are more influential than the orthodox organizations of private enterprise.' Prestigeful groups, he insisted, are not always effective as interest groups, but rather through 'personal friendships and connections with ministers and top civil-servants.' This observation is sometimes accompanied, as it was in this case, by the judgment that such behaviour is often covert and hence impossible to document systematically.

Several comments may be made regarding this perspective. In some cases, of course, it reflects an intellectual conviction that social behaviour is generally too variable and recondite to lend itself to empirical analysis, an observation which remains unproved. One rebuttal is implicit, it seems, in our earlier finding that 'representations by *prominent members* of our groups to government' was ranked first by the largest proportion (one-third) of directors as their single most effective political tactic. Similarly, both federal and provincial civil servants (N–214) agree that 'personal contacts with Cabinet members and higher civil servants' are the most effective methods used by the group representatives with whom they interact. This evidence suggests that personal lobbying commonly occurs in the specific context of interest group demands and is symbiotically related to their general political behaviour. 'Individual persons of stature' are indeed influential, but they usually exert such influence on behalf of and at the inspiration of some interest group.

Although somewhat difficult to maintain given the broad range of case study issues, a broad distinction may be suggested between the formative stage of policy issues and their implementation, with 'personal negotiations' probably tending to focus on the former. If some of our respondents are correct, business, industrial, and financial issues are especially likely to be the subject of personal negotiations between private and ministerial elites. The scope of this judgment is too broad, however, to be very helpful. Our case studies suggest that such negotiations sometimes occur in areas of defense spending, including shipbuilding and aircraft production, where the industries concerned are few in number, the funds involved are very large, and employment in one or a few ridings will be sharply affected by an adverse decision. In such cases, the synthesis of political and economic benefits encourages accommodation, while providing government an edge in the negotiations because the criteria for defense spending may be easily defined in terms of the over-riding national interest, if such becomes necessary. On the other hand, a great deal of such interaction occurs at the bureaucratic level, particularly regarding regulatory administration, in which the focus is often quite specific.

PERCEPTIONS OF POLITICAL EFFECTIVENESS

We consider first subjective perceptions of interest group effectiveness by MP's and directors. Here, as noted earlier, the weight one will give such judgments varies, but it may be well to remember that these are the considered opinions of sophisticated political practitioners, most of whom deal with interest groups on a sustained basis. Theirs is an expert judgment, in the usual sense of the term. However, not all of them interact with a cross-section of such groups, given the functional specificity emphasized earlier. It is also apparent that political ideology shapes such perceptions. In order to gain as precise a judgment as possible, each respondent was asked to name specific associations, rather than a general interest area. This proved difficult, since some respondents preferred not to name specific groups. Moreover, however positive they were that 'labour', 'business', 'high finance', or 'religious groups' were decisive, some found it difficult to name a specific association.

Beginning with the ranking of the general areas, precisely 50 per cent of Cabinet members (*N*–42) maintain that labour is the most effective interest group. Two-thirds of back-benchers conclude that labour and business–industry are *equally* powerful, while one-third of directors also name labour first, followed closely by business–industry. At the second level of effectiveness, ministers rank agriculture first while back-benchers and directors choose business–industry. At the third level, ministers rank business–industry first; back-benchers cite agriculture; and directors again rank business–industry. However, whereas the other two ranking groups are closely matched, agriculture is a very poor third. The consensus, it seems, is that labour is the most powerful interest group in Canada, with business–industry a strong challenger.

It is interesting that religious groups are ranked as the first choice, although narrowly, above professional groups, fraternal groups, and the mass media by interest group directors, although not by MP's or ministers. Indeed, among 14 categories of groups, religious associations rank third, following labour and business–industry. Further analysis reveals that 60 per cent of those directors ranking religious interests so high are from the Toronto area. This finding, parenthetically, is consistent with the earlier point that religious leaders are most likely to interact with Cabinet members.

Regarding specific groups in the labour area, the Canadian Labour Congress, the CSN, and the CNTU are most frequently cited. In the business–industry category, the Canadian Association of Manufacturers and Chambers of Commerce are typically mentioned, while among agriculture groups the Canadian Federation of Agriculture, the *Union Catholique des Cultivateurs* and the Ontario and British Columbia Federations of Agriculture are most frequently listed. The Canadian Medical Association and the Law Societies are often cited among professional groups. Among religious groups, the Catholic Church and the United Church are named most frequently by our respondents.

We indicated that these are subjective perceptions of effectiveness, a fact that is worth underscoring. Indeed, such judgments sometimes seem to be a reflection of political ideology as much as a disinterested appraisal of the groups concerned. For example, the largest proportion of business directors (one-third) ranked labour groups as the 'most powerful' in Canada, while the largest proportion of labour directors (54 per cent) ranked business groups as most powerful. It is almost axiomatic that individuals over-estimate the influence of those interest groups which seem most inapposite to their own normative preferences. Since the overwhelming majority of our respondents enjoy advantaged social positions, it is perhaps not surprising that labour would tend to be cited as the most powerful interest group. On the other hand, a similar tendency is apparent on the part of NDP members to regard business–industrial groups and the financial community as being most powerful.

Other evidence suggests, as we have indicated, that labour is somewhat less effective than these judgments suggest. One reason is the marginal legitimation it has in a putatively 'free-enterprise' society. Another is the fact that labour is not united in a way that could make its electoral power truly effective. As the Canadian Public Opinion polls indicate, most Canadians, including union members, believe that unions should not engage in political action. Moreover, it is clear that labour leaders do not receive the rewards that membership in their institutional power structures secures for elites in business and education and government. As John Porter shows, they are rarely appointed to prestigeful positions on the boards of universities or hospitals or foundations; they are not brought into the elite club system, nor are they given honourific political positions, such as a seat in the Senate. These conditions rest in part upon the hierarchical and anti-egalitarian residues in Canadian political culture and political conservatism, as traced in our introductory chapters.

More important, our own evidence indicates that labour does not usually rank high on the effectivness scale. If, for example, the Cabinet is the centre of formal power in the Canadian political system and access to it a symbol of legitimation, labour does not enjoy such largesse, since as we have seen, it generally tends to seek access at the back-bencher level. Moreover, labour's record as measured by its success in the case study issues indicates that her effectivness is not impressive compared with business and professional groups. When set against her copious resources in numbers and income, such findings suggest that interest group power in Canada rests in considerable measure upon subjective kinds of political resources, some of which are beyond the control of group directors. Among these seems to be a condition of public legitimation which provides an affirmative basis upon which an interest group can base its political claims. Groups that lack this resource may find that political elites are under little compulsion to honour their claims since they are not reinforced by pervasive societal support potentially demonstrable in the form of electoral sanctions.

Symbolic of the lack of such an affirmative social base is the fact that restrictive labour legislation has been passed recently in Ontario and British Columbia; that British Columbia and Ontario have no independent Departments of Labour, which are shared instead with other substantive areas; and that the NDP's financial reliance upon labour unions is often deplored, whereas the equally great reliance of the two major parties upon business and industry is generally accepted. Further evidence of labour's precarious legitimacy is seen in the fact that labour directors, compared with those in other areas, report a lower rate of felt approval in their interaction with

MP's. Indeed, the variation between labour and other groups is dramatic, with only 8 per cent ranking 'high', compared with 23 per cent for business and 17 per cent for welfare. Meanwhile, at the 'low' level, labour ranks highest with 30 per cent, compared with business at 15 per cent. That such perceptions are reciprocal is suggested by the fact that the same ranking exists regarding *directors'* imputations of legitimacy to MP's: labour is again low, with only 31 per cent indicating a high level of trust, followed by welfare at 43 per cent, with business significantly higher at 61 per cent.

The extent to which members are identified with association goals also explains some of the variation in effectiveness. According to their directors, 47 per cent of welfare groups and 41 per cent of business, compared with only 21 per cent of labour, have members who are 'intensely' committed to such goals and policies.

Another factor in effectiveness is probably the extent to which directors indicate that political action is among the proximate goals and services of their associations. If social or intra-organizational goals have top priority, interactions with governmental elites will necessarily be minimal. The most useful index here is probably the *amount of time* spent by the director in political interaction. This is another version of 'access' as considered earlier. Our items include a 'job analysis' of the director's role, which determines the allocation of his work-time among several activities, including 'services to members', internal administration, etc. A comparative analysis of these responses enables us to scale directors, i.e. associations, accordingly. We assume that those directors who spend most time on political interactions will probably be most effective. Political interaction is defined here as 'face-to-face contacts with MP's and civil servants.' Cross-tabulations

TABLE 7-1 *Distribution of interest group directors' work time*

Activity	Per cent spent on each activity			None
	10% 20% 30%	40% 50% 60%	70% 80% 90%	
Internal admin.	40	33	15	12
Service to members	40	33	10	17
Drafting speeches, public rels., etc.	40	2	1	57
Interaction: civil servants	30	1	1	68
Interaction: MP's	17	1	—	82

between such data and more precise indexes of demonstrated effectiveness will permit us to test such hypotheses. Table 7–1 presents the distribution among all directors.

Political interaction is obviously a marginal activity for the majority of directors, only 30 and 17 per cent of whom spend as much as one-third of their time, respectively, on interaction with civil servants and legislators. Three-fourths, however, spend over half their time on internal administration and services for their members. Public relations activity, which probably includes considerable indirect lobbying, is also somewhat more frequent than interaction with governmental elites. That interaction is almost twice as high for bureaucrats as for MP's is consistent with the earlier finding that the bureaucracy is the major general interest group target. Assuming that the time spent in political activity is a necessary condition of effectiveness, we next analyse which groups are included among those whose directors spend the most time interacting with MP's and bureaucrats. Here, it is perhaps not surprising that business, welfare, and labour groups rank highest, in that order.

Closely allied with time spent in political interaction as a criterion is the priority which interest groups ascribe to 'influencing government'. Our data include an item which asks directors to rank the major policy goals of their associations. Using the 190 groups who had employed lobbyists in the case study issue and presenting only the distribution for the first-named goal, we find the following scale of political orientation: business groups are first with 30 per cent; welfare groups next with 22 per cent; professional and educational groups follow with 14 per cent each; and labour is last with 10 per cent. When this ranking is compared with related variables, some interesting continuities appear. For example, when effectiveness in the case study is analysed (Table 7–15), the first three groups rank together in the upper ranges of the scale and labour again ranks lowest; again, when the frequency with which lobbyists are used in the case study is checked, business and welfare rank first and second, but labour is third, followed by professional and educational groups. In effect, the same groups rank similarly on all three variables.

These data narrow sharply the total universe of politically active groups and provide a better basis for the comparative analysis of effectiveness. Clearly, groups whose directors engage in little or no interaction with governmental elites are unlikely to be politically effective. At the same time, they provide a useful foil against which to set the some one-quarter of interest groups that are most active.

POLITICAL ACTIVISM AND INTEREST GROUP EFFECTIVENESS

We turn next to the task of determining any differences between politically active groups and the majority who are only peripherally involved in direct political action. Perhaps the best empirical basis for differentiating groups on this dimension is the amount of personal interaction between directors and members of the governmental elite. In the tables immediately following, we have combined directors' interaction with MP's and bureaucrats, designating 'high' interaction as that occurring at the 'frequently' level; 'medium' at the 'occasionally' level; and 'low' at the 'seldom' or 'rarely' level. An index of organizational resources, including such variables as size of budget and membership, SES of members, full-time employees and age, is used as a control. Table 7-2 presents the distribution.

Comparing the 'high' cells, we find the expected distribution, with the highest proportion (39 per cent) of those who rank high on effectiveness appearing in the 'high' category on activism and resources. Turning to the 'low' row on effectiveness, and comparing it with the 'high' columns on activism and resources, we find the expected gradient across the table: the proportion of those who rank low on effectiveness increases steadily as resources and activism decrease. Meanwhile, the largest proportions of those who are low on both activism and resources tend, as expected, to appear in the medium–low and low–low cells on effectiveness. On the whole, however, the relationship is not as strong or as regular as one would expect.

We have some fragmentary evidence that resourceful directors account for more of the variation in group effectiveness than the socioeconomic

TABLE 7-2 *Political activism, group effectiveness, and organizational resources*

	Political activism								
	High (118)			Medium (77)			Low (83)		
	Political resources of organization								
Effectiveness[a]	High	Medium	Low	High	Medium	Low	High	Medium	Low
	%	%	%	%	%	%	%	%	%
High	39	44	27	36	33	25	23	13	26
Medium	33	28	27	24	33	25	35	40	33
Low	27	37	47	39	33	50	42	47	41

X^2 = not significant of .05 K's tau B = $+.04$
[a]Effectiveness is defined here by the outcomes in the case study issue.

resources of the organization. A test of this proposition is presented in Table 7-3 which compares political activism and effectiveness, using the same indexes and controlling for directors' resources with an index based upon five items, experience, SES, memberships in voluntary groups, perceived identification of members with group objectives, and perceived legitimacy imputed to group political activity by legislators.

The distribution is irregular and the relationship not as strong as expected. There is only a slight tendency for the expected relationship to appear, as seen in the fact that one-third of those who rank high on both activism and resources also rank high on effectiveness, compared with 30 per cent of those at the low levels on these properties. At the low levels of effectiveness, the proportion of those who are low on effectiveness increases linearly as one looks across the table, with almost 70 per cent of those who are low on activism and resources also ranking low on effectiveness. Once again, however, the distribution is curvilinear and hardly supportive of the logically unassailable proposition that directors' resources and activism are positively related to group effectiveness.

Given these inconclusive results, it seems worthwhile to try one other analysis, using a different measure of effectiveness, while retaining the other indexes. Here, effectiveness is defined according to the directors' success in influencing the governmental elite through direct persuasion (see Table 7-4).

The relationship is not significant but positive, although quite irregular. Two-thirds of those who are high on both activism and resources (as well as those at the high–medium level) appear in the high cell on effectiveness, compared with just under one-fifth of directors who rank low on these

TABLE 7-3 *Political activism, directors' resources and group effectiveness*

	Political activism								
	High (105)			Medium (64)			Low (76)		
	Political resources of director								
Effectiveness[a]	High	Medium	Low	High	Medium	Low	High	Medium	Low
	%	%	%	%	%	%	%	%	%
High	33	18	30	42	44	25	30	12	25
Medium	35	36	46	15	22	50	27	41	6
Low	32	46	25	42	33	25	43	46	69

X^2 = not significant at .05 K's tau B = +.07
[a] Defined again by case outcomes.

182

TABLE 7-4   *Political activism, directors' resources and group effectiveness*

Effectiveness[a]	Political activism High (81)			Medium (47)			Low (59)		
	Directors' resources								
	High	Medium	Low	High	Medium	Low	High	Medium	Low
	%	%	%	%	%	%	%	%	%
High	68	67	36	36	17	23	16	—	19
Medium	28	19	43	55	67	69	28	56	56
Low	4	14	21	9	17	8	56	44	25

X^2 = significant at .05 K's tau $B = +.06$
[a] Defined by success of directors' lobbying efforts.

resources. The combined effect of resources and frequent contact, in sum, becomes decisive only when effectiveness is measured by the index of directors' persuasiveness, contrasted with the earlier use of the index based upon case study outcomes.

Since the use of three indexes causes so much attrition of cases, it seems useful next to discuss selected differences among the three group categories using the entire sample. The N's here are, high (153), medium (215), and low (253), again determined by their combined rates of interaction with MP's and bureaucrats.

SELECTED CORRELATES OF POLITICAL ACTIVISM

Political activism, interestingly, varies considerably according to area. Ottawa and Ontario have equal proportions (30 per cent) of the most active category (154), while Quebec has the lowest proportion of such groups. Notable differences also appear regarding directors' salaries, where those groups ranking high on political activism account for one-third of all salaries above $15,000, compared with 21 per cent and 14 per cent for the medium and low groups, respectively. Some tendency exists, too, for less active groups to rely more upon part-time voluntary directors, which is not unexpected. A somewhat larger proportion of highly active groups also cites 'helping government make wise policies' as their first policy goal, compared with the other two categories. Regarding the goals of members, a similar association appears, with three times as large a proportion of highly actives electing 'getting a better chance to express their will to government', compared with less active groups.

A substantial difference emerges when we consider the tactics ranked first in terms of *general* effectiveness where 40 per cent of the most active groups rank 'personal representations to government by prominent members' first, compared with only one-quarter and one-fifth respectively of the two other categories. Differences are also found regarding major targets, with highly active directors focussing more frequently upon bureaucrats than MP's, contrasted with their less active peers. Also, directors of active groups spend relatively more time in public relations and related activities directed toward the public, in what we have called indirect efforts to influence government policy. Political activism is also positively related to issue areas and success enjoyed in them; a substantially higher proportion of directors of the most active groups focus more successfully upon getting favourable legislation passed, compared with the others.

One of the most striking differences finds highly active groups considerably more likely than the others (one-fifth $v.$ only 4 per cent) to rank testifying at hearings as the most important service they provide for legislators. It will be recalled that Ottawa MP's ranked testifying at such hearings as the single most effective tactic of interest groups. Another related difference concerns directors' interactions with bureaucrats, where they rank serving on departmental committees higher than the other two categories. This is not unexpected, since only highly visible, well-legitimated clientele groups would be likely to have this close a relationship with government agencies.

Regarding self-perceptions of their major role, politically active directors are more likely to stress their function as a link 'between the organization and outsiders upon whom they depend to get things done', compared with the other two types.

A striking variation appears when political effectiveness is measured by the directors' judgments as to how often they have been able to persuade MP's and bureaucrats to come completely around to their own point of view through lobbying. Combining the two targets, we find that 44 per cent of the most active directors claim this high level of influence, compared with 33 per cent of the 'medium', and only 12 per cent of the 'low' group.

Perceptions of citizen knowledge and legitimation of interest groups also vary substantially among the three categories, with the most highly active directors being the most negative in both contexts. Over four-fifths of them believe that the ordinary citizen knows little about interest groups, compared with an average of 69 per cent among the two other groups. Again, one-half of them believe that the average man thinks interest groups have too much influence upon government policies, compared with just over one-third of their colleagues.

Similar differences appear regarding trust of governmental elites, which is expected in terms of interaction theory. Fully two-thirds of the highly active group indicate a high level of trust, compared with just over one-half and only one-third of the medium and low groups. Since the three groups were initially parcelled out on the basis of frequency of contact with governmental elites, we have here two elements of the interaction syndrome. The findings indicate, as expected, that highly political directors contact other segments of the political elite more frequently and trust them more completely than their less active brethren. Following the theory, we should expect these variations to be reflected in higher levels of political effectiveness. Using the case study outcomes as our index of effectiveness, we do indeed find the expected gradient: among the most active group, 47 per cent were completely or mainly successful, compared with 42 per cent among the medium group, and only 32 per cent among the least active.

The correlates of political activism should include some variation regarding the importance of the services that directors provide for governmental elites. Since they are the result of direct political interaction, such services may be useful in explaining variations in effectiveness among the three groups. Some kind of 'equalizer effect' may be at work, which might explain the unexpected fact that effectiveness is not very highly associated with hard resources. This may be because effective directors focus upon highly rewarding activities.

Following this path, we first determine what the most valuable service provided by directors is, by analysing the responses of MP's to this item. This reveals that the largest single proportion, one-fifth, ranks *receiving information on pending legislation* as the most important interest group service. We thus expect that the most active directors will spend somewhat more time on this activity than their less active colleagues. Table 7-5 tests the proposition.

The distribution strongly and significantly supports the proposition that politically-active directors, to a much greater extent than their less active colleagues, focus on the service regarded as most salient by MP's. Only 12 per cent of highly active directors rank low on this activity, compared with almost 80 per cent of those who rank low on activism. A glance at the high and low rows indicates the nice linearity of the distribution, which accounts for the highly significant X^2. The small N's in the table are an indication of the limited contact between directors and MP's on this dimension.

TABLE 7-5   *Association between political activism and directors' focus on service to legislators*

Information on legislation	Political activism			
	High (9)	Medium (37)	Low (60)	
	%	%	%	
High	45	22	12	(19)
Medium	11	30	10	(18)
Low	44	49	78	(69)

$X^2 = .001$ K's tau $B = .30$ Gamma $= .49$

Some further analysis (not shown here) indicates that directors at the 'medium' level spend the most time informing MP's about public opinion in ridings. Some continuity across the three categories exists, however, in that all of them spend the least effort on providing legislative support, in part, no doubt, because the parliamentary system does not typically provide for effective service in this area, given the limited influence of most back-benchers.

DISCONTINUITIES AMONG HIGHLY ACTIVE AND LESS ACTIVE
INTEREST GROUP DIRECTORS

Since this analysis of the political behaviour of interest groups and their directors has ranged widely, it may be useful to summarize the major differences found between the some one-quarter of all groups that are highly active politically and the remainder who are less so. The largest proportions of highly active groups are found in Ottawa and Ontario. Their directors tend to receive higher salaries on the average, although this may reflect mainly the comparative affluence of the two areas. Their favorite tactic is more likely to consist of 'personal representations by prominent members' to governmental elites. Meanwhile, their directors are more oriented toward the bureaucratic arena than their less active colleagues. Substantive differences also appear, with active directors more often concerned with getting legislation passed than with other activities. Testifying at hearings is ranked higher as the most important service they provide for MP's, compared with less active groups. Such directors are more likely to appear on departmental advisory committees. More importantly, they are more confident that they have been able to persuade legislators to come round to their own point of view. Somewhat unexpectedly, they have a less sanguine view of the average citizen's knowledge and his legitimation of interest groups. Meanwhile, a substantially larger proportion have a high degree of trust in governmental elites. Finally, they are more selective in the services they provide legislators, tending to focus mainly upon giving them information on bills, an activity which the latter value most highly.

BUREAUCRATIC PERCEPTIONS OF INTEREST GROUP EFFECTIVENESS

Next, we attempt to test comparative group effectiveness as perceived by the senior bureaucrats who interact with them on a sustained basis. Several indexes are available for this purpose. Each official, it will be recalled, was asked to present a 'significant' case involving one of the three or four interest groups having the most interaction with his department. Here again, the problem of precarious comparability arises in that interest groups necessarily strive for different goals, some of which are more difficult to achieve than others. Presumably, only a random sample of typical group decisions taken over a period of time would enable one to overcome this problem. Such a panel of decisions could be weighted according to difficulty by disinterested judges, to provide a firmer basis for determining relative group effectiveness. Since our resources did not permit this kind of intensive analysis, we must rely upon other alternatives, including the somewhat crude data provided by the case study and the general perceptions of higher civil servants.

With the possible exception of the group's perceived achievement of goals in the case study, these criteria depend upon the evaluations of participant observers. How much weight one attributes to such evidence is probably a matter of methodological fastidiousness and personal temperament. Ideally, of course, one should have some rigorous, independent measure of effectiveness, such as the case study outcomes attempt to provide, which can be set against various characteristics of groups to differentiate them. On the other hand, in an imperfect world, one might conclude that the evidence presented here is comparable to that used, for example, in a court of law where, if a witness can verify his facts by sense perception, credibility is granted. Thus our evidence is based upon the judgments of experts in their field, many of whom have had years of experience with the interest groups and lobbyists they are evaluating.

Despite its limitations, the case study issue is probably the best measure we have of group effectiveness. It provides an independent criterion and an empirical base upon which officials can make a judgment from their direct experience. It also reveals the closeness of the relationship between an agency and its major clientele groups, which is one vital aspect of effectiveness in the sense that a group must be accepted by the bureaucracy as a legitimate representative in order to enjoy the access and status upon which effectiveness partially depends. The case study data include a scale which measures the quality of group–agency interaction. The data show that one-quarter of the entire sample maintains that clientele groups 'are almost an integral part of the day-to-day activity of the department'. Provincial bureaucracies, moreover, are more than twice as likely as federal to interact at this level, 31 per cent *v.* 14. Another one-third indicate that 'their assumed reaction to what we do is usually taken into account during policy making'. As suggested earlier, these two conditions may be regarded as roughly analogous to the 'negotiation' (veto power) and 'consultation' levels of interest group–governmental interaction. Another 30 per cent affirm that clientele groups are 'only one of many factors that impinge upon our decisions'. Only one-tenth maintain that such groups 'have little or no effect upon our decisions'. These data are also useful in suggesting which agencies maintain the most intimate consultative relations with private groups. When this is analysed, we find that they exist mainly in the areas of business–industry (30 per cent), with the remainder scattered about among other agencies.

CORRELATES OF BUREAUCRATIC PERCEPTIONS OF EFFECTIVENESS

Interaction theory, as noted, holds that legitimacy is related to effectiveness as a by-product of shared activities. The strength of this relationship is apparent in Table 7-6, which indicates that fully two-thirds of all officials rank groups as either high or medium on effectiveness, on the basis of a specific, personal interaction. Here we find a nice linear association between legitimacy and effectiveness, with almost 90 per cent of the sample ascribing either a high or a moderate degree of trust to the groups cited in their case study issue as being directly involved in departmental affairs. The data provide strong evidence of the close normative ties between these two segments of the political elite.

Directly related to legitimacy and effectiveness, according to interaction theory, is the degree of contact between members of these elites. Indeed, from the earlier findings regarding legislators and directors, we may find this to be the strongest part of the interaction chain. Table 7-7 tests this hypothesis.

It should be noted that effectiveness is defined here by the *general* significance attributed to interest groups by officials. The association is positive

TABLE 7-6 *Association between effectiveness and legitimacy, case study*

Legitimacy[a]	Effectiveness			
	High	Medium	Low	
	%	%	%	
High	51	22	5	(82)
Medium	31	45	5	(76)
Low	18	33	90	(19)
	(60)	(60)	(57)	(177)

X^2 = significant at .001 K's tau B = .39
Gamma = .59
[a] 'Legitimacy' is defined by responses to the following item: 'How legitimate do you feel this particular group's position on this issue was, e.g. were its objectives and methods reasonable and appropriate?'

and significant, indicating again the strength of the two variables in shaping elite accommodation. Differences in perceived effectiveness are nicely linear in the expected direction across the high and low levels of effectiveness. It is also noteworthy that the global distribution is very strongly linear, with the strongest associations occurring in every case at the assumed level of effectiveness.

Another potential correlate of effectiveness is available in the relationship between the overall significance that officials attribute to interest groups in departmental policy-making and their perception of the general importance of the rule of interest groups. In effect, as Table 7-8 shows, this close relationship is characteristic not only of the case study experience, which

TABLE 7-7 *Association between interaction and effectiveness of interest groups in departmental policy-making*

Effectiveness	Frequency of interaction				
	High	Medium	Medium Low	Low	
	%	%	%	%	
High	34	26	21	11	(51)
Medium	57	59	56	36	(108)
Low	9	15	23	53	(35)
	(70)	(62)	(43)	(19)	(194)

X^2 = significant at .01 K's tau C = .23   Gamma = .36

may have been atypical, but also of the over-all behaviour of officials. The strength of this essentially functional relationship was demonstrated a moment ago in the relationship between legitimacy and effectiveness. One might speculate from this that interaction theory may prove more applicable to bureaucratic-interest group relations than to those of MP's. Table 7-8 presents the distribution.

Here again, a clear positive association is evident between the general perceptions bureaucrats have of interest group effectiveness and the strength of the role imputed to the major groups with which a department interacts on a functional basis.

An additional measure of effectiveness is provided by responses to the following item: 'What was the final *outcome* regarding this case; did the group concerned achieve its major goal?' Since officials were asked this question as an integral part of their analysis of a case study issue from their own experience, we have considerable confidence in these data. Because industrial groups proved to be so important and numerous (*N*–62), we have separated them from business groups with whom they have been included elsewhere. The following distribution occurs for the 'completely successful level' only (*N*–81): industry, 37 per cent; professional, 18; business, 12; intergovernmental relations, 12; labour, 8; welfare, 4; education, 3; agriculture, 3; and ethnic, 2. Industrial groups clearly dominate the effectiveness spectrum, as measured here.

Regarding specific groups, those in transportation and the construction industry ranked highest in nominations. Professional associations rank second, and among them medical, engineering, and teachers' groups are

TABLE 7-8   *Association between perceived signifi-cance of groups and their role in departmental policy-making*

| Significance of role | Perceived significance of interest groups | | | |
	High	Medium	Low	
	%	%	%	
High	38	21	24	(50)
Medium	42	36	18	(66)
Low	20	43	58	(75)
	(50)	(108)	(33)	(191)

X^2 = significant at .01 K's tau B = .21
Gamma = .34

TABLE 7-9   *Association between interaction and effectiveness*

	Frequency of interaction		
Effectiveness	High	Medium	Low
	%	%	%
High	59	8	8	(111)
Medium	26	55	38	(89)
Low	15	37	55	(194)
	(66)	(62)	(66)	

X^2 = significant at .001 K's tau C = .41
Gamma = .58

ranked highest in effectiveness. Business and intergovernmental organizations follow, with the Canadian Manufacturers Association, school boards, and municipal associations most frequently cited. Although labour's position below the sample mean is not unexpected, it is surprising to find welfare ranked so low, given its strong position using other criteria of effectiveness. Both labour and welfare have rather small N's, which suggests that they are under-represented in this particular subsample.

Our final and most dramatic example of interest group effectiveness *vis-à-vis* the bureaucracy turns again to the item concerning the extent to which officials indicate that they have been influenced by interest group agents at one time or another during their experience. We are anticipating our later analysis of interaction theory in presenting these data, but they are also relevant in the context of effectiveness. The criterion used here involves situations in which officials were influenced to the extent of altering their own position on an issue, using an unweighted index (see Table 7-9).

The data reveal that interaction is very strongly and positively associated with the tendency to be influenced by interest group representatives. The striking fact here, in addition to the impressive extent to which those who rank high on interaction also rank high on experienced influence (59 per cent), is the linearity of the distribution. In sum, the data presented in this section provide considerable support for the judgment that those directors who are politically active to the extent of making frequent representations to the bureaucratic elite enjoy a high level of effectiveness.

EFFECTIVENESS OF MAJOR TARGETS AND TACTICS

Our data include the relative effectiveness of the methods and the targets used by interest groups in their interactions with government. Once again, two bases of analysis are used: one involving group experience in the case study issue and the other their general patterns of interaction. Our procedure is to order all groups according to the success or failure achieved in the case study issue, and to use this as the bench-mark for determining the relative effectiveness of their targets and tactics. Most interest groups turned to the Cabinet as their primary target in the case study. Indeed, among those groups which employed lobbyists to represent them in the issue, fully 40 per cent focussed on the Cabinet. (The next target, civil servants, accounted for only 20 per cent). However, as Table 7-10 indicates, this did not always prove to be the most effective stratagem.

The largest proportion of successful groups, when all types of issues are combined, interacted with the bureaucracy, with the Cabinet and executive assistants tied for second. However, looking only at *frequency* of interaction, it is clear that the Cabinet is the preferred point of access. Whether it is also the most productive is problematic, by this measure, at least. Since executive assistants are often contacted as a result of a group's failure to secure an appointment with a minister, one may want to combine these two categories, which would, of course, increase the Cabinet's margin as the focal point of group access. These findings, in sum, do not sustain the common conclusion that access to the Cabinet is often difficult and, by implication, that interest group elites who penetrate at this level, should have a high probability of success. Indeed (not shown in Table 7-10), if one uses only the highest level of achieved success as a criterion, the bureaucracy's advantage is even more significant, 32 per cent *v.* 21.

Since a very high proportion of these issues involved group attempts to bring about change, while some of them also involved conflict, the fact that virtually one-half of the groups experienced a high level of success is perhaps another fragmentary bit of evidence regarding their effectiveness. On the other hand, if effectiveness is set aside and *access* is defined as the

TABLE 7-10   *Association between group effectiveness and target, case study*

Effectiveness	Bureaucracy	Cabinet	Exec. Asst.	Legislature	Other	
	%	%	%	%	%	
High	54	46	47	41	56	(202)
Low	31	28	53	42	33	(134)
Issue pending	15	26	—	17	11	(76)
	(106)	(160)	(17)	(59)	(70)	(412)

X^2 = significant at .01

index of where power lies, the Cabinet enjoys a substantial advantage over both civil servants and back-benchers. Of 425 directors reporting, 38 per cent focussed on the Cabinet, compared with 28 per cent on the bureaucracy and 15 per cent on back-benchers, while the remainder opted for 'other' sources. In general, this judgment is confirmed by back-benchers themselves (N-269), the largest proportion of whom (43 per cent) also rank the Cabinet as 'the element in the Canadian political system which receives the greatest amount of attention from lobbyists.' When asked why, fully 90 per cent offer variations on the theme 'this is where the power is.'

Next, we report briefly on the association between targets and types of issues. The Cabinet is the major focus in five of eight issue categories, including legislation, past and pending, administrative regulation and licensing, intra-organizational problems of policy, jurisdiction, and fund-raising, and an omnibus 'other' category. Only in licensing, fund-raising, and intra-organizational policy does the major focus shift to the bureaucracy. And only in one issue area, *pending legislation*, do back-benchers closely challenge the Cabinet as the centre of interest group attention.

The pattern of group behaviour in the *general* context differs considerably. Here again, effectiveness is determined by the case study issue, but the points of access are derived from the generalized experience of the groups. The frequency of targets and their relative utility are shown in Table 7-11.

Here, contrary to their case study experience, the largest proportion of effective groups (59 and 55 per cent) focus upon executive assistants to ministers and the judiciary. However, the N's are so small that the generalization is suspect. Those who have sought help through back-benchers rank next, followed narrowly by the bureaucracy. Somewhat unexpectedly, the Cabinet ranks lowest among the 'big three'. Despite the fact that legislators rank 'testifying before committees' as the most effective interest

TABLE 7-11   *Association between group effectiveness and target, general*

Effectiveness	Legis.	Bureau'cy	Judiciary	Cab.	Leg. Comm.	Ex. Asst.	Other	
	%	%	%	%	%	%	%	
High	52	51	55	47	38	59	52	(198)
Low	32	32	18	28	45	30	22	(123)
Issue pending	16	17	27	24	17	11	26	(76)
	(83)	(159)	(11)	(75)	(29)	(17)	(23)	(397)

X^2 = not significant at .05

group tactic, directors rank it lowest here. Such dissonance is surprising, since one would expect most politically-active directors to be aware of legislative judgments in this area, and as a result, to use this stratagem more frequently and perhaps with better effect. Unlike the previous table, the differences here are not statistically significant, and perhaps the major conclusion is that in their general interaction with governmental elites, interest groups select different targets than in the case study issue, but regardless of their target in the former context, the results are not likely to be very different, with the exception of legislative committees which have a substantially lower rate of effectiveness. It is also noteworthy that 40 per cent (N–159) of the total interactions occur between interest groups and the bureaucracy.

We turn next to any differences in effectiveness according to the substance of the case study issue. Assuming that these issues, which fall into seven major categories, provide a random sample across all types of groups, the data provide us with another basis for differentiating among them according to effectiveness. The findings provide an interesting commentary on the earlier judgment of a provincial minister that groups are typically not very effective regarding pending legislation because they are usually unaware of what is forthcoming. As Table 7-12 reveals, however, a significant proportion of them do indeed attempt, and successfully, to influence legislation *before* it passes.

Group margins of success are obviously highest in extra-governmental affairs, fund-raising and intra-organizational issues, but in the round they achieve their goals in almost two-thirds of the completed issues.

TABLE 7-12 *Association between effectiveness and substance of issue*

	Substance of issue									
Effectiveness	Fund-raising	Intra-org.	Reg. ad.	Jur.[a]	Lic-ense	Organ.	Bill	Law	Other	
	%	%	%	%	%	%	%	%	%	
High	64	60	56	53	50	40	48	38	53	(244)
Low	14	16	21	30	26	33	36	34	30	(150)
Issue pending	22	24	23	16	24	27	15	27	16	(91)
	(14)	(55)	(86)	(70)	(26)	(46)	(92)	(99)	(70)	(485)

X^2 = significant at .01
[a] This category concerns jurisdictional problems such as those encountered by labour unions.

Their skill in the game of accommodation is most apparent regarding administrative regulation and licensing, which are probably handled mainly by the bureaucratic elite, and in which, as suggested elsewhere, agency-group interactions tend to become quite sympathetic. Only regarding group efforts to modify existing legislation is the margin between success and failure narrow, although still positive. And this is not unexpected since modifying legislation already in effect seems considerably more difficult than amending proposed legislation or modifying rules and regulations set at the discretion of officials and regulatory agencies.

Another generalization shown by the comparative N's is that three-quarters of interest group issues are concerned with governmental issues, and especially pending and past legislation, administrative regulation, and licensing. Equally significant, with the exception of legislation already in effect, most groups fare quite well in their interactions with government.

This conclusion raises the point whether particular groups tend to focus on particular issues, which by inference would provide some evidence about their relative effectiveness. Analysis reveals that a concern with legislative issues varies considerably among groups depending upon whether a bill or a law is at issue. In the former case, labour and professional groups are equally involved, accounting for almost half of all types of groups ·concerned. Regarding laws, however, business groups are paramount, providing almost a third of all groups, with professional, labour, and welfare groups following in that order. Professional, educational, and business groups monopolize the licensing, concessions, and right-of-way issue area, providing over two-thirds of interaction. Business is most active in the area of administrative regulation with one-third of all cases, followed by labour and welfare which together provide one-quarter of the total.

Regarding non-governmental issues, intra-organizational affairs involve mainly professional, labour, and welfare groups. The only other category of any importance, fund-raising, finds welfare and social–recreational groups accounting for almost half of total group activity.

Turning next to the relation between tactics, targets, and achieved success, we look first at the general experience of interest groups. This item differs from others in combining both targets and tactics, and it is therefore not comparable with data concerning group behaviour in the case study (see Table 7-13).

Once again, although the differences are not significant, tactics that involve interaction with the bureaucracy, i.e. regulatory agencies, are found to be the most effective by the groups using them. This contrasts

TABLE 7-13 *Association between group effectiveness and general targets and tactics*

Effectiveness	General targets and tactics								
	Reg. ags.	Sp. hears.	Per. rep.	Public	Cab.	Comm.	Experts	Other[a]	
	%	%	%	%	%	%	%	%	
High	60	55	52	45	45	42	25	47	(205)
Low	7	27	31	39	31	26	33	43	(135)
Issue pending	32	18	17	16	23	33	42	9	(82)
	(50)	(22)	(140)	(49)	(69)	(51)	(12)	(29)	(422)

X^2 = not significant at .05
[a] 'Appeals to executive assistants' (N-6) have been combined with this category.

interestingly with the earlier generalization by directors that personal appeals by prominent members of their group was their single most effective tactic. Certainly, that tactic remains the most highly used, by a dramatic margin, but the present finding challenges its primary ranking, in terms of utility. Briefs to Cabinet and committees are substantially less effective in this context, and it does seem that the majority of briefs tend to have a *pro forma* quality, although their weight undoubtedly varies according to the influence of the group submitting them and its functional relevance to the issue concerned.

The exercise of group influence through special hearings ranks second in effectiveness, followed closely by personal appeals by members of the group. Note, however, that the latter accounts for fully one-third (N-140) of all tactics in terms of frequency. The low ranking of appeals by experts is unexpected, although it is partially explained by the high proportion of cases still pending in that category.

The frequency and effectiveness of group appeals to regulatory agencies suggests some support for the well-known tendency among them to become very closely intertwined with their respective clientele groups and to provide a sympathetic reception to the private groups concerned. There is an understandable tendency for functional imperatives to become a major factor in appointments to such agencies, resulting in some individuals moving from one sector of the private political elite to governmental posts, and back again. Indeed, it is almost a truism in Western societies that it is difficult to determine who is regulating whom with respect to the government agencies charged with such responsibilities, which include many departments as well as the special regulatory agencies. Intensive analysis by Professor Ronald Lang of the federal programme of drug legislation, during the period 1962-8, for example, suggests that the relationship between the Pharmaceutical Manufacturers Association and the Food and Drug Directorate, charged with control and supervision of the drug industry, especially with regard to the safety of their products, followed the usual pattern. Despite the fact that the Common's Special Committee on Drug Costs and Prices (1962) was concerned with both the safety and the cost of drugs produced in Canada, in part because of the Directorate's unfortunate authorization of the production and sale of Thalidomide, and regarding cost, because it was the use of brand-name drugs rather than their generic equivalents that accounted for their high price, the Director of the FDD testified before the Committee (1964) that 'he personally would always buy a brand-name drug, to ensure that he obtained the quality and efficiency guaranteed by the reputation of a well-known manufacturer'.[1] The Director retired shortly thereafter to become a member of the board of directors of CIBA, the Swiss pharmaceutical manufacturer. It should perhaps be added that his successor supported the Government's position, especially by his expert testimony, contrary to the PMAC, that 'there does not appear to be any significant difference between drugs sold under a generic name and those sold under a brand name. Similarly, imported drugs appear to be of the same quality as domestic production.'[2]

Canadian experience with so-called 'representative bureaucracy' at the departmental level is also relevant here. As John Porter concludes, 'the Departments of Veterans' Affairs, Agriculture, Fisheries, Health and Welfare, and Labour all have men in senior positions who during their careers have had experience in groups with which their departments came into contact. For example, there has always been a place for an ex-labour leader as Assistant Deputy Minister of Labour, and the top levels of Veterans' Affairs seem open mainly to former senior armed forces personnel, or those having some connection with the Canadian Legion.'[3]

Some comparison with the general tactics and targets reported above is provided by a summary of those used in the case study issue. Although each set of tactics tends to be different, there is some overlap, as indicated in Table 7-14.

[1] Lang, 'The politics of drugs: The Pharmaceutical Manufacturers Association of Canada and the Association of the British Pharmaceutical Industry (1930–1970)', doctoral dissertation, University of London (1972), pp. 205–6.
[2] *Special Committee on Drug Costs and Prices*, Appendix B., No. 30 (January 26, 1967), p. 2101.
[3] *The Vertical Mosaic*, pp. 449–50; 528–32.

TABLE 7-14 *Association between group effectiveness, targets, and tactics, case study*

	Targets and tactics							
Effectiveness	Members	Other groups	Public.	Cab.	Official	Exec. asst's.	Other	
	%	%	%	%	%	%	%	
High	53	51	51	50	45	38	54	(239)
Low	31	22	33	31	35	38	27	(145)
Issue pending	15	27	17	19	20	25	19	(86)
	(150)	(37)	(79)	(60)	(68)	(8)	(68)	(470)

X^2 = not significant at .05

Among those groups ranking high on effectiveness in the case study issue, the most common tactic is efforts to 'enlist their whole membership', followed closely by three external appeals. Since appeals to back-benchers and bureaucrats are separated in this item, it is not essentially comparable with earlier tables. We saw earlier that enlisting the support of members was a prime stratagem among directors, used essentially to secure advice and legitimation for further action. In some cases, governmental elites require that directors appear armed with a resolution from their members. Such action not only commits members to the collective group position and tactics, it also assures governmental elites that the director really has the green light from his group. This is a noteworthy matter, since it is a common belief among MP's that group leaders do not always represent the wishes of their members. Indeed, fully four-fifths of them disagree with any interest group claim that 'they speak for everyone in the social or economic sector they represent.' Such a generalization, of course, supports the claim of some MP's that they themselves represent the unorganized public.

Publicity campaigns, appeals to ministers and other groups follow the above tactic. Overall, the differences found are hardly substantial, and far from statistically significant. The combining of back-benchers and bureaucrats undoubtedly accounts for part of the small variance, but the differences among tactics across the high level are not impressive.

The relation between effectiveness and type of group provides another bit of useful evidence. It should be noted, however, that this is a rather unspecific measure, since it rests upon an undifferentiated lumping together of all groups within a given category, regardless of extensive differences in their political resources and the difficulty of achieving their objective in the case study issue. A major effect is to smooth out differences among groups. The item used here asked each director to indicate the extent to which his group had achieved its objectives in the case study issue. As noted earlier, since the distribution is spread fairly evenly along the scale, it seems valid to assume that directors did not select cases which placed themselves or their associations in a favourable light (see Table 7-15).

Professional, business, and welfare rank very similarly in the higher ranges of the effectiveness scale among the 'big four' of essentially economically-oriented groups and welfare. Labour, on the other hand, ranks lowest among all types of groups. Agriculture has not been included because the number of cases was too small to permit percentaging. Although fraternal–service groups enjoy the top ranking, the N's are too small for generalization. Despite their easy access to the Cabinet, religious groups rank quite low on achieved success, but here again the N's are too small to bear much weight. Given the fulsome expansion of higher education during the past decade, and their rather frequent nominations as being powerful by elites, it is unexpected that such groups do not rank higher on effectiveness.

It is important to repeat that the differences found here are not statistically significant, the data are based upon a single issue in the political life of these groups, and their respective goals varied substantially in difficulty. On the other hand, it seems virtually impossible to find a precisely comparative basis for effectiveness, since different kinds of groups will always be concerned with different substantive issues. In this sense, perhaps we must be prepared to accept a less rigorous standard of 'effectiveness', accepting, for example, the conventional practice in occupational life where judgments about individual 'success' are often made across occupational lines.

TABLE 7-15 *Comparative political effectiveness of interest groups, case study issues*

	Type of interest group									
Effectiveness[a]	Prof.	Bus.	Lab.	Wel.	F–S.	S–R.	Educ.	Rel.	Ethnic	Sample
	%	%	%	%	%	%	%	%	%	%
High	35	34	15	38	43	35	22	20	20	30	(108)
Medium	27	29	45	31	28	46	31	27	27	29	(134)
Low	38	37	40	31	28	19	47	53	53	41	(144)
	(60)	(75)	(66)	(70)	(14)	(28)	(49)	(15)	(15)		(386)

X^2 = not significant at .05 K's tau $B = -.02$
[a] 'High' effectiveness is defined by the response 'completely successful' in the case study outcome; 'medium' by the response 'mainly'; and 'low' by 'partially or not at all'.

THE EFFECTIVENESS OF LOBBYING

We saw earlier that lobbying was the most common of several kinds of technical aid, and that, in the case study issue, among 250 directors reporting having used special assistance, over three-fourths had employed lobbyists. It is also clear that lobbying occurs most frequently in two substantive areas: legislation and administrative regulation, with very similar intensity in each sector. Although it is difficult to demonstrate the effectiveness of lobbying, we have some evidence that such activities have a significant effect upon elite perspectives and evaluations of each other's role. Our interviews included an item which asked legislators and bureaucrats to indicate to what extent they have been influenced by lobbyists regarding political issues. Three levels of influence were prescribed: coming to question one's position on an issue; changing one's position toward that advocated by a lobbyist; and being influenced to the extent of coming to agree with his position. Since the highest levels of interaction occur between interest group agents and the bureaucracy, we begin with this sector (see Table 7-16).

Looking at the high and low levels of interaction and influence, we find a strongly significant and essentially linear association between them. Almost half of those officials who are high on interaction are also high on experienced influence, compared with only fifteen per cent of those who

TABLE 7-16 *Personal interaction with lobbyists and influence, bureaucrats*

Influence[a]	Frequency of interaction			
	High	Medium	Low	
	%	%	%	
High	45	34	15	(82)
Medium	40	38	12	(64)
Low	14	28	74	(49)
	(69)	(63)	(63)	(195)

X^2 = significant at .001 K's tau B = .36
Gamma = .49

[a] This index of influence was designed by weighting each of the levels of lobbyist influence, assigning one point for 'coming to question one's position'; two points for 'changing one's position toward that advocated by the lobbyist'; and three points for 'coming to agree' with his position on the issue.

rank low on interaction. Meanwhile, three-quarters of those who rank low on interaction also rank low on influence, i.e. group effectiveness. As noted elsewhere, influence tends to vary most sharply between the medium and low levels of interaction, with a dramatic increase in the low–low cell. In all, the data strongly support the interaction–influence segment of interaction theory. Earlier data indicate that the interactions referred to here mainly involve administrative rules and regulation where the civil service necessarily enjoys considerable latitude in order to handle the huge volume of activity.

The strong correlations in Table 7-16 (Tau B is .36 and Gamma is .49) underscore the comparatively greater cohesion existing between bureaucrats and directors, compared with that for MP's. In one context, this affinity is anomalous because, as we shall see later, members of the bureaucratic sample rank quite low on certain ideological dimensions that seem to be directly related to their occupational role. One of these is economic liberalism, which symbolizes a generally affirmative view of big government and its welfare components. Since the role of bureaucrats is precisely one of carrying out this expansive conception of government, they must experience some cognitive dissonance regarding such normative preferences and the inapposite consequences of their political role.

Our research design, unfortunately, did not include any analysis of what seems to be a nice example of role conflict. Logically, however, it seems that bureaucratic liaisons with interest groups must be explained essentially in terms of functional and interactional ties, rather than ideological ones. Perhaps there is an attending rationale that relationships between their own agencies and such groups are somehow qualitatively different from the generality of such whirlpools of mutual interest. There is also the weight of bureaucratic patterns of authority and continuity which tend to become unquestioned premises of action for the veteran officials who comprise our sample. The acceptance of existing structures becomes to some extent an operational necessity, given long-established agency-clientele alliances.

Their anti-big-government ideology, plus some random evidence, suggests however that senior officials are often reluctant participants in the expansive Canadian governmental system. One, for example, replying to an *ad hoc* question regarding the extent of his interaction with MP's, said, 'Oh yes, they are always coming in with some ill-conceived scheme.' Again, as reported elsewhere, another federal official insisted that he received more pressure from MP's than from interest group agents, but 'the Minister takes care of them'.

These speculations indicate that one should interpret the evidence in the previous table, and elsewhere, concerning the shared legitimacy and inter-action between bureaucrats and directors in terms that include the functionally-circumscribed role of most senior officials and their apparent tendency to honour the claims of their particular clientele groups, while retaining ideological preferences that often reject the expansive policy values of Ministers and back-benchers. In effect, while both sub-elites exhibit similar patterns of interaction and influence, their motivations are probably quite different in some such terms as suggested here.

Turning to both legislators and bureaucrats in the same context, we find a similar and almost equally positive relationship. Indeed, in part because a higher proportion of MP's say they have more intense interaction with lobbyists than bureaucrats, the assumed association again emerges very strongly. Influence is again defined by the most demanding level: coming to agree with a lobbyist's position (see Table 7-17).

Here, the relationship is nicely linear in the expected direction and it is strongly significant statistically. In the round, the data confirm that interaction is probably the critical variable in determining interest group influence. Fully half of those who rank high on interaction with lobbyists also rank high on influence, compared with only 31 per cent who rank low. Interaction seems to provide the opportunity for the exchange of information and other services which sustain the process of accommodation.

Meanwhile, the over-all distribution of the N's in the table reveals some interesting patterns of interaction. For example, 43 per cent of the governmental elite (N-194) interacts at the highest, 'frequently', level with lobbyists, and fully 80 per cent of them are found in the two highest cate-

TABLE 7-17 *Personal contact with lobbyists and influence, legislators and bureaucrats*

	Frequency of interaction			
Influence	High	Medium	Low	
	%	%	%	
High	50	46	31	(167)
Medium	36	33	22	(164)
Low	15	21	48	(120)
	(194)	(138)	(119)	(451)

X^2 = significant at .001 K's tau B = .21
Gamma = .31

gories of interaction. From another vantage point, about one-third indicate that they have come to agree with a lobbyist's position (the highest level of influence) 'occasionally'. Although the meaning of 'occasionally' is a subjective perception of respondents, virtually none of whom were influenced 'frequently' at this high level, the findings do provide evidence of the pervasive influence of lobbyists.

Perhaps most impressive is the fact that almost two-fifths (N–167) of the entire sample indicate that they have been influenced at one time or another to the extent of *coming to agree* with the position advocated by a lobbyist. Such a finding suggests again that interest groups make a potentially significant contribution to policy formulation in the form of substantive and ideological inputs, although this judgment is obviously more germane for bureaucrats than for legislators, almost all of whom are back-benchers whose role in policy determination is usually marginal.

SELECTIVITY AND EFFECTIVENESS IN LOBBYING

A final aspect of lobbying with direct implications for effectiveness involves the selectivity exercised by directors in contacting MP's. One would assume, for example, that party leaders, committee chairmen, and the members of important standing committees, and select committees as well, would be most salient for them. In this general context, it is interesting to determine whether directors, in their role as lobbyists, select MP's in terms of their assumed positions on policy issues, insofar as these are known. Do they contact legislators who agree with them or do they tend, as would seem logical, to focus their attention upon those who disagree but might be brought around to support their view? The item used here asked legislators, 'In your experience, are you contacted most frequently by lobbyists who agree with you on a particular bill or measure or by those who disagree?' An opportunity was also provided for them to answer '50–50'. We received interesting and conflicting explanations for many responses. Some MP's, for example, answered, 'Agree, obviously. Why should he contact me if he knows I am opposed to his views?' Other equally experienced members replied, 'Disagree; why should he waste time on me if he knows I agree with him?' A Quebec deputy, in affirming the latter view, concluded that 'One rarely hears from a contented cow.' A third variant, offered less frequently, maintained that 'They usually don't know what our position is.'

Our data enable us to generalize regarding the main drift among directors. Fully 70 per cent of back-benchers believe that lobbyists usually focus on those who *disagree* with them. Some variation appears. Ministers, for example, hold this view somewhat more often (three-quarters), with no differences between federal and provincial elites. Among back-benchers, no provincial differences exist, but Ottawa tends to rank somewhat higher, proportionately, compared with the others. Although it is only speculation, it may be that interactions occurring in a context of disagreement make a more lasting and even indelible impression upon MP's, with the result that their importance is magnified.

In the context of selective perception, it is significant that directors have a dramatically different view of their behaviour. Although many failed to answer, among those who did (N-280) almost two-thirds indicated they confined their contacts to MP's who *agreed* with their own view.

One might assume that pattern of selections would vary with the amount of trust directors have in the members with whom they interact. And such is indeed the case. Among those who believe that legislators generally agree with them, fully two-thirds trust MP's all or most of the time, compared with only 42 per cent of those who report that they usually contact members who disagree. Here, it seems, is another useful indication of the extent to which selective perception structures reality and political behaviour. Among directors who rank lower on policy agreement and trust, labour accounts for the largest proportion, with one-quarter, followed by business with one-fifth.

Following interaction theory, one might assume that a director's judgment of his personal effectiveness would also be affected by such conditions. Here, the test relies upon the item which asks directors to indicate how effective their lobbying efforts have been. Using only the most demanding criterion, 'How often have you been able to influence a member to the extent of his coming to agree with your position on an issue or a bill?', the analysis again reveals the expected gradient: 45 per cent of those directors who typically contact MP's who agree with their policies rank 'high' on perceived effectiveness, compared with 36 per cent of those who believe that MP's usually disagree.

The contrasting judgments of MP's and directors regarding selectivity suggest that directors tend to structure their interactions with legislators (and bureaucrats as well) in ways that reflect their own perceptions of the legitimacy of their groups, and in a generally positive direction. It will be recalled that significant majorities of directors regard MP's as cooperative allies rather than competitors; believe that legislators regard their attempts to influence government as legitimate; and feel they experience little consistent opposition from other groups. They are fully aware that the average man may tend to regard them with considerable ambivalence, but insofar as governmental elites and other interest groups are concerned, their perceptions are often positive. As suggested earlier, despite their realization that resources are not unlimited, they tend to regard society as a cooperative commonwealth.

In sum, it can be concluded that lobbying activities have sometimes proved quite effective in the bureaucratic arena, and especially in the area of administrative regulation. The highly focussed kinds of interaction brought about by the functional specialization which characterizes interest group–bureaucratic accommodation are probably a decisive factor. One suspects, too, that such interactions are eased by their relative depoliticization: in effect, the ideological component of policy formulation within the bureaucracy is probably quite low compared with that found in interest group–legislative interaction. Among the consequences may be a dampening of the potential for conflict and an impetus to conceptualize issues as 'merely' technological.

Beyond such positive inducements to accommodation is the relatively greater opportunity for policy makers in the bureaucratic arena to restrict the scope of participation to those private interests directly affected by the matter at hand. Indeed, it is probably true that the majority of issues are handled exclusively by the two elites concerned. In this context, it is worth underscoring the earlier conclusion of the vast majority of senior civil servants that it is very difficult for unorganized groups and those not directly affected by an ongoing issue to gain access into the decision-making process.

In effect, such positive conditions may act to reinforce consensus and legitimacy between interest groups and the bureaucratic elite, whereas legislators must more often function in the public arena, which may at times provide a reservoir of popular support but may also be more conducive to political conflict.

COMPARATIVE PATTERNS OF LOBBYING INFLUENCE

A useful means of determining the structure of lobbying effectiveness is to analyse the distribution of responses to the item which asks MP's and bureaucrats to indicate the frequency and the extent to which they have been influenced by directors. Table 7-18 is based upon a weighted index.

One-quarter of the entire legislative sample ranks at the 'high' level. The expected concentration appears at the medium level. Comparing only the 'high' level across the four areas (not shown here), Quebec has

TABLE 7-18 *Comparative lobbyist effectiveness,*
legislators and bureaucrats

Level of influence[a]	Legislators	Bureaucrats
	%	%
High	26	33
Medium	56	44
Low	18	22
	(269)	(214)

[a] The influence index was weighted as follows: Influenced by a director 'frequently', 4 points; 'occasionally',
3 points; 'seldom', 2 points; and 'rarely–never',
1 point. Cut-off points were 1–4 'low'; 5–8 'medium';
9–12 'high'.

the highest proportion with 35 per cent, followed by Ontario with 32 per
cent, British Columbia with 28, and Ottawa with only 21 per cent.

Not unexpectedly, given their high interaction rates and close functional
ties with directors, bureaucrats indicate a higher level of influence, with
one-third of the sample at the high level. Regionally, a dramatic variation
occurs, with over one-third of bureaucrats in Ottawa ranking 'high';
Ontario is next with just under one-quarter, followed by British Columbia
and Quebec at only 8 and 6 per cent, respectively. Here again, we have
some evidence of the critical role played in the accommodation of group
claims by the bureaucracy in Ottawa. It will be recalled that some directors
and back-benchers believe that major policy influence in Ottawa rests in
the hands of the bureaucrat, while ministers are seen as paramount in
Ontario. At the same time, by this index, Ontario bureaucrats are highly
responsive to group claims, compared with British Columbia and Quebec.

SOME TENTATIVE CONCLUSIONS REGARDING EFFECTIVENESS

Although we have no precise way of weighting their relative importance,
several criteria and correlates of interest group effectiveness have been
presented. Regarding the subjective judgments of political elites, it is clear
that large economic or producer types of groups are generally believed to be
the most effective politically. The capacity of groups such as the Canadian
Association of Manufacturers and the Canadian Labour Congress 'to
realize their own will in a communal action even against the resistance of
others involved in that action' is ranked highest by about half of the directors

and MP's. Religious groups rank a poor third regarding influence *vis-à-vis* government.

These subjective judgments, however, are only partially supported by our survey data. Welfare groups, for example, rank second only to business according to several empirical criteria of political effectiveness. Moreover, business, professional, and educational groups usually rank higher than labour, which despite generous shares of financial and membership resources, tends to lack the popular legitimacy often ascribed to business, welfare, and educational groups. Labour directors themselves attest to this condition, accounting for about one-third of all 'low' attributions on the group legitimacy scale.

Political activism, defined as the frequency of interaction between interest groups and governmental elites, has different effects when organizational resources and directors' resources are associated with effectiveness. It accounts for little variation in the former case, but is much more salient regarding directors' resources. When political activism and resources are correlated with type of group, a positive relation appears, with business groups exhibiting the strongest relationship.

When effectiveness is defined by the case study outcome and associated with governmental targets, we find that the most successful groups tend to interact with the bureaucracy, with the Cabinet ranking substantially lower. The Cabinet also ranks below the legislature in the general run of group political targets. Here, however, we may be encountering the levelling effect of averages. For example, some 40 per cent of all directors approached the Cabinet in the case study issue. This universe of 160 groups probably includes many with only marginal resources; one-quarter of them, for example, failed completely to achieve their goals. Such results, in effect, probably mask the fact that Cabinet-oriented groups also include many who possess major shares of political resources and are effective.

One clear finding is that the largest proportion of effective groups, again defined by case study outcomes, is found among those who deal with issues involving the bureaucracy, and particularly the regulatory agencies. (Among governmental issue areas, the lowest level of success is in dealing with laws.) When issues are correlated with groups, business types are involved most frequently in such areas, accounting for one-third of all groups involved. Four other kinds of groups, each accounting for about 10 per cent of the total distribution, contribute most of the remainder: welfare, professional, educational, and labour.

The other substantive area in which business groups dominate involves legislation, where once again they contribute about one-third of all interactions, followed by professional groups. Almost by definition, these types of groups are intimately concerned with regulatory problems and policy, the issue area in which group success is highest. So here again is evidence reinforcing the conclusion that 'economic' groups, with the exception of labour, are among the most politically powerful of Canadian interest groups.

Another empirical criterion of effectiveness is the judgment of interest group elites regarding the utility of their lobbying efforts. Here again, we found that business and welfare directors rank at the top of the scale. It is also clear that politically effective directors tend to spend their time somewhat differently than those who are less effective. They are more likely to focus upon highly valued services such as providing information to back-benchers on pending legislation, compared with other directors who attempt to inform them about constituency opinion, an area where most back-benchers feel they have little to learn.

A significant finding is that only about one-fourth of Canadian interest groups are highly active politically, when this condition is defined by the proportion of time directors spend interacting with governmental elites. When these groups are analysed, we again find that business, welfare, professional, and educational directors are most active. Not only do such groups tend to rank high on so-called 'hard' resources of income, access, and more extensive reservoirs of identification among their members, but they also monopolize the distribution on the important resource of legitimacy. Business groups enjoy the largest shares, followed by welfare, professional and educational groups. Labour, meanwhile, ranks lowest among all groups. It should perhaps be added that legitimacy is defined here by the subjective perception of interest group directors regarding the extent to which members of Parliament view attempts by their groups to influence them as legitimate. The behavioural consequences of such perceptions are well-established. To repeat I. W. Thomas' dictum, 'If situations are defined as real, they are real in their consequences.' The knowledge that governmental elites generally legitimate their role undoubtedly has beneficial consequences for those interest groups that enjoy this condition.

Finally, if the Cabinet is the cardinal source of power in the parliamentary system, the comparative frequency with which interest groups secure access there should provide an index of political efficacy. Based upon their *general* experience, the following scale appears: professional groups, 23 per cent; business, 20; education, 17; welfare, 11; and labour, 1.

PART III

THE STRUCTURE AND PROCESS
OF ELITE ACCOMMODATION

Having analysed the structure, role, and effectiveness of Canadian interest groups, we turn next to the processes of elite interaction and accommodation. The dimensions of interaction and accommodation are essentially four: behavioural, socioeconomic, ideological, and cognitive. The analysis includes an attempt to determine the relative influence of these dimensions upon elite interaction and interest group effectiveness.

CHAPTER 8

PATTERNS OF ELITE ACCOMMODATION

The basis of accommodation among the Canadian political elite is often functional and the process involves sustained interaction among its three subgroups. This pervasive functional thrust reflects the network of clientele relationships existing between government and interest groups, as well as the geography of political representation. As we have seen, groups seek access at several points, but most of them tend to focus upon the bureaucracy which handles the majority of the substantive claims they raise. The largest proportion, some 40 per cent, of all groups cite the bureaucracy as their major target, with Parliament and the Cabinet virtually tied for second.[1] A substantial proportion of federal legislators, moreover, insist that the civil service is the lodestar of the political system. As a result, we may safely assume that the most common pattern of elite interaction is between high-level bureaucrats and interest group representatives.

INTEREST GROUP INTERACTION WITH THE BUREAUCRACY

Several conditions are associated with this valence, not the least of which is the fact of executive dominance in the parliamentary system. The centre of power is surely the Cabinet, but its own effectiveness depends crucially upon the expertise and continuity provided by the civil service. Together, they provide the major governing impulse. In Ottawa, especially, some MP's maintain that higher bureaucrats are the true governors. Neither ministers nor back-benchers, the argument goes, really comprehend the situation. Their generalist backgrounds and the technical complexity of programmes, aggravated by the labyrinthine channels of the administrative system, make them highly dependent upon their permanent aides. This

---

[1] It may be significant, however, that business, religious, and educational groups rank the Cabinet a decisive second, compared with other types of groups.

judgment is under-scored by an interest group executive in Toronto who noted that his association, a highly regarded economic group, focusses on deputy ministers in Ottawa and ministers in Toronto because 'that's where the power is.'

The strong bureaucratic orientation of interest groups is also associated with the sheer volume of issues handled by the civil service, as well as its great discretionary power under the authority of delegated legislation. As a result, an interest group will be drawn into the bureaucratic arena much more frequently than it will turn to the Cabinet or to the ordinary member. Perhaps a rough quantitative index of the difference is the number of orders-in-council enacted annually by the Cabinet, amounting to thousands each year, compared with the number of laws passed annually by the House, which rarely exceeds sixty. A distinction must be made, however, between *frequency* and *importance*. We can say conclusively that interest groups interact most frequently with the bureaucracy; however, the present data say nothing about the substantive importance of such contacts.

Perhaps the main reason for the well-worn path between interest groups and the bureaucracy is their parallel functional structures. As noted earlier, this condition means that agency–clientele relationships will flourish between governmental elites and substantively-relevant groups. It should be noted that all sectors of the political elite are often drawn into these whirlpools of interest, which bring together not only the private interest and the bureaucracy, but the member from the riding or province in which the affected interest exists. In this context, to cite only one sample, it is noteworthy that representatives of tobacco-growing constituencies testified before the Federal Committee on Health, Welfare, and Social Affairs, 1968, during hearings on legislation to control advertising by the industry. William F. Knowles, Conservative member from Norfolk, for example, stated, 'I am here as an interested observer because the part of the country I come from is a major producer of tobacco. Also, as a farmer and producer of tobacco myself, I have an interest.'[1] The director of the National Association of Tobacco and Confectionery Distributors, also appeared, emphasizing that some 200,000 Canadians depended for their living upon the sale of tobacco and related products. 'We ask this Committee not to break up an industry which is part and parcel of all the other products that are being sold in Canada.'[2]

[1] *Hearings*, Standing Committee on Health, Welfare, and Social Affairs (Ottawa: Queen's Printer), 1968–9, p. 134.

[2] *Ibid.*, pp. 1774, 1787. Cited in Mark Wattenberg, 'The tobacco industry and the health controversy in Canada: a study in interest group politics' (M.A. Thesis, University of British Columbia, 1970.)

The pattern of access into the bureaucracy is highly structured, with one method being cited as first by fully 60 per cent of all bureaucrats (*N*–214), official appointments made by directors. The political milieu in which the higher bureaucracy functions is explicit in the fact that access through a Cabinet member is ranked second, by one-quarter of the sample, followed by access through an interested back-bencher, by almost one-fifth.

A final incentive for interest group penetration of the bureaucracy is the simple fact that access is easy. Fully 65 per cent of all officials maintain that such is the case, with those in Ottawa even more affirmative at 70 per cent. Moreover, one-third of them, the largest single proportion, come into 'frequent' personal contact with representatives of interest groups. Another 30 per cent interact at the 'occasionally' level.

This condition is in sharp contrast to the avenues of access available to non-functionally-related groups and the unorganized public. Here, while the majority of officials feel such groups can ventilate their views, 36 per cent of them believe that they find it hard to make such views known to government. This condition frequently results in calculated efforts by a public agency to create an interest group in order to generate claims upon itself. Indeed, as noted elsewhere, almost half the departments in our sample had done this. These conditions suggest again that, despite government efforts to widen its net, the channels of group–civil service interaction tend to be circumscribed within bureaucracy's functional design. More important, they underscore the critical role of interest groups as triggers of governmental action.

A distinction was made earlier between negotiation and consultation, in which the former referred to the practice whereby government merely discusses an issue with a group, while the latter characterized a situation in which the group concerned had a veto power regarding the issue. Like many nice theoretical constructs, this one proved to be difficult to handle empirically. It also seems to assume that most policy and programmatic initiatives originate within government, which seems doubtful indeed. The best index for operationalizing this concept is an item which asks civil servants to indicate the intensity of the policy role in departmental affairs played by the groups cited in the case study. When we equate the *negotiation* level of influence with the highest point on the scale, i.e. 'they are almost an integral part of the day-to-day activity of the department', and consign the remaining responses to the *consultative* level, we find that just one-quarter of groups have a veto power regarding their clientele agency. The largest proportion of these, just over half, is found in the area of health and welfare, followed by transportation with one-third.

Elite accommodation

In this general context, we turn to the going pattern of functional relationships. Before presenting summary data based upon interactions between specific types of agencies and their clients, it may be useful to report several *ad hoc* examples from the research. The first concerns a provincial director of a Health Department. A medical doctor with twenty years of experience in government, he indicated that 'the principal interest groups with which his department interacts' were two: the 'Provincial' Medical Association, of which he is a member, and the Canadian Pharmaceutical Association. When asked to specify the condition which 'best characterizes the relations of these groups to your Department', he ticked the second level on the influence scale, i.e. 'their assumed reaction to what we do is usually taken into account during our policy making.' With respect to the Pharmaceutical Association, he noted that 'the government buys millions of dollars worth of drugs, so we are quite a target for the drug people.' Moreover, 'many of us are members of Medical Association committees, which advise government from time to time; next year, one of our departmental doctors will be president of the Association.' The symbiotic relationship between some officials and their natural clientele groups is perhaps evident in this instance. Asked to indicate 'how effective' the Medical Association was in the case study reported, he placed it at the top of the scale as being 'very effective'.

Our second case involves a provincial agricultural agency, directed by a professional agronomist, with 22 years experience in his role. Three clientele groups were named as his principal contacts: the Provincial Fruit Growers' Association, the Vegetable Growers' Association, and the Nursery Association. As with the previous case, all were again ranked at the second level of influence. Regarding relationships with the most influential of them, he discussed an issue in which 'they came to...to discuss the problem with the Minister and I was asked to sit in.' This was the 'usual way' he became aware of a group's problem, which in this case concerned research on the conditions required to grow certain food products. Once again, this group ranked at the 'very effective' level in dealing with the department. In addition, discussing the inability of some interest groups to make their claims to the agency, he indicated that 'we help them organize', and gave an example of an agricultural interest which the department was trying to form into a group.

Concerning relations with clientele groups, he complained that some of his men were 'always on call, including Sundays'. They waited 'hand and foot' upon the farmers. Finally, when asked to rank several factors, including the public interest, party policy, and Government's expectations, which were considered when departmental policy was being made, he selected first 'the interests of the group most immediately concerned'.

Another example is from a provincial department of industry, headed by an economist with a graduate degree and 24 years of experience. He named four clientele groups as the major interests with which the department interacted: the Board of Trade; Council of Forest Industries; Mining Association; and the Fisheries Association. These groups were ranked at the third level of influence, i.e. 'They are only one among many factors impinging upon our decisions.' He indicated that he became aware of the issue through his Minister, to whom the group made its initial representations, but added that this was unusual since 'normally, groups go through channels; they only go higher if they don't get my approval.' Regarding the outcome, he maintained that the group concerned, the Board of Trade, had asked for an economic survey of a certain region, and that ('even though I wouldn't have given it first priority') the survey was carried out as requested.

The major tactic used by the Board in this issue, an initial approach to the Minister, was augmented by an appeal through the local MP. Our respondent ranked the group as being 'effective', i.e. at the second level on the scale, but qualified this by noting that such judgments depended entirely on the issue. Such groups were only 'moderately significant' in shaping departmental policy. He did not, moreover, regard the Board as a 'pressure group', since it used straightforward tactics which essentially involved calling, asking for help, and coming in to see him. The group's 'objectives and methods' in this issue were ranked as 'highly legitimate, since this is our job'. Here again, the seamless web often existing between private and governmental elites at the bureaucratic level is apparent. The rationale, as in the other examples cited, is generally one of 'service', in which the official tends to define his role within the parameters of function and representation of those groups which fall within his department's penumbra.

Another example which provides useful evidence of interest group–bureaucracy accommodation, concerns an engineer with 15 years experience in a provincial highway department. A member of many associations, including the interest group ranked first in terms of interaction with his department, he named nine interest group representatives, seven of whom he 'knew well socially'. The four clientele groups included: The Technical Asphalt Institute; American Asphalt Paving Association; the Provincial Road-Builders Association; and the Road Equipment Dealers Association. That agency–group interactions are not always functionally specific is indicated by his ranking of the Chamber of Commerce as being very effective in dealing with the Department. The reason, in his words, was 'constant pressure, by personal contact, by letter and by public pronouncements.'

Once again, as his predecessors, he ranked the groups at the second level of influence, i.e. 'their assumed reactions are usually taken into account during our policy making.' His case issue involved the creation of a new highway product in which, contrary to usual practice, his agency initiated negotiations with the private groups concerned. In an interesting manifestation of the exchange process, he noted also that it was not uncommon for departmental employees to be hired away by the firms represented by such interests.

Periodic meetings were held with technical experts of such firms when provincial road specifications were being reappraised and modified. Again, his department had also created an interest group, and his former Minister had been 'instrumental in the creation of the Provincial Road Builders' Association'. Our respondent also indicated that Imperial Oil had once sought support at the 'political level' in fighting a certain new specification. This example suggests that group access at the political, i.e. legislative level, is not always determined by whether an issue involves 'policy or administration,' but may also occur as a 'rear-guard' type of activity, enlisted only after the normal pattern of interaction has failed to produce accommodation.

Here again, in sum, there is some evidence of social, technical, and joint membership solidarity between the sectors of the political elite. However, since these are individual cases, they are useful essentially as illustrations.

One final illustration, at the federal level, suggests again the degree of functional specialization characterizing interest group–civil service interactions. Parenthetically, it should be noted that this functional drift dampens competition among the total universe of interest groups, since they tend to present different claims in different places within government. The interactions in which overt competition is involved are probably less frequent than those restricted to a single group–agency accommodation. Another larger consequence, which will be noted in more detail later, is the inhibiting effect that such a system has on over-all policy planning. Decisions, in effect, tend to be resolved segmentally, within the various functional centres. The corporatist legitimation for this process, moreover, makes it virtually impossible for any presumably disinterested, politically responsible agency to exercise system-wide coordination.

The federal department concerned is the Post Office; the respondent named four principal interest groups with which the department interacts. Most significant was the Newspaper Publisher's Association, which, of course, has a vital interest in postal rates and services. The Canadian Manufacturers' Association was ranked second, followed by the Direct Mailers' Association and the Graphic Arts Association. The Manufacturers' Association falls less precisely into the common functional scheme, which reflects its unusually broad concern with many matters of interest to its members. As with large union groups, its concerns and influence tend to proliferate beyond obvious direct economic interests to larger national questions of taxation, welfare, economics, and foreign affairs. Such broad scopes of interest are rather uncommon among interest groups, however, in part because of limits on their resources.

Regarding the level of influence of such groups, the respondent indicated that they were only one among many factors impinging upon decisions in the department. Nevertheless, he concluded later that interest groups generally played a 'highly significant' role in shaping policy in his Department. The case study, which involved representations by the Manufacturers' Association and the Direct Mailers regarding the postal rate increases of 1969, centred upon the groups' claim that they had received inadequate notice of the proposed changes and that, in any event, the changes themselves were ill-considered. Major tactics included letters and personal visits to him by the executive directors, representations to the Minister and to officials at lower levels in the Department. Personal conferences with responsible officials was the major single method used by the interest group elites with whom he dealt.

Regarding the role and legitimacy of such groups, the respondent was very positive. Not only were their methods and objectives in the case ranked as being 'highly legitimate', but his view of them was quite client-oriented. As he put it, 'they are our customers who should be served.' In the past, the Department had had no specific procedure for insuring that relevant groups and unorganized interests could 'make their interests known to the Department on any given issue'. As a result of the case study issue, however, it was planned that 'councils of users' would be formed to provide an appropriate avenue for such activities.

Having provided some *ad hoc* examples of interaction, we now turn to more systematic evidence of collective patterns of accommodation between the two elites. Table 8-1 is based upon the extent to which relationships between private groups and bureaucrats are functionally determined, as suggested by the examples presented above. The data used here are based upon an item which asked bureaucrats to cite the interest group which 'has had the greatest influence' in their department.

TABLE 8-1 *Functional continuities in interest group–bureaucratic interaction.*

Continuity[a]	Ed.	Agr.	Res. Mgt.	Health	Pub. Works	Lab.	Ind. Fin.	Trans.	Att. Gen.	Govtl. Affs.
	%	%	%	%	%	%	%	%	%	%
High	81	80	74	72	70	70	66	45	30	24
Low	19	20	26	28	30	30	33	55	70	76
	(11)	(10)	(23)	(29)	(23)	(10)	(36)	(43)	(16)	(11)

[a] 'High' and 'low' are based upon the relative proportions of the aggregate group nominations that fall directly within (high) or outside (low) the functional area served by the department concerned.

The data reveal that functionally-prescribed relationships are indeed common among our sample. Educational and agricultural agencies are closest to their clientele groups, followed by Resource Management and Health and Welfare departments. The low ranking of the Governmental Affairs and Attorney-General categories is perhaps explained by the fact that they have a highly generalized function, which encompasses groups of almost every kind. The only interest that appears more than once is the Bar Societies. These data also reveal something further about the earlier question of comparative political effectiveness. If, for example, we aggregate the types of groups nominated most frequently as being the 'most influential' within the various departments, we find that business and industry account for 46 nominations, compared with only 12 for unions. The construction industry ranks similarly, with 11 nominations. Among specific groups, the Canadian Manufacturers Association ranks first, with seven nominations, almost all of which are found within departments of Industry and Finance.

The significance of these patterns, of course, lies in their implications for cohesion between these two segments of the political elite. It is not unexpected that functionally-designed departments will tend to have such clientele relationships, but it is important to demonstrate that so much of elite interaction occurs within this framework. Given the broad discretion now possessed by the civil service, the question of how the so-called public interest is represented also arises. We are informed by just over half of civil servants that the public interest is the major single factor guiding their decisions, but given the lack of institutionalized mechanisms for expressing this interest, as indicated in the earlier evidence that outside, unorganized groups do not find it easy to participate in departmental policy issues, it is difficult to see how this factor is brought into play in any sustained, explicit manner.

It is important next to determine how much influence bureaucrats think clientele groups have on departmental policy. Even though such interactions are as close as suggested, they may not necessarily be perceived as having any decisive impact upon the shape of departmental policies. On the other hand, if our earlier generalization about the positive effect of social and ideological continuities upon elite cohesion is accurate, most officials should rank interest groups rather high on influence. The data in Table 8-2 are based upon the influence item mentioned earlier which asks, 'How effective do you think this interest group is in dealing with your Department?'

Here, education again ranks highest by a fairly substantial margin, which one would expect, following interaction theory. Otherwise, there is little continuity. Agriculture which had ranked very high in Table 8-1, is near the bottom and Resource Management is similar. On the whole, however, the distribution for all departments leans toward the middle-to-high end of the influence scale. The 'low' mean, for example, is only 7 per cent, compared with the 'high' mean of 27 per cent.

Influence, of course, rests upon several mutually-reinforcing bases. We have argued that functional cohesion is a vital basis for elite accommodation and it was indicated earlier that its members sometimes interchanged roles on the basis of such shared knowledge. One would predict, therefore, that bureaucrats would rank expertise highly as one basis of interest group influence within their departments. The following item was used to test this proposition: 'What in your opinion is the chief reason for the influence of the

TABLE 8-2   *Interest group influence upon public policy, case study*

Influence[a]	Ed.	Res. Mgt.	Health Welf.	Pub. Works	Lab.	Ind. Fin.	Att. Trans. Genl.	Govtl. Affairs	Agr.
	%	%	%	%	%	%	%	%	%	%
High	45	26	28	30	25	28	33	19	18	20
Medium	45	57	62	57	40	47	46	38	64	60
Low	10	4	3	9	15	14	4	6	—	10
N.A.	—	13	7	4	20	12	17	36	18	10
	(11)	(23)	(29)	(23)	(10)	(36)	(43)	(16)	(11)	(10)

[a] 'High' is based upon response #1 in the item; 'medium' is based upon responses #2 and #3; and 'low' is based upon response #4.

interest group ranked first above?' (i.e. in response to the question regarding the group which enjoyed the greatest influence within their department.) Three major reasons account for 60 per cent of the distribution. Among those who replied (N–181), just over one-fifth maintained that 'knowledge and expertise' was the major explanation. Another 19 per cent ranked 'mutual dependence between the group and ourselves' as first, while 17 per cent cited some variant of the size and power of the group as the salient quality.

The high ranking of 'mutual dependence' is also significant in the context of accommodation, suggesting again the extent to which these segments of the political elite define their relationship as a cooperative, problem-solving one. When set against the restrained appreciation that elites have of the extent of popular knowledge and awareness of interest group behaviour, it provides another bit of evidence that elites perceive their authority as both normatively and operationally legitimate.

Closely related to these patterns of influence, which are based upon the case study issue, is an item regarding the *general* significance of interest groups regarding the bureaucracy. This item asks: 'On the basis of your own experience, how significant a role do you feel interest groups generally play in helping you make policy in your Department?' One-quarter of all bureaucrats indicate that such groups are 'highly significant', while one-half ranked them as 'moderately significant'. Regarding functional areas, education again ranks highest, with almost half its senior officials characterizing interest groups as 'highly significant' in determining policy in their departments. Labour ranks second with 40 per cent; while Health and Welfare is third, with almost one-third ranking them at the highest level. Excepting Health and Welfare, the differences found throughout between the case study and the general experience of respondents again appear.

Interest groups, however, are not the only exogenous political forces to which bureaucrats respond. Other loci of influence include the expectations of the Government, parliament, party policy, and the public interest. Table 8-3 indicates the distribution, confined to Ontario and Ottawa to demonstrate national–provincial differences.[1]

Here, frequency of interaction with interest groups is linearly associated with perceived influence of groups at all levels of interaction for both sets of elites. Moreover, interaction is directly related to the over-all degree of influence attributed to all loci of influence (as shown by the row totals), again for both sets. The major differences in the two distributions appear in the progressions of the total row percentages, all of which are significant

[1] I am indebted to Scott Bennett for preparing this analysis.

TABLE 8-3 *Interaction and perceived loci of influence, civil servants*

Interaction	Loci of influence					
	Party	Public Int.	Parl.	Groups	Government	Total
Ontario:	%	%	%	%	%	%
High	4	15	3	10	12	44
Medium–high	6	7	3	2	5	23
Medium–low	2	6	2	4	5	19
Low	3	5	1	2	3	14
	—	—	—	—	—	—
	14	32	9	18	25	100
Ottawa:						
High	4	11	4	7	10	35
Medium–high	5	10	3	6	7	30
Medium–low	3	8	3	4	8	25
Low	1	4	2	.5	2	10
	—	—	—	—	—	—
	13	32	12	16	27	100

X^2 = not significant at .05.

in the top three rows. This indicates that interaction and perceived influence are much more skewed toward the highest level of interaction in Ontario, compared with Ottawa where the progression is very even through the first three levels, but falls off sharply upon reaching the lowest level of interaction. In Ontario, following the initial abrupt decline, the progression is quite even.

This cluster effect suggests that senior bureaucrats in Ontario interact intensely with a segment of interest groups that comprise a rather small proportion of the total interest-group population. Interaction in Ottawa, by contrast, appears to be more regular, and carried out across a wider spectrum of groups. This conclusion is supported by other evidence (not shown here) from directors who report a generally higher level of interaction with bureaucrats in Ottawa than with those in Ontario.

The table also indicates that the public interest ranks first as the major locus of bureaucratic influence (or responsibility), followed by the Government's expectations, with interest groups a strong third. Given earlier evidence regarding the ubiquity of departmental–clientele relationships, it may be that this expressed sensitivity to the public interest is mainly honourific. The somewhat marginal role of back-benchers in the political system is again suggested by the low ranking of Parliament's expectations, especially in Ontario.

Elite accommodation

It seems useful next to look at the normative bases of such perceptions of bureaucratic responsibility. Although officials are not always regarded as being philosophical about their social role, there seems to be a general tendency among men to develop some rationale which legitimates their authority. A glimpse of such a practice was provided earlier by the official who concluded that serving functionally-related groups 'was his job'. A similar commitment is explicit in the words of a Quebec official who, after indicating that the *Union Catholique des Cultivateurs* (the major agricultural group in the province) was 'almost an integral part of the day-to-day activities of the department', said, 'the department exists for these people'.

Another seductive rationale is the rather arid proposition that bureaucrats are mere instruments of their political masters, and hence have little opportunity or responsibility for honouring the larger public interest or adjudicating among the many demands presented to government. Such myths notwithstanding, it seems clear that the role of senior officials is precisely political, given their direct role in preparing, recommending, and making authoritative policy decisions regarding the allocation of national resources.

A dramatic example of bureaucratic initiative in policy determination concerns Bill C–190, introduced in 1967 under the Pearson Government, in an attempt to reduce drug prices through amendments to the Patent and Trade Marks Act. Although C–190 died, a similar measure was introduced in the twenty-eighth Parliament and became law in June, 1969. For some eight years before this time, committees in both the House and within the departments had considered various aspects of the policy. For our purposes, the instructive elements are two: the major thrust toward legislation, bitterly opposed by the Pharmaceutical Manufacturers' Association of Canada, was provided by senior civil servants; and there is considerable evidence that the Cabinet, with the exception of the Prime Minister, was very ambivalent about the entire policy.

Leadership was provided mainly through an interdepartmental committee of senior bureaucrats from several relevant departments, which met periodically over a number of years beginning about 1962, and ultimately presented the Cabinet with a Report which became the major basis for government policy. Among its signal contributions was empirical support for the proposition that drug prices in Canada were unduly high, indeed among the highest in the world. During this time a special committee on Drug Costs and Prices had been established in the Commons and it is in this context that the potential policy initiative of the bureaucracy is most clearly evident. Students of the issue agree that 'with the Privy Council as intermediary,

222

the civil servants suggested Committee staff, briefed the Committee Chairman and advocated policy, and provided data when requested. Later, less formally, they contacted and briefed potentially sympathetic witnesses, Committee members and newspaper reporters, and suggested criticisms of the written submissions from unsympathetic witnesses.'[1]

Another careful observer comes to a similar conclusion. Comparing Canadian and the British experience with drug legislation, in which 'politicians were the prime motivating force', Ronald Lang concludes, 'It is not equally clear that the same can be said of the Canadian drug programme, or of the manner in which the Government arrived at its policy on drug costs. While recognising the doctrine of ministerial responsibility, it is clearly evident that policy formation took shape from within the civil service, to be adopted later by the Cabinet. There is no evidence to suggest that the Cabinet, either individually or collectively, decided on a set of goals or directed the senior civil servants to formulate a policy which would have these goals implemented. Rather, it is the reverse which would appear to be more accurate – one in which the top civil servants in the six government departments concerned met regularly to set out a comprehensive programme which they believed would reduce drug costs in Canada. Having accomplished this, the bill of goods was then sold to a Cabinet which could see the political attractiveness of the scheme.'[2]

While this is a case study, from which one cannot generalize, its implications for conventional appreciations of Cabinet government and the potentials of bureaucratic initiative are clear. The highly political climate in which senior bureaucrats often function is also explicit in the fact that although the most frequent way lobbyists contact them is through direct appointments, the second and third ranking means is through a Cabinet member, followed closely by contact through a back-bencher. While unrepresentative, the following comment by an Ottawa bureaucrat is germane: 'I've had seven ministers with no experience of real pressure from interest groups, but MP's are different. They try to pressure me, but the Minister takes care of them.'

If the operational ethic of the bureaucratic elite is often one of 'representative bureaucracy', in which responsibility is keyed essentially to their client groups, such should be revealed in certain of their attitudes regarding the role of interest groups. The orientations suggested by the following evidence include functional specialization, clientele legitimacy and a service

[1] J. E. Anderson, 'The drug bill: aspects of the policy process', paper read at annual meeting, Canadian Association of Political Science, 1970, p. 11. [2] *Op cit.* p. 172.

definition of one's role. Here, in effect, one may observe the implementation of the corporatist ethos of Canadian political culture. The legitimacy ascribed to the going system is explicit in that not only do 87 per cent of senior civil servants maintain that interest groups perform a 'useful and necessary' role, but 80 per cent of them agree with the following specific rationale for a functional system of representation: 'Government departments are usually organized to represent discrete interests in society (e.g. business, agriculture, labour.) It is therefore reasonable that such departments should be mainly concerned with the social and economic interests in their special area.' Federal and provincial affirmations are virtually identical. Again, asked 'to what extent do the activities of interest groups generally contribute to the larger *public interest*, or are they usually focussed upon narrower interests', just over half indicate that such groups generally make a positive contribution to the public interest. Although less fulsome than those above, this affirmation is probably based upon the eminently pragmatic conclusion that the vigorous pursuit of discrete individual and group interests not only culminates in the general interest, but is, in logical terms, the only operational manifestation of that interest.[1]

THE CURRENCIES OF INTERACTION

We turn next to certain derivative benefits the bureaucracy receives in exchange for its service activities on behalf of clientele groups. As interection theory holds, social activity is initiated and maintained because those involved believe they arc 'making a profit'. Some mutually beneficial medium of exchange must flow between participants if existing patterns of interaction are to continue. The currencies may be extremely varied, ranging from subjective rewards of empathy, affection, loyalty, and the like through harder kinds of incentives including security, authority, power, and income. Many of these benefits, of course, surface at the political party level in the form of financial and ideological support, with the result that incentives at the bureaucratic level may seem relatively insignificant.

On the other hand, bureaucracy has its own political life and its own aspirations for security and growth. Such goals require fulsome support which, although its formal manifestation in such forms as appropriations and enabling legislation may lie within the governmental system, is likely to

---

[1] For impressive arguments that such is the case, see Bentley, *The Process of Government*, and Glendon Schubert, *The Public Interest* (Glencoe: Free Press, 1961).

depend in part upon the good will of organized client interests. As argued earlier, government may be regarded as the channel through which such support is allocated among the various great social interests, in a process which depends heavily upon the expertise and continuity provided by bureaucratic centres of power.

Our data enable us to specify the significance and distribution of some of the benefits which groups contribute to the accommodation process. It may be useful, however, to present the over-all distribution first. Information on the reactions of a department's clientele groups is ranked first by just over half of all bureaucrats (N–214), followed by participation in departmental advisory bodies and committees (one-quarter), with support for the department in the legislature, e.g. when appropriations are made, and helping draft legislation a very poor third (7 per cent). Some cognitive dissonance occurs here since directors themselves maintain that their participation in departmental advisory committees is their most important service. Moreover, they rank the other two services as being *equally* important to civil servants. Various services are ranked in Table 8-4 in terms of their comparative utility as perceived by senior officials. Only the distribution of the services ranked highest is presented.

Despite some discontinuity, there is general agreement among senior officials that interest group services are most valuable in the two areas of feed-back regarding clientele reactions to departmental activities and

TABLE 8-4 *Perceived utility of interest group services*

Service		Proportion ranking each service 'most important'								
	Ed.	Res. Mgt.	Health Welfare	Pub. Works	Lab.	Ind. Fin.	Trans.	Att. Genl.	Govtl. Affairs.	Agr.
	%	%	%	%	%	%	%	%	%	%
Information on clientele	18	8	45	47	60	56	60	43	55	60
Mem. on deptl. comms.	64	70	38	35	20	20	14	25	36	20
Support approps.	18	—	3	4	10	—	5	—	—	—
Helping draft legislation	—	—	7	—	—	6	2	—	—	—
Other	—	3	3	9	—	3	12	13	—	10
N.A.	—	18	3	4	10	15	7	19	9	10
	(11)	(23)	(29)	(23)	(10)	(36)	(43)	(16)	(11)	(10)

225

providing support and advice through participation in advisory committees of various kinds. Sharp variations occur regarding the 'information' service, however, with bureaucrats in Resource Management and Education ranking it substantially below the others, for reasons we are unable to explain. Meanwhile, both of these deviant categories rank very high on the second service, which seems to reflect certain functional characteristics of their respective fields.

These data, in effect, symbolize the pervasive functional cohesion existing between bureaucrats and directors, including prominent members of their groups who are brought in this way directly into the formal apparatus of government. The exchange process within the political elite is also evident in the value ascribed to group support for departmental budgets and participation in drafting and amending legislation. Since the latter seems to provide a seminal index of agency–clientele relationships, it may be useful to note that such ties are especially close in departments of Health and Welfare, Finance and Industry, and Transportation. Some substantial regional differences appear: Ontario bureaucrats, for example, rank much higher on the significance of interest group support for appropriations, compared with Ottawa. Ottawa officials, meanwhile, rank higher on the importance of group assistance in drafting legislation.

INTEREST GROUP INTERACTIONS WITH PARLIAMENT

We turn next to interactions between interest group representatives and back-benchers. Our sample of Cabinet members will be treated separately. Such interactions are somewhat anomalous, in that many knowledgeable observers, including back-benchers, insist that interest groups pay relatively little attention to Parliament because the ordinary member has such limited influence. As a *Union Nationale* deputy put it, 'Many times we don't know about a bill before it is presented on the floor. We learn about it in the newspapers.' A Quebec Liberal MP said similarly, 'An ordinary member can't do enough to make it worthwhile for a lobbyist to see him. It occurs at a higher level.' Nevertheless, about 30 per cent of interest group representatives spend some time interacting with ordinary members. The obvious question is, why is this so?

One explanation at the federal level is probably the growing importance of standing committees, which makes their chairmen and members more salient for group interests. Perhaps more significant is the division of labour in the parliamentary system whereby ministers are essentially concerned with substantive policy issues while back-benchers, almost by default, spend a great deal of time attending to the demands of their constituents for individual services and assistance of many kinds. The range of such claims is, indeed, coterminous with the vast scope of government operations. As David Hoffman and Norman Ward found in Ottawa, letters from constituents are primarily concerned with social welfare and job requests, averaging 80 and 45 per cent, respectively, when English and French-speaking back-benchers are combined.[1] Such claims, and particularly those from individuals with limited political interest and influence such as pensioners and recent immigrants, are often inspired by interest groups to which the individuals concerned may belong or which have a special concern for marginal groups.

We saw earlier, moreover, that a high proportion of Canadians feel considerable diffidence in approaching federal (and by inference, provincial) officials. As the national survey on citizens' attitudes toward government information found, there is a dramatic association between the quality of such relationships experienced by Canadians and their levels of interest, education and class. Over 40 per cent of upper-class individuals describe their interactions with officials as 'warm and cooperative', compared with only 23 per cent of lower-class persons. Only one-quarter of those whose interest in governmental affairs is high find such relationships 'cold and strained', compared with fully half of those whose interest is low.[2]

Faced with such psychic barriers, those with marginal resources often turn to interest group leaders to intercede for them with officials and MP's. If this is indeed true, it may explain the generalization offered by several members of the political elite that labour characteristically approaches back-benchers, whereas industry tends to gain access at the Cabinet level. As one provincial deputy minister maintained, 'I think industry would do this [lobbying] at the Cabinet level or at a departmental level with us. Organized labour is the opposite; they do it with the MLA.' Perhaps we may conclude that interest groups possessing generous shares of legitimacy and related political resources tend to function quietly within the system, according to conventional rules of the game. Outsiders, so to speak, tend to operate on its periphery and to employ provocative, publically-oriented stratagems. As we have seen, moreover, this distinction is not so much determined by 'hard' resources of income and membership, as by subtle

---

[1] *Bilingualism and Biculturalism in the Canadian House of Commons*, pp. 106–7.
[2] Morris *et al.*, 'Attitudes toward federal Government information', pp. 192–4.

kinds of social preferences and popular legitimations which often reflect conservative Canadian values.

From another vantage point, of course, the efficacy of these kinds of private political resources rests heavily upon the fact that they are also possessed by the governmental elite. Accommodation, in effect, is eased by a condition of consensual validation which makes such differential patterns of access natural, if not inevitable. However, this kind of an explanation rests in part upon a simplistic dichotomy between 'government' and private elites which is more likely to obfuscate than to ease political analysis. Instead, as our data suggest, governmental and private elites constitute an integrated political corps which, as will be shown in a later chapter, tends to be socially homogeneous.

Such conditions explain only part of the reasons for group penetration at the back-bencher level. The range of incentives is indicated in Table 8-5, which is based upon the following item: 'Given the Canadian system of party discipline and resulting limitations on the independence of members, why, in your opinion, do lobbyists and interest groups still attempt to influence individual members?' The majority of members believe that lobbyists think, however wrongly, that if they can persuade a sufficient number of back-benchers to support a given policy, they may be able, in caucus, to change the mind of the relevant minister (see Table 8-5).[1]

In the round, Canadian MP's generally agree that lobbyists approach them for three main reasons, the most compelling of which is the assumption that they can build a block of opinion among some members which may have an effect upon party leaders in caucus. This explanation might well have been combined with 'influencing the Cabinet', since both relate to the objective of exerting influence through back-benchers. Quite different is the second major explanation that lobbyists simply do not understand the parliamentary system, presumably meaning that members cannot in fact influence ministers through the caucus. Agreement on this judgment, however, is far from complete, and there is probably some variation among the parties in this regard. It also seems doubtful that interest group directors and their agents are naive about the system. It may also be that the recent strengthening of the committee system, which would make certain back-

---

[1] Federal members, at least, are ambivalent about the role of the caucus: while a majority agree that back-benchers have little opportunity to influence front-bench legislation, fully 80 per cent also disagree with the statement that 'the party caucus is not a place for influencing party policy', Hoffman and Ward, *Bilingualism and Biculturalism in the Canadian House of Commons*, pp. 159–60.

TABLE 8-5 *Members' explanations of why lobbyists approach back-benchers*

Explanation	Proportion ranking each variable			
	Ottawa	Quebec	Ontario	British Columbia
	%	%	%	%
Influence policy through caucus	50	35	32	41
Misunderstand system	13	8	8	6
Influence Cabinet	6	7	20	9
Weak party discipline	5	—	4	6
Lobbyist's duty	6	4	3	3
Personal reasons	2	6	10	9
Other	12	12	14	24
NA/DK	5	27	8	2
	(140)	(43)	(50)	(34)

benchers more salient for lobbyists, was not yet a factor in back-benchers opinion. Finally, the response concerning 'personal reasons' may symbolize the belief of some MP's that interest group directors attempt to justify their own role by contacting legislators, even though this is relatively ineffectual.

Interaction has often been conceptualized here as an asymmetrical process, with interest groups seeking access to MP's. Legislators also find it useful, however, to *initiate* contacts with group representatives. Their incentives include obtaining information which back-benchers *qua* generalists, typically without research facilities, badly need about the technical aspects of legislation and what we have called the ideological factor in policy issues. They must obtain information on both the operational consequences of governmental policies and the normative reactions to them, especially from articulate groups in their own ridings.

Such needs may be covered in four specific contexts: ascertaining the attitudes of constituents; securing information for writing speeches; obtaining information about pending bills; and mobilizing public support for a Government bill or programme. Our data indicate that the following proportions of MP's initiate contact in each of the above situations: 70 per cent, 60, 47, and 44, respectively. Securing information about the attitudes of their constituents ranks highest, followed closely by securing information for speeches. As noted, such dependence undoubtedly reflects the ordinary MP's lack of research sources.

Among Cabinet members, the pattern is quite similar, with the primary focus on the attitudes of constituents, but with somewhat higher dependence upon securing information about pending legislation among federal ministers, compared with back-benchers and provincial ministers. From these data, we may conclude tentatively that MP's are most likely to contact interest groups for information concerning constituent opinion and speech-writing, but substantially less so for the other two services. In the immediate context, however, the main thrust of these data concerns the bases and extent of interest group–legislative interaction.

More directly germane is the kinds of issues brought to back-benchers by interest group agents, compared with those presented to the Cabinet and civil service. Before examining this question, however, it may be helpful to summarize the distribution of such case study issues (*N*–484). Forty per cent concern legislation, divided equally between bills and laws. Administrative regulations are next, involving almost one-fifth, followed by two 'non-governmental' issues, intraorganizational problems (one-tenth), and fund-raising (almost one-tenth), leaving licensing, jurisdictional problems within or among groups, and 'others' to account for the remaining one-fifth. The vast majority of these issues, as noted earlier, involved attempts by the groups to bring about change.

Regarding the association between such issues and preferred interest group targets, the distribution shown in Table 8-6 occurs.

These data provide an over-view of both the substance and process of interest group–government interaction, in the case study context. Forty per

TABLE 8-6 *Substantive issues presented to governmental elites by interest groups, case study.*

Issue	Proportion ranking each target first					
	Back-benchers	Cabinet	Bureuacracy	Ex. Assts.	Other	
	%	%	%	%	%	
Laws	11	51	19	4	15	(92)
Bills	30	33	19	4	13	(90)
Intraorga'l policy	15	26	16	4	22	(27)
Licensing	13	54	21		13	(26)
Admin. regs.	13	41	21	3	19	(79)
Fund-raising	7	13	60	3	17	(30)
Group juris.	—	23	31	15	31	(16)
Other	6	36	24	1	22	(70)
	(60)	(154)	(107)	(15)	(50)	(406)

cent of all groups contact the Cabinet; 26 per cent turn mainly to the bureaucracy; while only 15 per cent focus on the legislature as their primary target. Putatively administrative issues, such as licensing and regulations, exhibit a similar valence. Only regarding pending legislation do groups approach back-benchers with an intensity similar to that accorded the Cabinet. And only in fund-raising and problems of group jurisdiction is the Cabinet's dominance superseded by the bureaucracy. Even the final 'other' category, consisting of a *pot pourri* of issues, neither significant nor structured enough to warrant detailed categorization, remains primarily a Cabinet province. Here, in sum, we have the clearest evidence of Cabinet hegemony in the process of elite accommodation.

As noted, however, this evidence is drawn from the case study issues, which are probably not entirely typical of the general pattern of interaction experienced by most groups. This proposition is shown to be true by responses to an item which asked directors 'which three of the following elements in the political system receive the greatest amount of attention from you and your association?' When the context is shifted to this level of group interaction with government, the distribution shown in Table 8-7 appears.

This evidence confirms that the case study issues evoke a somewhat different interaction pattern from that generally experienced by interest groups. Here, not surprisingly, the bureaucracy replaces the Cabinet as the primary target, with the same proportion of directors (40 per cent) seeking access there as had approached the Cabinet in the case study context. Back-benchers now come into their own, narrowly displacing the Cabinet

TABLE 8-7 *Major general targets of interest groups*

Proportion ranking each target first		
Target	Proportion	
	%	
Bureaucracy	40	(158)
Back-benchers	20	(80)
Cabinet	19	(74)
Legislative comms.	7	(27)
Executive assts.	5	(19)
Judiciary	3	(11)
Other	6	(24)
		(393)

as the second primary focus. My impressionistic judgment is that the difference between these two contexts is essentially one of frequency versus significance, with the case study generally tending to represent issues of critical importance to the group, which inspire attempts to penetrate the highest level of government, contrasted with general, run-of-the-mill issues which are handled according to their functional implications. Perhaps the difference is between issues in which technical considerations are paramount and those in which political or ideological elements are more pressing, with the divergent consequences for interaction seen in Tables 8-6 and 8-7.

Interaction theory suggests that directors must provide some tangible benefits and services to back-benchers if their relationship is to continue. Such benefits range broadly from inconsequential personal services and entertainment to vital matters such as information and campaign support. Such services also involve the resolution of conflicting preferences among their members and the presentation of a collective policy or programme to governmental elites. In effect, rationalization, information, and demands are the major currencies flowing from the interest group component of the accommodation process.

The utility ascribed by MP's and directors to such services tends to vary somewhat, which suggests that costs and benefits are not always synchronized as rationally as interaction theory maintains. The data include four specific interest group services, which are ranked by both MP's and directors. The highest ranking is 'providing information on pending legislation', which is considered the classic interest group input. This is ranked 'very important' by one-fifth of MP's, with no difference between federal and provincial samples. 'Helping me represent all community interests' is ranked second, by 18 per cent of both categories, followed by 'building legislative support' and 'helping me "sell" my own position to the public', by 15 per cent, with provincial MP's ranking this variable much higher than their federal colleagues. Finally, another 14 per cent rank 'informing me of the attitudes of my constituents' as being very important.

On the whole, directors tend to ascribe somewhat higher value to these services than legislators do. The greatest disparity (26 *v.* 14 per cent) occurs regarding the final item, attitudes of constituents, a group service which back-benchers tend to devalue somewhat. My impression is that they feel ambivalent about this particular activity, which touches very close to their own major role. Although the provision of information regarding legislation is valued most highly, it is unexpected that the difference is not greater, since as we saw earlier, pending legislation is the only case study issue where interest group access is shared almost equally between legislators and Cabinet.

Another bit of evidence indicating the extent of interaction between MP's and selected interest group representatives appears in a sociometric item wherein legislators are asked to name lobbyists in eight major interest areas. When interaction is scaled on this basis, the pattern shown in Table 8-8 appears, presented separately for federal and provincial MP's, including ministers.

Although this is not a very stringent test, since it asks only for the identification of lobbyists in major areas, including business, labour, professions, welfare, etc., it provides some evidence about interaction between these two segments of the political elite. Refusal rates were very high on this item, which proved somewhat unsettling since it asked MP's to name the lobbyists concerned. For example, no federal ministers, who are clearly a major target for most groups, were included in the 'high' category, and we have not reported them separately because of the resulting lack of confidence in the data. Provincial MP's tend to exhibit substantially higher rates of interaction, compared with federal, which is not surprising given the fact that they are, in geographical terms, at least, closer to their constituents and thus more accessible. It may be too that the high turnover rate (around 40 per cent) among federal MP's has a dampening effect on interaction.

A corollary of these findings is the fact that 45 per cent of federal and 55 per cent of provincial MP's indicate that they have, at one time or another, been influenced by a lobbyist 'to the extent that you began to question your position on an issue or a bill'. In the present context, the implications for influence are perhaps less significant than the fact that only 7 of 269 MP's failed to respond to this item, which indicates that regardless of the degree

TABLE 8-8 *Interaction between MP's and selected lobbyists*

Interaction[a]	Federal	Provincial
	%	%
High	22	30
Medium	22	29
Low	25	17
NA	30	24
	(140)	(127)

[a] 'High' is defined as knowing from 7–9 lobbyists; 'medium', 4–6; and 'low', 1–3.

of perceived influence, considerable interaction occurs between them and lobbyists.

THE CABINET AS SYMBOL OF ELITE ACCOMMODATION

In the context of elite accommodation, the Cabinet may be regarded as the prime symbol and ultimate agent of national synthesis among the political elite. Its cardinal role is patent in its representational criteria for appointment and the tendency, noted earlier regarding other consociational societies, to include proportionality and rotation within the dominant charter groups among such criteria.[1] Beginning with the first federal government of Sir John Alexander Macdonald in 1867, the pattern was cut by the inclusion in the Cabinet of George Etienne Cartier, Jean Charles Chapais and Hector Louis Langevin. From that time onward, the mould of one-quarter representation in the Cabinet for *French-Canadiens* continued unbroken until the 1960s when the proportion was increased to about one-third, in part as a result of aggravated strains on national unity brought by separatist demands, Quebec's insistence upon special status within confederation, and the Pearson and Trudeau Governments' receptivity to such claims. Regarding proportionality, it is interesting, and perhaps coincidental, that among the 16 Canadians who have held the office of Prime Minister, precisely four have been French-Canadians.

The Cabinet's role in elite accommodation is most clearly apparent in certain issues which have plagued relations between the Two Canadas historically. These are well known and will be mentioned only in passing, including the conscription issue in two world wars and the long-standing tensions regarding the funding and control of programmes in health, education, and welfare, as well as revenue sharing. The federal–provincial conference mechanism has been established to ease such problems. Other examples of accommodative politics include the fillip to French-Canadian nationalism symbolized by the Royal Commission on Bilingualism and Biculturalism, and subsequent legislation providing for bilingual government documents in certain areas of Canada. Quebec's insistence, mainly under the Lesage reform government, upon institutionalized means of federal–provincial consultation were honoured by the striking of a joint federal–interdepartmental committee charged with this task. At the cultural level,

[1] Among others, see N. McL. Rogers, 'Federal influences on the Canadian Cabinet' 11 *Canadian Bar Review* (February, 1933), pp. 103-21.

the Cabinet decision to situate the dramatically successful (and financially demanding) Expo 1967 in Montreal is germane.

Prime Minister Trudeau's bargain with Quebec (1972), whereby family allowance programmes are to be administered under provincial rules, again illustrates the historic pattern of accommodation at the highest level. The federal government's jejune bargaining position is perhaps evident in the Premier's observation that he was 'a little disappointed' that Quebec had not accepted the Victoria charter (1971) which had been adopted by all the other provinces. He 'now hoped Quebec would accept the charter since the federal decision respecting family allowances meets all the province's demands'.[1]

While such accommodations involve many problems, they are eased by the nonideological quality of the major parties and by the attending presence of the 'administrative politicians' who have usually managed the national political system. Such conditions also rest in part upon considerable social and normative cohesion among the political elite which has meant, with the exception of labour leaders, that interaction and accommodation among them has been relatively easy and productive. 'Political leaders', as John Porter concludes, 'seem to be easily accessible to the corporate elite'.[2] As we have shown, access and the expression of interest group demands are similarly fulsome between private elites and the bureaucracy. *Indeed, as noted earlier, virtually half of the departments in our sample have created interest groups in order to facilitate the expression of such claims.* The governmental sector, it may be said, is occupied with allocating something over one-third of Gross National Product and providing the framework of law and legitimacy within which this process occurs. Such is the context of political economy in which elite accommodation occurs, much of which is channelled into the Cabinet arena.

INTEREST GROUP INTERACTION WITH THE CABINET

The Cabinet, of course, is typically regarded as the centre of authority and power within the parliamentary system. Its members presumably control the machinery of government through their individual command of the great departments, while collectively, they determine the major outlines of

---

[1] The *Globe and Mail* (March 13, 1972), p. 1.
[2] *The Vertical Mosaic*, p. 533; for accounts of elite interaction in other institutional contexts, see *ibid.*, pp. 524–52.

national policy. Since interest groups seek access at critical points in the political system, we should expect frequent interaction between them and ministers. As we saw in the case study issue, most directors cite the Cabinet as their primary target. Indeed, among those who had employed lobbyists (N–181), 42 per cent had found access there. The extent to which such behaviour is institutionalized is explicit in the reply of the director of a prestigeful professional association to an item which asked if he ever contacted back-benchers: 'No, we go through *channels*, to Ministers and higher civil servants.'

Our data enable us to compare differences between Cabinet and back-benchers insofar as the frequency and substance of group access are concerned. In general, we may assume that back-benchers are usually approached regarding constituency services, whereas lobbyists approach Ministers mainly on substantive policy issues and major legislation.

Another incentive for approaching the Cabinet is the attempt to influence appointments at the highest levels of the bureaucracy and with regard to patronage appointments in various sectors. As is well known, the Prime Minister has the ultimate discretion in the assignment and transfer of deputy ministers, which means that clientele groups will at times advance their claims with him and with relevant ministers in an attempt to influence such appointments. Once again, similar conditions prevail at the provincial level, where one minister, for example, indicated in our interview that he had just seen two representatives of a Forestry Association who had called to press for the appointment of a certain individual as deputy minister, leaving with him a neatly bound statement supporting their claim.

This minister added that his relationships with interest group representatives were productive and extensive: 'I am very close to these people.' He not only saw them 'frequently' but had a high level of confidence in them. They were, moreover, 'quite influential' in shaping public policy. At the same time, he 'strongly disagreed' that interest groups actually represented *everyone* in their particular socioeconomic sector, as they sometimes claimed. Nor were they typically very influential in galvanizing support for legislation because 'in our system, they usually don't know beforehand what is coming up.'

Corroboration of the intensity of interaction between ministers and interest group representatives is found in the fact that the proportion of 'frequently' levels of interaction is substantially higher for ministers (N–42) compared with back-benchers (N–227), three-fourths $v.$ less than one-half. Although the N is very small (7), it is also noteworthy that 86 per cent of

TABLE 8-9 *Comparative psychopolitical resources of ministers and backbenchers*

	Ministers		Back-benchers	
Resource	Federal	Provincial	Federal	Provincial
	%	%	%	%
SES: upper-middle	86	66	73	67
Fathers' SES: upper-middle	30	23	26	25
Legitimacy: high	86	60	65	57
Sociometric ties:	57	40	38	52
'Pro-government'[a]	71	57	67	70
Interaction: high	86	66	40	54
	(7)	(35)	(135)	(92)

[a] 'Pro-government' ideology is based upon the following item: 'That government which governs least governs best' (reverse scored).

federal ministers rank at this high level, compared with two-thirds of their provincial counterparts.

We should also expect ministers to enjoy larger shares of psychopolitical resources, given their crucial leadership roles and the personal success and geographical availability that initially qualified them for appointment. Finally, following interaction theory, we should expect them to exhibit somewhat more positive attitudes toward interest groups and lobbyists. All these are empirical questions. We turn first to a comparative analysis of selected political resources which should be helpful in explaining some of any such differences. Table 8-9 presents the distribution, separated by role and region.

Although federal ministers,[1] compared with provincial, enjoy substantially larger shares of such political resources as higher education and occupation, which define socioeconomic status, it is noteworthy that federal back-benchers tend to have a much smaller advantage over their provincial colleagues. A related characteristic of both ministers and back-benchers is probably significant for elite accommodation, namely the fact that both groups have experienced considerable social mobility. For example, only one-quarter of our minister sample had fathers who ranked at the highest point on our scale, which includes over four-fifths of the present group. Mobility has been similarly dramatic among back-benchers, 70 per cent of whom are in

[1] It should be noted that our sample of federal ministers is so small as to make conclusions highly tentative. Our refusal rate with this subgroup was just over 50 per cent.

upper-middle-class strata, compared with only one-quarter of the total parent group. Canadian MP's, in effect, tend to be self-made men to a greater extent than often assumed. While the judgment can only be speculative, this recently-acquired status of many members of the political elite may have something to do with their brokerage role. It may be harder for them to take a position of independence regarding the business and corporate elites with whom they often interact in working out policy solutions.[1]

Regarding frequency of interaction and legitimacy, federal ministers again rank significantly higher than the others. Here again is a scintilla of evidence for the proposition that interaction is positively associated with imputed legitimacy. The association disappears, however, when we consider *federal* back-benchers, who are significantly lower than others on interaction, yet similar to provincial ministers and back-benchers in the degree of legitimacy imputed to lobbyists. Not astonishingly, federal ministers also rank highest on sociometric ties with group representatives. Here, a curious reversal occurs: whereas federal ministers rank substantially higher than their own back-benchers in this regard, the relationship is reversed at the provincial level, with a higher proportion of back-benchers naming such representatives.

Since we encountered considerable resistance to this particular question, the data must be interpreted with care. Ministers, for example, were more likely than back-benchers to reject this item, 40 per cent *v.* 24. Federal back-benchers, moreover, were much more likely to refuse than their provincial colleagues, whereas the refusal rate among ministers was virtually identical. Despite this refusal pattern, federal ministers rank highest on the variables concerned, and we can only speculate on what their relative position might have been had they, and provincial ministers as well, responded as freely as back-benchers.

Regarding 'pro-government' ideology, we noted earlier that the corporatist ethic and a positive appreciation of government's role in the private economy remained viable elements of Canadian political culture. While lip-service is paid to 'free enterprise'[2] and competition, the dominant orientation

---

[1] John Porter has shown similarly that Canadian political leaders have not been drawn from the highest socioeconomic strata: 'Only 16 per cent of the political elite came from families in which previous generations had occupied elite roles in the various institutional systems.' And again, 'It is certainly reasonable to conclude that top-ranking positions in the political system are not as attractive to those of high class origin as are top-ranking jobs within the economic system.' *The Vertical Mosaic*, p. 394.

[2] Like many political symbols, 'free enterprise' has no precise denotation. It is used here in its honorific sense as an idealized conception held by some individuals concerning

238

among political elites is toward the positive enlistment of government in virtually every sector of economic life. One finds, as a result, some evidence of a common anomaly of Western society, the recourse to government protection and subsidies in order to strengthen 'free enterprise'. Although such normative preferences will be analysed in detail later, it seems useful to consider this facet of them here as a resource that ramifies the ideological cohesion of governmental and private elites in their joint efforts to achieve national political stability through accommodation. Viewed as a political resource, this pro-government valence should be even more strongly held by federal ministers than by their provincial colleagues. Meanwhile, although regional variations probably exist, one would also expect ordinary members to share this norm widely.

Analysis indicates that this proposition is generally true. Fully 70 per cent of Canadian back-benchers (*N*–227) reject the individualistic, Lockeian premise that government is at best a necessary evil.[1] Provincial variations are dramatic, with Quebec ranking highest, at 87 per cent; followed by British Columbia (two-thirds) and Ontario (59 per cent). Ottawa shares the same ranking as British Columbia. Given its commercial–industrial thrust, it is not surprising that Ontario proves the least inclined to share this pro-government value, but surely the decisive conclusion is the consistent majority support for this appreciation among all back-benchers.

Our suggestion that ministers would tend to have a stronger pro-government orientation than back-benchers is not borne out, since 'only' 70 and 57 per cent, respectively, of federal and provincial ministers reject the proposition, compared with the average of 71 for back-benchers.

These preferences can be checked by another ideological item which maintains that free enterprise and democracy are necessarily interrelated. While some MP's might reject this proposition on the logical ground that there is no such equation, one assumes that the responses of most members mark either a pro-government or a 'free enterprise' orientation. If this is so, we should expect to find the proportion of MP's rejecting this proposition similar to that in the previous item.

Here, instead, it seems that back-benchers seek to have the best of both worlds. Having strongly endorsed the pro-government value in the earlier

relations between government and the private economy, in which the latter enjoys a great deal of autonomy in shaping its operating environment. Such a condition has rarely, if ever, existed, but this has little to do with the symbolic and rhetorical significance of the term.

[1] The specific item states: 'That government which governs least governs best.'

item, 56 per cent of them now manifest a similar, although less consensual, support for the inapposite proposition that 'democracy depends fundamentally upon the existence of free enterprise.' Provincial variations are again impressive, with two-thirds of Ontario's back-benchers supporting this prescription, followed by Quebec (60 per cent) and British Columbia with only 46 per cent. Just over half of federal MP's endorse this view, providing a fairly pervasive support for 'free enterprise' values.

This general configuration is sustained when ministers are analysed separately. Although the N is very small, only 55 per cent of federal ministers accept the generalization, compared with a substantially higher proportion of provincial ministers at 77 per cent. When provincial ministers are compared, they do not follow the gradient set by their back-bench colleagues: Ontario ministers, as expected, rank highest, with fully 90 per cent of them endorsing the free enterprise–democracy equation, but British Columbia's ministers are now second, with 80 per cent, followed by Quebec with almost two-thirds.

Here, in effect, we find an interesting variation between back-bencher and ministerial opinion, with the latter much more favourably disposed toward 'free enterprise'. Federal ministers, somewhat unexpectedly, are less favourably disposed than their provincial opposites, but the sample is quite small and the conclusion must be very tentative.

If consistency is a virtue, it seems that Ontario must be saluted, since its MP's rank lowest on rejecting the 'government is a necessary evil' norm, while ranking highest on the 'free enterprise' valence. On the other hand, if a high toleration for ambiguity is preferred, Quebec's status is impressive, since her deputies sustain the greatest ambivalence in supporting both government and 'free enterprise'.

Finally, concerning patterns of interaction, certain inter-provincial differences are germane. Regarding the intensity of interaction between interest groups and back-benchers, for example, the scale runs as follows: British Columbia has the highest rate, with 56 per cent of her MP's ranking high (twice a week or more), followed by Ontario with 40 per cent. In Quebec the rate falls sharply to only 23 per cent. Ottawa, meanwhile, ranks near the mean at 39 per cent. Further analysis reveals that Quebec's low position is characteristic of her ministers as well, only half of whom rank at the high level compared with over three-fourths in Ontario and British Columbia.

One would expect legitimacy to follow interaction in the assumed fashion. Taking only the highest level on the scale, i.e. trusting lobbyists 'all of the time', we do find the same gradient among the provinces: British Columbia ranks highest with 20 per cent; Ontario is next with 10 per cent, while Quebec is again lowest, with 5 per cent. Ottawa is relatively higher on legitimacy than on interaction, ranking in the upper range of the scale at 18 per cent, whereas she had been at the mean on interaction. Parenthetically, the same gradient appears again when one combines the first and second levels of the legitimacy scale, although the distance between each set of provincial members varies, with Quebec being closer to Ontario, but still ranking lower. Ottawa also occupies the same relative position.

Using another indicator of legitimacy, we find that about four-fifths of both Social Credit legislators in British Columbia and ruling party Conservatives in Ontario regard the efforts of interest group directors to influence them as entirely legitimate. Since the British Columbia sample includes three parties, it is necessary to demonstrate that the positive valence toward groups found there is not the result of the contributions made by parties other than Social Credit. When this is done, we find that the party differences are substantial: whereas half of the Liberal members (N–4) rank high on legitimacy, and one-third of the New Domocrats (N–10) do, only 10 per cent of Social Credit members (N–20) are found at this level.

In sum, the evidence is mixed regarding the question at hand. In an inter-provincial context, certainly Social Credit is not as unsympathetic to groups as Quebec's *Union Nationale* or Liberal parties, just over half of whose respondents rank low on interest group legitimacy, compared with her one-quarter. Indeed, combining all parties and all provinces, Quebec has the largest proportion of MP's at the low level of trust (51 per cent), followed by Ontario (44 per cent), and British Columbia with less than one-quarter. Perhaps we may conclude that despite Social Credit's ambivalence, the milieu for interest groups in the province is generally sympathetic. Certainly, there is ample evidence that interaction flourishes, despite any opposing philosophic tendencies on the part of the present Government. Perhaps functional interdependence tends to overcome ideological cleavages between party and groups, while the non-ideological posture of the political elite neutralizes the tensions that do arise.

This generally positive thrust is apparent in the experiences of interest group directors in British Columbia. When asked, 'To what extent do you feel legislators regard any attempts by your group to influence them as legitimate?', 47 per cent of them responded 'always', compared for example with 45 per cent in Ontario. About 80 per cent of both groups reject the judgment that 'interest group executives tend to regard legislators as competitors in a struggle to shape public policy'. Regarding their rapport with legislators, just over half in each province indicate that they trust legislators 'all or most of the time'. Meanwhile, British Columbia's directors enjoy a high level of felt efficacy: using the most demanding criterion of influence in the item concerning their efforts to influence MP's, over half of them report a high level of experienced influence, compared with just over one-quarter of those in Ontario.

Although I am anticipating the subsequent analysis of comparative elite values, it is interesting to speculate further upon the reasons for such variations. While Quebec's low ranking is not unexpected, it seems somewhat incongruous that British Columbia should rank higher on group legitimacy and interaction than the other provinces. The philosophy of the ruling Social Credit party, as expressed by some of its leaders, includes a tendency toward an individualistic conception of society in which interest groups are somewhat suspect, and in an interesting rejection of Durkheim's thesis, viewed as *barriers* between government and the 'people'. Interest group politics, in effect, is apparently defined in pejorative terms similar to those of western populism in the United States. In this context, one assumes that interest groups will be kept at arm's length, rather than being highly legitimated. Perhaps functional requisites have again triumphed over ideology, however, in that the Social Credit party has been obliged to work closely with major groups, especially given its dramatic thrust toward industrial development of the province. Explanation may also include the more fluid social structure which characterizes newer societies such as British Columbia, and which probably nourishes easier interpersonal relations, compared with Eastern regions of Canada. Presumably, lobbyists would benefit from this egalitarian milieu.

Following Durkheim's thesis of the functional need for *corps intermediaires* to bridge the gap in modern industrial society between the individual and government, Quebec's relatively low ranking on interaction and legitimacy suggests that the degree of organic solidarity or community consciousness required for fulsome interaction among the political elite is somewhat less developed than in British Columbia and Ontario. Given the patent cultural homogeneity of Quebec, however, this hypothesis seems questionable, suggesting that one must look to demographic factors such as social class and educational opportunity to sustain the generalization. Here, it may be that the residues of the structured class system of Quebec, and attending limitations on educational achievement among its citizens are more relevant.[1]

[1] What seems to be a fascinating empirical manifestation of such classical residues is

Such conditions tend to nourish more of an individualistic than an organic, corporatist conception of social life, with resulting limitations on the legitimacy and access of interest groups in the political system. Meanwhile, the tradition of educational elitism may account for the comparatively small proportion of individuals who turn to associational life as a means of interest accommodation (see Table 2-10). They would not always possess adequate shares of the personal resources which have usually been a prerequisite of democratic political and associational participation.

This thesis, of course, runs contrary to the main thrust of accommodation theory, which holds that ethnic and religious cleavages propel elites into mutual interaction to preserve stability. If the obverse of such conditions were sufficient, given her unusual cultural homogeneity, Quebec would obviously have little difficulty in maintaining a stable political equilibrium. Quebec's internal cleavages, in this sense, are not ethnic and religious, but based upon social class and political ideology, with more explosive consequences than those seen in other Western consociational societies.

found in the tendency of group directors in Quebec to designate their groups as *professional*, in many cases despite its obvious inapplicability in terms of the usual criteria. For example, 16 per cent of directors of business and labour associations categorized their groups as 'professional', including such anomalous cases as contractors' associations and chambers of commerce. This behaviour may reflect the traditional idealization of classical and professional learning and occupations in the province, compared with business and industry.

CHAPTER 9

THE STRUCTURE OF ELITE INTERACTION

The remaining chapters are devoted to an analysis of the bases of elite accommodation, separated into behavioural, cognitive, and affective components. Interaction theory will be used first to order the data regarding behavioural relationships among the political elite. In the next chapter, we shall turn to an analysis of instrumental values about the political system to determine whether members of the elite tend to share a certain cognitive structure regarding its operational nature and the role that interest groups play in influencing governmental policy. Finally, in the concluding chapters, certain social and ideological characteristics of the political elite will be presented. Our bench-mark assumption is that this constellation of behavioural, cognitive, and affective conditions provides the essential basis for the system of elite accommodation which characterizes the Canadian political culture.

INTERACTION THEORY: THE *I–L–I* SYNDROME

A brief restatement of interaction theory seems necessary at the outset. This theory functions at a relatively basic theoretical and empirical level, being concerned with personal encounters between individuals and groups. Essentially behavioural in focussing upon the incentives that mediate interaction, its essential formulation is that certain shared activities bring individuals together repeatedly, as in a work group situation, that such activities result in sustained interactions and exchanges which tend to produce shared sentiments or values. The latter, in turn, tend to encourage close normative ties among the actors and to encourage further interaction among them, with subsequent strengthening of the normative bonds. In an economic sense, the system may be seen as one of exchange, whereby all participants seek to 'make a profit' through exchanging valued currencies which may include such emotional gratifications as friendship, love, and empathy or instrumental rewards including prestige, influence, and income. In addition to this essentially economic basis, interaction theory rests upon the well-established psychological proposition that men tend to repeat experiences that are gratifying while terminating those that prove unpleasant.

As noted earlier, we have used this theory to order and explain interactions among legislators, bureaucrats, and interest group directors. It should be emphasized that we are dealing throughout with the operational, instrumental process of government, rather than with its isolated, dramatic, controversial issues which in some sense are only the patent manifestation of an ongoing, underlying reality which comprises the vast majority of governmental decisions. We have seen, for example, that interest groups focus mainly upon the bureaucracy. This is the milieu in which the vast majority of decisions regarding allocations of public resources are handled, usually with the knowledge and participation of only those immediately involved. In this sense, while Parliament is the focus of political and journalistic attention, the mainstream of decisions, and much of the policy that arises in their interstices, exists elsewhere.

Interaction theory leads us to predict that the frequency of interaction between the governmental elite and interest groups will be related to the normative trust or legitimacy that the former ascribe to the latter, and that both interaction and legitimacy will be positively associated with the effectiveness or influence that legislators and bureaucrats impute to interest groups directors or their agents.

As we have seen, interaction among the political elite is generally frequent and sustained. Legislators and civil servants derive various benefits from such interactions, including objective information regarding the consequences of proposed policies, the ideological posture of groups toward them, and various forms of support for or against such policies, according to the actors' positions. Legislators also receive such benefits as information concerning the attitudes of their constituents, the state of public opinion, and help in writing speeches, which requires a broad range of technical information since MP's are required to address themselves to many problems before many publics. Other instrumental benefits include political support which interest groups can provide in many forms including not only funds, but honorary appointments, awards, and speaking engagements at annual meetings – all of which receive publicity, which is sometimes regarded as a valued benefit for political actors.

Interest group directors also benefit from the exchanges that mediate the

245

interaction process, including legislative support for their group's policies in caucus, speeches, and the mass media. Prestigeful members of groups are brought directly into the governmental decision-making process through membership on boards, testimony before committees, the opportunity to submit briefs, the use of back-benchers to intercede with the bureaucracy regarding a multiplicity of claims by group members, the chance to determine or at least veto appointments to governmental positions affecting their substantive areas, the opportunity to enjoy governmental legitimation as the 'official' representative of their substantive field, and to receive direct subsidies to maintain their group, as well as to sustain its larger interest. Such are the currencies that mediate interaction among legislators, bureaucrats, and group directors. We shall now attempt to demonstrate the association between interaction and legitimacy, as well as the attending consequences for influence relationships among the political elite. Legislators will be analysed first.

LEGITIMACY, INTERACTION, AND INFLUENCE AMONG THE POLITICAL ELITE

Since interaction is the critical variable in the *I–L–I* syndrome, we begin by presenting the incidence of legislative interest group interaction in a single table, differentiated by region. The data are based upon a single, straightforward item which asked respondents how often they came into direct, personal contact with interest group representatives. Responses are scaled into three categories: *frequently* (defined as twice a week); *occasionally* (defined as twice a month); and *seldom* or *rarely*. No difficulty seemed to arise concerning the item and we feel that the responses are accurate. Table 9-1 presents the distribution for the entire sample.

Among legislators, British Columbia's very high ranking is noteworthy, especially since some observers have maintained that the highly individualistic, populist orientations of the Social Credit party tend to result in marginal legitimacy and, presumably, interaction with interest groups in that province. However, it is too soon to conclude that such is not the case, since it could be that high interaction is not positively related to legitimacy. This question will be considered later. Ontario's legislators also manifest a high rate of interest group interaction, which among other things probably reflects the substantial proportion of business-industrial groups there and the Conservative government's pro-business orientation. Ottawa's low ranking is somewhat unexpected, and I have no explanation for it. Quebec ranks even

TABLE 9-1 *Interaction with interest groups, legislators*

Legislators	Frequency of interaction[a]			
	High	Medium	Low	
	%	%	%	
Ottawa	42	30	29	(135)
Quebec	40	42	19	(43)
Ontario	57	33	10	(50)
British Columbia	78	19	2	(33)
	(129)	(81)	(53)	(263)

[a] 'High' is defined as 'frequently' (twice a week); 'medium' as 'occasionally'; and 'low' as 'seldom or rarely'.

lower, which if our theory is correct, should be manifest in low rates of legitimacy. Overall, it is noteworthy that the rates of interaction are generally substantial, with just over half of the legislators interacting at the twice-a-week or more level.

We turn next to the relationship between interaction and legitimacy or trust, which is assumed to be generally positive. A single item is used to define legitimacy, and interaction is based upon the usual criterion of the extent of personal contact between legislators and interest group representatives. Using the entire legislative sample, the distribution shown in Table 9-2 appears.

Here, as in a number of related, unreported analyses using different

TABLE 9-2 *Association between interaction and legitimacy*

Legitimacy[a]	Frequency of interaction			
	High	Medium	Low	
	%	%	%	
High	36	27	11	(74)
Medium	55	66	74	(165)
Low	9	7	15	(24)
	(130)	(79)	(54)	(263)

X^2 = significant at .05 K's tau B = .15   Gamma = .26

[a] Legitimacy is defined here by a single item: 'Some observers have concluded that most legislators do not regard the activities of lobbyists as a form of improper 'pressure'. What is your reaction to this judgment?' Response categories were 'strongly agree' (high); 'agree' (medium); 'disagree or strongly disagree' (low).

indexes, there is a significant relationship between the two variables. The strong curvilinear tendency often seen among legislators appears again, as a glance across the medium row indicates. The expected association is much stronger at the high-legitimacy level, where it is linear across the table, whereas the distribution across the low row varies considerably less.

Some substantial party variations are masked by this summary presentation. For example, an analysis of interest group interaction by party, controlled for legitimacy, provides the following relationships at the 'high–high' level: Conservatives (72), 35 per cent; NDP (37), 22; Liberals (105), 16; *Union Nationale* (23), 10; and Social Credit (18), 7 per cent.

It is interesting to consider whether the relationship is much different when viewed from the opposite direction, i.e. when legitimacy is made the independent variable. How important, in effect, is the extent to which legislators regard lobbyists as trustworthy in determining how much they interact with them? Table 9-3, differentiated by region, provides a tentative answer to this question.

Some dramatic, although not statistically significant, regional variations appear, Quebec, for example, ranks substantially lower than other regions in the high–high column, while British Columbia shows a strong positive

TABLE 9-3   *Association between legitimacy and interaction, by region*

Region	High (45)			Perceived legitimacy[a] Medium (119)			Low (95)			
	High	Medium	Low	High	Medium	Low	High	Medium	Low	
	%	%	%	%	%	%	%	%	%	
Ottawa	60	22	19	40	29	26	40	33	27	(135)
Ontario	63	38	—	53	37	10	58	27	15	(49)
Quebec	33	67	—	61	28	11	23	50	27	(43)
British Columbia	71	29	—	82	18	—	86	14	—	(32)
										(259)

$X^2 =$ not significant at .05 K's tau C = .08   Gamma = .24

[a] Legitimacy is based upon the following item: 'Some observers have concluded that relations between a legislator and a lobbyist are based essentially upon *mutual trust*. Regarding lobbyists you have known, how much would you say you could trust them?' Response categories were: 'all of the time' (high); 'most of the time' (medium); 'some or none of the time' (low).

relation at this level, but as one looks across the table, it becomes clear that legitimacy makes no difference in the extent to which Quebec's MP's contact lobbyists. Ottawa, on the other hand, exhibits more of the expected relationship, with 60 per cent of those who rank high on legitimacy also ranking high on interaction with lobbyists, compared with only 40 per cent who rank low. From the assumptions of interaction theory, members in this province tend to behave somewhat more consistently than the others. In effect, whereas MP's in British Columbia and Quebec tend to interact with lobbyists regardless of the extent to which they trust them, those in Ottawa (and Ontario) seem to be somewhat more selective. Obviously, this judgment applies only in a theoretical context, since there are several reasons why a legislator would want to interact as fully as possible with lobbyists, regardless of the legitimacy imputed to them.

One other variable may be used to test the interaction–legitimacy relationship. This deals with the important and topical question of the consequences of granting 'self-government' to various occupations, and particularly in such salient professional areas as law and medicine. Such delegations of governmental authority are coming under increasingly severe attack as issues appear in which the average layman may be led to believe that professional or occupational self-interest has been the primary motivation for actions taken under such authority. The extent to which legislators endorse the prevailing system and the extent to which this mandate is associated with interaction is apparent in the following data. The item used states: 'Certain occupational groups, including law and medicine, play a major role in determining the legal regulations under which they operate. Do you regard this sharing of governmental authority with such groups as necessary?' Fifty-two per cent of those who ranked high on interaction agreed that such delegation was required, compared with only about one-third and one-fifth at the medium and low levels.

It is noteworthy that 72 per cent of MP's believe that the going system of delegated authority is necessary, mainly because of the technical complexity of many of the areas concerned (41 per cent of the 72 per cent) and the high status of the members of some such groups (27 per cent). Meanwhile, however, just over half of all MP's have some reservations, which include giving such groups too much power, disadvantaging the majority, and undercutting the role of the legislator.

The most demanding criterion of influence is provided by an item which draws upon the direct experience of legislators with lobbyists. The specific question used is as follows: Some people are more influenced by lobbyists

TABLE 9-4   *Association between interaction and influence*

	Frequency of interaction			
Influence	High	Medium	Low	
	%	%	%	
High	47	45	24	(108)
Medium	39	37	43	(102)
Low	14	18	33	(47)
	(129)	(78)	(50)	(257)

X^2 = significant at .05 K's tau B = .14   Gamma = .22

than others. Thinking of yourself, how often have you been: influenced to the extent that you (1) began to question your position on an issue; (2) changed your position somewhat on an issue, or (3) came to agree with a lobbyist's position on an issue. Using a weighted index, we find the distribution shown in Table 9-4 among the entire legislative sample.

The relationship here is positive, essentially linear and statistically significant. The largest proportion of those ranking high on contact, 47 per cent, rank highest on experienced influence, compared with only 24 per cent of those who rank low on interaction. So far, the evidence indicates that interaction is positively associated with legitimacy and that interaction is also positively related to influence among our legislative sample.

Our next task is to determine whether legitimacy is related to influence as assumed by interaction theory. However, after examining several distributions, both collectively and by province, it became clear that no significant relationship exists between these two variables. Interprovincial variations appear, with Ontario ranking highest and Quebec lowest, but none of them are significant. Before turning to a test of the posited relationship among the three *I–L–I* variables, it seems useful to determine whether there is any association between legitimacy and influence, controlling for tenure. Fully half of Canadian MP's (1970) have served only 0–4 years; 75 per cent 0–9 years, and the turnover rate at the federal level is 40 per cent, so tenure may well have some effect on patterns of interest group influence. Table 9-5 tests for such.

Here again, the familiar curvilinear effect among legislators appears. Those in the 5–9 years category rank substantially highest on influence as measured here. First-term MP's, meanwhile, rank substantially lower, and those who have been in service ten years prove to be even less susceptible

TABLE 9-5   *Association between influence and legitimacy, by length of service*

Influence	Length of service					
	10 years + (58)		5-9 years (64)		0-4 years (114)	
	Perceived legitimacy					
	High	Low	High	Low	High	Low
	%	%	%	%	%	%
High	24	24	49	22	37	22
Medium	46	53	32	57	32	44
Low	29	24	20	22	31	35
	(41)	(17)	(41)	(23)	(68)	(46)

X^2 = not significant at .05 K's tau C = .12   Gamma = .19

to lobbyist influence. The differences in each high cell across the high influence row are quite marked. While one can assume that first-termers would tend to rely upon such agents for socialization into the going system, it is hard to explain why those in the second category would prove most receptive to their influence. In the case of veterans, it may be that they have discounted the aid provided by interest groups, in part because they have enough experience to make rather more independent judgments about policy issues.

ASSOCIATION AMONG INTERACTION, LEGITIMACY, AND INFLUENCE

Here, we will use the same interaction and legitimacy items used earlier in Table 9-4, and employ the highest level of influence from the 'lobbyist' item. Our expectation is that differing levels of interaction and trust should explain part of the variation in experienced influence.

The data indicate that there is a tendency for influence to vary as a function of legitimation (see Table 9-6). The proportion of those in the high and medium cells across the high influence level is significantly higher than those in the equivalent low cells, and there is the expected decline in the high–high column. A substantially higher proportion (41 per cent) of those who rank high on both interaction and legitimacy rank high on influence, compared with those (24 per cent) who rank high on interaction but low on imputed trust. Looking across the 'medium' row, no differences exist at the high level of legitimacy, although substantial differences appear among

TABLE 9-6   *Association among interaction, legitimacy, and influence*

	Legitimacy						
	High (158)			Low (91)			
	Frequency of interaction						
Influence	High	Medium	Low	High	Medium	Low	
	%	%	%	%	%	%	
High	41	43	23	24	20	25	(81)
Medium	37	32	37	51	53	35	(100)
Low	23	25	40	24	27	40	(68)

$X^2 = .05$ K's tau $C = .08$ Gamma $= .14$

those who rank low on this variable. Meanwhile, no variation occurs across the low row.

We saw earlier that several of the expected relationships held up when single items were used as indicators of interaction, legitimacy, and influence, and run for the entire sample. However, such summary tables not only tend to mask differences among the four areas, but the use of single-item indicators is less reliable than indexes based upon several items. A stronger mode of analysis involves the use of multiple-item indexes for legitimacy and influence, with the relationship controlled for trust. Unfortunately, such specification presents a problem in that the N's become quite small in some categories, with the result that the shape of the distribution is sometimes determined by differences in a relatively small number of cases. Despite such discontinuities, the analysis should reveal any general pattern among the three interaction variables (see Table 9-7).

Looking at the 'high' cells across the high influence row, it is clear that legitimacy has a curvilinear effect, and that it is related to interaction and influence in the expected way only at the high and low levels of legitimacy. Looking across the high row, 55 per cent of those legislators who are high on interaction and on trust are indeed high on experienced influence, but the distribution flattens out in the medium category and only in the low legitimacy–interaction category does the expected gradient reappear. Looking at the high columns, we find the expected decline in influence only in the high–high column.

In sum, although interaction is positively related to legitimacy, and while interaction is also positively associated with influence, legitimacy does not act consistently as a strong intervening variable between interaction and influence, insofar as these legislators are concerned, using these indexes.

TABLE 9-7   *Association among interaction, legitimacy, and influence*

	Legitimacy[a]									
	High (29)			Medium (87)			Low (116)			
	Frequency of interaction									
Influence[b]	High	Medium	Low	High	Medium	Low	High	Medium	Low	
	%	%	%	%	%	%	%	%	%	
High	55	54	—	28	31	28	30	22	13	(65)
Medium	36	46	25	47	54	50	37	53	60	(112)
Low	9	—	75	25	15	22	32	26	27	(55)
										(232)

X^2 = The relationships in the high legitimacy segment of this table are significant at .05, but the table itself is not.

K's tau B = .13   Gamma = .25

[a] The legitimacy index used here is based upon the following items: 'Some observers maintain that relationships between a legislator and a lobbyist are based essentially upon mutual trust. Regarding lobbyists you have known, how much would you say you could rely upon them?'; 'Most lobbyists are competent professionals who know their business'; 'Some observers feel that the activities of interest groups are often contrary to the public good. How do you feel about this?'

[b] The influence index is based upon weighted responses to the following 'lobbyist' item: 'Some people are more influenced by lobbyists than others. Thinking of yourself, how often have you been...' Three graduated levels of influence were specified, and weighted accordingly.

This conclusion, of course, is not based only upon the evidence presented here. Several multiple-item indexes of legitimacy and influence were constructed for analysis and run not only against the entire legislative sample, but against party and region. Despite some minor variations, such as the fact that Social Credit members (N–17) rank highest on the expected association by party, and that MP's in Ottawa (N–129) show the most positive relationship regionally, none of the relationships was statistically significant, and it is clear that, for legislators, the expected theoretical assumptions do not fully meet the empirical test.

One possible explanation involves the normative perception that many legislators have of interest groups and their agents, which may be described as one of a generalized symbolic approval of such groups as collectively necessary to round out the democratic representational structure, yet attended by a mildly ambivalent view of any given interest group as being too narrow to warrant fulsome approval. As a result, the legislator seems to conclude, 'Yes, we need interest groups to bring us information, and to express popular demands, but insofar as any single group is concerned, I am not going to be unduly influenced. Moreover, I *should* not be unduly influenced.'

Our data support this rationale. For example, fully three-quarters of the entire sample agree that 'the main function of an interest group is to define the interests of its partisans.' Moreover, 62 per cent agree that 'interest groups are necessary to compensate for the fact that legislators tend to represent geographical areas rather than social and economic interests', i.e. to round out representation.

As suggested earlier, these summary presentations mask interesting regional differences, as well as those of party. To some extent, the legitimacy imputed to interest groups seems to be a function of the degree of solidarity in the larger community. It may also, as touched upon earlier, be related to the attitudes of the major parties towards such groups. Some observers have maintained that the Social Credit party of British Columbia has highly ambivalent attitudes toward interest groups because of its individualistic, populist orientation which tends to define such groups as unnecessary intrusions between government and the people at large. Durkheimian social thought, on the other hand, regards such groups as an essential manifestation and instrument of a highly cohesive society, bound together by functional specialization and attending normative consensus.

Our evidence about British Columbia's position in this context is mixed, although it may be said that among legislators, her rates of interaction are the highest among the four areas. Moreover, combining the proportions of legislators in all provinces who rank at the 'all of the time' and 'most of the time' levels of trust, British Columbia ranks first with fully three-fourths; followed by Ottawa with two-thirds; Ontario with 56 per cent; and Quebec with 52 per cent. British Columbia also has the largest proportion of legislators (N–6) ranking at the 'all of the time' level. However, in terms of Social Credit's valence toward groups, it should be noted that none of these are members of the Party.

Another way of looking at this question is to determine the relative proportions of those who are high on trust *and* influence in each province: Ontario ranks first with 54 per cent; Quebec is next with one-half, followed by British Columbia with 38 per cent, with Ottawa at the bottom with only one-third. These data indicate the extent to which legitimacy and influence vary independently among legislators. Members in British Columbia and Ottawa, in effect, tend to have greater trust in interest group agents than their colleagues in the other provinces, but at the same time, they tend to be less influenced by them. Meanwhile, and somewhat anomalously, as our data suggest, Quebec generally ranks lower than the other provinces on interaction and trust, but medium on trust and influence, which is somewhat unexpected since many observers agree that hers is a homogeneous culture, which should encourage close normative integration among the elite. On the other hand, her attitudes are marked by a certain *incivisme*, increasing class tensions, and a political culture in which law and government are sometimes viewed as coercive impositions, rather than as legitimate expectations of a cooperative society.

PATTERNS OF INTERACTION BETWEEN BUREAUCRATS AND INTEREST GROUPS

As noted earlier, the bureaucracy is the point in the political system at which the greatest amount of elite interaction occurs, in order to carry out the sustained, largely routine affairs of government. Given the functional specificity of bureaucratic–group relations, we would expect the interaction level to be high and characterized by considerable mutual confidence and cohesion. The general atmosphere should be one of compromise, as both segments of the elite define their objectives within similar parameters of action and interest. In general, and with many exceptions, whereas MP's tend to deal with a constantly changing set of problems, presented by a broad range of group interests, some of which are inevitably conflicting and provocative, senior bureaucrats tend to operate in a more restricted milieu, often confined to repeated interactions with the same individuals representing the same interest. Even when individuals change, the substantive quality of a given interest and its policy preferences probably result in greater continuity in bureaucratic–group interactions than in those between lobbyists and back-benchers. Although ministers probably occupy some mid-point position on this variable, there too the frequent turnover and the reorganization fetish probably introduce considerable discontinuity into such interactions. The following data should provide some further evidence regarding such tentative conclusions, beginning with a summary analysis of interaction (see Table 9-8).

The evidence indicates that on the whole contact is somewhat less intense than that experienced by MP's, among whom the mean at the 'frequently' level is just over 50 per cent, largely inspired by British Columbia's unusually high rate (four-fifths), compared with the bureaucratic mean of only one-third. Interprovincial variations are also substantial, but not significant,

255

TABLE 9-8 *Interaction between bureaucrats and interest groups*

Bureaucrats	Frequency of interaction[a]			
	High	Medium	Low	
Ottawa	33	31	36	(87)
Quebec	16	34	50	(32)
Ontario	48	24	29	(46)
British Columbia	37	37	26	(35)
	(69)	(62)	(69)	(200)

X^2 = not significant at .05   *K*'s tau C = −.07
Gamma = −.10
[a] 'High' is defined as having direct, personal contact with interest group agents 'frequently' (twice a week); 'medium' as 'occasionally' (twice a month); and 'low' as 'seldom', or 'rarely'.

with senior officials in Quebec indicating the lowest rate of interaction. Ontario, on the other hand, ranks first by a clear margin, with almost half of its respondents at the high level. The difference between the interaction patterns of legislators and bureaucrats may be due to the fact that the absolute number of avenues of access and authority in the bureaucracy is vastly larger than those in the legislature. At the same time, substantive contacts are more specific. In effect, the interaction potential is less focussed, while the contacts are more specific, with the possible result that each official tends to see a smaller proportion of interest group representatives. Some evidence (considered later) indicates, moreover, that MP's tend to exaggerate their interaction with directors. Turning to the interaction syndrome, an analysis of the relation between interaction and legitimacy indicates that the relationship is weak and irregular. There is only a slight tendency for the expected positive relationship to appear.

Turning next to the association between interaction and imputed influence, we again assume that these variables will be positively related. It will be recalled that the case study issue included, for civil servants, an item which asked how significant a role was played by those private groups nominated as being most closely involved in departmental policy making. The response categories were: (1) they are almost an integral part of the day-to-day activity of the department; (2) their assumed reaction to what we do is usually taken into account during policy making; (3) they are only one among many factors impinging upon our decisions; and (4) they have little

TABLE 9-9   *Association between interaction and influence,*
case study

Influence	Frequency of interaction			
	High	Medium	Low	
	%	%	%	
High	29	26	23	(52)
Medium	38	48	17	(68)
Low	33	26	60	(80)
	(69)	(62)	(69)	(200)

X^2 = significant at .001 K's tau B = .16   Gamma = .23

or no effect upon our decisions. Items (1) and (2) are ranked as 'high' and 'medium', and we have combined items (3) and (4) as 'low' in Table 9-9, which provides an experientially-based test of the hypothesis that interaction is positively related to influence.

Here, the relationship is strongly significant, positive, but non-linear. In general, those bureaucrats who interact most frequently with interest group agents tend also to inpute the most vital policy role to them. Here, perhaps, the results reflect the cohesion that theoretically should follow the sustained functional patterns of interaction between bureaucrats and directors.

Another test of the interaction–influence hypothesis is provided by the item which asks bureaucrats (see Table 9–10) to indicate the extent to which they have been influenced at one time or another by a lobbyist regarding a departmental issue. Responses were scaled into 'frequently', 'occasionally',

TABLE 9-10   *Association between interaction and influence,*
general

Influence	Frequency of interaction			
	High	Medium	Low	
	%	%	%	
High	58	47	18	(79)
Medium	32	44	27	(66)
Low	11	8	55	(49)
				(194)

X^2 = significant at .001 K's tau B = .39   Gamma = .55

257

and 'hardly ever' and 'never' categories to provide a weighted index, with the results shown.

A very strong relationship between these variables is again evident, with experienced influence increasing steadily and dramatically with frequency of contact. The distribution is linear and the significance level is very high. We can feel quite sure from evidence such as this, and that in Table 9-9 that, *en bloc*, interaction among these two segments of the political elite often culminates in mutually satisfactory accommodations. As we have seen, bureaucrats quite naturally define their own roles in representational and service terms, which tend to legitimate group claims symbolically, but they are also influenced by direct personal interactions with those who present such groups. It should be noted, in passing, that we do not feel it necessary to specify these relationships further here because of the high degree of social homogeneity among the elite groups, which means, in effect, that many vital intervening variables are already being held constant in the relationships.

The association found in Table 9-10 is confirmed in a general context by the relationship between personal contact and the significance imputed by officials to interest groups in the area of bureaucratic policy-making. Almost half of those who ranked high on interaction (N–51) indicated that this role was 'highly significant', compared with only 22 per cent at the 'seldom–rarely' level of interaction ($X^2 = .05$). The pervasiveness of this relationship, moreover, is apparent in the fact that it is statistically significant among respondents in all areas. There is some internal variation, however, which merits analysis, as seen in Table 9-11. The index of influence is

TABLE 9-11   *Association between interaction and influence, by region*

	Frequency of interaction					
	High		Medium		Low	
			Experienced influence			
Region	High	Low	High	Low	High	Low
	%	%	%	%	%	%
Ottawa	34	31	45	18	16	51	(83)
Quebec	16	18	50	13	38	76	(33)
Ontario	58	34	25	26	16	44	(47)
British Columbia	58	27	33	45	8	29	(32)
							(195)

X^2 = significant at .10 K's tau C = .30   Gamma = .53

based upon the highest, 'coming to agree', level in the familiar 'lobbyist' item.

Strongly suggestive differences exist here, and the tau and gamma correlations are quite high. British Columbia and Ontario bureaucrats are much more subject to lobbyist influence than the other areas, whereas Quebec is least influenced by them. Quebec and Ottawa, meanwhile, rank surprisingly high (76 and 51 per cent) at the low–low level of interaction and influence, showing a palpable increase compared with their position at the medium level of interaction. In British Columbia, interaction has dramatically different effects upon influence at the high–high and low–high level.

The next step in the analysis of interaction theory involves the association between legitimacy and influence existing among bureaucrats as a correlate of their contacts with lobbyists. Even though interaction is not positively associated with legitimacy, it is quite possible that legitimacy may be independently related to influence. It will be recalled that no positive relation was found between them in the case of the legislators. Legitimacy is based here upon an item regarding bureaucratic perceptions of the reasonableness, objectivity, and propriety of group behaviour in the case study issue. Influence is based upon the extent to which the group achieved its goal (see Table 9-12).

Legitimacy and influence are indeed positively associated, as the data show. Almost 60 per cent of those ranking high on legitimacy also rank high on influence, compared with only 14 per cent of those who rank low. Such a strong relationship provides a basis for assuming that the *I–L–I* syndrome should prove more fruitful in the case of bureaucrats than legislators. The fact that lobbyists probably interact much more frequently with them than with back-benchers also lends credence to this assumption.

TABLE 9-12   *Association between legitimacy and influence, case study*

	Perceived legitimacy			
Influence	High	Medium	Low	
	%	%	%	
High	58	52	14	(88)
Medium	30	26	29	(45)
Low	12	22	57	(29)
	(77)	(69)	(16)	(162)

X^2 = significant at .001 K's tau B = .16
Gamma = .26

Since this test is based upon an important issue, drawn from the personal experience of respondents, we may have some confidence in the generalization that most bureaucrats tend to have sympathetic relations with their clientele groups. Such groups are regarded as both highly legitimate and effectual by about half of our sample and as merely 'successful' by another one-third. Only 16 per cent of the entire sample regards them as experiencing 'little or no' success. On the other hand, such relations may occasionally be viewed ambivalently by senior officials. As one in a provincial Department of Industry and Commerce said, 'These groups are frustrating for us, but they are effective. Most of them come through the various foreign offices who try to promote investment here. They usually want local financing and help in finding workers. They bargain with several provinces and take the best deal. Some are very skilful, especially if they have great experience in foreign investments.'

An even stronger relationship is found using another measure of influence which asks bureaucrats how effective interest group agents are 'in dealing with your department'. This item is somewhat broader in scope than that used previously since it asks about the several major groups usually affiliated with a department, rather than only about the group immediately involved in the case study issue (see Table 9-13).

Here again is suggestive evidence of the strong behavioural and normative ties underlying accommodation between bureaucratic and private elites. Looking at the low row on influence, for example, only about one-fifth of those who rank high on legitimacy are low on influence, compared with over four-fifths of those who rank low on legitimacy. This strong relationship is an interesting contrast to that found among legislators, and much of the variation is probably accounted for by the greater frequency of contact and

TABLE 9-13   *Association between legitimacy and influence*

Influence	Perceived legitimacy			
	High	Medium	Low	
	%	%	%	
High	51	22	7	(60)
Medium	31	45	7	(60)
Low	18	33	86	(57)
	(82)	(76)	(19)	(177)

X^2 = significant at .001 K's tau B = .38   Gamma = .56

the occupational ties among bureaucrats and group agents. For example, we shall find later that bureaucrats are much less likely to share the 'liberal' philosophy of expansive, easily-penetrated big government held by most Canadian legislators. This suggests that the reason for their rapport with lobbyists must be found in behavioural and affective ties, rather than in shared cognitive perceptions of how the political system works or in common ideological views of government's 'proper' role.

To some extent, this valence controverts the classical image of the official in the parliamentary system as an anonymous and impartial instrument, motivated essentially by legal–rational prescriptions. As Max Weber wrote, 'When fully developed, bureaucracy also stands, in a specific sense, under the principle of *sine ira ac studio*. Its specific nature, which is welcomed by capitalism, develops the more perfectly the more the bureaucracy is "de-humanised," the more completely it succeeds in eliminating from official business love, hatred, and all the purely personal, irrational, and emotional elements which escape calculation.'[1] Here, instead, we find a substantial proportion of officials bound closely to their clientele associates by common normative and functional perspectives.

ASSOCIATION AMONG INTERACTION, LEGITIMACY, AND INFLUENCE

Turning to the final part of the present analysis, we look at the association among the three interaction variables in the bureaucratic sample. Following interaction theory, and all else being equal, we assume that the activities that bring bureaucrats and lobbyists together will tend to produce and reinforce shared values that over time result in repeated interactions. Such behaviours, in turn, tend to have legitimating effects that culminate in increased influence for interest group directors and their agents.

Multiple-item indexes of legitimacy and influence will be used here in order to secure reliable instruments for measuring such effects. Indexes have the added value of smoothing out the normal curve distribution to some extent and thereby providing a more symmetrical basis for comparative analysis. As noted earlier, there is a tendency, especially among legislators, to choose the middle level of any response scale which results in some aggravation of the usual piling up of cases in the middle ranges of the distribution.

We begin by analysing the entire bureaucratic sample (N–217), using two indexes of legitimacy and influence, and running them against interaction

[1] *From Max Weber*, pp. 215–16.

defined again by the extent of personal contact among bureaucrats (see Table 9-14).

The relationship is significant and the correlations are high, indicating a strong relationship between the variables. Looking across the high row and down the high columns, although the differences are not great, the distribution is generally linear and the proportions appear as expected. The highest proportion of those who rank high on legitimacy and on interaction generally tend to rank highest on influence, as measured by these indexes. The proportions ranking high on influence decline sharply as one looks across the table, with only 11 per cent of those low on legitimacy and contact being high on influence. Perhaps the strength of interaction is manifested in the fact that one-third of those who rank low on legitimacy rank high, nevertheless, on influence. Since the relationships are statistically significant, we can feel reasonably sure that they are not spurious. Unlike legislators, when bureaucrats interact frequently with lobbyists and are influenced by them, they apparently develop confidence in them, which explains some of the variation in the total interaction process.

As suggested earlier, the ambivalent position of MP's on this score may reflect an essentially dualistic view of interest groups and their role in the

TABLE 9-14 *Association among interaction, legitimacy, and influence, bureaucrats*

	Legitimacy[a]								
	High (39)			Medium (47)			Low (62)		
				Frequency of interaction					
Influence[b]	High	Medium	Low	High	Medium	Low	High	Medium	Low
	%	%	%	%	%	%	%	%	%
High	63	70	11	62	38	17	55	37	33
Medium	32	20	33	23	50	40	36	52	10
Low	5	10	56	15	12	43	9	11	57

X^2 = significant at .05 K's tau C = .39   Gamma = .60

[a] Legitimacy is based upon a four-item index: the legitimacy imputed to the group by the official in the case study; responses to the item, 'Most lobbyists are competent professionals who know their business'; and 'In your opinion, to what extent do the activities of interest groups generally contribute to the larger public interest, or are they usually focussed upon narrower interests?'; and the official's response to the item regarding the necessity of delegating government's authority to private groups.

[b] Influence is based upon a weighted index comprising responses about the extent to which officials believe they have been influenced by interest group representatives.

political system. Such groups are viewed collectively and symbolically as essential and legitimate elements in a representative polity, but in an individual or specific context they are often perceived as being concerned mainly with their own limited interests and perhaps as exerting undue influence upon policy, compared with the unorganized majority of citizens. Interest groups, in effect, are differentiated from the 'public'. It is significant that many MP's use the expression, '*I* represent the public', when discussing the role of groups. They apparently regard themselves as a counterpoise to the directors who contact them, on the ground that there is a large, undifferentiated public 'out there' which doesn't know much about issues and relies upon MP's to represent the so-called public interest.

It is also true of course that legislators typically interact with group representatives in a somewhat different and generally less particularized and structured context than bureaucrats do. Whereas the substantive issue confronting a bureaucrat and his client is often governed by precedent and high technical imperatives, legislators deal with emerging policy, often heavily freighted with ideological implications. But the signal difference is probably the functional specialization and continuity of interest and representation of bureaucratic interactions, contrasted with the variety and scope of demands confronting legislators.

TABLE 9-15 *Association among interaction, legitimacy, and influence, legislators and civil servants*

	Perceived legitimacy[a]								
	High (158)			Medium (191)			Low (114)		
				Frequency of interaction					
Influence[b]	High	Medium	Low	High	Medium	Low	High	Medium	Low
	%	%	%	%	%	%	%	%	%
High	40	53	20	50	38	18	27	16	14
Medium	38	36	22	28	39	32	45	49	32
Low	22	11	58	22	23	50	28	35	54

X^2 = significant at .02 K's tau B = .19   Gamma = .31

[a] Legitimacy is defined here by responses to the following item: 'In your opinion, to what extent do the activities of interest groups generally contribute to the larger public interest, or are they usually focussed upon narrower interests?' Responses were: 'positive' (high); 'neutral' (medium); and 'negative' (low) contribution.

[b] The influence index is again comprised of responses to the item involving the extent of influence experienced by governmental elites through lobbying.

A final test is provided by combining the two governmental elites, in Table 9-15.

Although the distribution is curvilinear, the relationship among the three variables is strongly significant at the .02 level. A much larger proportion of those who are high and medium on perceived legitimacy and frequent interaction are high on experienced influence, compared with those who are low: an average of 45 per cent of those in the former category rank high on influence, compared with only 27 per cent of those who rank low on legitimacy and interaction. Looking at the high columns, the proportions decline significantly in the high and medium legitimacy categories. The very large proportions of the sample appearing in the low–low cells also support the expected relationship. It seems probable that these results reflect the influence of the relatively high proportion of respondents who ascribe high and medium amounts of legitimacy to interest groups and their agents, as measured by the item used here.

In concluding this chapter, which has focussed upon the interaction process and the role of legitimacy as an intervening variable between interaction and influence, the point should be made that however interesting this question may be from a theoretical standpoint, it is not always operationally decisive. More crucial from the standpoint of political analysis is the extent to which interaction among the political elite is associated with positive influence relationships. A useful way of punctuating such relationships is provided by Table 9-16 combining legislators and officials, using the same 'lobbyist' index of influence.

A strongly positive association between interaction and experienced influence (i.e. common interest group effectiveness) is again apparent. Looking at the total N's, we also see that fully one-third of the respondents

TABLE 9-16 *Association between interaction and influence, legislators and bureaucrats*

	Frequency of interaction			
Influence	High	Medium	Low	
	%	%	%	
High	41	38	18	(161)
Medium	35	40	28	(164)
Low	24	22	54	(119)

X^2 = significant at .001 K's tau B = .23   Gamma = .33

(*N*–161) categorize themselves as being at the highest level of influence. It is well to repeat that just over two-thirds of MP's perceive themselves as interacting at the twice-a-week or twice-a-month level. Among bureaucrats the individual rates are somewhat lower, even though the overall volume of interaction with groups is greater. Beyond this, it is important not to neglect symbolic interaction, whereby interest groups and their agents who have gained a recognized right of consultation within the formal political apparatus probably enjoy legitimation and influence without the necessity of sustained personal interaction. Experienced officials and legislators *know* what their position is on most issues, and often respond accordingly, a condition made easier by the relative continuity and specificity of group interests.

SUMMARY AND CONCLUSIONS

The analysis suggests various behavioural continuities among the governmental elite which provide a basis for the process of elite accommodation. Not only is personal interaction frequent among the political elite, but our data indicate that it is strongly and positively related to the influence exercised by group representatives upon those who direct the formal political apparatus. A similarly positive association exists between legitimacy and influence for bureaucrats (.001), but not for legislators. Interaction is also positively associated with legitimacy for legislators, but not for bureaucrats.

Although the expected *I–L–I* relationship is tentative among legislators, a positive association does exist among bureaucrats, and among the entire governmental elite when the two subsamples are combined. While this is theoretically satisfying, it has limited operational significance. The vital generalization is that considerable elite interaction occurs, culminating in an accommodation process in which private elites are ascribed considerable influence. This is not to suggest that interest groups make their demands good all of the time, nor that governmental elites are merely their agents. Only one-fourth of such groups are politically active; they vary widely in their political effectiveness; and the policy-making process is characterized by negotiation and compromise.

On the other hand, the main drift of the interaction analysis suggests that some modification is required of the traditional view that the parliamentary system enables Cabinet and bureaucratic elites to determine policy *in vacuo*, so to speak, using the expert civil service to iron out the technical and legal detail, without significant participation by interest groups. The Cabinet may enjoy such autonomy regarding back-benchers, but it seems doubtful indeed that the same can be said for its position regarding politically-active interest groups.

The process of elite accommodation also has other bases, which we have called socioeconomic, cognitive, and affective. Members of the political elite, in effect, probably share certain generalized social properties and definitions of the political system that seem to reinforce and reflect the behavioural continuities traced in this and earlier chapters. If such proves to be the case, we shall have some evidence that members of a given socio-economic stratum tend to share certain ideological preferences, contrary to the criticism that class strata are mere statistical artifacts. More important, any such continuities will suggest that such properties as social class and any attending dispositions have policy consequences. Such potentially integrative elements are analysed in the next three chapters.

CHAPTER 10

SOCIOECONOMIC BASES OF ELITE ACCOMMODATION

Having traced the critical interactional role played by interest group elites in the Canadian political system, we turn next to certain social continuities that ease accommodation between them and governmental elites. As noted earlier, the process of elite accommodation is associated with several deep-seated characteristics of the national political culture. Perhaps foremost among them is the complexity, diversity, and cleavages of Canadian society and the ethnic pluralism that tends to perpetuate this condition. A high degree of exclusivity among the various subcultures and the historic tensions between English- and French-Canada, aggravated by divisive regionalism, produce a deeply fragmented political culture. Compensatory factors such as a revolutionary tradition and a strong sense of national identity do not exist. As a result, national integration is precarious and instead of becoming positive agents of innovation, political parties tend to play a conservative, brokerage role.[1] Among the functional responses to these conditions is government through a process of elite accommodation.[2]

SOME CONDITIONS OF ELITE ACCOMMODATION

Elites are defined in any society as that minority which enjoys most of certain scarce and high valued resources such as security, prestige, income, and power.[3] Classical elite theorists, such as Mosca, Michels, and Pareto insisted that elite rule was a functional necessity in all societies, although

---

[1] This, of course, is an essential theme of John Porter's *The Vertical Mosaic*, especially Chapter 12. A half-century earlier, in a similar context, André Siegfried had called Canadian parties 'entirely harmless', *The Race Question in Canada*.

[2] See Chapter 1 for an outline of accommodation theory and its applicability to the Canadian socio-political milieu.

[3] For an empirical demonstration of this proposition, see Robert Presthus, *Men at the Top: A Study in Community Power* (New York: Oxford University Press, 1964).

each believed that elite power rested upon rather different resources, ranging through organizational capacity, certain psychological dispositions toward dominance and submission, as well as economic hegemony and control of certain key roles and institutions in society.[1] The conditions of elite rule are usually held to include self-consciousness, cohesion, and a collective will to action on the part of its members.[2] Beyond this, such rule is often believed to be eased by the small size of the elite and the attending fillip to cohesion.

Power, which is the essence of politics, may be defined, following Max Weber, as the capacity to achieve one's ends despite opposition. While power is often a means to some other end, such as wealth and social honour, it may also be highly valued for its own sake. It is also clear that in addition to the possession of political resources, the preconditions of power include a considerable measure of social and ideological cohesion among any elite. Our particular concern is with the extent to which such incentives and conditions exist among the Canadian political elite, defined empirically as our sample of some 1,150 interest group leaders, MP's and high-level bureaucrats in provincial and federal governments. We assume, in sum, that these three elites in concert play the major role in shaping and carrying out public policy, through a sustained process of mutual accommodation encouraged by a battery of compatible social, experiential, and ideological ties.

Given these assumptions, our task is to show, (1) that the political elite shares several values of class, education, and group membership that provide much of the basis for productive interaction among them, and (2) that such socioeconomic continuities are reinforced in turn by some measure of ideological and cognitive homogeneity that further enhances cohesion among them. The problem remains of explaining the discontinuity arising from the ethnic and religious diversity of English- and French-Canadian members of this elite. Accommodation theory handles this problem, it will be recalled, by ascribing a desire for compromise to such elites. Subcultural enclaves tend to be ethnically and culturally exclusive and unwilling to compromise, but their leaders are willing and able to function across these barriers and to work out mutually acceptable denouements. Theirs is an integrating and nation-building role. This condition introduces some

---

[1] *The Ruling Class* (New York: McGraw Hill, 1939); *Political Parties*, (Glencoe: Free Press, 1958); *The Mind and Society* (New York: Harcourt, Brace, 1935).
[2] For analyses of elite theory, see Geraint Parry, *Political Elites*; and James Meisel, *Myth of the Ruling Class* (Ann Arbor: University of Michigan Press, 1958).

tolerance into the system, explaining why a certain amount of social and ideological discontinuity can exist without disrupting the process of accommodation. Empirically, then, we shall not expect to find complete symmetry on either social or attitudinal dimensions, but rather that *as a group* elites are clearly different from those they govern.

One may suggest other incentives that account for cohesion among those who form the elite coalition. 'Nothing brings elites together so much as mutual respect which flows from sharing in the confraternity of power.'[1] Power may indeed be valued for its own sake, and it seems that members of any political elite may have well-developed appetites for power and its by-products of income, self-realization, and social honour. Moreover, since political elites tend to be eminently pragmatic, the process of sustained negotiation and consultation, of shifting alliances, that especially characterizes government by elite accommodation may prove neither disenchanting nor unreasonable in view of such contingent benefits. Beyond this, with respect to the accommodation of Quebec, is the well-known political calculation that it is virtually impossible for a political party to gain majority control of the federal government without substantial support from Quebec.

Accommodation among the political elite is also eased by certain institutional mechanisms, including various boards and commissions, comprising joint membership of its political, social, and economic segments. Porter, for example, in his analysis of elite relations cites the National Research Council, Ontario Advisory Committee on University Affairs, and the Canadian Council of Christians and Jews as examples of such interlocking mechanisms. Boards of Governors of universities are another common medium for such interaction.

Other similar instruments of elite interaction include a plethora of joint advisory boards and committees, seen mainly in the administrative sector of government, which determine and carry out government policies in virtually every substantive area where private and public interests coalesce. Interest groups have a legitimate claim to representation upon such agencies, which do not always include disinterested representatives of the public on the assumption that officials fulfill this role. As we have seen, however, the functional and clientele relationships between private and governmental elites at times challenge this assumption. Another common instrument of interaction, mentioned earlier in the context of typical interest group activities, is the practise whereby bureaucrats become members of substantively relevant interest groups. Nor do such officials play ordinary,

[1] Porter, *The Vertical Mosaic*, p. 532.

pro forma roles in such groups; often they become members of executive committees and they may at times assume the presidency of the group concerned. Such affiliations, of course, are perfectly understandable in terms of shared institutional and technological commonalities, despite any attending implications for representational and substantive introversion. The vital point here is that such symbiotic interactions provide further evidence of the nature and extent of the institutionalization of elite accommodation.

It is significant that neither party, industrial, ethnic, nor religious lines are typically decisive in this context, as suggested by the historic, however precarious, liaisons between English- and French-Canadian politicians at the federal and federal–provincial levels. The sharing of the Prime Minister-ship between members of the two charter groups is equally germane as an example of accommodation tactics which are common in many countries with similar cleavages.[1]

It is always necessary to emphasize that the theory of elite cohesion does not imply completely harmonious interactions nor complete ideological or cognitive consensus. Indeed, very bitter conflicts occur within and among the political elite, as is again clear from the recent political history of Ottawa–Quebec relations. Or from such dramatic controversies as the Trans-Canada Pipe Line case (1956); the prolonged Northern Ontario Natural Gas Company affair (1954–64); the expropriation and compensation of the British Columbia Power Corporation (1961); or the St. Lawrence Corporation proxy battle (1947–51).[2] All of these cases involved conflicts between the economic and political segments of the political elite, defined to include leading figures in the sectors represented by interest groups.

Nevertheless, some form of accommodation was eventually worked out in these, as in the vast majority of less spectacular issues with which our data deal. Perhaps the essential point is not that such isolated controversies break out, but that the process of elite accommodation has been able to preserve Confederation despite the pervasive disintegrative tendencies of the political culture.

SOCIOECONOMIC BASES OF ELITE ACCOMMODATION

Among the variables explaining the patterns of interaction presented above is socioeconomic homogeneity. Members of the political elite, in effect,

[1] Arend Lijphart, 'Typologies of Democratic Systems', pp. 63–4.
[2] Porter, *The Vertical Mosaic*, pp. 544–8.

share certain 'hard', relatively-fixed properties of education, occupational role, and socioeconomic status that may be differentiated from their cognitive and affective characteristics. One example of such structural properties is the patterns of interaction analysed in the previous chapter. It would be possible, of course, to argue that interaction by itself is the independent behavioural variable explaining the influence relations and attending accommodation found among the three sub-elites. However, not only do we want to establish additional bases of accommodation, but it could be that interaction is merely the inevitable consequence of the institutional roles played by each elite segment, that they are therefore forced to interact and in time, that such interactions tend to result in the shared norms that seem to exist. An additional independent explanation may lie in any common educational and class attributes shared among the political elite.

Although there are many definitions of social class, and some controversies as to its meaning and utility as an analytical tool, it has been widely, and I believe, profitably used in political analysis.[1] Some critics have insisted that the usual practice of determining class status by such *objective* indexes as occupation and education is inadequate, in part because individual self-perceptions are also significant in determining class stratification. Several issues are raised by this argument. One of them relates to the role of the researcher and whether he should be content to accept uncritically the judgments of his respondents on their class status or any other datum. It is well-known, for example, that many Canadians tend to dislike the very conception of class stratification.[2] They tend to believe that such distinctions are invidious, undemocratic, and anachronistic. Many of them tend to deny the existence of classes or to perceive themselves as being 'middle-class', insisting as they do that virtually everyone is in this category. If

---

[1] The relationship between class status and political ideology and participation, for example, has been frequently documented, with participation and political conservatism being generally positively associated with middle-and-upper-class status and with business, professional, and white-collar occupations. Among others, see Kahl, *The American Class Structure*, pp. 157–80; Richard Centers, *The Psychology of Social Classes* (Princeton: Princeton University Press, 1949), p. 120; Lane, *Political Life*, pp. 220–30; Van Loon, 'Political participation in Canada'.

[2] As John Porter remarks, 'One of the most persistent images that Canadians have of their society is that it has no classes. This image becomes translated into the assertion that Canadians are all relatively equal in their possessions, in the amount of money they earn, and in the opportunities which they and their children have to get on in the world.' *The Vertical Mosaic*, p. 3. A poll conducted by *Fortune* magazine (1948) found similarly that 80 per cent of Americans regarded themselves as 'middle-class'.

271

the researcher accepts such subjective judgments uncritically as representing the ultimate reality of class stratification among his sample, as distinct from the reality that respondents often tend to misperceive or inflate their objective class status, he is perhaps neglecting his own responsibility to report events as objectively as he can.

An interesting example of the extent to which elites tend to deny class stratification is seen in the responses of Canadian MP's to an item which asked for their subjective perception of their own status, with the results shown in Table 10-1.

Such a distribution is not unexpected, and perhaps especially among elite groups whose internalization of the ideology of equal opportunity (which class stratification is held to contravert) is often stronger than that of other strata, as we shall see in a moment. On the other hand, by objective indexes of education and occupation, it is clear that class differentiation exists in most societies. Certainly as we saw earlier, Canadian society is usually characterized as having rather strong elitist residues. This is perhaps especially apparent in the gradations in prestige attached to occupational roles, with the result that stratification is heavily influenced by occupation. In this sense, the scale of occupations often used in analyses of the labour force defines a rough social-class system.

Perhaps because the item was phrased somewhat differently, and because they are not equally concerned about public reactions to their views, interest group directors tend to show a subjective appreciation of their class status which is closer to their objective circumstances. Fully one-third place themselves in the upper-middle class, usually indicating that their *income* enables them to enjoy such a life style. Another 42 per cent define themselves as average middle-class people, while 14 per cent assign themselves to the working-class, which as indicated earlier is usually regarded as less invidious

TABLE 10-1
*Subjective class perceptions
of MP's (self-classification)*

	%
Never think in these terms	57
Upper-class	4
Middle-class	27
Working-class	11
N.A.	2
	(269)

than a 'lower-class' designation. At the same time, some reluctance to think of Canadian society in class terms is apparent in the fact that fully one-fifth fall into the 'forced choice' category, which means that some gentle probing was required to evoke a response. Moreover, refusals were high on this item, around one-seventh, with Quebec accounting for just over 60 per cent of them. Such evidence lends credence to the views of sociologists that the existence of class differentiations has been somewhat repressed in Canada, despite its aristocratic heritage.[1]

Regarding the claim that members of a given statistically-determined class do not necessarily share similar styles of life, values, chances for education or economic achievement, etc., this is in any given situation an empirical question. At the same time, a great deal of research indicates that socioeconomic status is often correlated with these, and other attributes. As indicated earlier, it has been shown that political participation and group membership are positively associated with education, income, and occupation, which are the indicators usually employed in determining class status. Individuals in similar class statuses tend to have similar aspirations for their children, to send them to the same types of schools, to share styles of consumption, to live in the same neighbourhoods, all of which is to say that those in different class strata tend to behave differently in these and other contexts. Even the diagnosis of mental illness has been shown to be partly a function of class differentiations.[2]

On the other hand, class-based voting in Canada has been found to be consistently the lowest among the four highly developed 'Anglo-American' democracies, Australia, Canada, Great Britain, and the United States.[3] Regionalism and religion have been the most salient dimensions of electoral behaviour. John Meisel's national survey (1965), nevertheless, indicates that a certain proportion (about 10 per cent) of Canadians rank themselves as 'upper-class' which suggests that class sensitivity is not unknown.

[1] Among others, see S. D. Clark who says, 'Canadian history has tended to be written as if social classes were something almost [sic] which did not exist', *The Developing Canadian Community*, p. 288; Porter, *The Vertical Mosaic*, pp. 3-6.

[2] For authoritative analyses of class, see A. B. Hollingshead and F. C. Redlich, *Social Class and Mental Illness;* and Kahl, *The American Class Stucture*. Some critics have insisted that class strata are merely artificial statistical categories and that there is no necessary social or normative continuity among members of strata determined in this way. On the other hand, one highly regarded study concluded that Americans did group themselves into class categories, especially when the invidious 'lower-class' designation was replaced by 'working-class', Centers, *The Psychology of Social Classes*, p. 78.

[3] Robert Alford, *Party and Society* (Chicago: Rand McNally, 1963), Chapter 9.

Elite accommodation

John Porter, similarly, has found class an effective, if imprecise, instrument of social analysis, useful in analysing such fundamental aspects of Canadian society as the extent of equality of educational opportunity, social mobility, and the distribution of income. As he concludes, 'the image of middle-class uniformity may appear plausible', but vast differences exist among classes in the quality of goods bought, levels of privacy obtained through housing accommodations, aspirations for their children, style of life, and so on.[1]

For such reasons we have made socioeconomic status a central element in our attempt to explain the process of elite accommodation. In order to ease some of the criticisms of class analysis, both objective and subjective indexes are used to discuss the socioeconomic status of our sample. The objective index is based upon father's and respondent's education and occupation, using an abbreviated version of the Hollingshead scale.[2] The subjective index is based upon the respondent's perception of his own class status.

Our assumption is that members of the three sub-elites will exhibit a considerable degree of homogeneity in objective terms of occupation, education, and family status. At the moment, we shall set aside the implications of any such homogeneity in terms of shared normative values. However, we shall argue later that sociometric continuities tend to culminate in collective personal identification among the members of a given social stratum. Such continuities ease the criticism that social classes are mere methodological artifacts. It is our subjective impression that the relatively small population of Canada and the small proportion of university graduates among its members, compared with that among the current political elite, most of whom of course would have been of college age during the 1930's, tend to restrict sharply the size of the national elite. As a result, considerable interaction occurs among them, accompanied by a degree of self-consciousness and cohesion not possible in a larger society in which greater educational opportunity and less out-migration have produced a larger middle-class. Certainly, at the very least, there is more cohesion among them than among the great mass of politically uncommitted individuals in the society. The evidence supporting this generalization was presented earlier when it was found that political attitudes and political participation varied greatly with socioeconomic status.[3]

[1] *The Vertical Mosaic*, p. 4; Chapters 1–6.
[2] *Op. cit.*
[3] Cf. Rick van Loon, 'Political participation in Canada', Nie *et al.*, 'Social structure and political participation'.

TABLE IO-2 *Socioeconomic continuities among the political elite*

| Category[a] | Proportion in each category | | | |
	MP's	Bureaucrats	Directors	National[b]
	%	%	%	%
I	43	75	20	7
II	28	22	48	11
III	26	3	19	28
IV	4	—	10	38
V	—	—	2	17
	(269)	(214)	(620)	

[a] The socioeconomic scale used here is based upon two variables, occupation and education, with occupation weighted × 7 and education × 3. For details, see A. B. Hollingshead and F. Redlich, *Social Class and Mental Illness.*

[b] The 'National' category is derived from Woods and Ostry, *Labour Policy and Labour Economics in Canada,* Table 26. This index provides a rough comparative scale to set against the elite distribution.

The effects of this restricted leadership cadre include a tendency to reinforce the system of elite accommodation. The scarcity of technically skilled talent, for example, which may be seen in the somewhat limited degree of functional specialization within the political elite,[1] manifests itself in a tendency for its members to move from one segment of the elite or from one institutional role, to another. It is as if there were not enough talent to man the various institutional substructures, resulting in a constant overload on the small reservoir available.

Such career patterns tend to reinforce cohesion among members of the elite, as they interact with one another in a variety of occupational contexts. It should be noted too that this condition is encouraged by the prevailing emphasis upon generalist styles of leadership, reflecting in turn the humanistic preferences of Canadian university education. Here, as in so many areas, residues of British models of conduct persist in Canadian life. In the

[1] This condition is most apparent, of course, among legislators. In this context, it is suggestive that a major argument for the substantial pay increases provided federal MP's in 1971 was the need to combat amateurism and high turn-over by making office more rewarding.

context, the effect is to legitimate patterns of leadership selection and behaviour that again facilitate elite accommodation.

Turning to the data, we present a summary (Table 10–2) showing comparative socioeconomic status among the political elite. It is immediately clear that the political elite includes a strikingly high proportion of socially advantaged members and that there is a considerable similarity among its three segments, especially when categories I and II are collapsed to form an 'upper-middle-class' stratum. Also, despite the somewhat tenuous comparability of the national index, it is clear again how atypical members of the political elite are. Generally, in occupational terms, the index ranges from so-called 'higher executive' roles through unskilled labour, as seen in Table 10–4. The extremely favoured position of senior civil servants (N–214) reflects the fact that being deputy ministers and assistant deputies, most of them were coded in the highest occupational category. This may have inflated their status somewhat. Meanwhile the substantial proportion of small businessmen among the legislators has the opposite effect, since this role is ranked lower in the occupational scale. Also involved is the impressive level of educational achievement among the bureaucrats (N–214), seen in the fact that they possess an aggregate of 299 undergraduate and graduate degrees. Comparable achievement for legislators (N–269) is 156 degrees, and only 184 for the more numerous and heterogeneous directors' sample.

Despite such differences, if one combines socioeconomic categories I and II, which correspond roughly to upper-middle-class levels, he finds MP's and directors closely matched, with about 70 per cent in these two highly advantaged statuses. The bureaucratic elite remains significantly more favoured. As suggested throughout, the Canadian political elite constitutes a highly atypical and advantaged stratum in the national social structure.

An interesting question is the extent of intergenerational social mobility experienced by members of the political elite. Given their own advantaged statuses, there is some tendency to assume that they have come mainly from middle- and upper-middle-class families, who have been able to transfer their own advantages to their children. Since our data include the education and occupation of fathers of the current elite, comparative rates of mobility can be determined. Analysis reveals that the Canadian political elite of today is comprised of men who have experienced a great deal of social mobility. While about a quarter had fathers who enjoyed highly advantaged statuses, the majority seem to be self-made men, as Table 10–3 suggests.

TABLE 10-3   *Social mobility among the Canadian political elite (proportions in socioeconomic categories I and II)*

	Current elite	Fathers	
	%	%	
MP's	71	24	(269)
Bureaucrats	97	31	(214)
Directors	68	24	(620)

Senior civil servants have experienced the greatest mobility, achieved mainly through their impressive levels of educational achievement.[1] Since most of these men are middle-aged and thus gained their university degrees at a time when educational opportunity was considerably more restricted than at present, their achievement is all the more remarkable. A similar generalization may be made about legislators, although their current status is somewhat lower. Directors were drawn from a much more varied social context, covering a broad range of interest groups and occupational roles. But they too have experienced a great deal of mobility.

From the standpoint of elite accommodation, it may be that any potentially dysfunctional consequences of the status disparity between the governmental and interest group elites are eased by the fact that only one-quarter of the directors are highly active politically, and they include a large proportion of highly advantaged individuals. When their socioeconomic status is analysed, however, we find that although fully 72 per cent of them are in status categories I and II, directors at the other two levels are quite similar, with just two-thirds in these categories. On the other hand, as noted earlier, the most active directors interact more frequently with the governmental elite, trust them more, believe they influence them more, spend more of their time on political activities and focus upon services that are more highly valued by legislators. Functional interdependence and normative ties thus tend to be stronger between them and governmental elites, even though socioeconomic differences are not very great.

Since occupational role is so important an element in encouraging functional accommodation and mutual feelings of legitimacy among the political

---

[1] A similarly high rate of educational achievement exists among members of the federal bureaucracy of the United States: 80 per cent had university degrees; one-quarter took MA's, W. Lloyd Warner, *et al., The American Federal Executive* (New Haven: Yale University Press, 1963), pp. 107–25.

TABLE 10-4 *Occupational status of Canadian political elite*
(*proportion in each category*)

	MP's	Bureaucrats	Directors	National[a]
	%	%	%	%
Higher exs.[b]	47	82	26	8
Lesser exs.[c]	24	18	46	10
Small business[d]	26	—	10	9
Clerical	2	—	10	18
Skilled worker	3	—	7	17
Semi-skilled	0.4	—	1	14
Unskilled	—	—	1	25
	(269)	(214)	(620)	

[a] Adapted from Woods and Ostry, *Labour Policy and Labour Economics in Canada.*

[b] Higher executives here include high-level managers, deputy-ministers and such independent professions as law, medicine, dentistry, and university teaching.

[c] Lesser executives include business managers, engineers, accountants, salesmen.

[d] Small business includes proprietors of various kinds, including farmers.

elite, it seems useful next to present the comparative occupational statuses of its three segments, again contrasting them with the national occupational distribution to indicate the extent to which they form a discrete stratum in the social structure (see Table 10-4).

In two sectors of the elite, we asked for the specific occupation the respondent had prepared for, or had performed before he entered parliament or interest group activity. Bureaucrats were categorized according to their position in the hierarchy. As noted, most of them were placed in the 'higher professionals' rubric, which may have inflated their SES somewhat. The 'national' column is again based upon Woods and Ostry. We have compressed the proportions so that our first three strata are roughly comparable to their proprietary, managerial, farm, and professional levels, i.e. a total of about 27 per cent of the national labour force. Other classifications exist. *Dominion Bureau of Statistics*, for example places about 16 per cent of the labour force in the professional, proprietary, and managerial categories, another 16 per cent in clerical and sales occupations, some 32 per cent in skilled and semi-skilled labour work, another 15 per cent in agriculture, and the remaining 20 per cent in unskilled labour. The Hollingshead scale includes a 'small business' category, in which farm owners are included, which we have had to collapse with the 'proprietors' category in the Woods–Ostry classification.

Given such variations, it is difficult to reconcile precisely the differences among the various classifications. The salient point is that the Woods–Ostry scale provides us with useful and detailed breakdowns for comparison between the political elite and the national labour force. It is immediately clear that the political elite is highly over-represented in the upper reaches of the occupational pyramid. Fully 50 per cent of them are found in the higher executive stratum, which includes professionals, high-level managers, and proprietors of large-scale businesses, compared with the national average of something like 8 per cent. The disparities continue as one descends the scale. Whereas only one-tenth of the Canadian labour force is comprised of 'lesser executives', fully 30 per cent of the political elite are in this category; clericals, skilled, and unskilled workers are also highly under-represented in the political elite. Only in the small-business category is the ratio between elite membership and the national socioeconomic structure similar. This unrepresentative condition, of course, is common in Western democracies and the Canadian elite is not unique in this respect. Our objective, however, is to demonstrate the relative homogeneity across the three sub-elites, and the attending difference between them and other citizens.

We noted earlier the special utility of the law in modern politics and management. Here again, we find considerable over-representation among the legislators, almost 30 per cent of whom are lawyers, compared with only about 3 per cent in the labour force in 1970. Indeed, of the half who have graduate degrees, 54 per cent have law degrees. Given the utility of legal training for governmental work, it is interesting to note that the proportion of lawyers among the other two elite groups is considerably smaller, i.e. 15 per cent among bureaucrats and only 3 per cent among the interest group directors. On the other hand, in terms of all types of graduate degrees, the differences are not as great: 53 per cent of the bureaucrats have advanced degrees, compared with 43 per cent of legislators and one-quarter of directors.

The remainder of degrees held by legislators are scattered about among business administration, medicine, political science, and 'others'. As noted earlier, their educational achievement is not as impressive as that of bureaucrats but superior to that of directors. Fifty-eight per cent have university degrees, compared with 86 per cent of bureaucrats and 56 per cent of directors. Despite such variations, the generalization again holds that this is a highly advantaged group which differs sharply on this dimension from the national educational structure, in which only about 10 per cent have university degrees. It is well known, of course, that both legislators and bureaucrats are highly unrepresentative of the general population in Western democracies,[1] and Canada is no exception. The salient point is the degree of socioeconomic homogeneity that exists among the political elite and the extent to which this condition eases the going system of elite accommodation.

Another property shared by the political elite is maturity. As might be expected of men who are at the apex of a bureaucratic career, senior officials have the largest proportion of individuals in the 50 years plus category (57 per cent), followed by directors (46 per cent) and legislators (41 per cent). If 45 years is taken as the cut-off point denoting middle-age and post mid-career status, the proportion increases to almost two-thirds among the entire elite, with virtually no difference among its components. Beyond the patent implication that the elite shares a common property of chronological maturity, its members are again unrepresentative of the larger population, only 25 per cent of which (1970) is over 50 years of age. With many exceptions, it may also be suggested that individuals of this age who enjoy highly favoured socioeconomic status are probably not likely to be characterized by excessive receptivity to change and innovation. Research on the politics of age suggests a positive association between advancing age and cynicism, alienation, and reduced participation and efficacy,[2] and while there is some doubt that such generalizations apply to political elites, it may be that the political conservatism of the bureaucratic elite (see Table 11-5) rests in part on this characteristic. Once again, in the immediate context, the important point is the extent to which the political elite tends to share yet another social property.

One final potential continuity is the extent to which the political elite shares a common intensity of group membership. As noted elsewhere, group membership is not characteristic of most men and women in Western society. Not including unions, comparative rates in Canada and the United States, for example, are as follows: about 50 per cent of adults belong to only one group; 32 per cent belong to two groups; and only 18 per cent

[1] A. Barker and M. Rush, *The British Member of Parliament and His Information* (Toronto: University of Toronto Press, 1970); H. B. Berrington and S. Finer, 'The British House of Commons', in *The Parliamentary Profession* 13 *International Social Science Journal* (1961); L. Hamon, 'Members of the French Parliament' in *ibid*; D. R. Matthews, *U.S. Senators and Their World* (New York: Vintage, 1960).

[2] Among others, see Presthus, *Men at the Top*, pp. 246–50, Nie *et al.*, 'Social structure and political participation' (September, 1969), pp. 819–25; Curtis, 'Voluntary association joining', p. 877; Milbrath, *Political Participation*, pp. 134–5.

TABLE 10-5 *Comparative voluntary group membership,
political elite and national*

Membership	MP's	Bureaucrats	Directors	National[a]
	%	%	%	%
One	35	18	32	51
Two	38	25	22	32
Three-or-more	27	57	45	18
	(106)	(198)	(451)	(2,767)

[a] Excluding union membership. Adapted from Curtis, 'Voluntary
association joining', pp. 874–5.

belong to three or more groups.[1] Clearly, individuals who belong to more
than one or two groups are atypical. Research indicates that multiple
membership is highly associated with education, political interest, and
socioeconomic status. Here again, one would expect the Canadian political
elite to rank dramatically higher on group membership. Table 10-5 presents
the findings, including the national distribution.

Not unexpectedly, members of the political elite share a high level of
voluntary group memberships, with an average of about 43 per cent belonging
to three or more such groups, well over double the proportion among all
Canadians. Officials, however, rank significantly higher at this level, while
legislators, in turn, rank substantially lower than bureaucrats. It is difficult
to explain the relatively low rate among the former, certainly it cannot
reflect less of an occupational need to 'win friends and influence people',
compared with other sub-elites. Comparison with the national membership
structure again indicates the atypical status of the political elite.

When we turn to the category of 'elite clubs', meaning such prestigeful
sanctuaries as Rideau in Ottawa, *Cercle Universitaire* or Garrison in Quebec,
York in Toronto, Mount Royal in Montreal, or Vancouver in Vancouver,
even greater differences appear. Legislators rank highest by a significant
margin; 40 per cent of them (N–269) belong to one or more elite clubs,
compared with one-quarter of directors, and only one-tenth of bureaucrats.
One striking difference involves the intensity of membership, with one-fifth
of directors holding memberships in four or five such clubs, compared with
the government elite who tend, when they do belong, to hold only one or
two memberships. Insofar as the entertainment of governmental elites is a

[1] James Curtis, 'Voluntary association joining: a cross-national comparative note',
36 *American Sociological Review* (October, 1971), pp. 874–5.

common activity of directors, such a difference is not unexpected. Since such clubs tend to be the special preserve of the Canadian economic elite, membership in them by some members of the governmental elite provides another index and an instrument of accommodation politics.[1]

Our research leads us to expect that business and industrial directors would probably emphasize such social interactions more than other types and that the directors of highly political groups would tend to have the largest proportion of multiple elite group memberships. In the case of political activism, this does prove to be true. Directors of low and medium groups, together, (N–457) account for only one-quarter of all elite-club memberships; while the most politically active directors (N–160) account for the remaining three-quarters. Regarding memberships and type of group, there is also a tendency for larger proportions of directors of business, industrial, and professional types of groups to belong to such clubs.

Having indicated the bases and extent of elite homogeneity along several 'property' dimensions, we turn in the following chapter to a review of selected ideological and cognitive perceptions existing among its members.

[1] For the pattern of elite club membership among economic leaders, see Porter, *The Vertical Mosaic*, pp. 304–5; Porter 'Economic elite and social structure in Canada', 23 *Canadian Journal of Economics and Political Science* (August, 1957) pp. 377–94.

IDEOLOGICAL, COGNITIVE AND AFFECTIVE CONTINUITIES

The main assumption to be tested here is that the interactional links and social continuities found earlier are augmented by a *rough consensus* among the political elite about the nature, utility, and propriety of the politico-economic system. This condition will be called 'cohesiveness'. Also assumed is a common appreciation among them of the process of accommodation whereby governmental power and largesse are shared with political actors representing the major functional sectors of Canadian society. There exists, we assume, a tacit acceptance of the legitimacy of interest group demands, the process by which they are reconciled, and resultant policy outcomes.

The political elite's collective identification with such values, which we shall call ideology, probably helps them sustain their vital role of accommodation, despite the centripetal tendencies of the Canadian political culture. The function of ideology is to explain such allocations of social power and resources, and more specifically, to justify the legitimacy of their control by political elites. The extent of cohesion along these lines will be determined by indexes made up of several items isolated by factor analysis.[1]

THE MEANINGS OF IDEOLOGY

A common element in most definitions of ideology is its rationalizing or valuational function. In effect, ideology plays a necessary role in reducing social tensions. 'Ideology is a system of beliefs, held in common by members

---

[1] The method of factor analysis used here is known as cluster analysis, whereby individual items are analysed to determine which ones form groups or clusters which measure the same dimension. Rotation was used to improve the loadings on the factors and to avoid overlapping among them. For a lucid explanation of various factor analytic techniques, see Dennis Palumbo, *Statistics in Political and Behavioural Science* (New York: Appleton Century, Crofts, 1969).

of a collectivity...a system of ideas which is oriented to the evaluative integration of the collectivity.'¹ Thus ideological explanations of events or ideas are often used to legitimate existing relationships among the various institutional structures of society, or, on the other hand, to justify their modification.

More specific and politically useful is Everett Carl Ladd's definition of ideology as a 'set of prescriptive positions on matters of government and public policy that are seen as forming a logically or quasi-logically inter-related system, with the system treating an area of political life that... typically includes such things as the structure of government, the distribution of power, the political objectives that the society should try to realize and how it should go about it, the distribution of the resources of the system, and the manner and bases of their allocation'.²

Stemming from Marx, Nietzsche, and Weber, ideology has thus often been concerned with the 'action-potential' of ideas, as distinct from their formal content. A related attribute often ascribed to ideology is its internal consistency as a set of reasonably coherent ideas. Such coherence may at times be sustained by repressing inapposite ideas or evidence. Thus another functional property of ideology is to provide a perceptual screen which attempts to order the inevitable contradictions of the real world.

Ideology is often comprehensive, embracing religious, economic, and intellectual spheres, as well as political. Although we are concerned here with the *political* ideology of the Canadian elite, such a categorization is probably an analytical fiction, similar to the attempt to exclude private leaders from the 'political' elite. For example, is the fact that some of our respondents object to heavy infusions of government funds during periods of unemployment a 'political' or an 'economic' facet of ideology?

In this context, we turn to the data concerning ideological dispositions among the political elite. We shall at the same time become aware of some aspects of the substantive content of their ideology. Our main purpose, however, is to suggest that shared beliefs provide another basis of social cohesion among the elite, which in turn eases their role of accommodation.

ELITE SELF-PERCEPTIONS OF LEGITIMACY

One facet of ideology which has suggestive implications for the morale and sense of legitimacy of any elite is the extent to which its members feel they

¹ Talcott Parsons, *The Social System* (New York: Free Press of Glencoe, 1964), p. 349.
² *Ideology in America* (Ithaca: Cornell University Press, 1969), pp. 7–8.

have a moral right to rule by virtue of distinctive competence. In Weberian terms, do they perceive their authority as legitimate? We saw that higher education (knowledge) is the most significant correlate of both political efficacy and activism. One aspect of competence relates to superior knowledge and, by inference, competence. In a sense, all such perceptions are comparative and relative: one does not ascribe competence in a vacuum, but against some salient reference point. In our research, it seemed that elites often measured their own knowledge and competence *vis-à-vis* those of the ordinary citizen.

This matter can be conceptualized in terms of Weber's bases for the legitimation of authority in political and bureaucratic settings: traditional, charismatic, and legal–rational. While legitimation in any life situation is often a composite of these attributes, they can be differentiated for analytical purposes. We suggested earlier that British generalist assumptions regarding leadership remained viable in Canada, and that such residues were essentially traditional and charismatic, and not always functionally apposite. However, our data on the occupational backgrounds of the political elite (Table 7–2) suggest that many of its members are well-qualified in legal–rational terms of specialized education and training. Supportive evidence is provided by the fairly high proportion of lawyers among them, almost one-third in the legislatures, as well as the fact that 45 per cent have graduate degrees.

On the other hand, there is some variation within each subsystem. The bureaucratic elite, for example, contains a large proportion of members with a general first degree. Among them ([N–186), humanities, political science, economics, pre-law, and pre-medicine account for almost half of all degrees. At the graduate level, where about half have degrees, there is naturally more technical specialization, with law and medicine accounting for forty per cent of all degrees. Economics and public administration provide another 15 per cent, with the remainder unknown. From these data, one may conclude that about half of all undergraduate and graduate degrees provide the technical education usually required for knowledgeable administration in a modern bureaucracy. As one might expect, given the similarity of their roles, federal and provincial bureaucrats tend to share similar levels of educational achievement: regarding graduate degrees, for example, 45 per cent are held by the Ottawa subsample, which accounts for 42 per cent of the total sample.

Since only about 8 per cent of Canadians have university degrees, compared with about three-quarters of the political elite, it is clear once again that we are dealing with a highly selective segment of Canadian society. In

285

this context, it is important to recall that these are mainly middle-aged men, whose degrees were earned at a time when such enjoyed considerably more scarcity value than at present. As a result, its members probably tend to be fairly confident of their capacity to direct the political apparatus.

A related aspect of the self-legitimation process is the extent to which elites impute knowledge and competence in general political affairs to ordinary citizens. Their judgments in this regard may be regarded as evidence of the extent to which its members converge on the belief that they possess both the knowledge and the moral right to exercise leadership. Any such consensus, moreover, will again suggest the extent of cohesion among them. Table 11–1 presents the distribution, using four items regarding the 'average citizen's feelings' about interest groups.

The first two items may be regarded as indicators of related citizen attitudes toward public affairs, with the first providing evidence of a self-regarding, somewhat narrow perspective toward interest groups, while the second evokes a broader philosophical conception of such groups. Such differences provide evidence of the political sophistication that elites ascribe to the rank-and-file, and upon which to some extent their own self-perceptions and behaviour are based. The third and fourth items deal with informational and attitudinal dimensions of citizen behaviour.

The data suggest a general similarity of opinion among elites regarding each proposition. Only in the final item, where directors tend, under-standably, to reject a statement which questions the legitimacy of interest

TABLE 11-1   *Elite perceptions of citizen knowledge and competence*

	Proportion agreeing			
	MP's	Bureaucrats	Directors	X^2
'He approves of and actively participates when they directly concern his interests.'	% 75	% 66	% 72	not sig.
'He regards them as useful and necessary representatives of the many interests in society.'	60	58	68	not sig.
'He probably knows little about activities of such groups.'	73	81	73	not sig.
'He probably feels they have an undue influence upon policy decisions.'	54 (257)	47 (203)	38 (624)	sig. at .05

groups, do we find a significant (.05) difference. Governmental elites also tend to be somewhat unrealistic on this point since, as we saw earlier, the average Canadian is likely to think that such groups do indeed have too much influence on public policy. Federal bureaucrats, however, are significantly less likely than their provincial opposites to endorse this judgment. Differences between federal and provincial back-benchers on this item are small; about 54 per cent of both elites agree, but ministers take a more sanguine view, with 'only' 40 per cent indicating that citizens think interest groups have too much influence.

The proposition concerning citizen knowledge of interest groups may be defined as an indicator of rank-and-file knowledge, as perceived by elites. *Three-fourths of them share the view that citizens know little about this vital aspect of policy making.* Inter-provincial differences range from a low of 68 per cent agreeing in Ontario, to 74 in Quebec, with British Columbia highest at 80 per cent. Once again, ministers rank lower than back-benchers, with 'only' 62 per cent accepting the generalization. Everything considered, bureaucrats have the least positive view on three of the four items; and directors are somewhat more favourable than back-benchers. It may be that the bureaucrats' highly negative appreciation of citizen knowledge reflects their tendency to be somewhat isolated from the public and any attending tension, as suggested in the earlier finding that almost two-thirds of Canadian adults (citizens and non-citizens) believe they become 'just a number' when they enter a federal government office.[1]

Such elite judgments about citizen attitudes towards groups have suggestive implications in the context of legitimacy and knowledge. On the one hand, they reveal that elite perceptions are not always accurate in this area, for as we saw earlier, there is considerable popular cynicism regarding the influence that 'big' interest groups are believed to have over Canadian governmental elites. *Such judgments, moreover, indicate that elites are much more likely to legitimate interest groups than the ordinary citizen.* In conjunction with the belief that citizens know little about interest group activity, this may encourage the tendency of elites to believe in their own legitimacy and competence, as well as in the going interest group system. Certainly, as shown earlier, there is some basis for the elite judgment that the average citizen is not always able to comprehend governmental affairs and that his attending feelings of inefficacy may induce him to perceive government and politics negatively .

[1] Morris, *et al. Attitudes Toward Federal Government Information*, p. 160.

Elite accommodation

Some evidence supporting these conclusions is available in comparative data on elite and rank-and-file alienation Alienation, of course, is a complex concept, composed of various states or feelings: powerlessness, meaningless, normlessness, self-estrangement, and isolation.[1] The items used here are a composite of powerlessness, normlessness, and estrangement from government and politics (rather than estrangement from self), often based upon some ambivalence regarding the honesty and competence of governmental elites.

We look first at the evidence regarding alienation among members of the political elite. Other research enables us to predict that rates for this variable would be very low, although it is interesting to speculate whether the limited effectiveness of the back-bencher in the parliamentary system will be reflected in the distribution. However, analysis reveals that the proportion indicating even a mild degree of alienation is so small that it seems useless to present the data separately. Well over 80 per cent of the political elite ($[N-1,085$) rank low on this dimension, as defined by a three-item index using standard items. It is interesting, nevertheless, that *powerlessness*, which incorporates a sense of political inefficacy, presents a typical normal curve distribution. Although powerlessness is often included as one component of alienation, our factor analysis indicates that alienation and powerlessness are independent, so a separate index was designed for powerlessness, to which we will turn shortly.

Considerable research indicates that alienation tends to occur most commonly among individuals who possess few political resources and who have not been socialized, either as children or adults, to expect to play a significant role in politics.[2] The sense of political powerlessness often tends

---

[1] Melvin Seeman, 'On the meaning of alienation', 24 *American Sociological Review* (December, 1959) pp. 783–91. For a useful survey of the literature and an attempt to clarify the concept, see Ada Finifter, 'Dimensions of political alienation', 64 *American Political Science Review* (June, 1970), pp. 389–410.

[2] Among others, see Presthus, *Men at the Top*, pp. 332–45; Almond and Verba, *The Civic Culture*, pp. 49–51; Milbrath, *Political Participation*, pp. 78–81; Agger, Goldrich and Swanson, *The Rulers and the Ruled* (New York: John Wiley, 1964), pp. 295–6; A. W. Finifter, 'Dimensions of political alienation', 64 *American Political Science Review* (June, 1970), pp. 389–410; and Lane, *Political Ideology*, p. 162. Some evidence indicates that alienation among ordinary citizens (as well as anomie and authoritarianism) may be due to 'response set' whereby those with 'socially subordinate' ethnic and class characteristics tend to agree with affirmatively-stated items. See, for examples, L. G. Carr, 'The Srole items and acquiescence', 56 *American Sociological Review* (April,

TABLE 11-2 *Rank-and-file alienation from government*[a]

		1965 (2,721)	1968 (2,767)
		%	%
'Do you think "quite a few", "hardly any", or "not very many" of the people running the government are crooked?'	Quite a few	24	24
	Not very many	37	37
	Hardly any/none	28	29
	DK/NA	10	10
'Do you think people in government waste "a lot", "some", or "not very much", of the money we pay in taxes?'	A lot	36	43
	Some	46	43
	Not much/any	13	8
	DK/NA	6	6
'Do you feel "all people" running government know what they are doing or that "quite a few" don't?'	All/most do	39	48
	Quite a few don't	52	46
	DK/NA	8	7
'Do you feel that people high in government give everyone a fair break or that some pay more attention to what the big interests want?'	Everyone a fair break	15	10
	More attention to big interests	75	83
	DK/NA	10	7
'How much of the time can you trust government to do what is right?'	Always	9	8
	Most of the time	49	50
	Some of the time	36	37
	DK/NA	6	5

[a] Some of these items have been abbreviated for convenience, and all figures have been rounded so columns do not always total 100.

to manifest itself in a generalized distrust of government and politics. It will be recalled that the Meisel national survey found that three-fourths of Canadians believed that voting was the *only way* they could influence government, and that substantial proportions of citizens ranked low on political efficacy. This belief is accompanied by considerable political alienation or cynicism, as indicated in Table 11-2.

Interpretation of these findings is difficult in some instances. Despite the ambivalence indicated in the first four items about government's honesty, economy, impartiality and competence, almost 60 per cent of Canadians indicate in the final item that they trust government to do the right thing 'always' or 'most of the time'. Some indication of the main drift of the distribution may be found, however, by averaging the sum total of *negative*

1971), pp. 287–92, and G. E. Lenski and J. Leggett, 'Caste, class and deference in the research interview', 65 *American Journal of Sociology* (March, 1960), pp. 463–7. Fortunately, the advantaged status of the Canadian political elite tends to obviate this problem here, although it may have affected the rank-and-file data cited elsewhere.

TABLE 11-3   *Rank-and-file trust in federal government, by province*[a]

Trust in Government	Quebec	Ontario	British Columbia
	%	%	%
High	9	5	6
Fairly high	20	25	25
Moderate	21	23	24
Fairly low	28	27	26
Low	22	20	19
	(3,733)	(4,592)	(1,253)

[a] Adapted from Morris, *et al. Attitudes toward Federal Government Information*, p. 164.

responses among the five items. When this is done, we find that almost two-thirds may, by this measure, be regarded as alienated. Moreover, if we include only those at the 'least positive' end of the scale on each item, we find fully 46 per cent among these two-thirds who may be characterized as being 'highly alienated' from government and politics. It is noteworthy that the values typically change very little between 1965 and 1968, although there is a noteworthy increase in the level of confidence in government's competence between the two periods.

General confirmation of these attitudes is available in the *Government Information* survey (1968) regarding rank-and-file trust in the federal government. Two items were used here: one concerning the belief that Ottawa provides honest information, and the other that the federal government usually lives up to its promises. Table 11-3 presents the distribution, controlled for the three provinces.

Here again, it is clear that the distribution is significantly skewed toward the 'low' end of the scale. Almost one-half of respondents in all three provinces rank 'low' or 'fairly low' in trust, as measured by the two indexes. Quebec is slightly more likely to distrust federal promises and information, but the differences are insignificant. This evidence, parenthetically, attests again to the precarious integration of the Canadian political culture, as seen in the tendency to make invidious distinctions between provincial and federal governments. Since over half of the Canadian people believe that the federal government handles the most important problems facing Canada, compared with only one-quarter who believe that provincial governments do, this is a particularly unhappy observation.[1]

[1] John Meisel, 1968 survey.

290

In sum, we may conclude that striking differences exist between the elite and rank-and-file regarding political alienation. Whereas the overwhelming majority of the political elite ranked low on this dimension, the findings reported above indicate that about one-half of two national samples manifest a high level of alienation and lack of trust in government. Psychologically, this gap has often been attributed to feelings of low efficacy. We are not denying, of course, that the sense of political powerlessness manifests itself in other, more positive ways. And indeed, part of the meaning of the current rise of consumer-oriented protest groups is no doubt attributable to such reactions. On the other hand, considerable research supports the relationship between felt powerlessness and rejection of the political system.[1]

In the immediate context, the evidence suggests another impetus toward cohesion among the political elite, based upon shared perceptions of political reality. It also punctuates the ideological separation between elites and the subcultures typically found in consociational societies, in which political stability is maintained essentially through accommodation among prag-matically-oriented elites. The problem confronting leaders is reflected in the ambivalence with which citizens view some aspects of elite competence, economy, and probity. Certainly, the national consensus often assumed to be a functional requisite of democratic stability is challenged by the data presented here. On the other hand, such strong underlying values as the deferential tradition and the acceptance of political authority implicit in the 'Old Tory' theory of leadership, as well as the federal elite's endorsement of the need for concessions to French-Canadian nationalism, provide countervailing forces that have sustained the national political system for a century.

ELITE COHESION ON SELECTED IDEOLOGICAL AND COGNITIVE DIMENSIONS

Having indicated some of the values that differentiate political elites from other citizens, we turn to the question of ideological cohesion among the political elite.

An attribute which one would expect to be shared among them is a well-developed sense of political efficacy.[2] This judgment is based upon both their

---

[1] Among others, see Lane, *Political Ideology*, p. 162; John E. Horton and Wayne Thompson, 'Powerlessness and political negativism', 67 *American Journal of Sociology* (1962), pp. 485–93.

[2] Robert Agger and D. Goldrich, 'Community power structures and partisanship', 33 *American Sociological Review* (August, 1958), pp. 383–92.

relatively high occupational and educational levels and their critical role in the political system. We anticipate some variation among sub-elites, for despite their social homogeneity, one would expect to find some normative discontinuity. A frequent observation regarding Canadian federal government, for example, is that high-level bureaucrats have become an autonomous centre of power, given their expertise and experience which provide them considerable leverage *vis-à-vis* their generalist masters in the Cabinet and Parliament. If this is so, we might expect to find higher rates of efficacy among bureaucrats than among members. It is also believed in some quarters that the talented group of men at the deputy-minister level have somewhat less than a fulsome regard for the competence of the average back-bencher. One item which provides hard evidence on this perception states: 'The average member is a competent political professional who knows his business.' Thirty per cent (N-214) disagreed with this judgment, and another thirty per cent 'didn't know'. As noted earlier, some evidence exists that senior bureaucrats regard back-benchers competitively, in part on the assumption that any increase in policy influence among them would be gained at their own expense.

In order to provide some bench-mark against which to set the felt efficacy of the political elite, we have prepared a summary (Table 11-4) which includes data from the Meisel survey of 1965 and the Hoffman–Schindeler

TABLE 11-4 *Comparative levels of political efficacy*

Efficacy[a]	Ministers	MP's	Bureaucrats	Directors	Nat'l[b]	Ontario[c]
	%	%	%	%	%	%
High	57	38	33	31	28	18
Medium	24	27	33	32	46	49
Low	19	34	33	36	26	33
	(42)	(211)	(208)	(601)	(2,721)	(1,598)

[a] Efficacy is based upon the following items: 'The old saying, "You can't fight city hall" is still basically true'; 'Most decisions in business and government are made by a small group that pretty well runs things'; 'The average man doesn't really have much chance to get ahead today'; 'Anyone in this country who wants to, has a chance to have his say about important issues'. Although the 'average man doesn't have . . .' item is often used as an alienation item, it emerged as part of this index through cluster analysis.

[b] Based upon the Meisel 1965 election survey, using such items as 'Voting is the only way people like me have any say about how the government runs things' and 'I don't think the government cares much what people like me think'.

[c] Adapted from the Ontario survey (1968) of political values of citizens. The cut-off points here were selected to provide as much similarity to those used in the present study as possible.

study of Ontario citizens in 1968–9. These valuable data provide us with a rough, but useful basis of comparison.

It must be noted that comparability is precarious in this table, except among the sub-elites in the present study. Different items were used in the 1965 and Ontario analyses and the cut-off points were not identical. It is questionable, indeed, whether the items used for such 'rank-and-file' surveys are entirely appropriate for elite analysis. For example, the national survey included the following items, 'Generally, those elected to Parliament soon lose touch with the people', and 'Voting is the only way people like me can have any say about how the government runs things.' Both are obviously unsuitable for governmental elites. The most we can say is that the items used tap similar dimensions of political efficacy, and that the cut-off points are roughly equivalent.

Looking across the high level, although the differences between the political elite (excepting ministers) and respondents in the two comparative surveys are smaller than expected,[1] there is a linear decline in felt efficacy from ministers to ordinary citizens. As expected, ministers rank significantly higher than back-benchers, bureaucrats, and the private elite group. Their advantage here would have been even greater had not just over half agreed that 'Most decisions in business and government are made by a small group which pretty well runs things', which was scored as an indicator of low efficacy. In any event, their responses provide another bit of evidence that 'democratic elitism' is widely perceived by those directly concerned as the going system of authority and decision-making in Canadian politics.

Substantial regional and inter-elite differences exist (not shown in the table). Quebec's elites, for example, rank lower than those in other areas. Ontario respondents tend to rank highest, followed by British Columbia and Ottawa. The variation among bureaucrats in the four areas is not very large. Ottawa ranks at the top with 37 per cent; British Columbia has 33 per cent; Ontario is next with 31 per cent, while Quebec has 29 per cent. Interest group directors range from 36 per cent who feel highly efficacious in Ontario, to 35 per cent in British Columbia, 33 per cent in Ottawa, with Quebec indicating only one-fifth at the high level. In view of the range and diversity of the directors' sample, it is unexpected that they would rank as close to the bureaucratic elite on this disposition.

[1] This may reflect the difference between responses based upon hypothetical perceptions of influence expressed by citizens and the presumably more reality-oriented judgments of experienced political elites who have fewer illusions about the extent of their influence as individuals.

In sum, it seems that although the rates of efficacy among the political elite are generally lower than one would expect from individuals possessing such large shares of political resources the range among them is not great, with the exception of ministers and of party differences, especially among the NDP sample, some 80 per cent of whom rank low on efficacy. The 'high' range among MP's includes about one-half Ontario members and one-third Quebec deputies; among bureaucrats, it descends from 37 per cent among Ottawa respondents to 29 per cent in Quebec; and regarding directors, the dispersion is from a high of 36 per cent in Ontario to a low of 21 per cent in Quebec. Quebec's low position confirms our earlier observations about its distinctive political culture, which seems somewhat less affirmative than that of the others.

Political and economic liberalism are important normative dispositions that mediate the process of elite accommodation. Although the dichotomy is sometimes tenuous, political dialogue often proceeds in terms of a left–right continuum, in which those on the 'left' are assumed to be generally more receptive to government penetration of the 'private' sphere, to a more active and positive role for government, to its use to equalize the dis-equilibria of power found in the market-place and to ease the shock of unemployment, sickness, and old age. Those on the 'right' sector of the continuum tend to resist such definitions of government's 'proper' role, and have their ideologies to justify such preferences. Obviously, no party or individual will adhere consistently to all the 'principles' of one or the other of these dimensions. Such differences in policy preferences are often characterized by the symbols 'liberal' and 'conservative', which may be somewhat confusing in the Canadian milieu since the terms are not synonymous with party labels. Some observers have argued that the major Canadian parties are not differentiable along such a continuum. Others, however, have found empirical differences in policy orientation between the Liberal and Conservative parties which suggest the terms 'liberal' and 'conservative' may be useful in characterizing them.[1]

We have therefore attempted to categorize the political elite on certain of these values. Because political liberalism has been found to include two discrete dimensions, *political* and *economic*, we will present them separately.[2]

---

[1] Cf. Allan Kornberg who found in a survey of the 25th Canadian federal parliament that Liberals could be distinguished from Conservatives on several policy issues, including Quebec and biculturalism, civil liberties, and 'welfare statism'. *Canadian Legislative Behaviour* (New York and Toronto: Holt, Rinehart and Winston, 1967), pp. 123–5.

[2] For evidence of this dichotomy which indicates that political elites tend to rank high on political liberties (free speech, etc.) and low on economic 'liberalism' (i.e. welfare

The use of such concepts provides an additional empirical basis for determining the extent of ideological cohesion among the political elite, as well as its substantive preferences.

A methodological note is required here. Two major types of statistical tests will be used in this chapter: chi-square and *t*-tests. Chi-square is used to determine whether the relative frequencies found among the elite sample within and across regions hold for the elite universe. Our criterion for significance will be the usual .05 level, which means that the relationship found could have occurred by chance only five times in a hundred. The second and more important objective, which involves testing our theoretical assumptions about the bases of elite interaction and accommodation, is to determine the *level of cohesion* among the political elite on selected ideological and cognitive dimensions. This requires another kind of test, which, unlike chi-square, can accommodate the small cells of N–30 and less which occur in the analysis and especially in Tables 11-16 to 11-22, where the use of two indices causes a high attrition of cases. More important, we require a test that can determine differences of means among sub-elites for the various test dimensions. The criterion for cohesion thus becomes the extent to which significant differences of means (again at the .05 level) on the several dimensions are found *within* regional sub-elites and *across* all sub-elites. The sums of such differences will be calculated and scaled in Tables 11-14, 11-15 and 11-23, to determine the extent of cohesion among the entire elite sample.

In the Table 11-5, political liberalism is based upon a multiple-item index developed through factor analysis which ensures that the items are strongly correlated. Regarding the distribution among the entire elite, only one-quarter rank high, 35 per cent are medium, while just under 40 per cent rank low. Regional and sub-elite frequencies are presented in Table 11-5.

Here, as with political efficacy, a general and fairly consistent tendency exists among the elite to rank rather low on this dimension. Some exceptions exist. Ottawa elites are generally more liberal and, looking at the 'high' column for all groups, it is immediately clear that British Columbia MP's rank highest on political liberalism. Each of its other subgroups, however, exhibits a small but noteworthy lower ranking compared with its counterpart (excepting Ontario directors) in other regions. Well over half of

programmes) while rank-and-file members of society tend to exhibit opposite tendencies, see Presthus, *Men at the Top*, p. 317. Evidence of these kinds of differences among Canadian university students, and by inference, among their parents, is presented in W. B. Devall, 'Civil liberties among English-speaking Canadian university students', 3 *Canadian Journal of Political Science* (September, 1970), pp. 439–40.

TABLE 11-5 *Political liberalism among the Canadian political elite*

	Political liberalism[a]			
Region/Elite	High	Medium	Low	
	%	%	%	
Ottawa				
Legislators	33	33	34	(137)
Bureaucrats	26	43	32	(89)
Directors	26	40	35	(101)
Ontario				
Legislators	27	35	39	(49)
Bureaucrats	22	43	35	(49)
Directors	19	30	51	(212)
Quebec				
Legislators	22	24	54	(41)
Bureaucrats	31	25	44	(32)
Directors	30	35	35	(186)
British Columbia				
Legislators	41	28	31	(32)
Bureaucrats	17	50	33	(36)
Directors	20	33	48	(107)
	(283)	(382)	(420)	

t-test =

across regions: all MP's v. all bureaucrats; all MP's v. all directors; and all bureaucrats v. all directors, no significant differences exist at the .05 level;

within regions: *Ottawa:* no significant differences;

Ontario: bureaucrats v. directors, significant at .05 (two-tailed t-test);

Quebec: MP's v. directors, significant at .01 (two-tailed t-test);

British Columbia: MP's v. bureaucrats, significant at .05 (two-tailed t-test). MP's v. directors, significant at .02 (two-tailed t-test).

[a] This index of political liberalism is based upon the following items: 'Democracy depends fundamentally upon free enterprise' (reverse scored); 'Everything considered, labour unions are doing a lot of good in this country'; 'An atheist or a communist should have as much right to make a public speech as anybody else'. These are standard items for measuring this dimension.

Quebec's deputies rank low on political liberalism; the disparity between them and British Columbia MP's is particularly striking. Meanwhile, British Columbia's bureaucrats rank substantially lower than their counterparts in other regions.

Among the three elites, MP's (except in Quebec) rank marginally highest among all groups in most areas. This is not unexpected since the toleration of dissent and ambiguity symbolized by political liberalism is often regarded as an essential element of the legislative role. On the whole, still looking at the 'high' level, it is interesting that the proportions found there are very similar in every case for directors and bureaucrats. A striking disparity exists among them, however, at the *low* end of the scale where directors in British Columbia and Ontario rank dramatically higher than either their counterparts in Ottawa and Quebec or bureaucrats in all regions, except Quebec.

As noted, a more precise way of determining the extent of elite continuity along these dimensions is by the comparison of means among regions and sub-elites, using the t-test. Statistical significance at the .05 level provides the criterion for such interpretations. *Across* regions, for example, none of the mean differences in political liberalism among any of the sub-elites are significant. *Within* regions, only four of the twelve possible combinations of sub-elite discontinuities prove significant: In Ottawa, no significant differences exist. In Quebec, MP's and directors are significantly different at the .01 level. Given the small N's involved in Quebec's case, the difference is remarkable, and attests again to the tendency of Quebec to differ from other regions. In Ontario, civil servants and directors differ significantly, while in British Columbia, MP's differ significantly from both directors and bureaucrats.

Given the relatively few significant differences in means found here, we conclude that a nice consensus exists among the political elite regarding this value. Indeed, the remarkable continuity among them is clear from a comparison of their respective means: MP's = 10.900; bureaucrats = 10.874; directors = 10.982. The over-all tendency of elites to rank only medium to low is somewhat unexpected because research usually reveals a strongly positive relation between SES and political liberalism.[1] Since members of the political elite are highly advantaged in social and economic

[1] Among others, see S. Stouffer, *Communism, Conformity and Civil Liberties* (New York: Doubleday, 1955); T. Adorno, *The Authoritarian Personality* (New York: Harper, 1950); J. R. Gusfield, 'Mass society and extremist politics', 27 *American Sociological Review* (1962), pp. 19–30.

terms, one would expect generally more positive loadings on this disposition. In sum, the conclusion seems warranted that the Canadian political elite, as defined here, shares a generally consistent disposition toward political liberalism as measured here.

We turn next to economic liberalism, which is defined in contemporary terms of 'big government' and the fulsome intervention of the state in the so-called private sphere, including an equilibrating role in economic and financial matters. Given the positive appreciation of government's role that has characterized Canada throughout its history, one would expect members of the political elite to rank fairly high on this value. On the other hand, some tempering of such inclinations results from certain policy issues included in the index, which proved unacceptable to some respondents. Federal aid to education, for example, tends to be rejected out of hand by many *Canadiens*, while the prospect of state-guaranteed economic security for every man, woman and child proved unacceptable to other respondents. The ambivalent position of most bureaucrats on political liberalism also suggests that as a group, with many exceptions, they might also rank low on this dimension. The distribution is presented in Table 11-6, by region and elite group.

Here, our predicted condition of relative homogeneity fails to appear as significant differences emerge in several contexts. Turning first to differences *across* regions, those between legislators and civil servants, as well as between civil servants and directors prove to be significant at the .001 level. For reasons to be speculated upon later, bureaucrats prove to be vastly more conservative politically than their legislative masters. Meanwhile, differences between the latter and directors on this dimension are not significant. The main drift is clear from a comparison of means: MP's = 18.715; bureaucrats = 16.385; directors = 18.432.

Within each region, which may be theoretically more crucial in the sense that each elite to some extent works in isolation from the others, with the result that internal cohesion is more important operationally within than across regions, strongly significant differences also exist. In every case, except for legislators and directors, they are significant at the .001 level in all regions. In effect, whereas MP's and directors have equally positive views regarding this dimension, bureaucrats differ sharply in rejecting the policy statements used here to characterize economic liberalism. That MP's and directors in British Columbia share very similar values adds another challenge to the assumption that the Social Credit party probably experiences some ideological dissonance *vis-à-vis* interest groups.

In sum, the 'pro-government' disposition symbolized by economic

TABLE 11-6 *Economic liberalism among the political elite*

Region/Elite	Economic liberalism[a]			
	High	Medium	Low	
	%	%	%	
Ottawa				
Legislators	37	44	20	(122)
Bureaucrats	28	30	42	(88)
Directors	41	36	22	(100)
Ontario				
Legislators	38	34	28	(47)
Bureaucrats	10	33	56	(48)
Directors	38	30	32	(210)
Quebec				
Legislators	40	43	18	(40)
Bureaucrats	12	30	58	(33)
Directors	35	46	20	(182)
British Columbia				
Legislators	47	43	10	(30)
Bureaucrats	11	42	47	(36)
Directors	42	43	16	(106)
	(359)	(393)	(289)	

t-test =

across regions, the following differences appear: all MP's *v.* bureaucrats, significant at the .001 level; and all bureaucrats *v.* all directors,
significant at the .001 level;

within regions: In all four regions, MP's *v.* bureaucrats are significant
at .001 (two-tailed t-test); and bureaucrats *v.* directors are significant
at .001 (two-tailed t-test).

[a] Economical liberalism is defined here by the following items: 'That
government which governs least governs best' (reverse scored);
'Economic security for every man, woman and child is worth striving
for, even if it means socialism'; 'If unemployment is high, the
government should spend money to create jobs'; 'A national
medicare plan is necessary to ensure that everyone receives adequate
health care'; 'More federal aid to education is desirable if we are
going to adequately meet present and future educational needs in this
country.'

liberalism reveals considerable variation by sub-elite. Among MP's, as with
political liberalism, British Columbia ranks substantially higher than others,
followed by Quebec, Ontario, and Ottawa, with very similar tendencies. On
the whole, among the three sub-elites, despite some inter-regional differences,
MP's tend to rank highest on this dimension, especially if one combines the

'high' and 'medium' categories, which is tempting given the common tendency for legislators to present themselves as being 'middle-of-the-road'.

Regarding directors, the variation is less pronounced. Ottawa and British Columbia's directors rank highest on this disposition, followed by Ontario directors, with those in Quebec sharing only a marginally lower measure of agreement.

Most striking, of course, is the consistent 'anti-welfare' posture of bureaucrats who rank dramatically lower in every region, compared with other members of the political elite. The position of those in Ontario and Quebec is especially low. These data suggest, contrary to the popular image, that bureaucrats do not always welcome the expansive role which Canadian government has assumed. Perhaps, too, there is some resentment among them of the tendency of ministers to propose large-scale policy ventures (many of which are stillborn, given interest-group opposition and the frequent rotation of ministers), leaving their implementation to the bureaucracy. To some extent, there is a built-in tension potential between politicians who may regard themselves as dynamic agents of change and bureaucrats whose natural inclination is probably toward continuity. The latter's specialized technical role, advantaged SES, long tenure (almost half have served 20 years or more), and comparatively high average age (57 per cent are over 50) may also contribute to this 'conservative' political valence.

Perhaps such disparities may be regarded as a 'frustration index', on which provincial civil servants rank near the top, while those in Ottawa find accommodation easier. With the exception of Ottawa, however, where deputy ministers play a vital policy role, any operational effects may be eased by the relatively weaker role of bureaucrats in the provinces surveyed here. The over-all distribution may also be treated as a rough index of the cohesion or consensus existing among regional sub-elites, with several of them revealing considerable dissonance on this dimension.

We noted earlier that despite low elite rankings on alienation, a disposition often regarded as one of its components, powerlessness, did emerge as an independent dimension, along which a normal distribution occurred. Before presenting the data on this variable, a caveat must be made regarding the relevance of political efficacy items for elites. It is questionable that such items are germane, on the ground that elites rank uniformly high by virtue of their copious resources and strategic political roles. On the other hand, it seems that this assumption, however logical, should be tested empirically in the Canadian milieu, and especially when back-benchers typically have little influence in policy-determination. As we saw earlier, the rates of political efficacy among the political elite are lower than one would expect. Table 11-7 provides a more intensive analysis of this related dimension, again differentiated by region and sub-elite.

Turning first to the analysis of means *across* regions, only one relationship, between MP's and directors, proves to be significant at the .05 level. As apparent in Table 11-7, this condition reflects the relatively high degree of powerlessness experienced by directors in Quebec and British Columbia. Their position is clear from a comparison of sub-elite means: MP's = 10.387; bureaucrats = 10.437; rising to 10.810 for directors.

TABLE 11-7 *Powerlessness among the political elite, by region*

	Powerlessness[a]			
Region/Elite	High	Medium	Low	
	%	%	%	
Ottawa				
Legislators	33	29	38	(135)
Bureaucrats	26	37	37	(89)
Directors	30	38	33	(101)
Ontario				
Legislators	32	21	47	(47)
Bureaucrats	40	29	31	(48)
Directors	31	33	36	(214)
Quebec				
Legislators	39	24	37	(41)
Bureaucrats	49	23	27	(35)
Directors	49	31	27	(135)
British Columbia				
Legislators	23	30	47	(30)
Bureaucrats	28	39	33	(36)
Directors	41	24	35	(103)
	(379)	(338)	(355)	

t-test =
across regions: MP's *v.* bureaucrats, significant at .05.
within regions: *British Columbia* MP's *v.* directors and bureaucrats *v.* directors, significant at .05 (two-tailed *t*-test).

[a] The index of powerlessness is defined by the following items: 'The average man doesn't really have much chance to get ahead today'; 'Most decisions in business and government are made by a small group that pretty well run things'; 'Anyone in this country who wants to, has a chance to have his say about, important issues'; 'The old saying, "You can't fight city hall" is still basically true.'

Elite accommodation

Within regions, considerable homogeneity exists, with the only exceptions appearing in British Columbia where differences on this dimension are significant between MP's and directors, and between bureaucrats and directors at the .05 level. Here again, we have a scintilla of evidence supporting the assumption that interest groups fare less well in British Columbia because of the ambivalence with which they are regarded by the Social Credit party. Despite this, directors in Quebec rank highest among all sub-elites on this dimension, with a mean of 11.563 *v.* 10.637 for the entire sample.

Some signal variations on this dimension (not included in Table 11-7) appear regarding party. Fully half of Quebec's *Union Nationale* members rank high on powerlessness, compared with only about one-fifth of Liberals and Conservatives, a distribution that may reflect the party's defeat by the Liberals during the course of the research. Among minority parties, 80 per cent of NDP members rank high on this dimension, reflecting in part their relatively low SES, compared with members of the two major parties.

Not unexpectedly, given their important role in policy-determination, Ottawa bureaucrats rank quite low on felt powerlessness, followed closely by their opposite numbers in British Columbia, with those in Quebec and Ontario ranking considerably higher than their counterparts. Meanwhile, directors in Quebec and British Columbia rank significantly above ($X^2 = .001$) those in Ottawa and Ontario. This evidence again lends some support to the proposition that the Social Credit Government does not provide the most hospitable environment for interest groups.

Quebec's singular ranking on powerlessness (almost 48 per cent of her political elite ranks high on this dimension) suggests that her political culture is distinct in the Durkheimian sense that a collective sense of solidarity and self-direction may be somewhat less developed than in other regions. It also suggests the survival of traditional, elitist patterns of authority, which tend to pervade political, as well as other social institutions. Combined with the discontinuities found regarding political and economic liberalism and the marginal legitimacy imputed to interest groups, this condition is both noteworthy and somewhat unexpected given the cultural homogeneity of the province.

Although highly speculative, it may be useful to consider the extent to which such tendencies are a residue of historical cultural values ultimately derived from France. Although relations with the mother country are obviously much different from those experienced by English-Canadians with Britain, certain symbolic interactions between Quebec and France

302

have continued despite Quebec's relatively greater isolation. Despite the resentment at being abandoned, so to speak, and certain historical discontinuities as seen, for example, in Quebec's imperviousness to the effects of the French Revolution, it seems that continental France has remained an honoured cultural and intellectual model for Quebec's French-Canadian leaders. Her preoccupation with French language and literature has strengthened such ties.[1] As the sociologist Marcel Rioux has said, 'The French-Canadian ideology has always rested on three characteristics of the French-Canadian culture – the fact that it is a minority culture, that it is Catholic, and that it is French.'[2]

In the economic sphere, too, entreprenurial styles in Quebec apparently correspond nicely to those in France. Family-owned enterprise, the persistence of particularistic, kinship-oriented criteria of employment, the reluctance to borrow from large financial institutions, and the attending inclination to remain relatively small – such preferences have also been characteristic of French enterprise.[3] This generalized security orientation may also symbolize a belief among the elite that it is not able to control the rate and direction of social and economic change in the province, which is strongly affected by *external* forces and institutions, including Ottawa and American financial interests. To some extent, a similar perception may underlie the unexpectedly high rates of felt powerlessness among the English-Canadian elite. Certainly these data raise questions about the pervasiveness of the new *élan* widely held to characterize Quebec's political leadership in the recent past.

Certain cultural and behavioural continuities may also be seen. Michel Crozier, for example, characterizes the French social system as one in which 'the prevailing view of authority is still that of universalism and absolutism; it continues to retain something of the seventeenth century's political theory, with its mixture of rationality and *bon plaisir*.'[4] Equally germane is the French insistence upon personal autonomy, even if it means restricting

---

[1] See, for example, *Le Conseil de la vie Francaise, Nothing More, Nothing Less* (Montreal: Holt, Rinehart and Winston, 1967), which speaks of the 'spiritual ties' between France and Canada, p. 46; Jacques Maritain, the French-Catholic philosopher, is cited in the context of French-Canadian culture. Quebec's programmes of educational, cultural and economic representation with France are also germane.

[2] 'Ideologie et crise de conscience du Canada francais', *Cité Libre* (decembre, 1955), p. 9.

[3] See, for example, N. W. Taylor, 'French Canadians as industrial entrepreneurs', 68 *Journal of Political Economy* (February, 1960), pp. 37–52; Taylor, *L'industriel canadien-francais et son milieu*, II *Recherches sociographiques* (April–June, 1961), pp. 123–50.

[4] *The Bureaucratic Phenomenon* (Chicago: University of Chicago Press, 1964), p. 222.

oneself to a somewhat narrow life space. Only during crises do people over-come their isolation and cooperate for community ends. Bureaucratic structure and norms, meanwhile, provide a sympathetic milieu for indulging both isolation needs and those of *bon plaisir*, described as the opportunity to wield 'virtually absolute authority' within a prescribed sphere.[1]

Concerning social change, it is not the rate of change that is different but the process by which change is achieved, which requires 'attacking the whole system'.[2] Bureaucratic rigidity explains part of this condition, which tends to lead to 'an irresponsible form of intellectual creativity', often attended by the view that 'great deeds are possible only during crises.'[3] Such per-spectives make the fullest internalization of community values difficult, since one must always be prepared to accept dramatic change.

At least some of these characterizations seem to apply to Quebec society today. Despite far-reaching moves toward urbanization, industrialization and secularization in the recent past, such factors as a preference among the young for careers in bureaucratic, collective enterprise; the emphasis upon preserving cultural traditions; the low rates of political participation as measured by group membership, seem to reflect French cultural legacies that make social change, as opposed to technological innovation, very slow, yet disruptive when it occurs. It should not be forgotten, meanwhile, that traditionalism in Quebec has probably been prolonged, as in English-Canada, by the fact that for decades thousands of enterprising individuals have emigrated to the United States, providing an escape valve for pressures toward change in Canadian society.

Obviously, such high-level generalizations are virtually impossible to prove or to refute. One's judgments reflect in part his general appreciation of the rate at which social change and political development occur within a society. My own view tends to be that the speed and ubiquity of *technological* change tend to distort somewhat our perceptions of social change, which lags considerably behind. In this sense, a society can have an urban physical culture inhabited by individuals whose value structure often remains essentially traditional.

COGNITIVE PERCEPTIONS OF INTEREST GROUP POLITICS

We have been discussing certain ideological dispositions of the political elite, to determine the extent of consensus and divergence among them regarding values that seem functionally related to their role of elite accom-

[1] *Ibid.* p. 224.   [2] *Ibid.* p. 287.   [3] *Ibid.* p. 228.

modation. Closely related to such dispositions are elite cognitions of the interest-group system. Our assumption is that such cognitions reflect more or less disinterested appraisals of 'how the system works', rather than normative judgments about its effects. We begin with the question, how much agreement exists among them regarding the political role and conditions of participation for lobbyists?

Here again, several indexes have been isolated using factor analysis. It should be noted that the following index refers only to lobbyist interactions with legislators. Our essential concern is with the extent of cognitive *consensus* among the political elite, and only peripherally with the substance of their views regarding the tactics presented (see Table 11-8).

Turning to the analysis of means *across* all regions, MP's and bureaucrats vary significantly (.001) from directors on their perceptions of interest group-lobbyist activities as defined by this index. Not surprisingly, directors exhibit a more consistent and positive view of such activities, with the possible exception of those in Ottawa, one-third of whom reject these characterizations of the lobbyist's role.

Within regions, a high level of cohesion exists among the Ottawa elite on this dimension, but significant differences in means emerge in the other regions. The strongest variations are in Ontario and Quebec, where, in the former case, MP's and bureaucrats differ at .05, and MP's and directors differ at the strong .01 level. In Quebec, both MP's and bureaucrats also differ from directors, at the .01 level. The same sub-elites vary in British Columbia at the .05 level. In sum, it is clear that governmental elites, except in Ottawa, part company with directors on this dimension. Given the directors' ego-involvement in this instance, the discontinuity is not unexpected. It is less easy to explain the divergence between MP's and bureaucrats in Ontario, which amounts to a split within the governmental family, so to speak. One explanation suggests itself: our legislative sample over-represents Ontario Conservatives to some extent, and they have been shown to be less sympathetic to interest groups (see Table 11-13) than members of the other parties. This may explain some of the difference found here, which is notably strong at the low end of the scale where just twice as high a proportion of MP's and bureaucrats rank low on agreement with the tactics index.

Across regions, strongly significant variations in means (.001) again appear between MP's and directors, and between bureaucrats and directors. Comparative global means are: MP's = 11.067; officials = 11.286; directors = 12.560. This general lack of cohesion reflects disagreements between governmental and private elites; perhaps because they perceive the interest group

TABLE 11-8 *Elite cognitions of the tactical role of lobbyists*[a]

Region/Elite	Proportion ranking			
	High	Medium	Low	
	%	%	%	
Ottawa				
Legislators	21	42	37	(124)
Bureaucrats	18	46	36	(78)
Directors	35	32	33	(82)
Ontario				
Legislators	21	23	55	(47)
Bureaucrats	31	42	27	(45)
Directors	40	38	21	(154)
Quebec				
Legislators	18	45	37	(38)
Bureaucrats	21	45	35	(29)
Directors	43	39	19	(135)
British Columbia				
Legislators	32	26	42	(31)
Bureaucrats	17	37	47	(30)
Directors	46	40	15	(81)
	(278)	(336)	(260)	

t-test =

across regions: MP's *v.* directors and bureaucrats *v.* directors, significant at .001;
within regions: *Ontario:* MP's *v.* bureaucrats, significant at .05; MP's *v.* directors, significant at .001;
  British Columbia: MP's *v.* directors, significant at .05; bureaucrats *v.* directors, significant at .05;
  Quebec: MP's *v.* directors, significant at .01; bureaucrats *v.* directors, significant at .01.
[a] The tactics index is comprised of three items: 'The lobbyist has become a service bureau for those members already in agreement with him, rather than an agent of direct persuasion'; 'The tactical basis of lobbyists is to assist members already on their side to persuade fellow members'; and 'The formality of the legislative process is often a roadblock for a lobbyist trying to present his position.'

system from a different vantage point, the latter tend to agree much more strongly with the prescribed conditions. Certainly, for example, it is not unexpected that directors would agree with the proposition that the legislative system often acts as a 'road-block for a lobbyist trying to present his position,' whereas governmental elites and particularly MP's, have a more positive view of the ease of interest group access (see Table 11-12).

Turning to the global degree of agreement with the tactical index, we find that just about one-third (*N*–278) of the political elite agrees strongly with these definitions of the lobbyist's role. Here, perhaps, we have some evidence that instruments and assumptions of political analysis designed for use in presidential systems are also perceived as relevant by elites in a parliamentary system. Evidence showing that interest groups tend to be similarly relevant in both structures, in the sense that their tactics may differ but their essential role and influence remain similar, has been found regarding France. Nor do they neglect ordinary members.[1]

A related cognitive dimension is the extent and character of the services or benefits that interest groups provide for legislators. These, in effect, are the currencies that mediate interaction between directors and MP's. Interaction theory, it will be recalled, posits that unless such exchanges are regarded as mutually beneficial by those involved, interaction will not persist.

One caveat is required, however, in that directors will probably tend to inflate the value of their contributions, with the result that significant differences will be more likely to appear here (Table 11-9) than in other contexts.

Clearly, governmental elites perceive these interest group services differently, and less favourably, than directors. Moreover, *across* all regions, there is a significant difference in means between MP's and bureaucrats, with the latter much more inclined to perceive such services as being useful to legislators. Ottawa's political elite ranks somewhat lower than the others, while Quebec is markedly more favourable, especially among its deputies. These differences are statistically significant at the .001 level. The cognitive gradient is clearly evident in the distribution of comparative sub-elite means: MP's = 11.004; bureaucrats = 12.188; rising sharply to 13.968 among directors.

Within regions, all differences in means among the sub-elites are significant, with only three exceptions: between MP's and bureaucrats in Ontario and between deputies and bureaucrats and bureaucrats and directors in Quebec. The greatest regional variation occurs in British Columbia where all three sub-elites differ at the strong .001 level. Among legislators, British

---

[1] Regarding France, after noting that the Cabinet and bureaucracy remain the major targets of interest groups, Henry Ehrmann says, 'Nevertheless, the National Assembly retains its importance for the business lobby as the maker and unmaker of governments'; again, speaking of the Fifth Republic, 'From the very beginning neither the "new look" in party life nor the electoral reform banned the action of interest groups from the parliamentary scene', *Organized Business in France* (Princeton: Princeton University Press, 1957), p. 218, 228; also, Jean Meynaud, *Les groupes de pression en France* (Paris: Colin, 1958) and *Nouvelles études sur les groupes de pression en France* (Paris: Colin, 1962).

TABLE 11-9   *Elite cognitions of the service role of interest groups*[a]

Region/Elite	Proportion ranking			
	High	Medium	Low	
	%	%	%	
Ottawa				
Legislators	6	37	58	(126)
Bureaucrats	24	34	42	(76)
Directors	38	31	32	(88)
Ontario				
Legislators	11	39	50	(44)
Bureaucrats	21	40	38	(47)
Directors	47	41	12	(173)
Quebec				
Legislators	31	41	29	(42)
Bureaucrats	36	42	23	(31)
Directors	58	27	15	(157)
British Columbia				
Legislators	6	31	63	(32)
Bureaucrats	22	38	41	(32)
Directors	49	42	9	(88)
	(322)	(336)	(278)	

t-test =

across regions: MP's v. bureaucrats, significant at .001 (two-tailed t-test);
within regions: *Ottawa:* MP's v. bureaucrats, significant at .01 (two-tailed t-test); bureaucrats v. directors, significant at .05; MP's v. directors, significant at .001.

> *Ontario:* MPs' v. directors, significant at .001 (two-tailed t-test); bureaucrats v. directors, significant at .001 (two-tailed t-test).
> *British Columbia:* all three relationships, significant at .001.
> *Quebec:* MP's v. directors, significant at .02 (two-tailed t-test).

[a] The service index is based upon three items: 'Interest groups provide indispensable information to legislators'; 'Interest groups help members line up support for their bills'; and 'Interest groups provide members valuable help in drafting bills and amendments.'

Columbia is farthest below the mean regarding the positive contributions of interest groups, which again adds a piece of evidence supporting the assumed anti-group orientation of the Social Credit party. On the whole, the most patent discontinuities are between MP's and interest groups, which is consistent with interaction theory in the sense that back-benchers, who comprise four-fifths of the legislative sample, interact less frequently with directors than do bureaucrats. More important, such interactions are likely to be less sustained and cohesive, since they are less likely to involve common functional interests and experiences. It seems possible, too, that the competitive image MP's have of some interest groups encourages them, perhaps unconsciously, to minimize group services. The salient explanation, however, is surely that MP's and bureaucrats (excepting ministers) do have a substantively different relationship with interest group representatives, in which the latter's services are sometimes vital to officials, but marginal to backbenchers.

The structure of the regional discontinuity encountered here is clearly apparent in Table 11-10, using the same index.

Here again, significant differences exist among regional elites. The variation between Ottawa and Quebec is especially striking, compared with British Columbia and Ontario whose political elites share very similar perceptions of the nature and value of interest group contributions to policy issues. Even though over one-third (N–322) of the sample indicates a high degree of consensus on this index, some possible explanations for the regional disparities revealed here may be suggested.

Ottawa's atypical position probably reflects somewhat more concern among MP's about the image of the federal government implicit in any admission that interest groups play so integral a role in policy issues. Among federal bureaucrats, it may be that interest groups are viewed competitively, since they are in effect the functional equivalent of research aides to backbenchers, and such information as they provide can be used to reinforce alternative policies to those now proposed and rationalized in large measure by senior officials. Federal officials may also have superior research and staff facilities that decrease their dependence upon the information and services provided by interest groups. Some support for these explanations is provided by the fact (not shown here) that only one-fifth of the Ottawa political elite agrees that the information and services provided by interest groups are 'a necessary part of governmental policy-making' or that such groups are

TABLE 11-10 *Elite cognitions of the service role of interest groups, by region*

	Ottawa	Ontario	Quebec	British Columbia	
	%	%	%	%	
High	20	37	50	34	(322)
Medium	34	40	31	39	(336)
Low	46	23	19	27	(278)

$X^2 = .001$ K's Tau $c = .23$

'necessary to make government aware of the needs of all citizens'. From this we may conclude that it is not only Social Credit members who sometimes question the utility of interest group political activity.

We saw also that many Canadians tend to have a negative view of the federal government, sometimes fed, it seems, by considerable selectivity on the part of provincial mass media, and that articulate groups tend to maintain a coordinated onslaught against some of its policies, as seen most recently in the Competition bill (1971) which was withdrawn by the Government.[1] The resultant sensitivity to such conditions may be reflected in the data presented here.

As noted earlier, there is some tendency among all governmental elites to deny or repress the extent to which interest groups play an active role in policy-determination, since this conflicts with conventional definitions of decision-making in Cabinet government. In this context, it is worth noting that careful observers have concluded that interest groups are more integrated into British parliamentary government than in the American separation of powers system.[2] There is some basis, therefore, for assuming that they are equally relevant in the Canadian parliamentary system.

A closely-related cognitive dimension that reveals, among other things, certain regional differences in Canadian political culture, is elite perceptions of the crucial informational role of interest groups. Here again, in Table 11-11, an index based upon factor analysis is used to differentiate regions and elites.

Here, since the *t*-test for each sub-elite *across* regions is significant at the .05 or higher level, we may conclude that interregional cohesion on this dimension is minimal. *Within* regions, we find a less pronounced degree of variation, with Quebec revealing the most cohesion. Meanwhile, Ontario's governmental elite shows a remarkably decisive rejection of this characterization of interest group indispensability.[3] Significant chi-square differ-

---

[1] Following the rotation of federal ministers early in 1972, the new Corporate Affairs Minister committed himself to 'substantial changes' in the legislation. Introduced in June, 1971, the bill 'ran into heavy fire from business', including more than 300 briefs and 'many hundreds of recommendations . . . by word of mouth and letter'. *Globe and Mail* (March 18, 1972), p. B1.

[2] Samuel Beer, 'Pressure groups and parties in Britain', 50 *American Political Science Review* (March, 1956), pp. 1–23.

[3] This disclaimer is in sharp contrast to the statement of the senior Ontario minister quoted elsewhere to the effect that 'It is very proper to have this third level of government (i.e., Chambers of Commerce and the Association of Mayors and Reeves) influencing us at the provincial and national levels'. These two groups, he added, had 'provoked' considerable legislation.

TABLE 11-11   *Elite cognitions of the informational role of the interest groups*[a]

Region/Elite	Proportion ranking			
	High	Medium	Low	
	%	%	%	
Ottawa				
Legislators	11	59	30	(138)
Bureaucrats	15	62	24	(89)
Directors	29	46	25	(104)
Ontario				
Legislators	4	59	37	(49)
Bureaucrats	8	56	35	(48)
Directors	25	50	25	(216)
Quebec				
Legislators	24	52	24	(42)
Bureaucrats	32	57	11	(36)
Directors	43	44	13	(187)
British Columbia				
Legislators	22	38	41	(32)
Bureaucrats	14	64	22	(36)
Directors	27	65	8	(109)
	(261)	(578)	(247)	

t-test =
across regions: MP's *v.* bureaucrats, significant at .05; MP's *v.* directors and
   bureaucrats *v.* directors, significant at .001, respectively;
within regions: *Ottawa*: MP's *v.* bureaucrats, significant at .05 levels.
   Ontario: MP's *v.* directors, significant at .001 (two-tailed *t*-test); bureaucrats
      v. directors, significant at .05 (two-tailed *t*-test);
   British Columbia: MP's *v.* directors, significant at .001 (two-tailed *t*-test);
      bureaucrats *v.* directors, significant at .001 (two-tailed *t*-test);
   Quebec: MP's *v.* directors, significant at .05 level.
[a] The information index is composed of two items: 'The information and services provided by interest groups are a *necessary* part of governmental policy-
   making' (italics added); and 'In a complex society like ours, interest groups
   are *necessary* to make government aware of the needs of all the people' (italics
   added).

ences appear among all sub-elites. Among MP's, Quebec ranks highest on
the acceptance of the index, followed closely by British Columbia, with just
under one-quarter each. Ontario and Ottawa rank much lower, with only 11
and 4 per cent, respectively. The tau *b* correlation between region and
informational role is a weak .04 for the entire legislative sample.

Among bureaucrats, the tau *b* increases to .11, indicating a somewhat more positive relationship between the two test variables. Quebec bureaucrats again rank highest, but those in Ottawa now assume second place by a narrow margin over British Columbia's senior officials. Not unexpectedly, given their *ex parte* position, directors prove to be much more positive on this dimension. Tau *b* is .15 and chi-square is a very strong .0001, due in part to the large sample size (*N*–615). The regional gradient remains very similar, with Quebec directors ranking highest (42 per cent), followed by Ottawa at 30 per cent, with Ontario and British Columbia having about one-quarter each. It should be noted, in conclusion, that the items used here are quite demanding, specifying that participation in policy-making by interest groups is not merely useful, but *necessary*. Some polarization among the elites tends to follow.

We turn next to another cognitive dimension bearing directly upon group behaviour and elite cohesion, the extent to which the political system is perceived as being 'open'. Do elites believe that exogenous groups and individuals have an opportunity to influence government? Is the MP's role seen as one of mediating among the claims of many discrete interests? On the basis of earlier evidence, one might expect elites in British Columbia and Quebec to be somewhat less likely to perceive the system in such terms. In the former region, any 'anti-group' valence of the Social Credit party might explain part of any such variation, while in Quebec the elitist tradition might be relevant. Table 11-12 presents the distribution for all regions.

Turning first to the analysis of means *across* all regions, only one significant difference appears, between MP's and directors, at the .05 level. Here, not surprisingly, interest groups directors are slightly less likely than members to perceive the system as being open. Indeed, the tau *b* correlation is − .05. Undoubtedly, the fact that only one-quarter of our interest group sample proved to be highly active politically, contributes to this condition. On the other hand, the variance among global means is marginal: MP's = 18,781; bureaucrats = 18.309; and directors = 18.261.

This conclusion is reinforced by the emergence of only one significant difference *within* regions, between MP's and directors in Ottawa, significant at the .02 level. Here again, the evidence suggests that interest group interactions with governmental elites are somewhat more intense and uninhibited at the provincial level than in Ottawa. At the same time, certain differences among the provinces tend to sustain earlier observations about comparative patterns of access. In Ontario and British Columbia, directors

TABLE 11-12 *Elite perceptions of the 'openness' of the political system*

Region/Elite	Openness of the system[a]			
	High	Medium	Low	
	%	%	%	
Ottawa				
Legislators	43	26	31	(126)
Bureaucrats	38	30	33	(80)
Directors	29	28	43	(89)
Ontario				
Legislators	49	23	28	(47)
Bureaucrats	46	31	23	(48)
Directors	36	36	27	(168)
Quebec				
Legislators	45	24	32	(38)
Bureaucrats	24	31	45	(29)
Directors	26	30	45	(142)
British Columbia				
Legislators	36	16	48	(31)
Bureaucrats	29	39	32	(31)
Directors	36	31	33	(88)
	(329)	(273)	(315)	

t-test =
across regions, MP's v. directors, significant at .05 (two-tailed t-test);
within regions: *Ottawa*: MP's v. directors, significant at .02 (two-tailed t-test).
[a] Openness is defined here by a four-item index: 'Information from all sides is necessary for the final vote'; 'Most legislators believe strongly in the right of petition'; 'Legislators often act as arbiters between the demands of many competing interests'; 'The democratic way of conflict-resolution is to include the opinions of outside, competing groups.'

rank above the mean, and above MP's, contrasted with Ottawa and Quebec where, as just noted in the case of Ottawa, they rank below.

If it is valid to assign disproportionate weight to the perceptions of directors on this condition, we may conclude that interest group access is probably most felicitious in Ontario and British Columbia, followed by Quebec and Ottawa. At the same time, given earlier comments about attitudes toward interest groups in British Columbia, it should be said that whereas her legislators rank lowest on perceived openness, with almost 50 per cent ranking at the bottom of the scale, her directors rank highest. As noted, the evidence on the question of the anti-interest group valence of the Social Credit party is highly mixed.

Among legislators, chi-square differences are not significant and tau *b* is − .02. Ontario ranks highest on perceived openness, with British Columbia, as noted, substantially lower than other regions. With the exception of British Columbia, MP's tend to rank higher than other subgroups, as expected from their political role. Some support for the hypothesis that Quebec would probably rank comparatively low on this dimension is provided by her bureaucrats who rank lowest among their subgroup. Since her directors occupy the same position, we have some evidence that access is more difficult in Quebec. On the other hand, Quebec's deputies rank second only to Ontario's in perceiving the political system as open to external influences, which is contrary to what one would expect and to our earlier finding that they ranked relatively low on interest-group legitimacy and interaction. MP's probably have an occupational preference for the somewhat idealized version of the political process incorporated in the openness index. It should be noted that 44 per cent of all legislators rank high on this dimension, compared with only one-third of bureaucrats and directors.

Directly related to openness is the affective perception elites have of interest groups and lobbying. These data enable us to check again the relative extent to which Canada's regional political cultures are hospitable to such activities. More important, they provide further information about the extent of 'consensual validation' existing among the elite regarding the going political system. This system, which has evolved through long experience and has demonstrated its survival capacity, might be expected to become an article of faith among those responsible for directing it. As a senior minister in Ontario remarked, after noting that the Chambers of Commerce and Association of Mayors and Reeves had 'provoked' considerable legislation, 'It is very proper to have this *third level of government* influencing us at the provincial and national levels' (italics added).

We expect, nevertheless, that elite attitudes will be tempered by several factors. Back-benchers, for example, who constitute the vast majority of the legislative sample, probably do not fully share the attitude just expressed by the Ontario minister. As we have seen, interest group legitimacy is somewhat precarious among legislators, despite the fact that interaction and influence are strongly related among them. There is also evidence that elites, in responding to our items, experience some conflict between the going realities of interest group politics and an idealized image of the political system. A manifest protective incentive is often at work, similar to that presented to most outsiders by the members of any self-conscious occupational group.

314

TABLE 11-13 *Elite negativism toward interest groups*[a]

Region/Elite	High	Medium	Low	
	%	%	%	
Ottawa				
Legislators	12	42	46	(123)
Bureaucrats	17	29	54	(87)
Ontario				
Legislators	27	51	22	(45)
Bureaucrats	33	31	37	(49)
Quebec				
Legislators	25	42	33	(40)
Bureaucrats	23	40	37	(30)
British Columbia				
Legislators	21	31	48	(29)
Bureaucrats	14	54	31	(35)
	(88)	(172)	(178)	

t-test =

across regions: MP's *v.* bureaucrats, significant at .001;

within regions: *Ottawa*, MP's *v.* bureaucrats, significant at .001 (two-tailed *t*-test).

[a] Interest group negativism is defined by four items: 'Individuals should take an interest in government directly, not through interest groups'; 'Most lobbyists are satisfied with a fair hearing not insisting on a specific conclusion' (reverse scored); 'There should be more objective information on issues from lobbyists and less persuasive tactics'; 'Such groups as the Canadian Labour Congress, The Canadian Manufacturers' Association and the Federation of Agriculture have too much influence upon government policy.'

Such dispositions are probably especially salient in Table 11-13, in which three of the four items regarding interest group and lobbyist activity are stated negatively.

For obvious reasons, directors are not included in this table. Analysis of means *across* all regions indicates that legislators and bureaucrats differ significantly regarding normative dispositions about interest groups and the activities of their representatives. *Within* regions, however, the level of cohesion is high, with only MP's and bureaucrats in Ottawa differing significantly among all regions.[1] Indeed, combining both sub-elites, we find that only about one-fifth rank high on the anti-interest group index. On the whole, governmental elites in Ontario rank somewhat higher than their

[1] A related but independent dimension, pro-lobby valence, exhibits an even higher degree of cohesion, with Ontario providing the only significant variation (see Table 11-14).

opposites on this disposition. For example, Ontario bureaucrats rank substantially higher than those in other regions on anti-interest group feelings, while those in British Columbia and Ottawa have the most favourable perception of them, as measured here. Among MP's, those in British Columbia and Ottawa rank substantially lower than their counterparts.

The explanation for the differences between MP's and bureaucrats (except in British Columbia) probably lies in the marginality of interaction between directors and MP's compared with that between directors and bureaucrats.[1] We saw earlier, too, that MP's ascribed only a precarious legitimation to interest groups, contrasted with bureaucrats. The latter, who are relatively more influential in Ottawa, also tend to receive more attention and deference from directors, relatively, than back-benchers who comprise four-fifths of our legislative sample.

Continuity and functional ties also provide a strong basis for cohesion between directors and bureaucrats, whereas MP's tend to be approached on an *ad hoc*, and even ceremonial, basis. As noted earlier, MP's sometimes regard interest-group leaders competitively, e.g., when the latter inform them of prevailing opinion in their ridings, a subject about which MP's pride themselves as being fully knowledgeable. The tendency for MP's to perceive interest groups as collectively suspect, but individually legitimate (when they represent relevant interests) is probably also at work. Finally, whereas MP's interact with a cross-section of groups, bureaucrats tend to see mainly those whose functional commitments and knowledge mesh with those of their agency.

COMPARATIVE ELITE COHESION

An index of comparative elite cohesion follows for the foregoing analysis; this is provided by a summary of the significant variations of means found among sub-elites for the dimensions analysed in Tables 11-5 through 11-13. Table 11-14 presents the total number of significant variations in means (*t*-test) among the nine dimensions concerned, *within* regions.

---

[1] Our earlier generalization, based upon the responses of MP's, indicated that interaction between them and directors was typically 'frequent' or 'occasional', and roughly comparable in frequency with that between directors and bureaucrats. When *directors* are asked about comparative levels of interaction, 20 per cent say they see bureaucrats 'frequently' (twice a week or more), compared with only 6 per cent for MP's. Back-benchers probably tend to exaggerate the extent of their contact with interest group directors.

TABLE 11-14   *Comparative elite cohesion on selected dimensions, within regions*[a]

	Total number of significant variations in means				
Dimension	Ottawa	Ontario	British Columbia	Quebec	Total
Powerlessness	0	0	2	0	2
Openness	1	0	0	0	1
Political liberalism	0	1	2	1	4
Economic liberalism	2	2	2	2	8
Anti-interest group[b]	1	0	0	0	1
Pro-lobby[b]	0	1	0	0	1
Service role	3	2	3	1	9
Informational role	1	2	2	1	6
Tactical role	0	2	2	2	6
Totals	8	10	13	7	38

[a] 'Cohesiveness' is measured by the total number of significant variations in means (*t*-test at .05) on each dimension, by region and sub-elite. Since the possible variation in each region ranges from 0–23, the scale was designed as follows: 0–8 equals 'high'; 9–16, 'medium'; and 17–23, 'low'.

[b] These two dimensions, for obvious reasons, include only the governmental elite. The pro-lobby dimension was not presented in a separate table.

According to the scale used here, the political elite ranges between the lower-high and mid-medium levels of cohesion. Quebec and Ottawa rank substantially higher than Ontario and British Columbia. *A chi-square test of regional totals, however, indicates that no significant differences exist among the four regions using these nine dimensions* ($X^2 = 3.8$; df $= 3$). It is noteworthy that four dimensions produce about three-fourths of the total dissonance: the ideological variable, economic liberalism, and three cognitive variables, service, tactics and informational role.

We must also test cohesiveness *across* the four regions, among the three sub-elites. Here again, the *t*-test is used to determine the number of significant variations (.05) among means. Table 11-15 presents the distribution.

It is clear that the political elite ranks in the upper-medium range of the cohesiveness scale, as measured by the nine dimensions used here. Each elite pair, moreover, has the same number of significant differences. Not unexpectedly, directors vary more than other sub-elites on cognitive dimensions regarding the utility of interest group services. Once again, only three of the dimensions account for most of the variation, but the set is somewhat different from that found among the elite as measured in Table 11-14.

TABLE 11-15 *Comparative elite cohesion on selected dimensions, across regions*[a]

Dimension	Total number of significant variations in means[b]			
	MP's *v.* Bur.	MP's *v.* Dirs.	Bur. *v.* Dirs.	Totals
Powerlessness	0	1	0	1
Openness	0	1	0	1
Political liberalism	0	0	0	0
Economic liberalism	1	0	1	2
Anti-interest group	1	0	1	2
Pro-lobby	0	0	0	0
Service role	1	0	0	1
Informational role	1	1	1	3
Tactical role	0	1	1	2
Totals	4	4	4	12

[a] Cohesiveness is measured by the total number of significant variations in means (*t*-test at .05 level) between each sub-elite pair on each dimension across all regions.

[b] Since a total of nine variations are possible for each elite pair on the nine dimensions, the scale was designed as follows: 0–3 = 'high'; 4–6 = 'medium'; and 7–9 = 'low'.

Anti-interest group valence differences are more frequent and service role is dramatically less salient. Here, no chi-square test is required to prove that no significant differences exist among the three sub-elites.

In sum, we may conclude that a medium-to-high level of cohesiveness exists among the Canadian political elite, as measured here. Such cohesion, reinforced by shared interaction, political roles, and the socioeconomic properties found earlier, clearly provides part of the explanation for the effectiveness of elite accommodation as a system for designing policy goals and allocating the public resources required to achieve them. We turn next to a further test of cohesion, using multivariate analysis of several of the same dimensions. At the same time, further evidence of the substantive drift of elite values will emerge.

ASSOCIATION BETWEEN IDEOLOGICAL AND COGNITIVE DIMENSIONS

Our next question is the way that such values as political and economic liberalism are associated with elite cognitions of the political system. We assume, for example, that political liberalism will be positively associated with 'openness' because it honours discussion, diversity and access. We also assume that governmental elites will rank higher on this association than

TABLE 11-16   *Association between political liberalism and perceived openness of the system*

Region/Elite	High (283)			Medium (382)			Low (420)			
	High	Med.	Low	High	Med.	Low	High	Med.	Low	
	%	%	%	%	%	%	%	%	%	
Ottawa										
Legislators	41	26	22	48	26	26	41	27	2	(125)
Bureaucrats	37	21	42	32	32	35	44	33	22	(80)
Directors	36	32	32	19	28	53	33	26	41	(88)
Ontario										
Legislators	42	33	25	44	31	25	58	10	32	(47)
Bureaucrats	64	18	18	44	28	28	38	44	19	(48)
Directors	30	36	33	37	33	38	38	39	23	(163)
Quebec										
Legislators	50	12	38	44	22	33	45	25	30	(37)
Bureaucrats	14	14	71	50	17	33	25	33	42	(25)
Directors	28	23	49	29	31	41	22	35	44	(88)
British Columbia										
Legislators	31	23	46	22	11	67	56	11	33	(31)
Bureaucrats	17	67	17	21	29	50	46	36	18	(31)
Directors	23	46	31	37	25	38	40	30	30	(88)

Column headings spanning sub-columns: "Political liberalism" over High/Medium/Low; "Openness of system" over the High/Med./Low sub-columns.

t-test =
across regions: bureaucrats, *Ontario v. Quebec*, significant at .05 (one-tailed *t*-test);
within regions: no significant differences.
X^2 = pooled for all sub-elites, not significant at .05.
Within regions, not significant at .05.
K's tau b = pooled for all sub-elites, − .03.

directors, who have no official obligation to entertain a range of demands. One always expects some variation, but the main drift should reveal a positive association between the two variables analysed in Table 11-16. It should be noted, parenthetically, that the test of elite cohesion here and in subsequent tables will be the presence of statistically-significant differences in means (*t*-test) across and within regions.

As the weak tau *b* correlation indicates, there is a mildly negative association between political liberalism and perceived openness of the system. The *t*-test analysis reveals only one significant difference, among officials in Ontario and Quebec. Similarly, the chi-square analysis confirms the absence of significant differences, so we must conclude that the assumed positive association between the two variables is not confirmed. Indeed, in several cases, those who rank highest on political liberalism rank about the same on openness as their less liberal counterparts. In others, notably Ontario and British Columbia MP's, the relationship is negative. The only trend in the expected direction occurs among Ontario bureaucrats and Quebec directors where a somewhat larger proportion of those ranking high on political liberalism also rank higher on openness, compared with those who rank low on liberalism. The most striking divergence is between bureaucrats in Ontario and Quebec, as indicated in the 'high' political liberalism sector.

Certain behavioural consequences seem to follow: as some of the other ideological preferences, political liberalism seems to be only tangentially associated with cognitions of the system which provide a sympathetic milieu for interest group access. (The relative influence of political liberalism, compared with other kinds of dimensions, will become clearer in the following chapter when regression analysis is used to determine the major variables affecting group interaction and effectiveness.)

As the total N's show, only one-quarter of the entire political elite ranks high on political liberalism. The proportion of these who also rank high on perceived openness attains or exceeds 50 per cent only in the case of Ontario bureaucrats and Quebec deputies. Looking at the high–high and low–high columns, MP's tend to approximate most closely the expected positive relationship between the two variables. British Columbia's MP's are a noteworthy exception, however. And indeed, all three of her sub-elites indicate a similar valence, a condition not found among elites in other regions.

The explanation for this unexpected association probably involves what might be called the disenchantment gradient, whereby liberally-oriented members of the elite, including many NDP members, tend to regard the system as being open mainly to powerful groups representing business and industrial interests. In any event, the neutral-to-negative posture of the elite on this relationship is clear enough, which suggests that other kinds of variables may be more useful in explaining the bases of elite accommodation.

Another dimension that seems relevant to cognitive perceptions of the political system is powerlessness. We saw earlier that roughly one-third of the political elite ranked high on this dimension. Given the tendency of the parliamentary system to relegate most back-benchers to constituency-oriented roles, with attending feelings of inefficacy among many of them, it is not unexpected that such dispositions exist. One way of measuring their

TABLE 11-17   *Association between powerlessness and anti-interest group valence*

	Powerlessness									
	High			Medium			Low			
	Anti-interest group valence									
Region/Elite	High	Med.	Low	High	Med.	Low	High	Med.	Low	
	%	%	%	%	%	%	%	%	%	
Ottawa										
Legislators	22	49	29	6	33	61	9	42	49	(122)
Bureaucrats	17	13	70	22	31	47	13	38	50	(87)
Ontario										
Legislators	46	36	18	30	50	20	14	59	27	(45)
Bureaucrats	37	21	42	29	43	28	33	33	33	(48)
Quebec										
Legislators	31	38	31	—	67	33	37	29	36	(39)
Bureaucrats	21	50	29	14	44	42	29	29	43	(28)
British Columbia										
Legislators	43	29	29	11	44	44	18	27	55	(27)
Bureaucrats	33	56	11	14	50	36	—	58	42	(35)

t-test =
across regions: bureaucrats, *Ottawa v. British Columbia*, significant at .05 (one-tailed *t*-test);
    directors, *Ontario v. Quebec*, significant at .05;
within regions: *Ottawa*, MP's *v*. bureaucrats, not significant at .05.
X^2 = pooled for all sub-elites, not significant at .05.
K's tau *b* = pooled for all sub-elites, .09.

effects is to determine the relationship between them and selected affective perceptions of the system. This is done in Table 11-17, using the anti-interest group index, and assuming a positive association between the two variables.

Comparing the high–high and the low–low columns, there is a slightly positive but not significant, tendency (except in Quebec) for those who rank high on felt powerlessness to rank higher on anti-group feelings than those who rank low. For example, 46 per cent of Ontario MP's who rank high on the control variable also rank high on powerlessness, compared with only 14 per cent of those who rank low on powerlessness. British Columbia and Ontario MP's share the same tendency while Quebec's deputies are atypical. Among bureaucrats, the picture is less clear. British Columbia respondents are similar to its MP's, revealing a very strong tau *b* of .32 and a gamma correlation of .50. For the others, powerlessness accounts for little variation in anti-group attitudes.

TABLE 11-18 *Association between powerlessness and perceived openness of the political system*

Region/Elite	High (317) High	Med.	Low	Medium (272) High	Med.	Low	Low (307) High	Med.	Low	
	%	%	%	%	%	%	%	%	%	
Ottawa										
Legislators	34	27	37	44	25	31	48	26	26	(123)
Bureaucrats	26	44	30	39	36	25	45	14	41	(80)
Directors	23	35	42	31	34	34	32	16	52	(89)
Ontario										
Legislators	43	21	36	30	30	40	62	24	14	(45)
Bureaucrats	32	37	32	50	21	29	57	36	7	(47)
Directors	33	37	29	36	40	25	36	34	30	(165)
Quebec										
Legislators	38	25	38	79	11	11	30	31	39	(38)
Bureaucrats	36	36	27	13	13	75	13	38	50	(27)
Directors	30	32	38	21	27	52	20	32	48	(138)
British Columbia										
Legislators	43	14	43	22	22	56	42	17	42	(28)
Bureaucrats	—	50	50	42	33	25	36	36	27	(31)
Directors	32	27	41	32	36	32	45	35	21	(85)

The column groups above are headed: **Powerlessness** — High (317), Medium (272), Low (307); and **Perceived openness of system** — High, Med., Low under each.

t-test =
across regions: bureaucrats, *Ontario v. Quebec*, significant at .05 (one-tailed *t*-test);
within regions: *Ottawa, Ontario*, MP's *v.* directors; *Ontario*, bur. *v.* dirs., sig. at .05.
X^2 = pooled for all sub-elites, significant at .05.
Within regions, not significant at .05.
K's tau *b* = pooled for all sub-elites, − .02.

Across regions, the differences in means among the sub-elites are statistically significant in only two cases, suggesting that members of the political elite share roughly similar dispositions in the immediate context. *Within* regions, only one difference is significant, in Ottawa, between the legislative and bureaucratic elites.

We determine next whether those who are high on powerlessness, some of whom have shown a tendency toward an anti-interest group valence, also tend to perceive the political system as being relatively less open, compared with those who rank low on powerlessness. Theoretically, one might assume that those who feel low on power would, in effect, try symbolically to restrict competition in their particular arena by characterizing the system as being relatively closed to penetration by external influences. As anxiety, powerlessness may be associated with a tendency to prefer structured situations in which relationships and outcomes are relatively unambiguous. Given the bureaucratic ethos of Canadian society,[1] such security-oriented preferences might prove especially appealing. This assumption is tested in Table 11-18.

Here again, although the *t*-test reveals only two significant variations in means across the entire sample, some dissonance occurs. Among Ottawa and Ontario MP's, for example, the expected negative association appears, as those who rank low on the control tend to rank high on perceived openness. Tau *b* is −.21 among Ontario MP's; 62 per cent of those who rank low on powerlessness rank high on openness. A similar gradient appears among Ottawa legislators, although tau *b* falls to −.11. Powerlessness, however, explains little variation in British Columbia, while Quebec's deputies are again atypical as shown by the fact that tau *b* becomes slightly positive. Some regional cohesion is apparent in Quebec since her bureaucrats and directors show the only substantially positive correlation among the entire sample, with tau *b*'s of .24 and .12, respectively.

Turning to bureaucrats, those in Ottawa and Ontario rank substantially higher than their counterparts on the expected relationship. Ontario officials, for example, have a tau *b* of −.22 and a gamma of −.34. Almost 60 per cent of those who are low on powerlessness rank high on perceived openness, compared with only 7 per cent of those who rank low on the control. The largest proportion of Quebec officials (75 per cent) appear at the medium level of powerlessness, in the low openness cell. Also, 50 per cent of those in the low powerlessness category rank low on perceived openness, and tau *b* changes to a positive .24, which means that they tend to define the system as closed, with attending implications for security and non-competitive behaviour. A substantial variation exists between them and bureaucrats in British Columbia where 36 per cent of those who rank low on powerlessness rank high on openness.

Among directors, Ottawa and Quebec are similar, and contrary to the assumed association, in that about half of those who rank low on felt power are also low on perceived openness. Tau *b*, however, is a neutral .02. Those in British Columbia who rank low on powerlessness tend to regard the

---

[1] See, for example, Clark, *The Developing Canadian Community*. For a socio-psychological analysis of bureaucratic structure and values, see Presthus, *The Organizational Society* (New York: Vintage Books, 1965).

TABLE II-19 *Association between political liberalism and anti-group disposition*

	High (283)			Political liberalism Medium (382)			Low (420)			
Region/Elite	High	Med.	Low	High	Med.	Low	High	Med.	Low	Total
	%	%	%	%	%	%	%	%	%	
Ottawa										
Legislators	15	46	39	13	31	56	10	49	42	(121)
Bureaucrats	13	9	78	17	36	47	21	36	43	(87)
Directors	9	27	64	17	34	49	50	14	36	(85)
Ontario										
Legislators	44	11	44	18	53	29	26	68	5	(45)
Bureaucrats	27	27	46	33	33	33	35	29	35	(49)
Directors	18	35	47	20	29	51	28	40	32	(92)
Quebec										
Legislators	11	44	45	44	11	56	38	33	29	(39)
Bureaucrats	29	43	28	29	29	43	14	50	36	(28)
Directors	15	28	57	16	35	49	25	39	36	(139)
British Columbia										
Legislators	27	18	55	—	50	50	30	30	40	(29)
Bureaucrats	—	33	67	12	65	24	25	50	25	(35)
Directors	18	35	47	20	29	51	28	40	33	(92)

Above the sub-column headers a spanning label reads: Anti-interest group disposition

t-test =
within regions: Ottawa – MP's *v*. directors significant at .05;
across regions: MP's, *Ottawa v. Ontario* significant at .05.
Pooled K's tau $b = -.12$.
$X^2 = $ *across regions:* not significant at .05;
   within regions: Ottawa, all sub-elites, .01.

system as open, and tau b becomes negative, at $-.15$. The association is very weak in Ontario.

We turn next to the association between political liberalism and anti-interest group disposition. As noted earlier, there is a tendency among the elite to differentiate between interest group activities and lobbying, with the latter being quite suspect, while the former are generally regarded as legitimate. From earlier evidence, we predict that the association between the variables will be generally negative. Table II-19 presents the distribution.

The Canadian elite exhibits some variation, both in substance and in cohesiveness. Among legislators, with the exception of those in Ontario, who show a strongly significant X^2 relationship (.03), the predicted relationship is weak and negative. The Ontario tau b is $-.15$ and gamma $-.22$. Regional correlations are highest among the Quebec sample, with a tau b of $-.22$ and a gamma of $-.34$, falling in Ottawa to .03 and .05, respectively. None of the X^2 associations even approach significance at the .05 level. Moreover, the means test reveals only two significant differences: in Ottawa between MP's and directors; and, across regions, between MP's in Ottawa and Ontario. This particular variation, parenthetically, is the strongest found among all sub-elites on all dimensions across all regions.

Among bureaucrats, the expected relationship, significant at the .07 (chi square) level, emerges only in Ottawa, with a tau b of $-.21$ and a strong gamma of $-.33$. *Almost 80 per cent of officials who rank high on political liberalism rank low on anti-group attitudes, compared with only 13 per cent of those who rank high on the control.* British Columbia has the strongest correlation, with tau b of $-.28$ and gamma of $-.44$. Although X^2 is only .23, the distribution follows the expected pattern, with two-thirds of those who rank high on the control variable ranking low on anti-group feelings, compared with no cases in the high anti-group cell. Ontario bureaucrats reveal almost no support for the assumed relationship; and only Quebec exhibits a midly positive association, with a tau b of .09 and gamma of .14. However, the Quebec N's are so small in several cells that the evidence is marginal.

The strongest correlations (tau $b = -.28$; gamma $= -.42$) and X^2 association (.007) are found among interest group directors in Ottawa, among whom political liberalism is very strongly associated with low anti-group attitudes, with almost two-thirds of those ranking high on the control ranking low on the anti-group dimension. Not unexpectedly, the same expected negative relationship appears among other directors, with Quebec somewhat stronger than Ontario and British Columbia. As noted elsewhere, the pro-lobby index is independent of the interest group dimension, so the differences in the relationship found between the two are not inapposite. (It should be noted that the association between political liberalism and pro-lobby attitudes was not consistent among regions, contrary to our assumption.)

An ideological dimension which should be positively related to cognitive perceptions of interest group politics is economic liberalism. This variable it will be recalled, symbolizes a generalized preference for 'big government,' including its use as a means of easing the dislocations of unemployment, old age, and ill-health. As noted earlier, the Canadian political elite ranks quite low on this dimension, yet there is a pool of about one-third of them who

TABLE 11-20 *Association between economic liberalism and perceived openness of the system*

Region/Elite	Economic liberalism								
	High (332)			Medium (359)			Low (269)		
	Openness of the system								
	High	Med.	Low	High	Med.	Low	High	Med.	Low
	%	%	%	%	%	%	%	%	%
Ottawa									
Legislators	42	26	33	44	18	38	39	52	9	(111)
Bureaucrats	26	35	39	52	16	32	36	39	26	(79)
Directors	31	33	36	31	28	41	25	11	63	(87)
Ontario									
Legislators	69	13	19	25	38	38	62	15	23	(45)
Bureaucrats	60	20	20	47	27	27	41	37	22	(47)
Directors	36	34	30	46	35	20	27	41	33	(162)
Quebec									
Legislators	50	25	25	58	12	29	14	43	43	(36)
Bureaucrats	33	33	33	44	11	44	14	36	50	(26)
Directors	35	29	37	21	35	44	25	19	56	(138)
British Columbia									
· Legislators	46	23	31	33	8	58	33	—	66	(28)
Bureaucrats	66	—	34	21	43	36	29	43	29	(31)
Directors	32	35	32	41	32	26	33	20	47	(86)

t-test =
across regions: no significant differences.
within regions: MP's *v*. directors, *Ontario*, significant at .05 (one-tailed *t*-test);
X^2 = pooled for all sub-elites, no significant differences.
      pooled for regions, *Ottawa*, MP's *v*. bureaucrats; MP's *v*. directors; directors *v*. bureaucrats, significant at .05.
K's tau *b* = pooled, .05.

strongly endorse this disposition. Our assumption is that this segment of the elite, with its preference for 'big government,' will exhibit a generally positive association with the openness dimension, which relates essentially to the extent to which the political system is seen as open to interest group penetration. Table 11-20 presents the distribution.

Only one significant difference of means occurs, indicating a general consensus on this dimension. Among all sub-elites, Ontario MP's rank highest above the elite mean at 2.500, compared with 2.132 for legislators,

2.049 for bureaucrats, and 1.951 for directors. Ontario MP's also rank highest on the positive association between economic liberalism and perceived openness; however, they also rank similarly at the low end of the liberalism scale. Ottawa exhibits a similar tendency. In Quebec and British Columbia, the frequencies follow the expected gradient, but the relationship is not significant.

Bureaucrats are less consistent, exhibiting the expected positive association in Ontario, British Columbia and Quebec, but revealing an inverse relationship in Ottawa. Two dramatic variations stand out among them. One is the extent to which those in British Columbia differ from their counterparts in endorsing the expected positive association between liberalism and openness of the system. Tau *b* equals .14 and gamma is a fairly strong .22, and fully two-thirds of those who rank high on liberalism also rank high on perceived openness, compared with only about 30 per cent of those who rank low. The second appears among Ontario bureaucrats, 60 per cent of whom appear in the high–high column, compared with 41 per cent of those who rank low on economic liberalism. Directors in Ontario and British Columbia rank well below their respective governmental elites on this association, but the *t*-test differences among directors and governmental elites are not statistically significant.

A final context in which ideology may affect elite cognitions of the system concerns the relationship between economic liberalism and the affective dimension, pro-lobby. One would expect, theoretically, that the two variables would be positively related, since the preference for 'big government' characterizing those who rank high on economic liberalism seems to subsume a generalized acceptance of the lobby groups which benefit from such expansiveness, and whose demands inspire and legitimate most governmental programmes. On the other hand, we are now aware of the ambivalence of elites toward lobbying activities which may cause some variation. Table 11-21 presents the data.

The *t*-test analysis reveals only one significant difference of means among the 15 possible combinations, again suggesting a high level of cohesion on this dimension. Comparing the high columns across the table, it is clear that MP's rank either neutral or negative on pro-lobby feelings, controlled for economic liberalism. Indeed, the pooled tau *b* among them is a fairly strong − .23. Quebec and Ottawa reveal the most striking rejection of the assumed positive association. Perhaps the explanation is that those MP's who wish to restrict the penumbra of government programmes reject lobbyists and lobbying as advocates of expansion. Insofar as MP's define lobbyists as

TABLE 11-21 *Association between economic liberalism and pro-lobby valence*

Region/Elite	High (332)			Economic liberalism Medium (359)			Low (269)			
	High	Med.	Low	Pro-lobby valence High	Med.	Low	High	Med.	Low	
	%	%	%	%	%	%	%	%	%	
Ottawa										
Legislators	23	48	30	27	50	23	46	33	21	(120)
Bureaucrats	36	20	44	27	58	15	30	38	32	(88)
Directors	36	31	33	50	34	16	60	5	35	(91)
Ontario										
Legislators	18	41	41	19	44	38	17	50	33	(45)
Bureaucrats	20	60	20	44	31	25	33	48	19	(48)
Directors	32	21	48	37	32	32	37	26	37	(184)
Quebec										
Legislators	29	20	50	48	18	35	57	29	14	(38)
Bureaucrats	50	50	—	20	30	50	33	28	39	(32)
Directors	45	34	21	37	25	38	30	24	46	(154)
British Columbia										
Legislators	29	43	29	33	25	42	—	67	33	(29)
Bureaucrats	25	50	25	27	53	20	18	47	35	(36)
Directors	28	48	25	37	29	34	50	43	7	(95)

t-test =
across regions: directors, significant at .05 (one-tailed t-test);
within regions: no significant differences.
X^2 = pooled for all sub-elites, no significant differences at .05;
within regions, *Ottawa*, significant at .05.
K's tau b = pooled, $-.04$.

competitors in governmental policy-making, this might also be a partial explanation for the negative valence among MP's.

Meanwhile, bureaucrats in Quebec tend to sustain the expected positive relationship, although this is not true of their counterparts in other regions and especially in British Columbia. With the exception of those in Quebec, directors reject or are neutral on the assumed association. On the surface, this seems anomalous, since the system of expansive government symbolized by economic liberalism seems entirely consistent with a generally positive view of groups and their lobbying activities, and especially among directors. Some parochialism may be at work here, whereby directors tend, as MP's, to legitimate their own and ideologically-related groups, while rejecting the majority of others.

Contrary to our assumptions, then, the tendency is for economic liberalism to be either only precariously or inversely related to a pro-lobby disposition. Quebec MP's provide the best example, where less than 30 per cent of those who rank high on economic liberalism, defined generally as a 'pro-big government' posture, also rank high on pro-lobby values. *Meanwhile, among those who rank low on economic liberalism, almost 60 per cent rank high on pro-lobby attitudes.* Similarly, only some one-quarter of Ottawa MP's who are high on this dimension rank high on such attitudes, compared with 46 per cent of those who rank low on the control variable.

In sum, most members of the political elite indicate little or no connection between their preferences for expansive government and approval of the political activities that often spark expansion. Selective perception is probably at work here, as governmental elites tend to deplore interest groups collectively, while honouring the claims of those seen as ethically, occupationally, and politically relevant.

It may be useful to indicate comparative pro-lobby orientation by regions, for legislators and bureaucrats. Reporting only the proportion of MP's ranking *high*, Ottawa leads with 53 per cent, followed by a sharp decline in Quebec to 24 per cent, with Ontario and British Columbia having 13 and 11 per cent, respectively. For bureaucrats, Ottawa is again high with 42 per cent, Ontario is next at 28, followed by Quebec with 17 and British Columbia with only 13 per cent. In effect, with the exception of Ontario, MP's tend to rank somewhat higher on this dimension than civil servants. Here, also, is another bit of evidence for the thesis that British Columbia's political culture includes a patent anti-group bias. It is also possible that although the political 'conservatism' of bureaucrats may have influenced their somewhat marginal (except Ottawa) perceptions of interest groups, it is apparently only in Quebec that these dispositions have any marked dampening effect upon their interactions with directors. Interactions rates, it may be recalled, were significantly lower (Table 9-8) between Quebec bureaucrats and directors, compared with other regions.

Since economic liberalism varies considerably among legislators in the four regions, it may be useful to specify the relationship a bit further by determining its effect upon pro-lobby attitudes, controlling for party. For example, British Columbia's parties ranked significantly higher on economic liberalism than those in other areas, yet one doubts from previous evidence that this disposition will manifest itself in a strong pro-lobby valence.

TABLE 11-22 *Association between economic liberalism and pro-lobby valence, by party*

	Economic liberalism									
	High (91)			Medium (96)			Low (49)			
Party				Pro-lobby valence						
	High	Med.	Low	High	Med.	Low	High	Med.	Low	
	%	%	%	%	%	%	%	%	%	
Liberal	16	55	30	30	45	24	40	20	40	(94)
Conservative	36	36	27	25	46	12	39	42	18	(65)
New Democrats	27	30	43	50	25	25	—	—	—	(34)
Social Credit	—	50	50	33	22	44	—	67	33	(16)
Union Nationale	40	20	40	38	13	50	50	33	17	(19)

X^2 = not significant at .05 K's tau b = $-.10$

Another discontinuity might well occur regarding Liberals who are generally high on interaction but marginal on trust regarding interest groups. For these two parties, any positive effect of economic liberalism will probably disappear in the distribution shown in Table 11-22.

Although none of them are significant, substantial variations exist among the parties. It may be useful to begin by indicating their comparative positions on economic liberalism (not shown): NDP and Social Credit rank at the top with three-fourths of their members at the high level, compared with only 30 per cent among Liberals, Conservatives and *Union Nationale* MP's.

Regarding Table 11-22, Liberals clearly rank lowest on the association: looking at the high cells across the row, an inverse relationship appears, in which only 16 per cent of those who rank high on economic liberalism, compared with 40 per cent of those who rank low, manifest high pro-lobby attitudes. New Democrats show the strongest negative correlation (tau b = $-.15$). Considering only the distribution under high economic liberalism, 27 per cent rank high on pro-lobby values, compared with 43 per cent who rank low. Conservatives show a slightly positive association, while Social Credit members rank either medium or low on pro-lobby feelings, regardless of their posture on economic liberalism. Finally, among Quebec's *Union Nationale* deputies, a somewhat larger proportion of those who rank low on economic liberalism rank high on pro-lobby attitudes, compared with those who rank high on the control variable.

Explanations for the Liberal, NDP and Social Credit variance may include the fact that the Liberal sample is largely composed of federal MP's who, as the ruling party, may be surfeited with interest group demands and thus ambivalent about them. We also saw earlier that Liberals tend to rank low on interest group legitimacy, a variable that could also be intervening in the present association. NDP members seem to have a distinct anti-lobby bias, a disposition that is obviously shared by many Social Credit MP's.

Other explanations for the discontinuities found throughout the distribution probably include the pervasive ambivalence that some members feel toward interest groups and lobbying. Minor party members sometimes regard groups pejoratively because they associate them with the business–industrial community which supports the major parties ideologically and financially. It also seems that Social Credit members have a generalized scepticism about interest groups, even though interaction is not much affected thereby. Finally, among all parties, affective dissonance persists because many MP's tend to perceive themselves as the representatives of some mythical and presumably ethically-superior 'public interest', which is challenged by the claims of interest groups with whose aims and behaviour they disagree.

Once again, we turn to the extent of elite cohesion as measured by the number of significant variations in means found among elites in Tables 11-16 to 11-21. Table 11-23 presents the frequencies.

Since each regional set of sub-elites has a potential total of 18 variations, it is clear that they all rank quite high on cohesiveness. Moreover, the total scores among regions are clearly too small to be significantly different.

TABLE 11-23   *Comparative elite cohesion on selected dimensions, within regions*[a]

Dimensions	Total number of significant variations in means				
	Ottawa	Ontario	British Columbia	Quebec	Total
Economic liberalism *v.* openness	0	1	0	0	1
Economic liberalism *v.* pro-lobby	0	0	0	0	0
Powerlessness *v.* anti-group	1	0	0	0	1
Powerlessness *v.* openness	1	2	0	0	3
Political liberalism *v.* openness	0	0	0	0	0
Political liberalism *v.* anti-group	1	0	0	0	1
Total	3	3	0	0	6

[a] Each region has a total of 18 possible significant differences and the cohesiveness scale is defined as follows: 0–6, 'high'; 7–12, 'medium'; and 13–18, 'low'.

Elite accommodation

Regarding cohesiveness *across* regions, in order to vary the basis for determining cross-regional cohesion, *each* sub-elite has been compared across all regions, rather than in pairs as in Table 11-15. MP's are compared with each other, as are bureaucrats and directors. Cohesion, in effect, is being measured along a different dimension. Here, the three sub-elites exhibit virtually the same pattern and no table seems required. *A total of only seven significant variations occurs among them on the six dimensions.* Since the potential total of variations is 36 for each sub-elite, it seems that cohesion, as measured here, is again quite high on the ideological and cognitive dimensions included in the analysis.

In sum, we conclude that the Canadian political elite tends to share an impressive degree of continuity along the several dimensions covered in the past few chapters. Interaction between the governmental elite and the one-quarter of interest groups who are most active politically; their shared socioeconomic properties; their strategic political roles; and as just seen, the pervasive cohesion among them on selected ideological and cognitive dimensions, all tend to provide behavioural and affective commonalities that enable them to interact effectively. Our assumption that elite cohesion may be conceptualized in 'national' terms is supported by the finding that cohesion *across* the three sub-elites is the same, if not lower (see Table 11-15), than *within* regions. Obviously, as the distributions in the various tables in this chapter have shown, there is some discontinuity among elites on many of the test dimensions, but the salient point is that it usually clusters around the respective means. To the extent that such differences are not statistically significant, we may conclude that cohesiveness is high.

CHAPTER 12

THE STRUCTURE OF VARIANCE

Regarding the analysis of our findings in terms of the theories of interaction and elite accommodation, the evidence is generally supportive. Our assumption that elite accommodation is mediated by a certain amount of socio-economic, behavioural, cognitive, and ideological cohesion proved generally valid in the context of socioeconomic variables and the assumed association between and among interaction, legitimacy, and interest group influence. In effect, socioeconomic continuities and political roles among the elite are reinforced by behavioural variables, which jointly sustain the process of elite accommodation.

COGNITIVE AND IDEOLOGICAL VARIANCE

On the other hand, although our expectation that members of the political elite would exhibit a rough consensus upon various ideological and cognitive dimensions was sustained, neither structure proved to be as mutually consistent as predicted. The discontinuities in cognitive appreciations of interest group services, tactics and information were particularly striking. Using comparisons of means and calculating whether differences among regions and sub-elites were statistically significant, the following generalizations emerged. Political liberalism and the positive association between it and interest group legitimacy, and between economic liberalism and perceived openness of the political system proved to be generally shared. Similarly, very few significant differences in means appeared on such univariate dimensions as powerlessness, affective perceptions of lobbying, and openness of the system.

Some variation appeared on other dimensions, however, particularly on such associations as political liberalism $v.$ anti-interest group disposition, where senior officials sometimes ranked differently, and significantly lower,

333

than MP's or directors. Given their vital role in mediating the comprehensive welfare and subsidy programmes of Canadian governments, senior officials must experience considerable role conflict. Again, on the association between felt powerlessness and perceived openness of the political system, Ontario's governmental elites ranked significantly higher, for example, than the Quebec elite which ranged evenly along the scale.

The most suggestive disparity appeared regarding cognitions of the service role of interest groups, to which legislators proved to be significantly less likely to attribute importance, compared with bureaucrats. Legislators tend to be more likely than bureaucrats to exhibit a generalized anti-interest group disposition. There was also some deviance regarding the tactical role and conditions of participation of interest groups in the political system, which may reflect the distance between the assumed weakness of such groups in the Canadian parliamentary system and the reality of the sustained participation of the one-quarter of groups that are highly-active in policy formulation.

The evidence regarding interaction also revealed some dissonance concerning the central role of the higher bureaucracy in accommodation, contrasted with that of back-benchers. It will be recalled that about half of all MP's indicated that they interacted 'frequently' with directors, which suggests a substantial measure of (or opportunity for) accommodation. Other data, however, indicate that back-benchers tend to misperceive the intensity of such contacts. For example, when *directors* are asked how often they interact 'frequently' with back-benchers, compared with bureaucrats, the proportions are 20 per cent for bureaucrats, but only 16 per cent for MP's. Moreover, the association among interaction–legitimacy–influence is only weakly positive for MP's (see Tables 9-6 and 9-7), but strongly so for bureaucrats (see Table 9-14), with a very high gamma correlation of .60, again suggesting that interaction patterns are very different among the two.

Another possible explanation for such role differences is that even when interaction between directors and governmental elites is roughly similar in intensity, it is *substantively* different. Interest group interaction with senior bureaucrats, in effect, is continuous, functionally-specific and critical, while tending to be *ad hoc*, functionally diffuse, less operationally-significant, and perhaps even ceremonial among back-benchers. Many back-benchers clearly rely upon lobbyists for information that will enable them to challenge Government policy in caucus, or, if in opposition, by questions on the floor. In the main, however, they are not in a position to use such information effectively, especially from the standpoint of the interest group concerned, which suggests that directors interact with them for reasons oriented rather more toward constituent needs than toward policy. It may be recalled, moreover, that a substantial proportion of MP's attributed such interaction to the failure of directors to understand the parliamentary system.

Interaction theory suggests another partial explanation: the exchange of valued benefits provides a persuasive extra-ideological incentive for accommodation. Despite their highly articulate opposition to some aspects of governmental programmes and policies, interest groups continue their participation in the process of accommodation. Bureaucrats, as noted, are apparently able to sustain a similar ambivalence, since they tend to rank very low on political and economic liberalism, yet persist in their task of allocating public largesse on an impressive scale. In part, then, and despite any cognitive and ideological tension, perhaps members of the political elite sustain their accommodative roles because such result in the exchange of highly pragmatic benefits, including re-election, appropriations, new programmes and governmental subsidies, all of which are undoubtedly reinforced by personal gratifications of self-realization, service, and achievement.

INTERACTIONAL, IDEOLOGICAL, AND COGNITIVE EFFECTS

The evidence suggests, in effect, that 'hard' properties of role, function, interaction and exchange are perhaps more decisive in shaping the process of elite accommodation than ideological and, less surely, cognitive perceptions. One useful way of further testing this formulation is through multiple regression analysis which specifies the relative influence of selected independent variables when measured against a single dependent variable. Since one of the most crucial elements in accommodation is the *effectiveness* of interest groups in dealing with governmental elites, it will be used as the dependent variable (i.e. the variable to be explained in the following analysis). Effectiveness is operationalized by the item which asked MP's and bureaucrats to indicate the extent to which they had been influenced by lobbyists at one time or another. A large number of ordinal variables that seemed to provide the best explanation for any variance in effectiveness were analysed, including political and economic liberalism, powerlessness, SES, voluntary group membership, occupation, education, tenure and four items regarding elite perceptions of the average man's attitudes toward interest groups.[1]

As all statistical techniques, multiple regression makes several assumptions about the data used in the analysis. The major ones include at least an ordinal level of measurement, a linear relation between each independent variable and the dependent one, and that no relationship exists between the independent variables.

TABLE 12-1   *Zero-order correlations between interest group effectiveness and selected independent variables, legislators and bureaucrats*

Dimension	Legislators	Dimension	Bureaucrats
Pro-lobby valence	.36	Interaction	.48
Information	.28	Powerlessness	.23
Tactic	.25	Tenure	.22
Economic liberalism	.14	Pro-lobby valence	.21
Party position	.13	Anti-interest group	.17
Interaction	.09	Political liberalism	.08
Powerlessness	.08	Socioeconomic status	.07
SES	.08	Information	.02
Legitimacy	.04	Legitimacy	.01
Tenure	.01		
	(81)		(162)

$$R^2 = .26 \qquad\qquad R^2 = .31$$
$$F = .05 \qquad\qquad F = .05$$

The dimensions having the largest zero-order correlations are presented in Table 12-1, for MP's and bureaucrats.

These data indicate that behavioural, property and affective dimensions are indeed more decisive than ideological dispositions in explaining the variation in effectiveness. Economic liberalism, political liberalism and powerlessness appear as ideological variables in both sets, but they rank (excepting powerlessness for officials) in the middle and lower ranges of the scale. The affective disposition, pro-lobby valence, has the strongest correlation for legislators, while interaction is most critical for bureaucrats. Interaction is dramatically higher for bureaucrats, suggesting again that the process of elite accommodation is more functionally-relevant for them than for back-benchers. Our theoretical reliance upon interaction is thus confirmed by the fact that it appears in both sets, and is fully twice as strong as the next most significant dimension for bureaucrats. Tenure ranks in the middle range among bureaucrats, but is marginal for MP's. The reasons probably include the fact that whereas 70 per cent of the former have been in harness fifteen years or more, and a quarter have served over twenty-five years, fully three-quarters of the legislators have been in office nine years or less, and almost half have served less than four years.

Although the comparative impact of ideological dimensions is somewhat marginal, the strength of powerlessness *vis-à-vis* bureaucrats is both noteworthy and unexpected, given their critical role in accommodation and the discretion they enjoy. One might have expected that MP's, four-fifths of whom are back-benchers, would have been more affected by this variable, yet the correlation is only moderate. Powerlessness' impact will become clearer when we turn to the relative variation explained by each dimension. Economic liberalism, upon which bureaucrats ranked quite low, exhibits relatively moderate strength for MP's.

Such cognitive dimensions as information and tactics are strongly correlated for legislators, while the former is very weak for bureaucrats. The strength of information among MP's is unexpected, given their marginal endorsement of this dimension in earlier analyses. Nevertheless, the disparity between them and bureaucrats on this dimension is entirely consonant with the well-known difference in their respective research facilities. The distance between the remaining affective dimensions, anti-interest group and legitimacy, is somewhat unexpected, although the earlier interaction analysis provided a forecast regarding legitimacy's inconsistent role. Finally, the three property dimensions SES, party position and tenure vary considerably between the two sub-elites, with tenure being very low among MP's.

Turning to the signal question of the *amount of variance* explained by these dimensions, interaction is dramatically the strongest variable among bureaucrats, accounting for 23 per cent of the total variation. Among legislators, however, it explains only .002 per cent. *In the round, among bureaucrats, the 9 variables in Table 12-1 account for 31 per cent of total variation, while the 10 included for legislators account for 26 per cent.*

Among bureaucrats, in addition to the 23 per cent contributed by interaction, pro-lobby and tenure add 2 per cent each; economic liberalism adds 1; interaction and powerlessness account for approximately 1 per cent each; and the other five per cent is scattered about among the remaining variables.

Among legislators, 5 of the 10 variables presented in Table 12-1 account for virtually all the variance. Pro-lobby attitudes account for 13 per cent, while economic liberalism contributes 3 per cent, followed by tenure and tactics which add another 5 per cent. Legitimacy and party role account for an additional 2 per cent each, while interaction, information, socioeconomic status, and powerlessness provide the remaining approximate 1 per cent.

In the main, with the exception of economic liberalism, these data suggest that behavioural, property, and affective variables are more salient than ideological ones in the interest group influence process. Some support for one aspect of interaction theory rests in the strong ranking of the pro-lobby variable among MP's, reinforcing the theoretical assumption that affirmative dispositions toward lobbyists can be positively related to interest group effectiveness.

In sum, the analysis provides a scale of the major variables that contribute to interest-group effectiveness in the process of elite accommodation. Although all types of dimensions are included, the scale is dominated for bureaucrats by the behavioural variable, *interaction*, with other dimensions such as pro-lobby valence and tenure contributing much smaller increments to the total variation. Among the Canadian legislative elite, an affective disposition, pro-lobbying, accounts for precisely half of the total explained variance.

MAJOR CORRELATES OF INTERACTION

Given its crucial role in the accommodation process, it seems useful to analyse further the major correlates of interaction. Several regression analyses were again performed, including all types of dimensions; those having the strongest correlations were combined, with the results shown in Table 12-2.

Clearly, property and behavioural dimensions tend to be more significant than other types of variables. Party role, tenure and committee position are most strongly correlated with interest group interaction among legislators. Moreover, just three of these 10 dimensions account for over three-fourths of the total explained variation, providing a clear gain in parsimony compared with earlier regressions (not shown). Among the three, tenure, committee role and party position dominate with some 3 per cent each. Powerlessness accounts for another 2 per cent, while most of the remaining 3 per cent is explained by legitimacy, pro-lobby valence and group effectiveness. The tendency of some observers to conclude that the parliamentary system has a monolithic effect upon interest group behaviour and influence in Canadian politics, characterized by neglect and lack of differentiation among back-benchers, is challenged by the fact that party and committee role are so significant as explanatory variables. That lobbyists are selective in contacting back-benchers, despite their marginal policy roles, is clearly evident in the impact of committee role.

As shown earlier, tenure (when legitimacy is controlled) has an interesting curvilinear association with group effectiveness (see Table 9-5), being most positive in the middle range (5–9 years) intermediate among neophytes (0–4), and weakest among MP's who have served a decade or more. Perhaps, through experience and the opportunity to develop alternative sources of information, the latter have acquired sufficient independence to discount the services provided by interest group representatives.

338

TABLE 12-2 *Zero-order correlations between selected independent variables and interaction, legislators and bureaucrats*

Dimensions	Legislators	Dimensions	Bureaucrats
Party role	.27	Effectiveness	.47
Tenure	.21	Powerlessness	.23
Committee position	.20	Service	.21
Powerlessness	.09	Perception – 4[c]	.19
Legitimacy	.08	Tenure	.16
Perception – 1[a]	.06	Group membership	.11
Effectiveness[b]	.06	Socioeconomic status	.04
Pro-lobby valence	.03	Legitimacy	.04
Economic liberalism	.01	Economic liberalism	.04
	(85)	Information	.02
			(156)

$R^2 = .14$
$F = .05$

$R^2 = .32$
$F = .05$

[a] 'The average man approves of and actively participates in interest groups when they concern his own interests.'

[b] 'This dimension relates to the experienced effectiveness of directors in their lobbying role.'

[c] 'The average man feels that interest groups have too much influence upon governmental decisions.'

Among bureaucrats, interest group effectiveness in lobbying has the highest correlation by a considerable margin, while the remaining high-ranking correlations are divided among property and cognitive values.

Turning to the proportion of total variance explained, 32 per cent, group effectiveness accounts for almost half. Powerlessness ranks second, with almost 5 per cent. The cognitive dimensions, perception and service follow, with 4 per cent each, tenure contributes another 3 per cent, and the remaining 2 per cent is shared almost equally among group membership and socio-economic status. It is noteworthy that service, a dimension that ranked very low in the analysis in the previous chapter, and especially among MP's, now appears as a salient explanatory variable in both correlational and explained variance contexts.

In sum, when tested against two of the most critical variables in interest group politics, interaction and effectiveness, we find that affective, behavioural, property and cognitive dimensions explain considerably more variation than ideological ones. Among ideological dimensions, economic and political liberalism and powerlessness appear among the final set of variables, but for both sub-elites they tend to exhibit substantially lower zero-order

correlations than property and cognitive dimensions such as group effectiveness, information and service. Regarding explained variation, two exceptions
occur, involving bureaucrats in the context of interaction, where powerlessness ranks in the middle range; and pro-lobbying, which is critical among
MP's in the context of effectiveness.

REGIONAL VARIATION ON SELECTED DIMENSIONS

Given the critical role often ascribed to regionalism in Canadian politics, it
seems useful to analyse the relative values of several dimensions, controlled
for region (see Table 12-3). At the same time, the interaction effects of yet
another combination of selected dimensions will become apparent. MP's
and senior officials are presented separately, and only the R^2 and RSQ
changes (i.e., the amount of variation explained) are included. The dependent
variable is *interaction*.

Using this set of ideological, cognitive, affective, and property dimensions,
and looking at the amount of variation explained by each, we find considerable difference among the four regions. The utility of information, for
example, is clearly much more salient for MP's in Quebec and Ontario than
for their colleagues in Ottawa and British Columbia. Since legislative
research and information facilities are quite limited in all systems, these
differences must reflect other influences. In British Columbia, it is tempting
to attribute them to anti-group attitudes, while in Ottawa they may be due
to limited interaction, compared with British Columbia MP's.

TABLE 12-3 *Comparative regional variation on selected dimensions,
among MP's, by interaction*

Dimension	Ottawa		Ontario		Quebec		British Columbia	
	R^2	RSQ	R^2	RSQ	R^2	RSQ	R^2	RSQ
Information	.04629	.04629	.13615	.13615	.21906	.21906	.02655	.02655
Leg. committee[a]	.05772	.01143	.17325	.03710	.23923	.02018	.07260	.04605
Legitimacy	.06164	.00393	.24455	.07127	.24238	.00315	.11798	.04538
Perception – 1	.06212	.00048	.24553	.00098	.24496	.00258	.29033	.17235
Perception – 2	.09737	.03525	.28276	.03723	.25229	.00733	.34289	.05256
Econ. liberalism	.10859	.01123	.28608	.00331	.27915	.02686	.34363	.00074
Pol. liberalism	.11926	.01067	.29121	.00514	.29592	.01677	.38199	.03835

$F = .05$

[a] This dimension is made ordinal by ranking the committee position of respondents, i.e.
chairman, vice-chairman, member.

Perception – 2, relating to elite judgments about the extent of affective consensus among ordinary citizens regarding the social role of interest groups, is highly salient in British Columbia, Ontario and Ottawa, ranking second in each of these regions, but quite marginal in Quebec. In the sense that MP's tend to seek consensual validation of their views, as part of their representational ethos, such cognitions probably reinforce any legitimacy they may personally ascribe to interest groups. There may be an association between this assumption and the fact that Quebec ranks lowest on legitimacy, or more precisely, that legitimacy explains the least variance there among the four regional elites. British Columbia's high ranking on Perception – 1 is striking, since this ranks lowest among all variables in other regions.

The ideological dimensions, political and economic liberalism, also vary substantially. Quebec and British Columbia rank highest on such values, with the latter being more influenced by political liberalism and the former by the economic segment of this dimension. Ottawa ranks mid-way on the scale, while Ontario's variation is affected very little. These variations seem to nicely reflect the political cultures of Quebec and British Columbia, particularly the traditionalism and elitism of Quebec, which contrasts with the egalitarianism of British Columbia, perhaps symbolized by its socialist Government.[1] Such variations are surely bound up with the demographic character of the two provinces, including the greater influence that immigration has had upon politics in British Columbia, but our data do not permit us to do more than speculate about such underlying explanations.[2]

Turning to the total explained variation, we again find substantial differences, ranging from a high of 38 per cent in British Columbia to Ottawa's low of 12, with Ontario and Quebec being virtually the same, about 30 per cent. Generalizing about the major dimensions in each province, we may conclude that cognitive dimensions, e.g. information, rank highest in Ottawa and Quebec, while the affective disposition, legitimacy, is most salient in Ontario, and the cognitive dimension, Perception – 2 ranks dramatically

---

[1] John Porter, for example, says 'The large proportion of foreign-born adults who were residing in the prairie provinces and British Columbia and who were therefore "captured" in the system in which they found themselves may be one factor, in addition to many others, including economic ones, to account for the radicalism of the west.' *The Vertical Mosaic*, p. 36.

[2] While most observers agree that regionalism is a signal element in Canadian politics, the task of isolating the salient variables and their effect on political behaviour has only begun. See, among others, William P. Irvine, 'Assessing regional effects in data analysis', 4 *Canadian Journal of Political Science* (March, 1971), pp. 21–4, which indicates the infinite complexity of the problem.

TABLE 12-4 *Comparative regional variations on selected dimensions among bureaucrats, by effectiveness*

Dimension	Ottawa		Ontario		Quebec		British Columbia	
	R^2	RSQ	R^2	RSQ	R^2	RSQ	R^2	RSQ
Pol. liberalism	.00794	.00794	.00424	.00424	.00200	.00200	.00323	.00323
Interaction	.21116	.20322	.35758	.35335	.41639	.41439	.25163	.24841
Tenure	.25241	.04125	.37712	.01954	.44288	.02649	.25314	.00151
Perception – 2	.30376	.05134	.38047	.00335	.44789	.00501	.30842	.05528
Econ. liberalism	.30743	.00368	.38473	.00426	.57705	.12916	.30878	.00035
Powerlessness	.37121	.06378	.38481	.00008	.59125	.01420	.32987	.02110
Perception – 3	.37884	.00762	.40568	.02087	.61085	.01960	.33249	.00262
Perception – 1	.38269	.00385	.41163	.00595	.69911	.08826	.34746	.01497
Group member.	.38291	.00022	.43090	0.1927	.75398	.05487	.34922	.00176
Perception – 4	.38867	.00576	.44755	.01665	.77029	.01631	.36853	.01931
SES	.42125	.03258	.44823	.00067	.77139	.00110	.37571	.00719

$F = .05$

highest in British Columbia. Committee role, however, is virtually as strong as legitimacy in Ontario.

We turn next to a similar analysis for bureaucrats, using a different set of variables and running them against interest group *effectiveness*, defined by the extent of influence directors believe they have experienced in lobbying senior officials. Table 12-4 again presents only the R^2 and *RSQ* changes.

It is immediately apparent, scanning the *RSQ* column, that interaction is the crucial dimension in explaining variation in lobbying effectiveness in this set of variables. Substantial differences, nevertheless, characterize the bureaucratic elite in the four regions: Quebec and Ontario exhibit the highest ranking on this variable, and Quebec is considerably higher than Ontario. Yet, the proportion of the total variance accounted for in Ontario is about three-quarters, compared with just over half in Quebec. British Columbia ranks similarly high, about two-thirds in these terms. Here, we have further evidence that behavioural dimensions are critical in explaining elite accommodation. The only other variable even remotely approaching the strength of interaction is economic liberalism (13 per cent), among the Quebec sample.

Ideological dimensions of some strength include powerlessness, which was found earlier to be inversely associated with perceived openness of the political system. This dimension ranks quite high in Ottawa (.06378), which is somewhat unexpected given the saliency of the bureaucratic role in the federal capital. The substantial position of political liberalism found among British Columbia MP's disappears among its bureaucrats, and indeed it ranks very low among elites in all regions, as does economic liberalism, with the notable exception of Quebec.

Cognitive dimensions regarding the 'average man's' perception of interest groups are generally weak, with the exception of Perception – 1 and Perception – 3 in Quebec and, for the latter, in Ontario. Perception – 4, regarding the judgment that average citizens believe interest groups have too much power *vis-à-vis* government, reveals some cognitive dissonance between federal and provincial officials, as it explains about 2 per cent of variance among the latter and virtually nothing among the former.

Among three property dimensions, tenure explains 4 and 3 per cent of variation in Ontario and Quebec, falls to 2 per cent in Ottawa, and virtually disappears in British Columbia. One would expect tenure to be quite salient, given the characteristically long service of the vast majority of these senior officials. However, as noted earlier regarding MP's, the influence of tenure on interest group effectiveness can be curvilinear, being highest at the middle levels.

Membership in various types of voluntary groups has some weight in Quebec, Ontario and British Columbia, but virtually none in Ottawa. Such memberships, it may be recalled, were quite low among federal officials, which may account partly for the distribution here. Socioeconomic status again differentiates federal and provincial sub-elites, as it accounts for over 3 per cent in Ottawa and virtually nothing in the provinces. Certain attributes of political culture among the latter might seem to have inspired some variation among them, yet the evidence from this particular set of variables indicates otherwise. The marginality of class, moreover, is apparent in Tables 12-1 and 12-2 where its correlation strength is limited.

Comparing the overall distribution, the combined variables explain a substantial proportion of the total variation. In general, it may be noted, these proportions are higher than those found when the same sets of variables are run against *interaction*. The relative weight of each variable tends to change substantially when the total set is altered, but interaction generally explains most of the variation in effectiveness when it is included. Although a combination of dimensions has been used here in an effort to broaden the analysis, it may be of interest that the highest single example of explained variation occurred when the nine dimensions used in Chapter 11 to measure cohesion were combined in one set. In the case of Quebec officials, these ideological and cognitive dimensions accounted for almost 80 per cent of the total variation between the set and interest group effectiveness. Among them, a single dimension, economic liberalism, accounted for fully 46 per cent of total variance, followed not very closely, by perceived openness and powerlessness.[1] However, as seen earlier, when ideological variables are included with the whole range of dimensions, and especially property dimensions of tenure, committee role, and interaction (which is essentially a function of political role), they tend to become marginal, both in number and intensity, compared with the 'hard' variables just mentioned. As our test of interaction theory reveals, legitimacy is not a necessary intervening variable between interaction and influence.

Elite accommodation, in sum, is mainly a function of political role and interaction, in which such other dimensions as ideology, cognition and affect (to a lesser extent) provide incentives that are in some sense peripheral. With some exceptions, Canadian governmental elites seem to be motivated essentially by a managerial ethic, rather more than by ideological commitment.

[1] Since this is an exploratory research study, which others may want to develop further, I have from time to time included such somewhat tangential information to provide evidence of research avenues that may be worth investigation.

PART IV

INTEREST GROUPS IN THE CANADIAN POLITICAL SYSTEM

We turn finally to a brief review of some pragmatic consequences of the going system of elite accommodation, including such positive achievements as preserving the nation against strong disintegrative forces. Other consequences include some narrowing of access and participation in the political system. Questions also occur about the operational effects of the allocation of national resources by an essentially ad hoc process of interest group politics.

CHAPTER 13

THE CONSEQUENCES OF ELITE ACCOMMODATION

Although they are necessarily very highly generalized, it seems useful to conclude with a brief survey of several pragmatic consequences of elite accommodation suggested by the study. Such consequences, which deal mainly with the costs of the system must be treated at two levels: political integration at the national level and the operational consequences of elite accommodation in an instrumental context. The first level usually involves dramatic, highly visible confrontations between Ottawa and Quebec or other provinces, centring upon questions of federalism, revenue sharing, et cetera. Obviously, programmatic issues are sometimes involved, but the major thrust is usually concerned with what are tacitly regarded as 'nation-saving' concessions by the national government to the claims of provincial or regional autonomy. The second level is concerned with routine, often essentially economic, decisions hammered out among the political elite, of which the case studies outlined earlier are examples.

Clearly, at the first level of accommodation, the overall consequences of elite accommodation have been benign in the critical sense that Confederation has been maintained, despite the ethnic, cultural, religious, and regional cleavages stressed earlier. That the compromises reached are temporary and that the equilibrium is precarious is clearly apparent in Quebec's explosive nationalism and the centripetal force of self-conscious regionalism as manifested, for example, in British Columbia's cavalier posture *vis-à-vis* Ottawa. Nevertheless, on balance, the process has maintained the solvency of the Canadian nation for over a century, and this is a tremendous achievement.

The positive consequences of elite accommodation also include a generally viable, popularly-tolerated system of resource allocation, but here, one suspects, tensions will become greater as more Canadians look even further to government to provide security against the periodic dislocations that, perhaps inevitably, confront a nation so heavily dependent upon external,

347

often uncontrollable, forces for its social and economic development. In very broad terms, the conflict between welfare and 'economic' criteria of resource allocation will probably become more intense as resources are strained by increasing welfare, health and educational programmes, often launched at the expense of traditional economically-oriented criteria. The decision of the Ontario Government to cut back its support of higher education (1972) is only one example in which the balance may be said to have swung back toward economically-oriented assumptions. Such tensions are symbolized by the behaviour of interest groups. To a great extent, their resolution will be fought out among groups advocating sharply different criteria for the allocation of public funds.

In this context, the existing system of elite accommodation structures the conditions of interest group participation in certain ways that will affect, and be affected by, the outcome of the emerging confrontation. Although our conclusions are somewhat speculative, it seems important to suggest some of the consequences, for both federal and provincial systems, of the present centralization of decision-making in the hands of the Cabinet, higher bureaucrats, and functionally-relevant interest groups.

One salient by-product tends to be a neglect of comprehensive, long-range social and economic planning in favour of case-by-case, uncoordinated, incremental policy-making. There tend to be few, if any, overarching priorities for ordering the system in directions that will permit industrial rationalization to overcome inapposite claims of protectionism. The going assumption is that the claims of virtually all major articulate groups are equally legitimate and should be honoured, a consequence encouraged by the fact that such claims, as we have seen, tend to appear in substantively and administratively watertight compartments. Governments everywhere, of course, are organized essentially along functional lines, so it is quite understandable that accommodation will proceed in this segmented fashion. Political incentives aggravate the resulting fragmentation and proliferation, as ministers, senior civil servants and interest group leaders indulge their natural enthusiasm for growth within their respective sectors. Party ideologies such as the well-known Liberal managerial style are also germane.

The larger outcome is a relatively uncontrolled expansion of activities,[1]

---

[1] From 1966 to 1971, total expenditures by all provincial governments increased by over 80 per cent, Dominion Bureau of Statistics, 46 *Canadian Statistical Review* (January, 1971), p. 6. Meanwhile, spending by all levels of government increased by over 300 per cent from 1960 to 1968. United Nations, *National Accounts Statistics* (1969), pp. 97–108.

without much qualitative differentiation among the competing claims of major social interests.[1] Theoretically, the Cabinet is supposed to provide the ultimate synthesizing force, but given the counter-pressures suggested in this analysis, such hardly seems the case. Efforts are made to ease the resulting proliferation by task force surveys and management studies, often motivated by 'efficiency' incentives. But these, however useful some of their recommendations, are beside the point in this context. It is the larger, over-all programmatic aspects of government that require rationalization, not the management aspects of existing programmes. Perhaps here, however, one is being equally beside the point in contemplating rational solutions for a governmental process powered essentially by brokerage incentives. If parties gain and maintain office by expanding their distributive parameters, it is probably useless to insist that the uncoordinated reconciliation of most group claims results in collective hypertension.

A second consequence of the going system of elite accommodation is a reinforcement of the *status quo* in terms of the existing pattern of distribution of public largesse and political power. Functional ties and established clientele relationships tend to crystallize existing power relationships. As we have seen, it is understandably difficult for new or substantively weak interests to penetrate the decision-making process. Inertia also plays a part as the influence of those groups which have gained legitimacy in their various sectors is reinforced through sustained contact and the weight of cumulative loyalties. The perhaps inevitable inequalities in political resources among interest groups mean that government, to some extent, is pushed into the anomalous position of defending the strong against the weak. While the governmental elite plays an equilibrating role in welfare areas, much of its energy is also spent reinforcing the security and growth of interests that already enjoy the largest shares of the net social product. Here again, the fundamental problem is the unequal distribution of political resources that characterizes all societies. But some easing of its consequences might occur if governmental elites played a more qualitative role in resource allocation, based upon broader criteria than those now in effect. Conforming to established influence structures is, to some extent, the understandable but easy way out.

[1] As Karl Mannheim insists, 'If we are to direct social forces effectively, we must not remain absorbed in the continued pursuit of short-run interests. The new form of policy can only succeed at a much higher level of consciousness with a taste for experimentation.' *Man and Society in an Age of Reconstruction* (New York: Harcourt, Brace and World, 1941), p. 7.

The tendency of governmental elites to reinforce the going distributive system also reflects, as we have shown, the socioeconomic, interactional, and (to a lesser extent) ideological continuities existing between them and politically-active interest group leaders.

Also at work is the natural desire of those who enjoy major shares of power and security to retain them. Here the ramifications seem international in scope, as evidenced by the current tendency of Canadian bureaucratic elites in certain sectors to deplore economic and intellectual competition from abroad. Speaking of such efforts in an economic context, one wise interest-group leader concludes, 'It may not greatly matter to a foreign investor if he chooses to come to Canada and subjects himself to special restrictions. The important question is what such a treatment does to Canadian society. We have not permitted discrimination in the past... because we had a sizeable problem of creating unity in an odd and disparate country. We cannot afford now to introduce discrimination and new factors of disunity.'[1]

Meanwhile, another fillip to the *status quo* follows as the major parties are necessarily (again from the standpoint of pragmatic politics) constrained to listen most closely to those groups in Canadian society who can contribute the most generous shares of financial support and respected public endorsement of their policies. As long as parties require huge amounts of money to compete successfully in national and provincial political arenas, it is difficult to see how the existing system can be modified. Perhaps the growth of latent, mass-oriented consumer groups is one answer, but here the incentives for organizational viability and continuity are rarely as strong as those enjoyed by groups organized around producer interests. To some extent, a fuller understanding that modern governments tend *not* to play an equilibrating role in the contest among badly matched publics may have an effect. Such an appreciation, however, depends upon greater educational opportunity at the advanced levels to enable more citizens to comprehend the going system of elite accommodation and to develop the resources required to participate in it. From such sources may come the incentives and knowledge required to stimulate a more competitive, and hence more democratic, interest group politics.

Such a development bears directly upon a third consequence of the existing process of accommodation, the extent to which it tends to restrict meaningful participation to those with a direct substantive interest. Here

[1] R. M. Fowler, address to the Canadian Pulp and Paper Association, *The Globe and Mail* (29 January 1972), p. B2.

again, while desires of the political elite for dispatch and expertise provide eminently desirable incentives, the perhaps unanticipated consequences include a heavy reliance upon consultation with interested groups and a tendency to define problems as essentially technical, with the implication that 'political' considerations are probably illegitimate and certainly devisive. Here again, the 'Old Tory' theory of authority is germane, since it aggravates the technological drift, while at the same time it encourages the constriction of the boundaries of participation in policy making. The assumptions of Cabinet government and the jejune policy role of back-benchers are among the institutional factors that reinforce the traditional, and somewhat astounding, assumption that the major policies of government are properly formulated in secret.

Given the weight of such elements of Canadian political culture, some long-term resocialization regarding leadership and rank-and-file participation will be required before traditional models of policy-making can be modified. Such again is a long-range solution requiring both time and increased equality of educational opportunity, buttressed by a realization among young people that the higher learning has other objectives than occupational success. These ends, in turn, will probably require some modification of elitist conceptions of higher education which still enjoy considerable support among advantaged social groups, as seen in current fulminations about the high costs of university expansion and successful attempts to cut back graduate education. Given the small proportion of university graduates in Canadian society, and the technical and scientific manpower required to sustain a modern industrial economy, this policy seems anomalous indeed. Whether Canada can, or should, continue to rely so heavily upon immigration for its supply of highly skilled and professional manpower is of course a moot point.

In sum, while the going success of elite accommodation has much to commend it, it tends to result in an incremental, uncoordinated expansion of governmental and private programmes, without adequate direction by the only institution possessing the legitimacy and authority to do so, government. A crystallization of existing patterns of resource allocation follows, which makes the introduction of new scientific, technical and economic directions difficult as they strike against established influence structures, based largely upon long-standing, functionally-determined, agency–clientele relationships. The rational consideration of policy alternatives is correspondingly inhibited so that, despite the flurry of plans and programmes, task forces, and reorganization schemes announced by ministers naturally anxious to be regarded as innovative, the more things seem to change, the more they remain the same. Power continues to meet with power, through the process of elite accommodation.

Finally, the going system has significant implications for those who take democratic participation seriously. Symbolized by the tradition of governmental secrecy, Cabinet hegemony, and the weakness of back-benchers in the formulation of policy, the consequences include a virtual monopoly of access by established groups which tend to enjoy major shares of political resources. One by-product is a built-in disposition toward inequity, which only the governmental elite can ease by widening the channels of participation. It is clear that some governmental leaders are aware of this problem and are attempting to liberalize the system. But their own advantaged positions in the social structure and their preferences for going values make it extremely difficult to interact with representatives of less-advantaged groups. There is also some evidence that political elites sometimes obfuscate the substance of policy issues for tactical reasons.[1] Such stratagems, which are surely encouraged by the complexity of many public issues, yet deny the essential educative function of parties, are part of the quasi-participative ethos.

In addition to such social, ideological and tactical restraints, there is the vital issue of practical politics which, all else being equal, compels governmental elites to defer to those who command the most powerful institutional structures in finance, industry and the mass media. Indeed in some cases, they are the same individuals. Meanwhile, elections require vast amounts of funds and support from those who can provide them. Thus the barriers to a more participative political culture include social and ideological discontinuities between political elites and ordinary citizens, as well as the brute economic calculus of successful party politics. Equally important is the lack of political sophistication and interest on the part of large proportions of Canadians, again reinforced by residues of elitist values, the assumptions of the parliamentary system, and limitations on the opportunity for higher education which is critical in distributing larger shares of political resources among more citizens. These traditional preferences and their institutional manifestations are obviously changing, but societies tend to

---

[1] H. G. Thorburn, for example, has shown how the Conservative Government aggravated the inherent complexity of anti-combines legislation (1959–60) in order to ease its efforts to meet the expectations of the organized business and financial community while avoiding any alienation of the public, which was only tangentially involved in the accommodative process, 'Pressure groups in Canadian politics', p. 169.

change more slowly than we assume. In part, our misperception rests upon the assumption that technological change is accompanied by equally rapid social evolution. What seems to occur, instead, is the well-known 'cultural lag', now evident in the tension between the Canadian thrust for economic development and scientific progress and the attending search for national identity mainly to be found in traditional values that often seem inapposite to the former aspiration.

A METHODOLOGICAL NOTE

The following brief summary of the methods used and some of the problems involved in the study is included to make the bases of our findings clearer and to provide possible guidelines for those who may want to do similar kinds of research. Since the most crucial element in survey research is the sample, we begin there.

SAMPLING PROCEDURES

Four sites were selected for the analysis: Ottawa, British Columbia, Ontario, and Quebec, mainly on the ground that they include about three-fourths of the total population of Canada and account for a similar proportion of gross national product. Three elite groups (N–1,123) were included: legislators, bureaucrats, and interest group directors, and a somewhat different sampling base was used for each. The legislative sample (N–269) was drawn using a technique called sequential sampling, whereby one is able to determine the sample size needed to reach a certain level of confidence as the research proceeds. We decided to aim for a .05 level of significance, which required a sample of about *50 per cent* of the universes, given the size of the Parliaments included. Such a sample was drawn and successfully administered, with the exception of Quebec where we received somewhat less cooperation than in other sites. As a result, our Quebec sample of deputies includes 43 per cent of the universe, rather than the 50 per cent reached elsewhere. In all cases, with the exception of Ontario where Conservatives are somewhat over-represented, the distribution of the sample is quite closely representative of the legislative universe, as indicated in Table A-1.

The interest group sample (N–640) was also selected with the aim of achieving a .05 level of confidence. Current telephone directories provided

354

TABLE A-1 *Representativeness of Canadian parliament samples* (*N*–269)

	Party distribution	Sample
	%	%
Ottawa (June, 1968)		
Liberal	58.7 (155)	53.9 (76)
Conservative	27.3 (72)	30.5 (43)
New Democratic	8.3 (22)	12.0 (17)
Creditiste	5.3 (14)	3.6 (5)
Independent	.4 (1)	.0
British Columbia (Sept. 1966)		
Social Credit	60.0 (33)	58.8 (20)
New Democratic	29.1 (16)	29.4 (10)
Liberal	10.9 (6)	11.8 (4)
Ontario (1967)		
Conservative	51.9 (56)	61.5 (32)
Liberal	23.9 (29)	19.2 (10)
New Democratic	17.1 (20)	19.2 (10)
Quebec (1968)		
Union Nationale	51.9 (56)	52.4 (22)
Liberal	46.3 (50)	47.6 (20)
Independent	1.9 (2)	.0

the universes. Every category that included 'interest groups' was covered, e.g., trade associations, religious, ethnic, fraternal, union, social welfare groups, etc. In large cities such as Montreal and Toronto, the resulting pool contained about 1,200 groups. Our criteria of selection were four: each group selected had to have a telephone, a director, major income from non-public sources, and status as a non-profit organization. We tried in every case to interview only the appointed, permanent director of the group, but in some one-quarter of the cases we were obliged to interview the president or the director's assistant. Because the number of groups in each universe was quite high, we were able to obtain the desired significance level by drawing an approximate *one-quarter* of each universe. Although our primary interest was in the *political* behaviour of interest groups, we decided that a random sample of all groups was the proper way to proceed, rather than try to make any *a priori* judgments about 'political' *v.* 'nonpolitical' groups. In all cases the samples were drawn using random-number tables, from alphabetical lists of the universes.

The civil servant sample (*N*–214) was selected somewhat differently, mainly because our major objective was a universe that contained a functional cross-section of senior bureaucrats in major departments who would, it seemed, be most likely to come into contact with interest group representatives. Preliminary discussions indicated that, although group access occurs at virtually every level in the civil service hierarchy, the most significant and frequent interaction probably occurs at the top levels of the service. We therefore used salary and classification levels to select a universe of 2–3 per cent of those officials at the top of the provincial and federal civil services. From this pool we drew an approximate *20 per cent* sample. For these reasons, unlike the legislative and interest group director samples, the bureaucrat sample constitutes only a tiny segment of the total universe. However, it includes a cross-section of higher officials in all *major departments* (i.e. not including special agencies or Crown corporations) in the several research sites.

INTERVIEWING PROGRAMME

The interview schedules were designed and pre-tested well before the field research began. The French translations required for the Quebec schedules were done by academics in Quebec and checked for accuracy and equivalence by French-Canadian political scientists.[1] Our conclusion, following the research, is that any difficulties in this area are less a result of semantic or translation inadequacies than of cultural and nationalistic tensions which complicate communication between English and French-Canadians. As noted, our refusal rates were highest in Quebec, partly for such reasons.

As a group, however, federal Ministers proved to be most difficult to contact. Our refusal rate among them, for example, was about 50 per cent.

Our interviewing programme began with a letter to those on the sample lists, explaining the project in rather general terms. We indicated that we did not expect them to reply, but that the project secretary would be calling them for an appointment within the following two weeks. Follow-up letters were used when potential respondents asked for further information. When required, at least a half-dozen follow-up calls were made to reluctant respondents. In most cases, we received remarkably good cooperation. Although there was some tendency for some respondents to be unsympathetic

---

[1] 'Interest groups' for example, was rendered as '*corps d'intermediaries*', rather than 'groupes de pression', which is more common, but less useful because of its pejorative connotation and theoretical distance from the positive Durkheimian conception of such groups used in this analysis.

with behavioural research,[1] even those who were most sceptical usually participated in the study.

Several reasons may account for such cooperation. One was clearly our sponsorship by the Canada Council, which was mentioned in the initial letter. In addition, we stressed the potential utility of the research findings for university courses, which drew upon the 'public service' orientation which so select a group might be expected to possess. Finally, we emphasized the confidential nature of the study, assuring respondents that all reports would be either anonymous or in statistical form. Certainly, another helpful condition was the fact that Canadian political elites have not been saturated with survey research interviews. Finally, we benefited from the tendency of highly committed individuals to *want* to talk about their careers and programmes.

The author was assisted in each city by graduate student interviewers in law, political science and sociology. Each interviewer was carefully instructed as to the character of the study; its objectives; and the usual interviewing techniques. Such instruction is of course critical. French-speaking respondents were provided with bi-lingual interviewers and French-language schedules. One expensive facet of bi-lingual research, which we neglected to budget adequately, was the high cost of translation, especially regarding the case-study issues.

It is desirable to employ interviewers in the city where the research is being done. Not only is this more economical, but access is usually eased by the institutional attachments and personal acquaintances that they bring to the project. Working from a university is also helpful for similar reasons. Legitimacy and felicitious access are vital in all research and institutional connections are invaluable in this regard. In every site except one, we established our research headquarters in a university.

Our interviewing system was actually a mutation in the sense that it combined questionnaire and standard interviewing techniques. Approximately half of the schedule was first administered by the interviewer, after which the respondent was asked to complete the remainder by himself while the interviewer waited. In this way, it was possible to answer any questions the respondent might have, and to secure a very high return rate. Length of interviews varied from about one hour each with the legislator and bureau-

---

[1] For an account of the problems faced by pioneers in Canadian behavioural research, see David Hoffman and Norman Ward, *Bilingualism and Biculturalism in the Canadian House of Commons*, Chapter 3.

357

crat schedules to some one and one-half hours with the interest group schedule.

Another somewhat novel aspect of the research was the inclusion of a transcribed 'case study' issue in the bureaucrat and interest-group director interviews. This came in the middle of the interview, after rapport had been established, and focussed upon a 'significant and recent' case in which the respondent had either made or received a demand. Refusals here were surprisingly low, probably because rapport was well-established by that point in the interview. Respondents were asked to talk freely about the issue, although interviewers were instructed to ensure that they answered a certain block of questions, responses to which were entered in the schedule as they spoke. Usually, about 15–20 minutes was required for this part of the interview, which proved to be among the most valuable segments of the research, even though such materials are inevitably idiosyncratic and must therefore (with the exception just noted) be used essentially as illustrative material.

The time frame of the Canadian research included the years 1967–71. Every effort was made to complete each geographical area fully before passing onto the next. This proved almost impossible, however, particularly due to the difficulties and delays encountered in Quebec City, mainly with deputies. Coding of completed questionnaires went on constantly at our York University headquarters, along with transmission of the data to IBM cards, for ultimate processing onto CDC tapes and analysis, using the Statistical Package for the Social Sciences, developed at the University of Chicago. Computer programming and analysis were carried out at the State University of New York – Buffalo. The various techniques used for analysing the data are discussed in the text. The attempt to order the data using the theories of elite accommodation and interaction is also explicit in the analysis.

Given the extremely detailed work involved in such a project, including the considerable amount of accounting, correspondence and appointment detail, it was necessary to employ a full-time project secretary, in addition to the appointment's secretary employed in the field in each research centre.[1] Depending upon graduate students for coding and preliminary analysis proved less satisfactory than the use of virtually full-time assistants, mainly because of the turnover among the former and their heavy commitments to their own work. Moreover, the practice of graduate students working closely with a comprehensive research programme, from which in some cases their

[1] The role of the appointments' secretary is obviously critical, requiring tact, intelligence, and knowledge of the project's general aims, all heavily larded with persistence.

own dissertations will emerge, is not yet established in Canadian universities. Nor are programming and computing facilities always adequate. Such problems aggravate the normal difficulties and tensions of large-scale survey research, and as suggested earlier, they tend to be a reflection of certain deep-seated cultural values in Canada, which are themselves worthy of intensive research.

Little need be said about the interview instruments.[1] Given the well-known problems of coding open-ended items, such were held to a minimum. The instrument contains five discrete sections: the usual biographical items; the case study (for bureaucrats and directors only); a general section on elite interaction with groups; a long scaled section on attitudes toward lobbyists and interest groups;[2] and a concluding section on political values.

THE CANADIAN RESEARCH CULTURE

Some difficulties in language did present themselves, although these proved operationally surmountable. Since the larger research programme included a comparative analysis of interest group behaviour in the United States, identical items were used in all instruments. Given differences in political structure and language, we were obliged to modify certain items, but these were very few in number and in the main, no serious communication or semantical difficulties arose, outside of certain cultural differences based rather more upon nationalistic values than upon linguistic or conceptual differentials. Perhaps the greatest of such barriers occurred within the Canadian context, between French-Canadians and English-Canadians who exhibit quite substantial differences in temperament, historical experience, political legitimation and socio-cultural definitions of reality.

Such problems, of course, confront all cross-cultural research, and especially that between Western and non-Western societies. In this per-spective, comparative research within the North American continent is not too difficult, with the possible exception of the Quebec situation. Certainly, despite the fundamental differences in political culture outlined in Chapter 2, English-Canadians and Americans have little difficulty in *understanding* each other. Yet, at the same time, the lack of a behavioural research tradition and

---

[1] I will be glad to supply a set of these schedules and complete data sets upon request.
[2] This section was drawn from earlier research by Harmon Ziegler and Michaer Baer, *Lobbying : Interaction and Influence in American State Legislatures* (Belmont, California: Wadsworth, 1969) to whom I am grateful for permission to use part of their question-naire.

attending institutional back-up, particularly in programming, result in serious difficulties for the researcher.

On the other hand, changes are obviously underway. A nucleus of young Canadian scholars, trained in the most advanced behavioural methods, is beginning to turn its skill to *Canadian* social and political institutions. Equally important, funding agencies such as Canada Council are providing the generous support required to sustain behavioural research. Building upon the analytical realism of S. D. Clark, John Porter and Frank Underhill, we can expect within the next decade a *risorgimento* in Canadian social and political science, in which the 'new men' will push the field beyond its ideological focus to one of cool analysis. Some of these scholars will follow Max Weber's admonition, 'Drill hard boards', accepting perhaps more fully the need to become full-time outsiders. The evidence, of which the present study is on example, is appearing.[1]

Meanwhile, despite pervasive discontinuities, symbolized by their discrete political stuctures, it is a signal fact that the ubiquity, role, and (less surely) the effectiveness of interest groups in Canada and the United States tend to be quite similar.[2] The generalization waits to be destroyed by more precise specification of the conditions under which this is so.

[1] For an impressive example in the area of judicial behaviour, see John Hogarth, *Sentencing as a Human Process* (Toronto: University of Toronto Press, 1971).

[2] For comparative data, see Presthus, *The Third House: Interest Groups in Politics* (forthcoming).

INDEX

access, among groups, 14, 127, 312
  comparative, by region, 313
  directors perceptions of, 313
  ease of, in bureaucracy, 213
accommodation, theory of elite, 3–18,
  59–63, 64–5, 78, 88
  allocative functions of, 4, 8, 9
  and cultural exclusivity, 16–17
  and joint membership, 269–70
  application to provinces, 111n
  as function of political role and inter-
    action, 335–44
  Cabinet's role in, 234
  conditions of, 62–3, 78
  consequences of, 347–52
  extra-ideological incentives for, 335
  functional bases of, 10–17, 78–9, 88
  hypotheses regarding, 63
  limitations of, 351–2
  major variables affecting, 336, 339, 340,
    342
  'nation-saving' role, 4, 268, 222, 234, 347
  rule of proportionality in, 9, 234, 270
  status quo orientation, 349–50
  see also, Lijphart, A.
affective cognitions of groups, 314–16, 321,
  327–8
  critical role in effectiveness, 336
age, as potential group resource, 137
agriculture, 109, 111
  close clientele relations in, 218
alienation, *see* political alienation
Almond, G., 5, 41
American Asphalt Association, 215
anti-lobbying, as elite norm, 314–16
  in British Columbia, 329
  index of, 315
  see Social Credit Party
ascriptive values, 29–30, 51, 303

v. achievement orientation, 32
Association for the Advancement of
  Christian Scholarship, 72
Association Cycliste Canadienne, 72
Association of Deans of Pharmacy of
  Canada, 162
Association of Mayors and Reeves, 314
authority, Weber's categories, 29
  deferential patterns of, 14, 28–37, 49, 61,
    83
  'Old Tory' theory of, 9, 48, 127, 291, 351
  French view of, 303

back-benchers, limited policy role, 179,
  211, 221, 226–7, 236, 320, 351, 352
  ambivalence toward groups, 314
  ambivalence toward service role of
    groups, 308–9, 334
  cited as lobbyists, 77
  competitive view of groups, 309, 316
  conceptions of 'public interest', 331
  disenchantment among, 37
  'free enterprise' ideology, 238–9
  high turn-over among, 34
  idealized image of political system, 314
  initiation of contact with groups, 229–30
  judgment regarding bases of lobbyist
    access, 203–4
  judgment why lobbyists approach them,
    228–9
  political efficacy among, 292
  pressure on bureaucracy, 223
  prestige level of, 36
  'pro-government' ideology, 239, 325,
    327
  symbolic approval of interest groups,
    253–4
  tendency to exaggerate interaction, 316n,
    334

Index

Index

nationalism, moderate, as requisite of accommodation, 14
'nation-saving' impulse, of elites, 4, 268, 347
  in Pearson Government, 222, 234
  in Trudeau Government, 234–5,
  see accommodation theory, functional requisites of
  see also, Lijphart, A.
New Democratic Party,
  low efficacy among, 294
  pro-group valence, 330
  selective perception of groups, 177, 320
Newspaper Publishers Association, 216
Nietzsche, F., 284
Nursery Association, 214

occupational specialization, and groups, 64
occupational status, 36
  among political elites, 125–6, 278
  national structure of, 278
'Old Tory', theory of leadership, 48–9, 127, 291, 351
Olson, M., 73–4, 76, 119
Ontario,
  economic liberalism in 299–300
  elite efficacy in, 294
  elite powerlessness in, 301–6
  hegemony of ministers, 206
  lobbyist influence in, 205
  perceptions of citizen knowledge, 287
  political liberalism in, 295
  variation, on selected dimensions, 340–4
  see also, subject headings
Ontario Dental Association, 100
Ontario Federation of Agriculture, 177
openness, of political system, 312–14, 317, 318, 322, 325–7, 332
  index of, 313
Orange Order, 100
Orders-in-Council, 147, 212
ordinal variables, 335, 340n
'organic society', *see* corporatism
organized labour,
  effectiveness of, 190
  high subjective evaluations of influence, 206
  precarious legitimacy of, 156, 169–70, 178–9, 208
  socioeconomic resources of, 131–2, 139
Ostry, S., 278
Ottawa,
  economic liberalism in, 299–300
  elite efficacy in, 294

elite powerlessness in, 301–2
influence of bureaucracy in, 206
hegemony of civil servants, 206
lobbying effectiveness in, 205–6
perceptions of citizen knowledge, 287
political liberalism in, 295
variation, on selected dimensions, 340–4
  see also, subject headings
'overlapping group membership', theory of, 15–16, 74

Parato, V., 61
Parliament,
  ambivalence toward groups, 316
  as 'closed' system, 34, 351
  as system of institutionalized deference, 37
  concentration of power in, 37
Parti Québécois, 55, 57
particularistic, bases of evaluation, 30–4
  values in Quebec industry, 303
  in bureaucracies, 32
party role, as vital basis for group contact, 339
patronage, of Prime Minister, 9, 37
  in Quebec, 57
Pearson government, 9, 222, 234
perception, influence on behaviour, 129, 208
  regional variations among, 340–4
Pharmaceutical Manufacturers Association,
  as pressure group, 197
  see Lang, R.
policy,
  consequences of elite accommodation, 348–52
  differences among parties, 249n
  idealogical component of, 205
politics, defined, 70
political activism, defined, 47n
  among citizens, 42–3
  among groups, 207
  and education, 47
  and effectiveness, 183–6
political alienation,
  among ordinary citizens, 289–91
  among political elites, 288–9, 291, 300
  among youth, 33
  in Quebec, 85
political change, in Quebec, 58–9, 304
  and emigration, 304
political conservatism, among governmental elites, 295, 300
political culture, defined, 20

Index

Porter, J., 34, 53, 59, 83, 84, 143, 154, 168, 178, 197, 235, 269, 274, 360
Posgate, D., 57, 58
  see participation, Quebec
power, defined, 268
  and interaction, 339
  negotiatory v. consultative among groups, 86, 213
  powerlessness, among elite, 300–2
  see political efficacy
powerlessness, 300–2, 318, 332, 336, 339
  index of, 301
  regional variations in, 342
  relation with anti-group valence, 320–2
  relation with openness of system, 322–4
Presthus, R., 41
prestige, ranking of occupations, 169, 169n, 170
'primal' collective goals, 107, 118
professional groups, 119, 207
  see interest groups
pro-lobbying, as elite norm, 315n, 317, 328, 336, 339
  by region, 329
  by party, 330
proportionality, rule of, 9, 9n, 234, 270
Protestant ethic, 33
Provincial Road-Builders Association, 215–16
psychic barriers, 227
psychopolitical resources, of directors, 123, 128–31
'public interest', 224
  as bureaucratic goal, 221
  as group goal, 100–1, 117–18
  as myth, 65
  contribution of groups to, 224

quasi-participative politics, 38–58
  see political culture
Quebec,
  and French cultural influences in, 302–4
  as traditional society, 55, 58–9
  attitude to federal aid to education, 298
  economic liberalism in, 299–300
  educational achievement, 56
  elite efficacy in, 294
  elite powerlessness in, 301–2
  extractive industries, 110
  lobbyist influence in, 205–6
  low rates of elite-group interaction, 329
  perceptions of citizen knowledge, 287
  political change in, 22, 56–8
  political liberalism in, 295

quasi-participative system, 52–3
  refusal rates in, 85
  variation on selected dimensions, 340–4
  see Crozier, M.
  see also, subject headings
Quebec Chamber of Commerce, 99
Quebec City, 358
Quebec College of Physicians and Surgeons, 162
Questions, planting of, in parliament, 162–3
'quiet revolution', 22, 58
Quinn, H., 49, 52, 56

'reactive tactics', of groups, 159–61
regionalism, 340–4
regulatory agencies, and interest groups, 207
religiosity,
  and social conservatism, 51
  critical role of, in Quebec, 51–2
  decline of, in Quebec, 53
  influence of, in English-Canada, 50, 51–2
  leaders, and access to Cabinet, 154
  ubiquity of groups in Ontario, 110
  see Clark, S. D.
'representative bureaucracy', theory of, 197, 223
research,
  bureaucratization of, 82, 85
  cross-national, problems of, 359–60
  methods, 94–5, 354–59
residues, traditional, 31, 31n
Resource Management, Department of, 226
resources, comparative,
  and political activism, 207
  of directors, 124, 208
  of groups, 114–17, 133
  psychopolitical, 123, 128–31
  socioeconomic, 124, 131–2, 139
response set, 288n
Retail Council of Canada, 102
Rioux, M. 303
Road-Equipment Dealers Association, 215
Rocher, G., 59
Royal Canadian Air Force, 100
Royal Institution for the Advancement of Learning
  within the Province of Quebec, 100
Royal Textiles Association, 100

sample, of study, 94–5, 109, 354–6
  representativeness, of legislative, 355
Schindeler, F., 47, 292

selective access by groups, 144–8
selective incentives, of members, 73, 118–19
   see Olson, M.
selective perception, 329
   see Thomas, I.
self-government, by groups, and MP attitudes toward, 249
self-legitimation, process, 285–6
semantical, problems in cross-national research, 82–5
senate, functional representation in, 27–8, 30
   vestigial, symbolic role of, 30n
separatism, 55, 58, 58n
service role, of groups, 307–10, 317–18, 334
   cognitions of, by regions, 309
   index of, 308
Siegfried, A., 18, 50, 143
size, of membership, as resource, 131–3
   of annual budgets, 132–3
social change, 58, 204, 304, 351–2
social class,
   among citizens, 275
   among highly-active and less-active directors, 277
   and deference, 35
   and education, 56–7
   and working-class, 57
   as a resource, 123, 132
   as sociological construct, 274
   as statistical artifact, 271
   continuity, among elite, 271–2, 275–6
   denial of, 271–2, 273n
   mobility among elite, 276–7, 277
   objective, of political elite, 238n, 275
   of directors, 124, 175
   subjective index of, 35
Social Credit Party, 94
   assumed anti-group valence of, 298, 302, 308, 313
   pro-group valence, 330–1
social mobility, among elite, 276–7
   among French-Canadians, 57
   and educational opportunity, 59, 351
social polarization, as requisite of con-sociationality, 15
socialization, *see* political socialization
Société Saint-Jean-Baptiste, 100
Society for Relief of Strangers in Distress, 100
State University of New York – Buffalo, 358
status quo, reinforcement of, by elite accommodation, 350–1

structural–functional theory, 88–91
subjective perception, 129, 176, 202, 206, 208
substance of issue,
   and effectiveness, 194–5
suffrage, slow evolution of, 46

tactical role, of groups, index of, 306
tactics,
   elite cognitions of, 306–17
targets, governmental, of interest groups, 153–5, 156
   and effectiveness, case study, 192–3
   and effectiveness, general, 193–4
   in case study, 156–8
   in general experience, 152–4
Taylor, N., 33
Technical Asphalt Association, 215
technical assistance, use by groups, 137–8
technology, and definition of problems, 351
tension potential, among groups, 135
tenure,
   among directors, 126–7
   among MP's, 34
   effect upon influence and legitimacy, 250–1
   regional variations in, 342–3
   role in effectiveness, 336
   role in interaction, 339
testimony at hearings, as group service, 159, 166–7, 184
t-tests, use of, 295–7
theory, as explanation, 87–8
   used in present study, 87–94
theory of selective incentives, 73, 118–20
   see Olson, M.
Thomas, I., 129, 208
time, allocation of, by directors, 179–80
Toronto Musicians Association, 100
traditional values, 29–30, 55–9
   and bureaucracy, 32, 323
   and class, 30
   and religion, 51–2
   as basis of authority, 28–9
   survival of, 29, 55, 304
Transportation, Department of, 226
Trudeau, P., 26, 29, 59, 234–5
Truman, D., 74
trust,
   and influence, 204
   and policy consensus, 204
   in federal government, 44–5, 290
   of directors in MP's, 204
   see legitimacy

Index

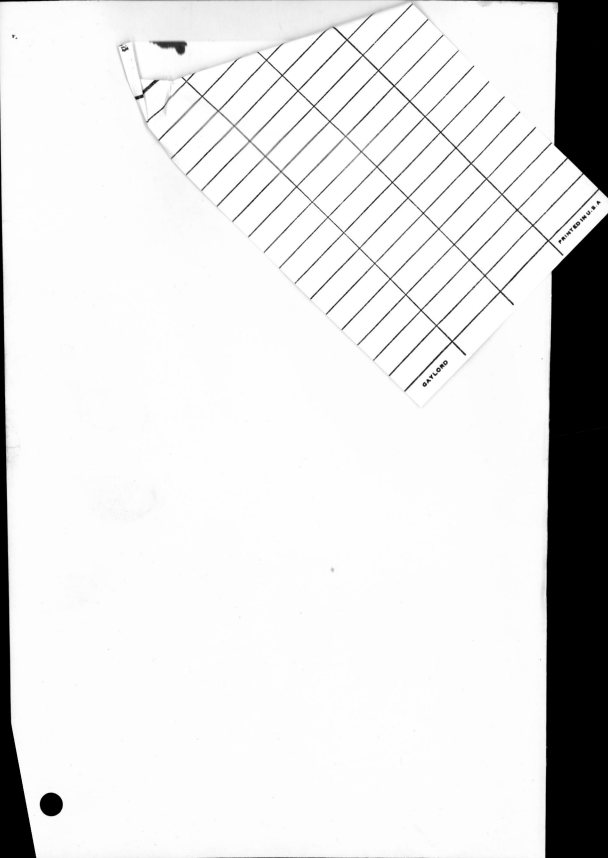

PRINTED IN U.S.A

GAYLORD